ATLANTIS
OF THE WEST

By the same author

Picts and Ancient Britons

ATLANTIS OF THE WEST

THE CASE FOR BRITAIN'S DROWNED MEGALITHIC CIVILIZATION

PAUL DUNBAVIN

ROBINSON

London

Constable & Robinson Ltd
3 The Lanchesters
162 Fulham Palace Road
London W6 9ER
www.constablerobinson.com

First published in the UK as *The Atlantis Researches*
by Third Millennium Publishing, 1992

This revised and updated edition published by Robinson,
an imprint of Constable & Robinson Ltd, 2003

A copy of the British Library Cataloguing in Publication
Data is available from the British Library

ISBN 1-84119-716-5

Printed and bound in the EU

10 9 8 7 6 5 4 3 2 1

Contents

Preface

Ask most people what they know about Atlantis and they will probably say they have heard something about a continent that supposedly disappeared beneath the sea long ago, during some great conflagration. They may perhaps think that it has some connection with the occult, or with UFOs, or with the spirit world – such is the range of comment available on the library shelves. If these are your interests then *Atlantis of the West* is probably not for you!

Perhaps you view the problem from a more rational standpoint and, like myself, you simply have an overpowering interest in the ancient past. In that case I am sure you will find something here of interest to you; but I warn you that you must approach the matter with an open mind! If you cannot conceive that a supposedly sixth-century Welsh tale about a lost land in the Irish Sea might, in fact, describe the same reality as Plato's 12,000-year-old submergence, then again, this book is probably not for you. Or if, like Professor Marinatos, you find it unthinkable that 'England' or some other island in the Atlantic might become detached and sink, then you will surely have great difficulty with my conclusions.

At the outset, my goal was solely to research a theory of changes in the Earth's rotational characteristics, these being a likely cause of past ice ages and climatic change. In seeking evidence of the most recent shift in the axis, I began to study the various references within mythology which might have some bearing upon that subject, Atlantis being then just one myth among many. Increasingly I came to see a remarkable degree of congruence within evidence drawn from quite unrelated sources.

A pattern began to emerge that agreed surprisingly well with published scientific evidence. Whenever that pattern suggested that a vital clue *should* be available from a certain source, then it was always there to be found; the pieces just fell into their proper place. As far as possible I have tried to let the evidence speak for itself, with only the minimum of comment to hold it together. If I have presented my material well then you must surely arrive, unaided, at very similar conclusions.

1

Lost Atlantis

In a more religious age, it might have been considered an act of blasphemy to suggest that the story of Noah's flood might be just a myth like any other. For to call something a myth is to imply that it is not really true. The scientific revolution, which began with Lyell and Darwin in the nineteenth century, has all but relegated the Flood to the status of a myth. Few people today dare to suggest that it might be a memory of a real event; and the view that the world we inhabit is the result of millions of years of gradual erosion and evolution is now the one in all the textbooks. Somewhere in this process of scientific rationalization we have lost something of immense value. It is time to consider once again the role that sudden catastrophic changes have played in human development.

There are many myths and legends from around the world that remember a flood catastrophe in remote antiquity; but of these, surely the most controversial is Plato's Atlantis. The story of the 'lost continent' that supposedly disappeared beneath the waves of the Atlantic Ocean some 12,000 years ago has caught the imagination of every generation since Plato; but as yet there has been no really satisfactory theory to explain it. If there really was a flood in ancient times, then it remains surprisingly resistant to scientific enquiry.

The Atlantis story is told within two of the dialogues of Plato, the *Timaeus* and the unfinished *Critias*. They are believed to be among the last works written by Plato shortly before *The Laws*, which he left incomplete on his death in 348 BC. The feature that sets the Atlantis story apart from most other myths of its type is that Plato presented it as a true history, complete with a chronology. We are faced with the fact that the most respected philosopher of ancient Greece believed it to be true.

The *Timaeus* is primarily a work of theology and cosmogony of

which the Atlantis dialogue is only a part of the introductory
section. It takes the form of a conversation between Timaeus,
Socrates, Hermocrates and Critias, Plato's cousin. Critias is asked
by Socrates to relate a story told him by his grandfather, the elder
Critias, of the ancient and unrecorded achievements of the city of
Athens.[1]

> In the Egyptian Delta, at the head of which the river Nile divides,
> there is a certain district which is called the district of Sais, and
> the great city of the district is also called Sais, and is the city from
> which King Amasis came. The citizens have a deity for their
> foundress; she is called in the Egyptian tongue Neith, and is
> asserted by them to be the same as the Hellenes call Athene; they
> are great lovers of the Athenians, and say that they are in some
> way related to them. To this city came Solon, and was received
> there with great honour; he asked the priests who were most
> skilful in such matters about antiquity, and made the discovery
> that neither he nor any other Hellene knew anything worth
> mentioning about the times of old. On one occasion, wishing to
> draw them on to speak of antiquity, he began to tell about the
> most ancient things in our part of the world – about Phoroneus,
> who is called 'the first man', and about Niobe; and after the
> Deluge, of the survival of Deucalion and Pyrrha; and he traced the
> genealogy of their descendants, and reckoning up the dates, tried
> to compute how many years ago the events of which he was
> speaking happened. Thereupon one of the priests, who was of very
> great age, said: O Solon, Solon, you Hellenes are never anything
> but children, and there is not an old man among you. Solon in
> return asked him what he meant. I mean to say, he replied, that in
> mind you are all young; there is no old opinion handed down
> among you by ancient tradition, nor any science which is hoary
> with age. And I will tell you why. There have been, and will be
> again, many destructions of mankind arising out of many causes;
> the greatest have been brought about by the agencies of fire and
> water, and other lesser ones by innumerable other causes. There is
> a story, which even you have preserved, that once upon a time
> Phaethon, the son of Helios, having yoked the steeds in his father's
> chariot, because he was not able to drive them in the path of his
> father, burnt up all that was upon the earth, and was himself
> destroyed by a thunderbolt. Now this has the form of a myth, but
> really signifies a declination of the bodies moving in the heavens
> around the earth, and a great conflagration of things upon the
> earth, which recurs after long intervals; at such times those who
> live upon the mountains and in dry and lofty places are more

liable to destruction than those who dwell by rivers or on the sea-shore. And from this calamity we are preserved by the liberation of the Nile, who is our never-failing saviour. When, on the other hand, the gods purge the earth with a deluge of water, the survivors in your country are herdsmen and shepherds who dwell on the mountains, but those who, like you, live in cities are carried by the rivers into the sea. Whereas in this land, neither then nor at any other time, does the water come down from above on the fields, having always a tendency to come up from below; for which reason the traditions preserved here are the most ancient. The fact is, that wherever the extremity of winter frost or of summer sun does not prevent, mankind exists, sometimes in greater, sometimes in lesser numbers. And whatever happened either in your country or in ours, or in any other region of which we are informed – if there were any actions noble or great or in any other way remarkable, they have all been written down by us of old, and are preserved in our temples. Whereas just when you and other nations are beginning to be provided with letters and the other requisites of civilized life, after the usual interval, the stream from heaven, like a pestilence, comes pouring down, and leaves only those of you who are destitute of letters and education; and so you have to begin all over again like children, and know nothing of what happened in ancient times, either among us or among yourselves. As for those genealogies of yours which you now recounted to us, Solon, they are no better than the tales of children. In the first place you remember a single deluge only, but there were many previous ones; in the next place, you do not know that there formerly dwelt in your land the fairest and noblest race of men which ever lived, and that you and your whole city are descended from a small seed or remnant of them which survived. And this was unknown to you, because for many generations, the survivors of that destruction died, leaving no written word. For there was a time, Solon, before the great deluge of all, when the city which now is Athens was first in war and in every way the best governed of all cities, and is said to have performed the noblest deeds and to have had the fairest constitution of any of which tradition tells, under the face of heaven. Solon marvelled at his words, and earnestly requested the priests to inform him exactly and in order about these former citizens. You are welcome to hear about them, Solon, said the priest, both for your own sake and for that of your city, and above all, for the sake of the goddess who is the common patron and parent and educator of both our cities. She founded your city a thousand years before ours, receiving from the Earth and Hephaestus the seed of your race, and afterwards she founded ours, of which the constitution is recorded in our sacred registers to be 8,000 years old. As touching your citizens of 9,000 years ago, I will briefly inform you of their laws and of their most famous action; the exact particulars of the whole we will hereafter go through at our leisure in the sacred registers themselves. If you compare these very laws with ours you will find that many of ours are the counterpart of yours as they were in the olden time. In the first place, there is the caste of priests, which is separated from all the others; next, there are the artificers, who ply their several crafts by themselves and do not intermix; and also there is the class of shepherds and of hunters, as well as that of the husbandmen; and you will observe, too, that the warriors in Egypt are distinct from all the other classes, and are commanded by the law to devote themselves solely to military pursuits; moreover, the weapons which they carry are shields and spears, a style of equipment which the goddess taught of Asiatics first to us, as in your part of the world first to you. Then as to wisdom, do you observe how our law from the very first made a study of the whole order of things, extending even to prophecy and medicine which gives health; out of these divine elements deriving what was needful for human life, and adding every sort of knowledge which was akin to them. All this order and arrangement the goddess first imparted to you when establishing your city; and she chose the spot of earth in which you were born, because she saw that the happy temperament of the seasons in that land would produce the wisest of men. Wherefore the goddess, who was a lover both of war and of wisdom, selected and first of all settled that spot which was the most likely to produce men like herself. And there you dwelt, having such laws as these and still better ones, and excelled all mankind in all virtue, as became the children and disciples of the gods.

Many great and wonderful deeds are recorded of your state in our histories. But one of them exceeds all the rest in greatness and valour. For these histories tell of a mighty power which unprovoked made an expedition against the whole of Europe and Asia, and to which your city put an end. This power came forth out of the Atlantic Ocean, for in those days the Atlantic was navigable; and there was an island situated in front of the straits which are by you called the Pillars of Heracles; the island was larger than Libya and Asia put together, and was the way to other islands, and from these you might pass to the whole of the opposite continent which surrounded the true ocean; for this sea which is within the Straits of Heracles is only a harbour, having a narrow entrance, but that other is a real sea, and the land surrounding it on every side may be most truly called a boundless continent. Now in this island of Atlantis there was a great and wonderful empire which had rule over the whole island and several others, and over parts of the continent, and furthermore, the men of Atlantis had subjected the parts of Libya within the columns of Heracles as far as Egypt, and of Europe as far as Tyrrhenia. This vast power, gathered into one, endeavoured to subdue at a blow our country and yours and the whole of the region within the straits; and then, Solon, your country shone forth, in the excellence of her virtue and strength, among all mankind. She was pre-eminent in courage and military skill, and was the leader of the Hellenes. And when the rest fell off from her, being compelled to stand alone, after having undergone the very extremity of danger, she defeated and triumphed over the invaders, and preserved from slavery those who were not yet subjugated, and generously liberated all the rest of us who dwell within the pillars. But afterwards there occurred violent earthquakes and floods; and in a single day and night of misfortune all your warlike men in a body sank into the earth, and the island of Atlantis in like manner disappeared in the depths of the sea. For which reason the sea in those parts is impassable and impenetrable, because there is a shoal of mud in the way; and this was caused by the subsidence of the island.

The rest of Plato's Atlantis story is told in the *Critias*. Once again it commences with an introductory dialogue between the same four characters. Critias relates from memory the story that Solon brought back from Egypt.[2]

Let me begin by observing first of all, that nine thousand was the sum of years which had elapsed since the war which was said to have taken place between those who dwelt outside the Pillars of Heracles and all who dwelt within them; this war I am going to describe. Of the combatants on the one side, the city of Athens was reported to have been the leader and to have fought out the war; the combatants on the other side were commanded by the kings of Atlantis, which, as I have said, once existed greater in extent than Libya and Asia, and afterwards when sunk by an earthquake, became an impassable barrier of mud to those voyagers from hence who attempt to cross the ocean which lies beyond.

Critias continues by describing the condition of the ancient state of Athens – the land of the Hellenes. In the time of Atlantis, Greece too was a very different place, with a climate fit for the gods and their children, and where a beautiful race of farmers and herdsmen tilled the then lush soil. The calamity that befell Atlantis was no localized event, for its effects extended as far into Europe as the Aegean. Great earthquakes destroyed Athens – just as the sea engulfed the Atlantic island. The Acropolis, says Plato, is but a relict; all that remains after a great deluge washed away the surrounding land in a single night.

> Many great deluges have taken place during the nine thousand years, for that is the number of years which have elapsed since the time of which I am speaking; and during all this time and through so many changes, there has never been any considerable accumulation of the soil coming down from the mountains, as in other places, but the earth has fallen away all round and sunk out of sight. The consequence is, that in comparison of what then was, there are remaining only the bones of the wasted body, as they may be called, as in the case of small islands, all the richer and softer parts of the soil having fallen away, and the mere skeleton of the land being left.

Critias extols the virtues of the ancient Hellenes and then goes on to describe the history and institutions of the Atlantic empire.

> Yet, before proceeding farther in the narrative, I ought to warn you, that you must not be surprised if you should perhaps hear Hellenic names given to foreigners. I will tell you the reason of this: Solon, who was intending to use the tale for his poem, inquired into the meaning of the names, and found that the early Egyptians in writing them down had translated them into their own language, and he recovered the meaning of the several names and when copying them out again translated them into our language. My grandfather had the original writing, which is still in my possession, and was carefully studied by me when I was a child. Therefore if you hear names such as are used in this country, you must not be surprised, for I have now told how they came to be introduced. The tale, which was of great length, began as follows:-
> I have before remarked in speaking of the allotments of the gods, that they distributed the whole earth into portions differing in extent, and made for themselves temples and instituted sacrifices. And Poseidon, receiving for his lot the island of Atlantis, begat children by a mortal woman, and settled them in a part of the island, which I will describe. Towards the sea, half-way down the length of the whole island, there was a plain which is said to have been the fairest of all plains and very fertile. Near the plain again, and also in the centre of the island at a distance of about

fifty stadia, there was a mountain not very high on any side. In this mountain there dwelt one of the earth-born primeval men of that country, whose name was Evenor, and he had a wife named Leucippe, and they had an only daughter who was called Cleito. The maiden had already reached womanhood, when her father and mother died; Poseidon fell in love with her and had intercourse with her, and breaking the ground, enclosed the hill in which she dwelt all round, making alternate zones of sea and land larger and smaller, encircling one another; there were two of land and three of water, which he turned as with a lathe, each having its circumference equidistant every way from the centre, so that no man could get to the island, for ships and voyages were not as yet. He himself, being a god, found no difficulty in making special arrangements for the centre island, bringing up two springs of water from beneath the earth, one of warm water and the other of cold, and making every variety of food to spring up abundantly from the soil. He also begat and brought up five pairs of twin male children; and dividing the island of Atlantis into ten portions, he gave to the first-born of the eldest pair his mother's dwelling and the surrounding allotment which was the largest and best, and made him king over the rest; the others he made princes, and gave them rule over many men, and a large territory. And he named them all; the eldest, who was the first king, he named Atlas, and after him the whole island and the ocean were called Atlantic. To his twin brother, who was born after him, and obtained as his lot the extremity of the island towards the pillars of Heracles, facing the country which is now called the region of Gades in that part of the world, he gave the name which in the Hellenic language is Eumelus, in the language of the country which is named after him, Gadeirus. Of the second pair of twins he called one Ampheres, and the other Evaemon. To the elder of the third pair of twins he gave the name Mneseus, and Autochthon to the one who followed him. Of the fourth pair of twins he called the elder Elasippus, and the younger Mestor. And of the fifth pair he gave to the elder the name of Azaes, and to the younger that of Diaprepes. All these and their descendants for many generations were the inhabitants and rulers of divers islands in the open sea; and also, as has been already said, they held sway in our direction over the country within the pillars as far as Egypt and Tyrrhenia. Now Atlas had a numerous and honourable family, and they retained the kingdom, the eldest son handing it on to his eldest for many generations; and they had such an amount of wealth as was never before possessed by kings and potentates, and is not likely ever to be again, and they were furnished with everything which they needed, both in the city and country. For because of the greatness of their empire many things were brought to them from foreign countries, and the island itself provided most of what was required by them for the uses of life. In the first place, they dug out of the earth whatever was to be found there, solid as well as fusile, and that which is now only a name and was then something more than a name, orichalcum, was dug out of the earth in many parts of the island, being more precious in those days than anything except gold. There was an abundance of wood for carpenter's work, and sufficient maintenance for tame and wild animals. Moreover, there were a great number of elephants in the island; for as there was provision for all other sorts of animals, both for those which live in lakes and marshes and rivers, and also for those which live in mountains and on plains, so there was for the animal which is the largest and most voracious of all. Also whatever fragrant things there now are in the earth, whether roots, or herbage, or woods, or essences which distil from fruit and flower, grew and thrived in that land; also the fruit which admits of cultivation, both the dry sort, which is given us for nourishment and any other which we use for food – we call them all by the common name of pulse, and the fruits having a hard rind, affording drinks and meats and ointments, and good store of chestnuts and the like, which furnish pleasure and amusement, and are fruits which spoil with keeping, and the pleasant kinds of dessert, with which we console ourselves after dinner, when we are tired of eating – all these that sacred island which then beheld the light of the sun, brought forth fair and wondrous and in infinite abundance. With such blessings the earth freely furnished them; meanwhile they went on constructing their temples and palaces and harbours and docks. And they arranged the whole country in the following manner:-

First of all they bridged over the zones of sea which surrounded the ancient metropolis, making a road to and from the royal palace. And at the very beginning they built the palace in the habitation of the god and of their ancestors, which they continued to ornament in successive generations, every king surpassing the one who went before him to the utmost of his power, until they made the building a marvel to behold for size and for beauty. And beginning from the sea they bored a canal of three hundred feet in width and one hundred feet in depth and fifty stadia in length, which they carried through to the outermost zone, making a passage from the sea up to this, which became a harbour, and leaving an opening sufficient to enable the largest vessels to find ingress. Moreover, they divided at the bridges the zones of land which parted the zones of sea, leaving room for a single trireme to pass out of one zone into

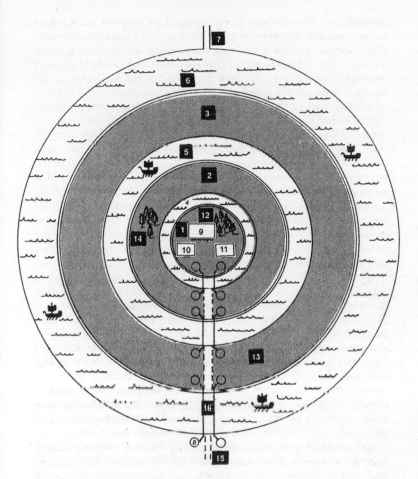

Fig. 1.1 A popular reconstruction of the city of Atlantis based on Plato's description.

1 Central Island
2 Middle Ring Island
3 Outer Ring Island
4 Inner Harbour
5 Middle Harbour
6 Outer Harbour
7 Canal leading to the plain
8 Towers

9 Shrine of Poseidon
10 Palace
11 Fountains
12 Palace Gardens
13 Racecourse
14 Gardens
15 Canal to the sea
16 Bridges

another, and they covered over the channels so as to leave a way underneath for the ships; for the banks were raised considerably above the water. Now the largest of the zones into which a passage was cut from the sea was three stadia in breadth, and the zone of land which came next of equal breadth; but the next two zones, the one of water, the other of land, were two stadia, and the one which surrounded the central island was a stadium only in width. The island in which the palace was situated had a diameter of five stadia. All this including the zone and the bridge, which was the sixth part of a stadium in width, they surrounded by a stone wall on every side, placing towers and gates on the bridges where the sea passed in. The stone which was used in the work they quarried from underneath the centre island, and from underneath the zones, on the outer as well as the inner side. One kind was white, another black, and a third red, and as they quarried, they at the same time hollowed out docks double within, having roofs formed out of the native rock. Some of their buildings were simple, but in others they put together different stones, varying the colour to please the eye, and to be a natural source of delight. The entire circuit of the wall, which went round the outermost zone, they covered with a coating of brass, and the circuit of the next wall they coated with tin, and the third, which encompassed the citadel, flashed with the red light of orichalcum. The palaces in the interior of the citadel were constructed on this wise:- In the centre was a holy temple dedicated to Cleito and Poseidon, which remained inaccessible, and was surrounded by an enclosure of gold; this was the spot where the family of the ten princes was conceived and saw the light, and thither the people annually brought the fruits of the earth in their season from all the ten portions, to be an offering to each of the ten. Here was Poseidon's own temple which was a stadium in length, and half a stadium in width, and of a proportionate height, having a strange barbaric appearance. All the outside of the temple, with the exception of the pinnacles, they covered with silver, and the pinnacles with gold. In the interior of the temple the roof was of ivory, curiously wrought everywhere with gold and silver and orichalcum; and all the other parts, the walls and pillars and floor, they coated with orichalcum. In the temple they placed statues of gold: there was the god himself standing in a chariot – the charioteer of six winged horses – and of such a size that he touched the roof of the building with his head; around him there were a hundred Nereids riding on dolphins, for such was thought to be the number of them by the men of those days. There were also in the interior of the temple other images which had been dedicated by private persons. And around the temple on the outside were placed statues of gold of all who had been numbered among the ten kings, both them and their wives, and there were many other great offerings of kings and private persons, coming both from the city itself and from the foreign cities over which they held sway. There was an altar too, which in size and workmanship corresponded to this magnificence, and the palaces, in like manner, answered to the greatness of the kingdom and the glory of the temple.

In the next place, they had fountains, one of cold and another of hot water, in gracious plenty flowing; and they were wonderfully adapted for use by reason of the pleasantness and excellence of their waters. They constructed buildings about them and planted suitable trees; also they made cisterns, some open to the heaven, others roofed over, to be used in winter as warm baths; there were the kings' baths, and the baths of private persons, which were kept apart; and there were separate baths for women, and for horses and cattle, and to each of them they gave as much adornment as was suitable. Of the water which ran off they carried some to the grove of Poseidon, where were growing all manner of trees of wonderful height and beauty, owing to the excellence of the soil, while the remainder was conveyed by aqueducts along the bridges to the outer circles; and there were many temples built and dedicated to many gods; also gardens and places of exercise, some for men, and others for horses in both of the two islands formed by the zones; and in the centre of the larger of the two there was set apart a race-course of a stadium in width, and in length allowed to extend all round the island, for horses to race in. Also there were guard-houses at intervals for the main body of guards, whilst the more trusted of them were appointed to keep watch in the lesser zone, which was nearer the acropolis; while the most trusted of all had houses given them within the citadel, near the persons of the kings. The docks were full of triremes and naval stores, and all things were quite ready for use. Enough of the plan of the royal palace.

Leaving the palace and passing out across the three harbours, you came to a wall which began at the sea and went all round: this was everywhere distant fifty stadia from the largest zone or harbour, and enclosed the whole, the ends meeting at the mouth of the channel which led to the sea. The entire area was densely crowded with habitations; and the canal and the largest of the harbours were full of vessels and merchants coming from all parts, who, from their numbers, kept up a multitudinous sound of human voices, and din and clatter of all sorts night and day.

I have described the city and the environs of the ancient palace nearly in the words of Solon, and now I must endeavour to represent to you the nature and arrangement of the rest of the

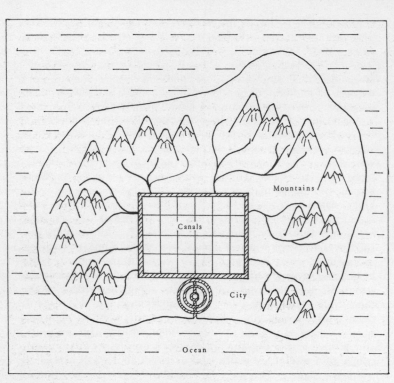

Fig. 1.2 A popular representation of Atlantis based on Plato's description.

land. The whole country was said by him to be very lofty and precipitous on the side of the sea, but the country immediately about and surrounding the city was a level plain, itself surrounded by mountains which descended towards the sea; it was smooth and even, and of oblong shape, extending in one direction three thousand stadia, but across the centre island it was two thousand stadia. This part of the island looked towards the south, and was sheltered from the north. The surrounding mountains were celebrated for their number and size and beauty, far beyond any which still exist, having in them also many wealthy villages of country folk, and rivers, and lakes, and meadows supplying food enough for every animal, wild or tame, and much wood of various sorts, abundant for each and every kind of work.

I will now describe the plain, as it was fashioned by nature and by the labours of many generations of kings through long ages. It was naturally for the most part rectangular and oblong, and where falling out of the straight line had been made regular by the surrounding ditch. The depth, and width, and length of this ditch were incredible, and gave the impression that a work of such extent, in addition to so many others, could never have been artificial. Nevertheless I must say what I was told. It was excavated to the depth of a hundred feet, and its breadth was a stadium everywhere; it carried round the whole of the plain, and was ten thousand stadia in length. It received the streams which came down from the mountains, and winding round the plain and meeting at the city, was there let off into the sea. Farther inland, likewise, straight canals of a hundred feet in width were cut from it through the plain, and again let off into the ditch leading to the sea: these canals were at intervals of a hundred stadia, and by them they brought down the wood from the mountains to the city, and conveyed the fruits of the earth in ships, cutting transverse passages from one canal into another, and to the city. Twice in the year they gathered the fruits of the earth – in winter having the benefit of the rains of heaven, and in summer the water which the land supplied, when they introduced streams from the canals.

As to the population, each of the lots in the plain had to find a leader for the men who were fit for military service, and the size of a lot was a square of ten stadia each way, and the total number of all the lots was sixty thousand. And of the inhabitants of the mountains and of the rest of the country there was also a vast multitude, which was distributed among the lots and had leaders assigned to them according to their districts and villages. The leader was required to furnish for the war the sixth portion of a war-chariot, so as to make up a total of ten thousand chariots; also two horses and riders for them, and a pair of chariot-horses without a car, accompanied by a horseman who could fight on foot carrying a small shield, and having a charioteer who stood behind the man-at-arms to guide the two horses; also, he was bound to furnish two heavy-armed soldiers, two archers, two slingers, three stone-shooters and three javelin-men, who were light-armed, and four sailors to make up the complement of twelve hundred ships. Such was the military order of the royal city – the order of the other nine governments varied, and it would be wearisome to recount their several differences.

As to offices and honours, the following was the arrangement from the first. Each of the ten kings in his own division and in his own city had the absolute control of the citizens, and, in most cases, of the laws, punishing and slaying whomsoever he would.

Now the order of precedence among them and their mutual relations were regulated by the commands of Poseidon which the law had handed down. These were inscribed by the first kings on a pillar of orichalcum, which was situated in the middle of the island, at the temple of Poseidon, whither the kings were gathered together every fifth and every sixth year alternately, thus giving equal honour to the odd and to the even number. And when they were gathered together they consulted about their common interests, and inquired if any one had transgressed in anything, and passed judgement, and before they passed judgement they gave their pledges to one another on this wise:-

There were bulls who had the range of the temple of Poseidon; and the ten kings, being left alone in the temple, after they had offered prayers to the god that they might capture the victim which was acceptable to him, hunted the bulls, without weapons, but with staves and nooses; and the bull which they caught they led up to the pillar and cut its throat over the top of it so that the blood fell upon the sacred inscription. Now on the pillar, besides the laws, there was inscribed an oath invoking mighty curses on the disobedient. When therefore, after slaying the bull in the accustomed manner, they proceeded to burn its limbs, they filled a bowl of wine and cast in a clot of blood for each of them; the rest of the victim they put in the fire, after having purified the column all round. Then they drew from the bowl in golden cups, and pouring a libation on the fire, they swore that they would judge according to the laws on the pillar, and would punish him who in any point had transgressed them, and that for the future they would not, if they could help, offend against the writing on the pillar, and would neither command others, nor obey any ruler who commanded them, to act otherwise than according to the laws of their father Poseidon. This was the prayer which each of them offered up for himself and for his descendants, at the same time drinking and dedicating the cup out of which he drank in the temple of the god; and after they had supped and satisfied their needs, when darkness came on, and the fire about the sacrifice was cool, all of them put on most beautiful azure robes, and, sitting on the ground, at night, over the embers of the sacrifices by which they had sworn, and extinguishing all the fire about the temple, they received and gave judgement, if any of them had an accusation to bring against anyone; and when they had given judgement, at day-break they wrote down their sentences on a gold tablet, and dedicated it together with their robes to be a memorial.

There were many special laws affecting the several kings inscribed about the temples; but the most important was the following: They were not to take up arms against one another, and they were all to come to the rescue if any one in any of their cities attempted to overthrow the royal house; like their ancestors, they were to deliberate in common about war and other matters, giving the supremacy to the descendants of Atlas. And the king was not to have the power of life and death over any of his kinsmen unless he had the assent of the majority of the ten.

Such was the vast power which the god settled in the lost island of Atlantis; and this he afterwards directed against our land for the following reasons, as tradition tells: For many generations, as long as the divine nature lasted in them, they were obedient to the laws, and well-affectioned towards the god, whose seed they were; for they possessed true and in every way great spirits, uniting gentleness with wisdom in the various chances of life, and in their intercourse with one another. They despised everything but virtue, caring little for their present state of life, and thinking lightly of the possession of gold and other property, which seemed only a burden to them; neither were they intoxicated by luxury; nor did wealth deprive them of their self-control; but they were sober, and saw clearly that all these goods are increased by virtue and friendship with one another, whereas by too great regard and respect for them they are lost, and virtue with them. By such reflections and by the continuance in them of a divine nature, the qualities which we have described grew and increased among them; but when the divine portion began to fade away, and became diluted too often and too much with the mortal admixture, and the human nature got the upper hand, they then, being unable to bear their fortune, behaved unseemly, and to him who had an eye to see grew visibly debased, for they were losing the fairest of their precious gifts; but to those who had no eye to see the true happiness, they appeared glorious and blessed at the very time when they were becoming tainted with unrighteous ambition and power. Zeus, the god of gods, who rules according to law, and is able to see into such things, perceiving that an honourable race was in a woeful plight, and wanting to inflict punishment on them that they might be chastened and improve, collected all the gods into their most holy habitation, which, being placed in the centre of the world, beholds all created things. And when he had called them together he spake as follows:-

There ends the *Critias*. Precisely what mighty Zeus may have intended next we shall never know, for the *Critias* has apparently never been anything more than a fragment. Plutarch records it as being incomplete in Roman times. We know from the text of the

Timaeus that the *Critias* was intended to be its sequel. The *Critias* also tells us that Hermocrates was to be allowed to speak next, and it may be supposed that what was to follow was a more detailed account of the war with Athens and the destruction of Atlantis, as briefly alluded to in the *Timaeus*.

The source that Plato cites for the story rests on firm ground. In the *Timaeus*, we are told that Critias heard the story from his own grandfather when he was a mere boy of 10. His grandfather was then nearly 90 years of age. The elder Critias had in turn been told the story by his father Dropides who was a friend and relative of Solon, its original Greek source. This time-scale is just about credible to fill the period between Solon's time and Plato.

Solon lived some 200 years before Plato, between about 640 BC and 560 BC. He is said to have vouched for the truth of the Atlantis story and Plato evidently considered him beyond reproach. For Solon was one of the Seven Sages of Greece and celebrated for his honesty and wisdom. Plutarch, in his biography of Solon, tells us that he repealed the harsh laws of Draco and gave Athens a new and fairer constitution.[3]

Solon is then said to have left Athens for 10 years to allow his laws to take effect and it is during this period of his life, around 590 BC, that he visited Egypt. According to Plutarch he spent quite some time in Egypt discussing philosophy with two priests, Psenophis of Heliopolis and Sonchis of Sais. The source from which Plutarch derived these names, and his knowledge of Solon's life, is uncertain. He quotes a fragment of Solon's poem about the River Nile and informs us that Solon had intended to introduce Atlantis to the Greeks in the form of a poem. There is little reason to doubt that Plato passed on the story much as Solon recorded it, but its detail seems too clear to be reliant on the memory of a 90-year-old man and a 10-year-old boy! We cannot know whether it was ever fully written down before Plato's time, or prove that the Greeks did not introduce errors during the 200 years between Solon and Plato.

Critias tells us in his narrative that Solon recovered the original meaning of the Egyptian names and translated them into Greek – and that Solon's notes were still in his possession. If one is further prepared to believe that Solon accepted the story in good faith from his Egyptian hosts, then it must be concluded that Atlantis was a genuine tradition of Egypt, surviving at least until the XXVIth Dynasty. We should not therefore assume that it was widely known; Solon may have spoken to the last surviving priest who took an interest in the ancient inscriptions. It would seem that if the story turns out to be mere fiction after all then the responsibility must rest with the Egyptians.

We are told that Solon recognized the names of many Greek heroes of legend. It is not clear whether Plato links the great catastrophe with the Greeks' own flood of Deucalion, or with the legend of Phaeton, or indeed any other event in Greek mythology. He only hints at these possibilities, leaving any interpretation to the reader's imagination.

There must be a question mark too, over Solon's own interpretation of the story. If Atlantis is indeed based upon a genuine tradition of Egypt in the sixth century BC, then it must already have been a very old story – even if it is not as old as the priests themselves believed. If Atlantis was destroyed by a world-wide flood catastrophe, as the *Timaeus* suggests, then how did such a detailed history come to be preserved? Were the traditions preserved orally for a period? How soon after the events were they first committed to writing? One must conclude that the Atlantis legend may at best hold a core of truth, but it should not be treated as an accurate record of remote events; its apparent crispness and detail are a tribute to the writing skills of Plato alone. As a source of ancient history the Atlantis story can be accorded no more status than any other legend that has reached us from ancient times.

With the possible exception of Posidonius, not one of the later writers and historians of the classical era believed Plato's story.[4] It should not be assumed that there was any great debate about Atlantis among classical historians. It seems to have attracted no more than passing references. Just as today, some accepted the tale willingly, others dismissed it. Then as now, there was no middle ground in the debate. In fact the Atlantis legend makes far more sense if we treat it as an Egyptian rather than a Greek story. The very fact that the later Greek and Roman historians, wise men all, failed to reconcile Atlantis with the conventional mythology, speaks volumes about the unique content of Plato's narratives.

2

In Search of a Legend

There can be no doubting the historical existence of the priests of Sais. Like Solon, Herodotus also visited Sais at some time around 454 BC. He describes the Temple of Athene and mentions the scribe who kept the register of Athene's treasures.[1] Herodotus, too, came away from Egypt with a sense of the fabulous antiquity of the Egyptian state but makes no mention of anything resembling Atlantis.

The Greeks equated their own goddess Athene, the Roman Minerva, with the Egyptian goddess Neit (sometimes Neith or Net) who is known to have been one of the oldest Egyptian deities. Her cult was widespread in Lower Egypt during the First and Second Dynasties (c.3100–2700 BC) where she was worshipped as the mother of the gods. Archaeological evidence confirms the existence of her temple. It occurs on an ivory label discovered by Flinders Petrie at Abydos.[2] The inscription records the building of a temple to Neit at Sais by Horus Aha, son of Menes the first king of Egypt. Nothing now survives of the temple itself.

The Neoplatonist philosopher Proclus (AD 412–85) wrote a long commentary on the *Timaeus* and quotes other Atlantis sources which have not survived. He relates that a Greek named Crantor (c.335–275 BC), a student of Plato's academy and the earliest commentator on Atlantis, vouched for the truth of Plato's Egyptian sources. Crantor is said by some authors to have visited Sais himself to verify the sources of Solon and to have found there a temple column decorated with hieroglyphs, upon which the history of Atlantis was written. Unfortunately, he left us no additional information. In fact, what Proclus actually had to say about Crantor is somewhat less positive than this:[3] 'Crantor adds, that this is testified by the prophets of the Egyptians, who assert that in these particulars [which are narrated by Plato] are written on pillars which are still preserved.' It is rather less certain on this evidence that the inscriptions were actually at Sais. Similar inscriptions are mentioned by the Egyptian historian Manetho, as cited by Syncellus, and the Jewish historian Josephus also describes pillars, the Siriadic Columns.[4, 5] He records that the god Set, *at a time before the Flood*, erected two columns, one of brick and one of stone, to preserve the records of the past. The pillar of brick, he maintains, 'remains in the Siriadic land [Egypt] to this day'.

Manetho's *Book of Sothis* is now preserved in only a few fragmentary references by Josephus and Syncellus.[6] The latter records that the inscriptions were translated from 'sacred language' by Agathodaemon and deposited in the temple shrines of Egypt. The sacred books were subsequently included by Manetho in his *Book of Sothis* and presented to King Ptolemy II Philadelphus in the third century BC.

If Crantor did indeed see an inscribed column of Horus Aha's temple at Sais, then it would place the roots of the Atlantis legend far back into the Archaic period of Egypt. But this is a tenuous link indeed, for although Neit was an ancient deity, her religion achieved its greatest prominence only very late.[7] Her cult enjoyed a revival during the Saite Dynasty when Psammetichos achieved independence from Assyria and established his capital at Sais. Many Old Kingdom monuments were restored at this time, including the pyramids, as Egypt enjoyed its final period of independence. Sais continued to flourish after the Persian conquest in 525 BC and further embellishment of the temple was funded; the building of a great new gateway is subsequently recorded by Herodotus. Solon's visit would have taken place at the very height of Neit's restored popularity and we may presume that much restoration of her temple had already taken place.

Proclus quotes a further lost work, the *Ethiopic History* of the Greek geographer Marcellus, who wrote in the first century AD. His account is evidence that other reports of a lost Atlantic island must have once existed.[8]

That such and so great an island once existed, is evident from what is said by certain historians respecting what pertains to the external sea. For according to them, there were seven islands in that sea, in their times, sacred to Proserpine, and also three others of immense extent, one of which was sacred to Pluto, another to Ammon, and the middle [or second] of these to Neptune, the magnitude of which was a thousand stadia. They also add, that the inhabitants of it preserved the remembrance from their ancestors, of the Atlantic island which existed there, and was truly prodigiously great; which for many periods had dominion over all the islands in the Atlantic sea, and was itself likewise sacred to Neptune. These things therefore, Marcellus writes in his Ethiopic History.

Now it is necessary to be careful with this passage before any conclusions can be drawn from it. First, the names of the gods are Roman, Neptune being the equivalent of the Greek god of the sea, Poseidon. Second, we must ask what purpose it served within a book of Ethiopian history. This does not refer to the modern state, but to a mythical race. Diodorus Siculus also describes seven islands within his story of the voyage of Iambulus.[9] In this story, Iambulus was kidnapped by Ethiopians and carried off to seven fabulous islands. Although these were in the Indian Ocean rather than the Atlantic, their description bears more than a little resemblance to some of Plato's ideas. The reference by Marcellus to the 'external sea' is therefore significant, as at times the name 'Atlantic' was applied to the entire ocean surrounding the known world. The name derives from that of the Titan Atlas and was used by Herodotus to denote the ocean 'beyond the Pillars of Heracles'.

It is the reference to the three larger islands that is most revealing. This is not a description of Atlantis, as some have thought, but a reference to three Atlantic islands which were known to the older classical historians. The central island of the three preserved a tradition about its own remote past, which would seem to bear a resemblance to the Atlantis legend. Perhaps if we find this island then we find Atlantis. But again caution is needed; nothing is known of this Marcellus and he could simply have been reading Plato!

There is another very different tradition that superficially bears little resemblance to Plato's account; and it is preserved in the histories of Diodorus Siculus. Diodorus of Sicily wrote in the time of Julius Caesar between 60 and 30 BC, but little more is known about him. The references to the Atlantians are contained in his third book, within a passage describing the Libyan myths of the Amazons and the Gorgons.

The style of Diodorus was an attempt to rationalize the myths of the Greeks and other nations. He believed that such myths were but an account of very ancient history and the gods merely the kings and heroes of ancient times. For this he has been much criticized and some of his rationalized myths considered even more incredible than before! This is perhaps a little unfair since at least he did not neglect the myths as did other writers, and as a result he is for some of them our only source. Most of his own source material came from the *Kyklos*, a mythological encyclopaedia written by Dionysius of Mitylene who worked in Alexandria during the second or first century BC. Little is known of Dionysius either, except that he had a reputation for falsely quoting earlier writers. However, he did have at his disposal all the lost sources of the Great Library of Alexandria.

According to Diodorus, there once existed a race called the Amazons, which was ruled entirely by its women.[10] Among the Amazons it was the custom for the women to indulge in warfare and for this reason their breasts were not allowed to develop, lest they became a hindrance in fighting. The name Amazon literally means 'breastless'. These Amazons lived on an island called Hespera, which was situated in the marsh Tritonis. They had not yet invented agriculture and lived on the milk of sheep and goats together with the fruit of certain trees which were abundant on their island. This island 'was of great size' and the marsh that surrounded it lay near the mountain called Atlas by the Greeks.

The Amazons conquered all the cities of their island with the exception of a 'sacred' city, which lay near a volcano. Next, the Amazons set about the conquest of the nomadic Libyan tribes and founded a city within the marsh Tritonis which they named Cherronesus. This word literally means 'peninsula' indicating that it was built on a promontory of land overlooking the marsh. Not satisfied with the extent of their conquests, Diodorus tells us that they then set about a conquest of the Atlantians.[11]

the Amazons embarked upon great ventures, a longing having come over them to invade many parts of the inhabited world. The first people against whom they advanced, according to the tale, was the Atlantians, the most civilized men among the inhabitants of those regions, who dwelt in a prosperous country and possessed great cities; it was among them, we are told, that mythology places the birth of the gods, in the regions which lie along the shore of the ocean.

Now the Amazons themselves are a fascinating subject for study, but they will not be discussed here except when they are able to tell us something relevant to the Atlantians and the cataclysm that engulfed them. Diodorus does not mention Atlantis as such, only the 'Atlantians' and 'the land of the Atlantians' and this may be significant. Upon entering their land the Amazons, led by their queen Myrina, defeated the Atlantians in a battle in which they captured the city of Cerne. They slaughtered all the men and burned the city, an act which so terrified the Atlantians that they surrendered the remainder of their cities without further bloodshed.

The Atlantians honoured Myrina and agreed to do whatever the queen commanded. Amazons and Atlantians in effect became allies. Myrina had the city of Cerne rebuilt and named in her own honour, and extended friendship to the Atlantians. This submissive policy by the Atlantians seems to have succeeded, as they persuaded the Amazons to attack their own long-standing enemies, the Gorgons. These people, the Amazons exterminated entirely, but for a few who took refuge in a forest.

Both the Amazons and the Gorgons are mentioned elsewhere in Greek mythology in entirely different contexts, but these traditions are quite unique to Diodorus Siculus. Of the eventual fate of the Amazons and the Gorgons, Diodorus cites the Greek myth that they were entirely destroyed by Heracles when he visited the west. However he also relates another myth:[12] 'The story is also told that the marsh Tritonis disappeared from sight in the course of an earthquake, when those parts of it which lay towards the ocean were torn asunder.' The marsh Tritonis is traditionally identified with the seasonal lake in modern Tunisia known as the Chott El Jerid, but this does not seem to be the place described by Diodorus. Evidently, the Tunisian lake still exists and has not sunk into the sea. We are only told that it was 'near the ocean which surrounds the Earth' and close to Mount Atlas. If this implies the modern Atlas Mountains of Morocco then perhaps we should look somewhere off the Atlantic coast of that country for a potential site.

We may be mistaken to make any association between Mount Atlas and the Atlas Mountains of today. Diodorus gives no indication that he really knew where it was. According to Herodotus the highest mountain in the region was named for Atlas because the local inhabitants considered it to be a pillar of the heavens; and in Greek mythology the Titan Atlas is said to have supported the sky on his shoulders. However, in his histories, written around 450 BC, Herodotus does briefly acknowledge two tribes living in the western Sahara in his own day, called the Atarantes and the Atlantes, the latter named after the mountain.[13] Beyond the sand belt lived the Ethiopians: a name which the later Greeks freely applied to any black Africans. However, Pliny informs us that the entire race of Ethiopians, including some known as 'White Ethiopians', were formerly named Atlantia.[14] The implication therefore must be that the name Atlantians derives from a North African tribe or race.

The name Mount Atlas was applied to several mountains by the ancient writers. Speculation as to where it really lay was just as rife in classical times as it is today and it makes all the geography associated with these legends open to suspicion. Plato himself makes no mention of Mount Atlas – only that many mountains surrounded the great plain at the centre of Atlantis. Mount Atlas as a pillar of the heavens was also described by Marcellus, as cited by Proclus.[15]

> According to Heraclitus, he who passes through a region very difficult of access, will arrive at the Atlantic mountain, the magnitude of which is said to be so great by the Ethiopic historians, that it reaches to the aether, and sends forth a shadow as far as five thousand stadia.

This gives us some further clues about Mount Atlas. It must have been situated near the coast, with its summit often obscured by clouds. It may have been a volcano, or perhaps quite a small mountain giving the illusion of great height to the Ethiopians, unfamiliar with cloudy skies. The length of the shadow is perhaps an indication that it was located somewhere in the northern latitudes where midday shadows are longer. A tropical people would naturally associate a long shadow with great height.

Diodorus goes on to relate the myths of the Atlantians about the origin of the gods.[16] They contain many recognizable elements of Greek and Phoenician myth, but with significant differences. The first king of the Atlantians was Uranus. He was the first ruler to gather all the people within the protection of a walled city, to give them laws, and to show them how to cultivate and store fruits. He is also credited with great military and scientific achievements.

he also subdued the larger part of the inhabited earth, in particular the regions to the west and the north. And since he was a careful observer of the heavens he foretold many things which would take place throughout the world; and for the common people he introduced the year on the basis of the movement of the sun and the months on that of the moon, and instructed them in the seasons which recur year after year.

Not surprisingly, on the basis of these achievements, Uranus was considered a god and was worshipped as the king of the universe. His children inherited the name Titans from their mother Titaea; and his eldest daughter Basilea went on to receive the accolade of 'Great Mother' in recognition of her skill in raising her younger brothers.

Diodorus relates more of the achievements of the Titans, which need only be summarized here as they merely confuse the Atlantians still further with the Greek myths. The dynasty of the Atlantian kings is then described. Basilea went on to make an incestuous marriage to her brother Hyperion and gave birth to two children Helios and Selene. Since these names mean respectively the Sun and Moon, it is easy to see in this and the achievements of Uranus a garbled creation myth of the kind found in all mythologies. At a later time Hyperion was put to death for attempting to usurp power, after which the kingdom was divided between the sons of Uranus.[17]

the most renowned of whom were Atlas and Cronus. Of these sons Atlas received as his part the regions on the coast of the ocean, and he not only gave the name of the Atlantians to his peoples but likewise called the greatest mountain in the land Atlas.

Atlas is portrayed as a great astronomer. Diodorus mentions him again in his fourth book, within his rationalized account of the story of Heracles. He credits Atlas with the discovery of the 'spherical nature of the stars'; and as such the father of all Greek astronomy. It is for this reason, Diodorus goes on to say, that the myth grew up about him in later times as the giant who supported the sky on his shoulders. The ultimate fate of Atlas was to be whisked away from the summit of Mount Atlas by strong winds while making his astronomical observations. Here, however, Diodorus may be confusing Atlas with another mythical figure whom Pliny called Atlans, son of Libya.[18]

Beneath the obvious differences in the accounts of Plato and

Diodorus, it is possible to find common ground. In Plato's tradition, the Atlantians are said to have conquered 'Libya as far as Egypt', whereas the rival tradition places them in western Libya – this being the name which the Greeks applied to the whole of Africa west of Egypt. The Amazons may thus have conquered only a colony of Atlantis. The cultivation of fruit also figures strongly in both versions. The *Critias* relates that the Atlantians took both a summer and a winter crop from their irrigated plain in what seems to have been a Mediterranean climate of dry summers and wet winters. It cannot be assumed that any of our modern crops are intended here and it may well be that the crops were cultivated fruits. If we are to believe Diodorus, then Atlantis dates to a time before the cultivation of grain.

The conquests of the Atlantians are another common thread. In the Platonic tradition, the Atlantians conquered the islands in the Atlantic, most of Europe as far as Tyrrhenia, and Libya up to the borders of Egypt. By Tyrrhenia, probably the entire Italian peninsula is intended, since the next proposed conquest was to be Greece. The tradition derived from the Libyan myths says only that they conquered all the regions to the west and north.

Atlas is a major figure in Greek and Phoenician mythology with a web of contradictory stories surrounding him. Hesiod, in *Theogony* makes him son of the Titan Iapetus and grandson of Uranus.[19] The enigmatic figure of Atlas is common to both Atlantian traditions. In both versions, the country and the ocean around it are named after him, but there all similarity ends. Plato describes him as receiving only the best part of the island of Atlantis from his father Poseidon and it is his descendants who go on to build a vast empire over many generations. He mentions nothing of either Uranus or Cronus. In contrast Diodorus makes Uranus the conqueror, leaving only a part of his empire to his son Atlas.

A further link between the two stories lies in the worship of an 'earth-mother' or virgin goddess figure and the apparent equality or even pre-eminence of women within society. This is exhibited by the Atlantians' reverence of Cleito, the mother of the gods. It is also illuminating to compare the descriptions of the Amazons with Plato's comments concerning the women of ancient times.[20]

Solon said that the priests in their narrative of that war mentioned most of the names which are recorded prior to the time of Theseus, such as Cecrops, and Erechtheus, and Erichthonius, Erysichthon, and the names of women in like manner. Moreover, since military pursuits were then common to men and women, the men of those days in accordance with the custom of the time set up a figure and image of the goddess in full armour, to be a testimony that all animals which associate together, male as well as female, may, if they please, practice in common the excellence which is typical of their kind.

Both traditions end with a cataclysmic destruction in the regions of the west. Plato's Atlantis disappears beneath the sea in a time of great earthquakes, leaving behind it impenetrable mud beyond the Straits of Gibraltar. However since Diodorus is primarily concerned with the Amazons, he tells us that it was the marsh Tritonis that disappeared beneath the sea following an earthquake. We are left to wonder what happened to the Atlantians. Significantly, both traditions are traceable to ultimate sources in Egypt, where many mythological references may be found denoting the west generally as 'the land of the dead'.[21]

These two separate traditions of Plato and Diodorus Siculus, together with the various commentaries upon them, are all the evidence that exists about Atlantis and the Atlantians. All that has been written on the subject by more recent authors can be resolved to these few references. Many of them have neglected the tradition of Diodorus entirely, but it has to be included in any complete study. The two sources are so contrasting in both their origin and content. One is offered as history, traceable through respected figures such as Plato and Solon back to a written account in ancient Egypt. The other is presented as mythology by a reputedly dull author, citing an untrustworthy source.

Plato's Atlantis is commented upon by other Greek and Roman writers. Aristotle considered it just a fictional embellishment to Plato's philosophy and it has to be said that Plato displays more interest in the perfection of the political institutions than in Atlantis as history. However, the philosopher Posidonius (*c.*135–59 BC) thought that some truth lay behind the legend; and Pliny quite happily accepted the west coast of Africa as its location.[22, 23]

Speculation as to the likely location of Atlantis has continued unabated ever since. The early Christian and medieval writers saw the legend as a memory of the Garden of Eden, which similarly lay in the west. The calamity which destroyed Plato's isle fitted neatly with the biblical Flood. However, the fabulous antiquity claimed for Atlantis had to be rejected as it conflicted with the biblical chronology. The European discovery of the American continent led to suggestions that it might have been the site of Atlantis; and the various islands of the Caribbean also had their proponents.

In modern times, the most influential writer on the subject has been Ignatius Donnelly. In 1882 he published his famous book, *Atlantis: The Antediluvian World*, which soon became the major reference work of the new pseudo-science of 'Atlantology'. Donnelly was the first to propose that the similarity of cultures between the New and Old Worlds might be derived from a common source: a lost continent in the middle of the Atlantic. He drew on obvious similarities, such as the building of pyramids by both the Egyptians and the Central American cultures, among others, as evidence of this. He also linked the destruction of Atlantis with the biblical Flood and noted the similarity of traditions about the Flood on both sides of the Atlantic.

Donnelly really started the whole idea of Atlantis as a sunken mid-Atlantic continent. Since Donnelly, various authors have taken up this theme with differing degrees of credibility. The German writer Otto Muck placed his island on the Mid-Atlantic Ridge, to be sunk amid volcanic convulsions, following the impact of a comet in 8498 BC. Another German writer, Jurgen Spanuth, equated the Atlantians with the mysterious 'Sea Peoples' who raided Egypt around 1200 BC. He made a soundly argued case for the submerged land around Heligoland and the Danish coast as the site of Atlantis. The historian and Atlantologist Lewis Spence suggested that the remnants of the lost continent were to be found in the islands of the Caribbean, where shallow water covers areas which were above sea level during the last Ice Age.[24]

However, the theory that has come to hold sway with modern archaeologists and prehistorians is the Minoan theory. On this hypothesis Plato's story is to be treated as a fable, based on a distant memory of the Minoan civilization on the Aegean island of Crete. Plato simply placed his island out in the Atlantic so that it could never be found. To make this theory work, Plato's date of 9,000 years before Solon's time has to be discarded and it is proposed that the date has somehow been multiplied by a factor of ten. This would then give a date of only 1500 BC which is about right for the end of the Minoan civilization.

The civilization of Minoan Crete flourished at its height between 1950 BC and 1450 BC, its existence being largely unsuspected before the excavations of Arthur Evans at the palace of Knossos. That Minoan Crete was a great maritime trading nation with riches rivalling Plato's Atlantis is beyond doubt. Its influence extended to the Cyclades and to the mainland of Greece. Its trading relationship with Egypt is also established by the various finds of Egyptian artefacts in the ruined palaces; but the existence of this entire civilization had been forgotten by the time of later classical Greece, except perhaps in legend.

The palaces of Crete show signs of destruction by a series of earthquakes in the years before 1450 BC and these were almost certainly associated with a massive volcanic eruption on the island of Thera (Santorini) only 100 kilometres to the north of Crete. The Thera eruption is thought to have been one of the largest of modern times and would certainly have sent great tidal waves and clouds of airborne ash and pumice in the direction of Crete. However, there is evidence that the Minoan civilization was able to survive for a further century beyond this time. Thera itself has also been proposed as the site of Atlantis following the excavation of the Bronze Age ruins of Akrotiri.[25]

Atlantis has also had its charlatans and tricksters, in fact probably more of these than serious theorists! Perhaps the strangest concerns the American clairvoyant and faith healer Edgar Cayce, who claimed to have discovered that many of his hypnotized clients had lived before and were, in fact, reincarnated Atlantians! From the testimony of hundreds of his clients he built up a picture of an advanced technological society, the equal of our own, which had been destroyed in a nuclear catastrophe in 10,000 BC. Space does not permit a review of all the other more ludicrous ideas linking Atlantis with colonists from Mars, extraterrestrial gods and the rest. It is hardly surprising that any new theory is immediately dismissed by sober-minded archaeologists and historians.

All these bizarre ideas together with all the best-intended research have left the subject of Atlantis in a state of limbo. Even the best of the theories is unsatisfactory for one reason or another and the sheer weight of published material is staggering. The entire subject tends to be dismissed as fiction. Any serious researcher is instantly labelled a 'catastrophist', or something worse, and is relegated to the fringes of science. Just recently, Atlantis has earned itself an entry in *The Dictionary of Imaginary Places*, where it vies for attention along with such locations as Toad Hall, Dracula's Castle and Toyland! It would appear that not only the lost continent, but the very legend itself, has sunk into the depths.

If the truth behind the Atlantis legend is ever to be discovered, then we must return to the original ancient sources and begin again. In addition, Atlantis must be seen in its proper context as merely one of many recollections of a great prehistoric cataclysm. Any suggestion that Thera or Crete is the site of the sunken island has to be immediately rejected. If Solon's sources can indeed be traced back to Archaic Egypt then this would mean that the legend predates the catastrophe itself by about 1,500 years! In any case, the popular Minoan theory completely ignores the evidence of Diodorus Siculus. Both Plato and Diodorus clearly assert that Atlantis was located in the Western Ocean.

Some have also suggested that the name 'Atlantis' is merely Plato's shorthand for 'an Atlantic island'. He asserts that the island was situated 'In the true ocean beyond [or opposite] the Pillars of Heracles'. In Greek mythology, Heracles placed his pillars at the entrance to the Mediterranean and this is the name usually applied to the Straits of Gibraltar by classical writers. Part of Atlantis faced Gadeira. Plato knew where this country was and expected his readers to know. It can be positively identified with the region around Gades, the settlement founded by the Carthaginians in southern Spain on the site of the modern city of Cadiz.

The island was also 'of great size'. The *Timaeus* puts its size at 'larger than Libya and Asia put together'. We cannot know how large Plato thought this to be, but, interestingly, Herodotus used the same form of words to describe the whole of Europe between Spain and the Caspian Sea.[26] It is this very precise size and location that has been the undoing of the Atlantis legend. Modern theories of plate tectonics simply will not permit a large land mass ever to have existed in the Atlantic. There is ample evidence that the sea level has risen during the 12,000 years since the end of the last Ice Age, drowning many coastal areas. But currently accepted theories say that the melting at the end of the Ice Age was a gradual process; the sea level did not rise 'in a single day and a night' but over hundreds of years. The majority of human population centres lie close to sea level. Why should we doubt that a vast amount of human prehistory lies far out on the continental shelves, awaiting the archaeologist?

The weakest link in Plato's description of Atlantis is its supposed great antiquity. The legend is far too detailed and precise to be 12,000 years old. It is inconceivable that a historical account of any kind could have survived through this vast expanse of time. If the story is 12,000 years old then it surely cannot be accurate. If it is accurate in all its detail then it cannot be 12,000 years old.

This very precise dating is based upon the estimate of the antiquity of Egyptian civilization given to Solon by the Egyptian priest. He believed the Egyptian state to be 8,000 years old in his own day, with Atlantis 1,000 years older still. Herodotus calculated a similar time-scale himself for the antiquity of Egypt, also based on information supplied by Egyptian priests; and so it is the accuracy of the Egyptians' own religious chronology that has to be challenged.[27] It is Plato's very precise chronology that has received all the attention; and far less credence has been given to the statement that Atlantis was submerged only shortly before the founding of the Egyptian state. Modern Egyptology offers a very firm date for the formation of a unified Egypt. Both archaeological and documentary evidence place the beginning of the First Dynasty at about 3100 BC. A date of around 3300–3000 BC is therefore the favoured era to look for evidence of Atlantis. If we are to find evidence of a catastrophic event which could hide a large land mass beneath the ocean then it should be sought during this period.

Before it is possible to pursue such enquiries we must define precisely what we are looking for. It is no longer satisfactory to suggest that the Atlantic basin can open up and swallow a continent. Regardless of whether you consider the history or the science to be of the greater interest, the two strands of enquiry are inseparable. The physical processes of the Earth itself must be appreciated. Before we can ask how it might be possible for a land mass to disappear beneath the sea, it is first necessary to investigate precisely what is meant by the term 'sea level'. This is the problem that will be addressed in the next few chapters and it will be quite some time before the subject of Atlantis can be examined again.

3

The Figure of the Earth

The planet upon which we live is usually described as a sphere, an approximation which suffices for most practical purposes. More accurately, it is an oblate spheroid or ellipsoid. Its rotation causes it to bulge at the equator, giving it an equatorial radius of 6,378.16 kilometres compared with its polar radius of 6,356.775 kilometres, a difference in sea level radius of just over 21 kilometres. Small though this seems compared to the scale of the Earth, it has a profound effect on its behaviour.

In fact, the figure of the Earth is very close to the predicted shape of an ellipsoid of revolution that its dynamics demand. The sea level corresponds to an 'equipotential surface', that is to say, the sea level at every point conforms to the height where the attraction of the Earth's gravity pulling it down is balanced by the centrifugal force of rotation tending to throw it outwards. The solid surface also corresponds closely to this theoretical shape. At its highest point it deviates only 8.9 kilometres above the mean, at the lowest ocean trench just over 11 kilometres. But since the Earth is not of uniform density, the equipotential surface does not conform precisely to a perfect ellipsoid, but undulates slightly above and below it due to gravity anomalies. This more irregular surface is termed the geoid. The direction of gravity is perpendicular to the geoid at every point on its surface. It can be represented as the calm ocean surface and its ideal continuation through the continents.

The surveyors and mapmakers soon ran into difficulties when they tried to map the curvature of the various parts of the Earth's land surface. At local level, the shape of the land surface was found to fit best with a series of local ellipsoids rather than the predicted shape for the world as a whole. The curvature of North America fitted best with a particular ellipsoid, Europe with another, Africa different again, and so on. Each of these when extrapolated to the entire globe would give differences of the order of hundreds of metres in predicted heights. It can now be seen more clearly that the 'best fit' ellipsoid differs slightly for each of the continents.

The modern theory of plate tectonics is a development of the earlier theories of continental drift. In 1912 Alfred Wegener, a German meteorologist, first put forward the theory in a credible form, although several earlier theorists had noted the correspondence in the shapes of the continents on either side of the Atlantic Ocean. According to this theory, the present disposition of the continents results from the break up, around 270 million years ago, of a single supercontinent.

The mid-ocean ridges are now known to be the sites where oceanic crust is manufactured by continuous volcanic activity. Where two sections of oceanic crust clash head-on, the crust is forced down into the interior creating the deep ocean trenches; and mountains are created as the continents override the oceanic crust. These independent portions of continental and oceanic crust are termed 'plates', from which the whole science of plate tectonics takes its name.

The continents of Europe and North America can now be seen to have drifted apart as a result of the activity at the Mid-Atlantic spreading ridge, over a period of millions of years. By contrast, the Mediterranean is a region of mountain formation. It is all that now remains of the former Tethys Ocean. The mountain ranges of southern Europe were formed as the northward drift of Africa pushed the former oceanic crust into and under the Eurasian continent.

The eastern Mediterranean and Aegean Sea remains a tectonically active region and earthquakes are a frequent occurrence throughout Greece, Turkey and the Caucasus. To the west this gives way to vulcanism, with active volcanoes in southern Italy and Sicily; but the most explosive volcanoes are reserved for the Aegean, where there is evidence of recent massive explosive eruptions. The largest recent outburst in this region was that at Thera (Santorini) about 3,500 years ago, which has been associated with the demise of the Cretan civilization. The destructive plate margin extends westwards, where it meets the Mid-Atlantic Ridge near the Azores.

By contrast, the Eurasian continental land mass can be seen to be the largest stable block of the crust. It extends from Spain in the west, along its mountainous southern boundary as far east as

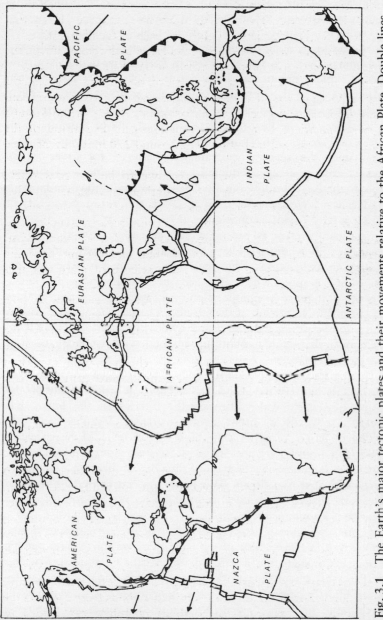

Fig. 3.1 The Earth's major tectonic plates and their movements relative to the African Plate. Double lines indicate spreading ridges. Serrated lines show subduction zones.

Indonesia and the Pacific Ocean. To the north, the Mid-Atlantic Ridge gradually tails off in the Arctic Ocean.

The tectonic theory is now so well established that it has been a revolution in geological thinking. It explains so many geological phenomena that it is surely correct in most of its detail. Not only does it explain mountain building and the similarity between the palaeontology of the continents, but it also explains the occurrence of earthquakes and volcanoes. For the plate boundaries are areas of weakness in the Earth's crust. The locations of volcanoes and earthquake zones correspond very closely with the plate boundaries, with the severest earthquakes reserved for areas where oceanic crust is being subducted beneath continents. Old theories such as the 'land bridge' once proposed to have linked India with Madagascar have been swept away. Gone, too, is any possibility of a sunken Mid-Atlantic continent.

Continental crust is fundamentally different from that of the ocean bed. It is much older and lighter and consists mostly of granite, an association of light silica-based minerals, whereas oceanic crust is composed of heavier basalt containing rather less silica. It is this difference in composition and lower density that enables the continents to remain at the surface, whereas the oceanic crust is continuously subducted and recycled into the interior. There is no mechanism that could explain the subduction of even a fragment of continental crust.

Geologists and geophysicists have also put together a picture of the Earth's internal structure. Seismology, the study of the propagation of seismic waves through the interior of the Earth, has provided a wealth of circumstantial evidence. The discovery that the Earth has a 'crust' is attributed to Andreijei Mohorovicic in 1909. He found that the speed of seismic waves produced by earthquakes changes at the base of the crust, indicating a change in the structure at that depth. This boundary has come to be named after him, the Mohorovicic Discontinuity or 'the Moho'; the region beneath is known as the *mantle*.

Seismic waves can also reveal the structure even deeper down. An earthquake gives rise to two types of seismic waves, which propagate through the interior of the Earth. Compression waves (or P waves) travel fastest and generally arrive first at the seismometer. Shortly afterwards arrive the shear waves (or S waves). Shear waves have the property that they cannot be propagated through a

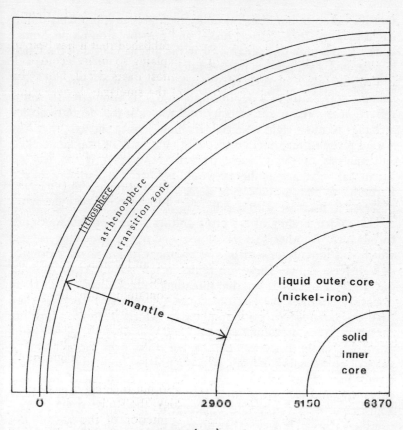

Fig. 3.2 The principal layers of the Earth.

liquid and this has been used to establish the existence of a *liquid core* at a depth of around 2,890 kilometres. The P waves are strongly refracted at the core–mantle boundary.

The mantle above seems to be a remarkably uniform layer at whatever geographical position is investigated; however it does show evidence of layering, indicating a gradual change of composition or chemical phase, with depth. It consists largely of olivine, a dense silicate mineral rich in magnesium and sodium. By contrast the high density of the core leads to the conclusion that it is a

swirling ocean of liquid metal under high pressure, probably dominated by a mixture of iron, nickel and possibly iron oxide. Somewhere deep within this ocean of iron the magnetic field of the Earth
is generated, by a process not yet fully understood.

Evidence also suggests that within this liquid core, a *solid
metallic core* exists at a depth of about 5,150 kilometres. A sharp
refraction and rise in the velocity of P waves at this depth indicates
a change to more rigid material. Its high density suggests that it is
a solid phase of the outer core consisting mostly of iron and nickel;
and analysis of the P wave pattern shows that it too has an
equatorial bulge just as theory would predict. The flattening of the
Earth due to its rotation can be detected even at these depths and is
observed to decrease with depth.

Our understanding of the crust and its processes also continues
to advance. Another feature of the mid-ocean spreading ridges,
which was initially missed by the oceanographers, is the existence
of transform faults. These are faults in the oceanic crust running
out at right angles from the spreading ridges themselves. Their
discovery removed the last objections to tectonic theory, as they
gave the oceanic crust a boundary at which it could adjust its
curvature to the prevailing ellipsoid and thus obey the demands of
gravity. Clearly, if a continental plate drifts over the millions of
years of geological time from, say, the polar regions to the equator,
it must move from a flatter part of the ellipsoid to one of increased
curvature, and vice versa. In a theory of gradual spreading, slow
adjustment of curvature takes place at these transform faults. The
continental crust, however, has no such mechanism and presumably
each continent must retain the curvature equivalent to the part of
the Earth on which it formed.

Theories do exist that could explain how the continental blocks
can, at least partially, adjust their shape and height. Recently, the
analysis of shear waves has revealed yet another unexpected surprise. In the 1980s geophysicists gave up waiting for earthquakes
to produce shear waves and began to probe the crust with shear
waves of their own. For the first time, this revealed that in certain
cases the waves from a single source can be split, arriving at the
detector polarized along a specific direction and thus implying that
a diffraction has taken place. The conclusion is that the crust, and
possibly also the upper mantle, is riddled with fluid-filled cracks of
random size and orientation. The existence of such cracks would

allow the crust to flex with the stresses of geological processes, by the squeezing of water or magma from one crack to another. It would appear that the Earth's crust is designed to be somewhat flexible.

On a much larger scale, deformations of the crust have been explained by the theories of *isostasy* and *eustasy*. The continents can be modelled as 'floating' on top of the heavier mantle at their equilibrium height, just as an iceberg floats on water. Indeed, the average height of all the oceanic crust is about 4,500 metres below sea level whereas that of the continents is only 100 metres above it. The oceans fill the troughs in between and, fortunately for us, some of the continental crust is left above the sea for us to live on. Only at the volcanic spreading ridges do islands of oceanic crust break the surface, of which bleak Iceland is the only large example.

Precisely how much of the continental crust is exposed above sea level at any epoch varies according to the amount of water locked up in the polar ice caps and in living matter. In the recent geological past, the polar ice caps have been larger and consequently the sea level lower. At times the ice caps have disappeared altogether allowing a raised ocean to transgress much more of the continental shelves, forming shallow seas. Today shallow seas cover only a small area of the globe, of which the prime example is the European continental shelf around the British Isles. Other examples of shallow continental shelves exist off Argentina and between Australia and New Guinea. Variations of the sea level due to this exchange are termed *glacial-eustasy*.

If the additional weight of a polar ice cap is added to a continent, then the crust is depressed into the mantle. This is observed to occur in both Greenland and Antarctica, which would lie mostly below sea level without their ice cover. By the same token, oceanic crust should therefore rise during periods when the polar ice caps are larger, due to the loading of ocean water thus removed from it. This compensatory mechanism is known as *isostasy*. Evidence to support these theories comes from the apparent rise of land in areas such as Scandinavia and Canada. These regions were formerly covered by polar ice sheets and may still be adjusting to the removal of the ice burden.

All these changes, and the theories that describe them, rely on gradual effects. Current theory dictates that eustatic effects are primarily driven by changes in world climate acting over hundreds of years. Eustatic effects drive isostatic responses, which keep the Earth's surface close to the ellipsoid shape, imposed by the strait-jacket of its mass and rate of rotation. Although such processes may be considered rapid on the geological time-scale, they are scarcely noticeable within a human lifetime.

Another idea proposed before the theories of plate tectonics took hold was that of polar wandering. Throughout the nineteenth and early twentieth centuries, palaeontologists continued to uncover fossil evidence of tropical life forms in sediments at high polar latitudes. Evidence exists, too, of former ice sheets in the Sahara and the world-wide existence of coal measures – fossilized tropical swamps – had to be explained. Various theories were advanced to explain the wandering of the rotational axis within the Earth over millions of years, interchanging the polar and tropical regions. Such phenomena can now all be readily explained in terms of continental drift and the polar wandering theories have fallen out of favour. However, there is nothing to rule out the occurrence of both polar wandering and continental drift.

If we leave aside, for the purposes of illustration, the question of how a change in the position of the rotational axis might occur, then it is possible to draw some interesting conclusions. As has been described, the Earth's land surface corresponds very closely to the geoid, as defined by the surface of the calm ocean. If the position of the rotational poles were to be displaced to a new geographical location, then the spheroid would have to move with them. The centrifugal acceleration at every point on the Earth's surface would be altered. The fluid oceans would rapidly conform to this new geoid, probably within just one or two revolutions. However the solid body of the Earth would be unable to react quite so quickly; depending how rigid the crust is considered to be, it would take somewhat longer to adjust to the new geoid.

Another possibility to consider is a change in the rate of rotation, or, rather, a change in the length of the day. Again leaving aside how this might happen, its effect may be seen. An increase in speed would 'flatten' the ellipsoid, thus increasing the equatorial bulge. The oceans would immediately adjust to the new ellipsoid causing increases in sea level at latitudes below 45°, with decreasing sea level at latitudes above 45°. For a slowing down of the rotation, the effect would be reversed.

The argument usually cited against any major change in the

length of the day during the recent geological past is that no obvious 'piling up' of the oceans is observed in either polar or equatorial regions; but all that this really implies is that the solid Earth has also had sufficient time to adjust its figure. If it has ever occurred then, as with polar wandering, we would only be able to detect it from the evidence which such a temporary change of sea level would leave behind in the form of raised or submerged shorelines.

Pierre Laplace, the great French mathematician, was the first to describe mathematically the surface geometry of an ellipsoid of revolution. His equations remain at the heart of modern geodesy and geophysics. He described what would happen at the surface of the Earth following a shift of the rotational axis and saw in it a mechanism that could explain the biblical Flood. A change in the characteristics of the Earth's rotation would cause the oceans to leave their beds and transgress the land, wiping out human and animal life on all but the highest peaks. Although he wrote in an era when it was the norm to explain all geological phenomena as the consequence of the deluge, we may still accept many of his conclusions today.

The oceans would indeed transgress the land surface in many places, but elsewhere new land would be revealed as the seashore moved further out. The vertical and horizontal directions at each point would be altered. All our carefully constructed level surfaces would become slopes. Our tall modern buildings would no longer be vertical and most would collapse. Rivers would be forced to change their courses, as the flowing water took the shortest route to the lower level; and lakes would be tipped out of their beds. There is a tendency to regard the sea level and our everyday perception of 'up' and 'down' as fixtures of our world, but they are intimately tied up with the rotational dynamics of the planet we live on. It is only the constant rotation of the Earth on its axis that allows us an illusion of stability.

Consider the implications of even a small change in the position of the rotational poles. The maximum effects would be felt along the great circle of longitude (see figure 3.3), passing through the new and old pole positions. The effects would diminish proportionately to the east and west until at 90° east and west of the line hardly any sea level change would occur. The new equator would also cross the old equator at 90° east and west of the line of greatest effect and these are the only two points, on opposite sides of the Earth, at which geoid height would remain unchanged.

If the body of the Earth is treated as totally rigid (which it surely is not) then the change in land heights at various points can be estimated. Proceeding on a theoretical journey from the new North Pole towards the new equator along the line of greatest effect, we would first pass through a region where the sea level is depressed to the new ellipsoid, but the solid crust retains its former curvature. However, proceeding on from the new equator to the new South Pole, the effect would be reversed. The new ellipsoid is above the old ellipsoid and the sea level rises to it, drowning the former land surface. Continuing the journey, we would pass through another

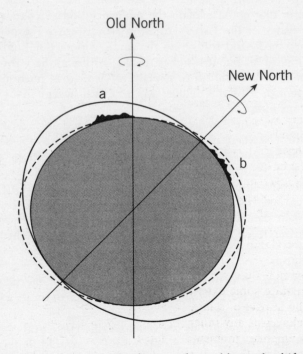

Fig. 3.3 A greatly exaggerated view of a sudden pole shift through 45°. As the oceans conform immediately to the new ellipsoid, the land mass at 'a' is submerged, while the formerly submerged continent at 'b' is revealed. There are two opposite quarter-spheres where the sea level has fallen and two where it has risen.

region of lowered sea level on the way back to the equator, followed by a further zone of sea level rise between the equator and the North Pole. The effects would be repeated exactly in alternate quarter-spheres. There are two quarter-spheres where the sea level would fall and two where it would rise. The geodetic effect at any point on the Earth's surface would be repeated precisely at its antipodes.

The magnitude of the geodetic effect can be roughly estimated. The greatest possible change would be for a pole shift through a full 90°, interchanging the poles with the equator. The geodetic effect would then be equivalent to the full 21 kilometres of the equatorial bulge. But there is no need to consider such an extreme case as this. For a shift of just a single degree of latitude, the predicted change in radius near the equator would be of the order of 6–7 metres, and a similar amount at the poles. The greatest effect would occur at mid-latitudes, where a latitude change from, say, 45° to 46° would imply a change in sea level of about 373 metres. Even a pole shift of just a fraction of a degree would be enough to cause noticeable effects around world coastlines, especially at temperate latitudes. Here, then, is a mechanism that could hide an island beneath the sea 'in the course of a single day and a night'; not because the island has sunk – but because the natural level of the sea has risen!

It must be borne in mind, however, that the foregoing illustration is greatly oversimplified. The geophysicists regularly monitor tiny shifts in the position of the rotational poles and infer from them much about the internal structure of the Earth. Any significant change in the rotational characteristics of the planet, of the kind under consideration here, would have to follow a complex transitional phase.

A common misconception is that a shift of the rotational axis would require some external force to be applied to the Earth, for which the impact of a large meteorite or comet is often cited. The Earth behaves as any other rotating body and in any such interaction its angular momentum must be conserved. The angular momentum can be visualized as a vector acting northwards along the axis of rotation. If some external force acts to change the direction of this vector then the whole planet must move with it and the geographical location of the rotational poles on the surface of the Earth would remain unchanged. Polar wandering is quite a

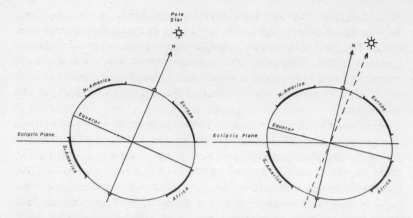

Figs. 3.4 and 3.5 The effect of a change in the obliquity of the rotational axis *in space*; the tilt to the ecliptic is altered, but the geographical position of the poles remains constant.

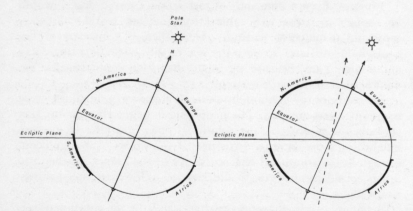

Figs. 3.6 and 3.7 An illustration of a change in the *geographical* position of the rotational poles; the axis continues to point in the same direction in space and the Earth adjusts relative to it.

different consideration. It implies a change in the geographical position of the axis within the Earth, which does not necessarily imply any change in angular momentum. A shift of the rotational axis only requires the Earth to distort its shape somewhat such that its mass distribution is altered. The instantaneous rotational axis would then no longer coincide with the axis of maximum moment of inertia. In a rotating body with unconstrained axes, this condition is unstable. Either the axis of rotation must move to coincide again with the maximum inertia axis, or, conversely, the body must deform so that it becomes symmetrical about the new axis.

A fair analogy here would be an unbalanced motor car wheel. In a perfectly balanced wheel, the centre of gravity of the wheel coincides with the centre of the wheel's axis; but if a tyre wall bulges, or uneven tread wear takes place, the centre of gravity could be displaced from the ideal position and the wheel would wobble. This manifests itself as a nasty bumpy ride which the driver can feel through the steering wheel. The condition is easily corrected by adding weights to the wheel rim so as to bring the centre of mass back to the centre of the axle. No external forces cause the wobble, only a change in the mass distribution of the wheel itself. The wheel tries to change the position of its axis, but cannot as its axle is fixed.

The astronomer Thomas Gold considered just such a change in the mass distribution of the Earth.[1] A rotating planet has no fixed axis, and so it is free to wander if the mass distribution were to change. By way of illustration his theory considered the rapid building of a mountain on some part of the crust. This would leave the rotation unstable or 'excited', as the planet would no longer be rotating about its axis of maximum moment of inertia. The axis must then migrate so as to pass through the new centre of mass, and to maximize the moment of inertia by placing the new mountain at the greatest possible distance from the axis. This can only occur when the rotation has changed such that the new mountain is placed on the equator. Gold considered that such a migration would require many millions of years. No external forces act. Throughout this process the angular momentum vector continues to point in the same direction in space. The movement should therefore be visualized as one of the planet relative to the axis, rather than as a change in the obliquity of the axis itself.

The discussion up to this point has conveniently side-stepped the problem of how such a migration of the axis could occur more rapidly. In considering changes over the geological time-scale it is perhaps acceptable to argue that a pole shift could occur as a result of imperceptibly slow processes; however a shift on a shorter time-scale requires altogether different consideration.[2]

An instantaneous shift requires a sudden redistribution of mass to take place on or within the planet, such that the axis of maximum moment of inertia is torn away from the axis of instantaneous rotation. A wobble must then develop as the two axes try to realign themselves once again. The imbalance would set up temporary isostatic strains in the crust and mantle. Some areas of the crust would suddenly find themselves above their position of isostatic balance and would therefore tend to sink. Conversely those portions of the crust now below it would tend to rise. These combined movements would continue until the two axes again coincided and the wobble would be extinguished. Within this transitional period there is scope for dramatic changes to occur at the surface, especially on a planet with an ocean.

A chicken-and-egg argument arises here. How could such sudden movements of mass occur within the Earth? In simple language, this means massive earthquakes; the sudden rise, fall, or lateral movement of large parts of the crust and interior. Rotational imbalance would cause sudden mass movements, but sudden mass movements are necessary to explain the initial imbalance! While no external forces are required to explain a pole shift, they are needed to account for the initial rotational imbalance. It is difficult to avoid the conclusion that a force external to the Earth is required to start the process.

To find such a process, one must look to the other planets of the solar system. Little is known about the geology of our planetary neighbours and theories are inevitably driven by what can be most readily observed: the effect of impact phenomena on their surfaces. The Earth would have as many impact craters as the Moon but for the combined effects of weathering and tectonic activity. We can also observe that planets such as Mercury and Venus, which scarcely rotate at all, are almost perfectly spherical and show few signs of tectonic activity. However, on planets such as Mars and the outer planetary moons there is ample evidence of surface cracks and rills indicative of geological activity, as well as the expected flattening of their shapes due to their rotation. These planets have clearly had to adjust to the effects of impacts; why should the Earth be considered differently?

Perhaps the fall of a comet is not the only possible external influence upon our planet. Gravitational interaction, or a magnetic interaction with some other astronomical body have been variously proposed from time to time.[3] Gravitational or 'tidal' forces have to be ruled out, by considering the minimal effect of the Moon's gravity on the Earth. The Moon regularly raises tides in the oceans and the so-called bodily tides are a small but detectable phenomenon. There is no evidence that these could cause sudden movements of mass, and in any case the Earth has endured these strains throughout its existence.

It would seem that if one is determined to contest the gradualist consensus of modern geology, then impact phenomena have to be considered as the only feasible cause, either directly or indirectly, of catastrophic events. If a sizeable extraterrestrial object has impacted the Earth in, say, the last 10,000 years, then it has left no obvious remains for us to find. Those who argue against such a possibility would cite the absence of a suitably large and recent impact crater, or any other evidence of such an unwelcome visitor. Surely, the argument goes, a meteorite or comet impact large enough to trigger a geological catastrophe would have to be so large that we could not fail to detect some physical evidence of it. Just because no direct evidence of a recent impact is known, is this really sufficient proof that it has not occurred?

There is really nothing new about the association of comets with disaster. Every new comet that our ancestors saw in the sky was accompanied by prophecies of doom and this fear must have been based on a genuine memory of a close encounter in the remote past. Proclus, in his commentary on the *Timaeus*, saw a comet as the most likely explanation of the legend of Phaeton.[4]

And it will be among the number of things that may be easily accomplished, if it is supposed that this Phaeton was a comet, which being dissolved produced an intolerable dryness from vehement heat. For this supposition is generally adopted. Porphyry therefore says that certain signs may be assumed from the motion of comets. For when this motion is towards the southern parts it is indicative of tempests, towards the north of dryness from excessive heat, towards the east of pestilence, and towards the west of fertility. The disappearance of a comet is said to be destruction by thunder.

4

Target Earth

Some 4,600 million years have elapsed since the formation of the solar system and the Earth. As the swirling solar nebula collapsed to form the Sun, it left behind a variety of debris rotating in a thin disc along the plane of its equator. This material would have consisted of the kind of matter that astronomers can observe in the galactic nebulae today. As well as dust and gas, there would have been larger chunks of matter, ranging from dust size to several kilometres in diameter.

Initially, the composition of the solar nebula would have been fairly homogeneous. The larger bodies would have been composed of a mix of iron, stony silicates and ices, mixed together in various proportions. But once the Sun's nuclear reactions began, the volatile constituents were vaporized and blown by the solar wind to the outer parts of the nebula, leaving the remaining iron and stony bodies to collide and condense into the inner planets. Today, this process of accretion is virtually complete, but even now a little of this loose material remains to bombard the planets occasionally.

That the Earth has suffered from collisions with these minor bodies throughout its history is not in doubt. Studies of the cratering histories of the Moon and the other inner planets reveal that the rate of cratering has declined dramatically to only one-ten-thousandth of that of 4 billion years ago. The first billion years of the Earth's existence were dominated by impact events!

Today the Earth is still subject to continuous bombardment from small chunks of interplanetary material. The majority burn up in the upper atmosphere, but if they survive to strike the surface they are termed *meteorites*. Most of these objects are of the stony type, consisting of silicates and a little iron, but about 7 per cent are of the heavy iron type. These consist of roughly 90 per cent iron, with the rest nickel and a few trace elements. Although many thousands of meteors enter the Earth's atmosphere every year, they are usually quite tiny; of those discovered on the surface, the largest weighed only about 70 tons. Larger objects by far still roam the inner solar system; and these are the *asteroids*. Only the larger ones can be observed, but the term is generally used to describe any minor planetary body in orbit about the Sun, ranging from bodies hundreds of kilometres in diameter down to observable limits.

Evidence for the occasional impact of these larger bodies is drawn from the existence of the small- and medium-sized craters on the Moon, together with the few that exist on the Earth. The best known of terrestrial craters is the Barringer crater in Arizona. Although impressive in appearance, it is quite small by the standards set elsewhere in the solar system. At 1.2 kilometres in diameter, it is the best-preserved large crater on Earth and is thought to be between 25,000 and 40,000 years old; the body that formed it was probably no more than 30 metres in diameter. Many larger and more heavily eroded craters are known, such as the circular Lake Manicouagan in Quebec, Canada, which is about 60 kilometres in diameter and thought to be 210 million years old. Another, the Popigai crater in Siberia, has a diameter of 100 kilometres and is estimated to be 39 million years old.

The most surprising factor is not the existence of such craters, but rather their relative scarcity. There should be more evidence than we find of smaller, more recent impacts. It could be argued that smaller craters would erode very quickly to the point where they become unrecognizable. Many more may exist in jungle or polar regions, but by far the majority of impacting bodies must have fallen into the oceans. The oceans make up nearly 71 per cent of the Earth's total surface area, and so it can be estimated that for every crater found on land, three more objects of similar size must have hit the oceans.

There may be other reasons for the scarcity of discernible cratering. A circular impact crater implies that the projectile impacted at quite a steep angle. For each of these there must also have been others that impacted at a shallow trajectory, leaving a less obvious scar. As with circular craters, these would soon be eroded by rivers or landslip, or fill up with water such that they become indistinguishable from any other kind of lake; the less circular the impact scar, then the less natural erosion would be required to disguise it.

There is another group of astronomical bodies which occasionally cross the orbit of the Earth and they are the *comets*. These are the remnants of the frozen volatile components of the early solar nebula. A sizeable population of these icy bodies reside in permanent orbits on the outer edge of the solar system. Occasionally, chance gravitational interaction diverts a few of them into the inner solar system, where they suffer the same fate as their primeval brothers. The frozen volatiles are vaporized and blown off to form the spectacular tail that we recognize as a comet.

The composition of comets, long a source of speculation, has now been largely settled. The Giotto probe investigated Halley's comet during its 1986 return and was able to confirm the hypothesis that a comet is little more than a 'dirty snowball'.[1] Its head, or coma, was observed to consist of 80 per cent, by volume, of water. Other ions present indicated the presence of carbon, sulphur and their oxides together with larger dust particles. The nucleus was found to be a dark irregular body about 15 kilometres long by 10 kilometres wide.

Halley's comet is just a typical example of a comet that has become trapped in the inner part of the solar system and is gradually losing all its icy constituents. The fact that sufficient remain to form a bright tail is evidence that it must have become trapped in its present orbit during only the last few thousand years, probably due to a close encounter with one of the outer planets. Other shorter period comets are known which have such poor tails as to be barely distinguishable from asteroids. The theory is unproven, but asteroids themselves may be only the remains of very old comet nuclei. Indeed all the evidence indicates that comets contain some rock and that asteroids can contain icy material. There may well be no sharp distinction between the two types of object.

Most of the asteroids, including all the really large ones, reside in orbits between Mars and Jupiter. However, a number of smaller objects are now known, with orbital periods similar to that of the Earth. They are all so small that they can be seen only during a close approach. One of these, named Icarus, came within 6 million kilometres of the Earth in 1968; another, Hermes, passed within only 1.2 million kilometres of us in 1937 and has not been seen since. As recently as 23 March 1989 the tiny asteroid FC1989 crossed the Earth's orbit at a distance only twice that of the Moon, travelling at a speed of 20 kilometres per second.[2] This is surely evidence enough that such close encounters are a regular occurrence.

We may therefore conclude that the Earth has experienced many more comet and asteroid impacts than may be detected from the cratering evidence alone. Not only have many fallen into the sea, but also many more may have impacted at shallow angles and therefore not left anything now recognizable as an impact scar. To form a circular crater the impacting body must strike at an angle greater than about 10–30°. At trajectories more oblique than this the crater may become elongated, or ricochet effects may spread the ejecta over a much wider area.[3]

The Earth may be likened to a 'target' in space. The gravity field

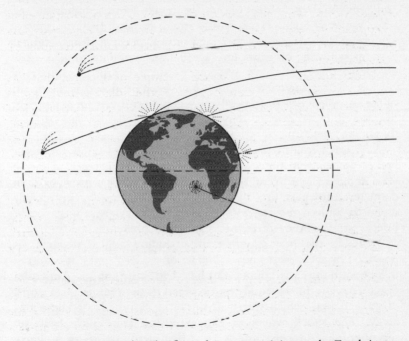

Fig. 4.1 Target Earth! The flux of comets arriving at the Earth is not homogeneous. The vast majority arrive out of the ecliptic plane; and this suggests that the majority of high-latitude impacts should be at an oblique angle. For a near-tangential encounter the impacting body may bounce off again into space.

of the Earth extends out into space to many times its diameter; but to form a circular crater the incoming comet must hit the 'bull's-eye'. It is to be expected that a far larger number of these randomly aimed projectiles would enter the outer rings of this target and thus be drawn inwards to impact at shallow angles. Clearly the size of this target, or capture zone, depends on the size and velocity of the approaching body. A comet travelling slowly has a far larger capture zone than one of equivalent mass travelling at a high velocity.

Theoretical studies have shown that the most likely angle of incidence for an impacting body is 45°. A quarter of all events should occur at less than 30° with near-tangential events being quite rare. However the tendency for solar system debris to orbit close to the ecliptic modifies this estimate such that shallow-angle and tangential encounters should be much more common in the polar regions.[4] Such objects would streak through the atmosphere, skimming the surface of either land or sea, perhaps disintegrating, perhaps bouncing off again into space after giving up some of their energy to the Earth. Firm evidence of such oblique encounters is elusive; but grazing comet impacts have been proposed as the origin of the so-called 'oriented lakes' and a geologically recent crater field discovered in Argentina may have been made by just such a 'bouncing' meteorite.[5]

Additional confirmation that this principle must apply for larger bodies comes from observation of the tracks of meteors, shooting stars and the slightly larger meteors of the order of a metre or so in diameter, known as 'fireballs'. Very few are observed to fall steeply to Earth. Indeed the majority of shooting stars are tiny particles, briefly visible as they graze the upper atmosphere.

Probably the best example of a shallow-angle encounter is provided by the largest known impact of modern times. It occurred in Siberia in the early hours of 30 June 1908: the famous 'Tunguska event'. An enormous explosion occurred in the remote taiga north of Lake Baikal, which was heard in cities hundreds of kilometres away. The shock waves of the explosion were picked up on seismographs in Irkutsk and were at first attributed to an ordinary earthquake. Clouds of dust thrown up by the explosion caused an unusual glow in the night skies of Europe for several days afterwards.

The intervention of wars and revolutions sadly prevented investigation of the area until nearly 20 years later when the Soviet scientist Leonid Kulik took an expedition to the area. Kulik expected to find an enormous crater like that in Arizona, resulting from the fall of a meteorite, but instead he found something much more interesting. Over an area several kilometres in diameter, trees had been stripped of their leaves and branches, charred and blown over. From the higher ground he could see that the fallen trees formed a 'fan' pattern as if they had all been blown over by the force of the blast.[6] He was unable to find any sign of a crater, only a series of small shallow depressions filled with swamp water. The entire area showed evidence of intense heat and burning.

He was also able to collect eyewitness accounts from some of the local inhabitants. One peasant described how 'a huge fireball that covered an enormous part of the sky' had appeared out of the north-west. An intense flash of light and heat had burned the shirt from his back and forced him to take shelter. At that moment an enormous explosion had blown him off his feet, leaving him unconscious for several minutes. Some witnesses described a firestorm, which had destroyed the forest and their reindeer. Others confirmed that before the fall the Tungus region had been normal green forest and that all the devastation was entirely due to the fall and the fire that followed.

Later expeditions were able to survey the site in greater detail. Every tree had been blown down over an area some 30 kilometres in radius. No debris from the impacting body was found in this region, however the 1962 expedition of Florensky found a trail of meteoric dust over an area 250 kilometres to the north-west of the zone of devastation. Magnetite and silicate particles less than a millimetre in diameter were discovered in the soil.

Florensky concluded that the Tunguska object was a comet nucleus; entering the atmosphere from an east-south-easterly direction it exploded in the atmosphere above the zone of destruction, scattering micrometeoritic debris to the north-west. He considered that this was consistent with the approach of a small comet, unobserved as it moved across the daylight sky.[7] It hit the Earth, as he put it, 'squarely on the side'. In fact it shows that the angle of approach was almost tangential in this case and that the entire force of the impact was small enough to be absorbed within the atmosphere. The unstable and highly reactive ions found in a comet head would react explosively on contact with the air; the water which composed the bulk of the comet's nucleus simply dissipated leaving little trace. All this destruction was caused by a lump of dirty ice at most 100–120 metres in diameter!

If encounters with cometary debris of equivalent scale to the Tunguska object are to be expected every few hundred years, then we should expect to find references to such visitations in historical records and legends. Clube and Napier conclude that as many as fifty impacts of equivalent size could have occurred in the last 5,000 years! Many ancient myths and legends exist that could be descriptions of a comet fall, and some of these will be studied later. The legend of Phaeton alluded to by Plato and immortalized in poetry by Ovid, is but one example.[8] One other will suffice for this discussion. Diodorus Siculus describes something that sounds remarkably similar to the eyewitness accounts of the Tunguska event.

Diodorus describes a frightful monster, the Monster of the Aegis, which attacked Phrygia (Asia Minor) and burned the land such that even in his own day the region was known as 'Burned Phrygia'.[9] Diodorus tells us that the Aegis then burned up the forests over a wide area extending as far as India and returning to burn parts of Lebanon, Egypt and Libya, to disappear in the 'regions of the west'. It finally fell to Earth in the Ceraunian forests, a region that can be tentatively identified with Epirus, or perhaps the Caucasus. It is impossible to attach a date to a legend such as this but we may assume that it is much older than the classical era.

If the somewhat convoluted path taken by the Monster of the Aegis is overlooked, the legend would seem to describe a perfect example of an oblique comet impact. It may be that the simultaneous impact of several cometary fragments is being described here. Another possibility is that the Aegis was a single comet, which orbited the Earth once or twice, grazing the atmosphere in several places and bouncing off again, before it finally fell to its destruction. The devastation would survive long after the eyewitnesses had died, leaving their children in no doubt that the monster described by their parents was real. Human imagination then did the rest!

Much recent discussion has centred on the possible climatic effects of a major impact in remote prehistory. Comet impacts are now seriously proposed as the boundary events of major geological periods. A popular theme is the effect of the dust clouds which would be thrown up into the upper atmosphere, blocking off the rays of the Sun. The force of an impact might trigger volcanic activity, sending yet more clouds of dust into the air and lowering the temperature of the entire world. Dust clouds like these, we are told, may have killed off the dinosaurs, freezing and choking them into extinction. But there has been very little discussion of the possibility that a comet impact might trigger geodetic effects, or of the outcome of an impact in the ocean. Scientific discussion centres on the possibility of gigantic impact events occurring at intervals of tens of millions of years. The lesser impacts which must have occurred in the intervening periods are just not considered powerful enough to cause lasting geological changes.[10]

It is worth while at this point to investigate the effect of an impact in the ocean. Since the ocean is a much softer medium than rock, the shock would push aside a water-crater much larger than would occur on land. Vast quantities of water would be thrown high into the atmosphere. The crater would really be no more than a huge splash. The splash would rapidly subside but energy would be carried away from the point of impact in the form of waves. The enormous power of such waves is difficult to appreciate, but we may compare them to the waves generated by underwater earthquakes.

The Japanese have regularly experienced such 'tidal waves' throughout their history and have even given them a name: 'tsunami'. The huge waves generated by Pacific earthquakes can travel across the entire Pacific Ocean, halfway round the world, without dissipating. When they finally reach the shallower water of the continental shelves their amplitude increases until by the time they reach the shore they may be hundreds of metres high. Tsunamis have been known to pick up and deposit ships far inland.

The tsunami caused by an oceanic impact would be at least as impressive. For a large impact, waves a kilometre or more in height could be expected. When these reached a continent their destructive power would be awesome. They would have the capacity to inundate the low-lying coastal areas for hundreds of kilometres inland. These waves alone could transport an enormous mass of water right round the world and any such sudden movements of mass would disturb the Earth's rotational balance. The axis of maximum moment of inertia would be dragged away from the axis of rotation and a nutation would develop. The world-wide geodetic effects described previously could then be expected to occur.

Once again the possibility of a shallow-angle impact must be considered. It is easy to imagine the effect that the Tunguska comet would have had if it had hit the ocean instead of the land. A comparable object would slice a long 'furrow' in the ocean and push a great slug of water ahead of it. In these circumstances the entire energy of the comet might be expended in transporting a mass of ocean water around the planet, not to mention the disruption of the atmospheric weather systems.

An impact of comparable energy on land would not affect the oceans in this way. Certainly the result would be analogous to a particularly violent earthquake, but the potential for it to affect the rotational balance is greatly reduced. Unless the worst effects were felt in a tectonically unstable region, then probably the worst outcome would be violent world-wide volcanic activity. The apparent lack of evidence for recent large impacts argues strongly that any recent falls must have occurred in the oceans. It is also a strong indicator that they were comet impacts rather than silicate or iron meteorites. If the impacting comet nucleus were sufficiently large, then it would survive its short journey through the atmosphere and oceans, to expend its remaining energy in an impact on the ocean floor. Its geological effects would then scarcely differ from those of an impact on land, but with the additional destructive power of the oceanic disturbance.

The problem remains: do cometary impacts possess sufficient energy to cause the scale of geodetic effects outlined in the previous chapter? A massive impact would surely have left some trace, and so the question has to be asked: are there any circumstances in which geodetic effects could be triggered by quite a small object, one small enough to be undetectable a few thousand years later?

In considering the impact of a smaller body, its velocity becomes much more significant. Comets may approach the Earth from all directions, with velocities varying from 11 kilometres per second to as much as 72 kilometres per second.[11] The magnitude of these velocities becomes apparent when one considers that the average velocity of a rifle bullet lies in the range 15–30 kilometres per second. At these high energies, even a body of very modest mass has catastrophe potential.

The angle at which the comet strikes the surface also becomes highly significant. A perfectly vertical strike is most unlikely. For any other angle, the force exerted on the point of impact can be resolved into its horizontal and vertical components. Only a part of the energy would be wasted in the impact itself. The rest would be transferred to the Earth as a shock wave propagated in the direction of the projectile. If the impact occured at a steep angle, then most of the energy would ultimately go into modifying the Earth's orbital motion. If the angle were to be shallower than 45° then the greater part would be exerted as a rotation of the Earth's outer shell. As has been discussed, there is every reason to believe that oblique, or near tangential, impacts should be fairly common, especially among those occurring at high latitudes.

In the case of a near tangential impact, most of the energy of the comet would be manifested as a turning couple, about an axis at right angles to the direction of impact. The impact event may be considered as exerting an angular impulse upon the Earth. An impulse is a large force acting for only a short period of time, during which momentum is transferred. In this case, the linear momentum of the comet through space would be converted into the angular momentum of the Earth's rotation.

A simple analogy may help with the visualization of this. Consider a stationary billiard ball resting on a table. If you strike this ball with the cue exactly at its centre, then the linear momentum of the cue is transferred to the ball as a simple linear impulse, causing it to slide across the table. However, if you strike the ball near the top, then it will instead begin to roll. In this case, the linear momentum of the cue is for the most part converted into the rolling momentum of the ball. This exchange of energy can be represented as an angular impulse.

At first sight it may seem absurd to suggest that an object as small as a comet would be able to affect the rotation of a body as massive as the Earth. Indeed for a comet or asteroid to have a kinetic energy equivalent to the Earth's rotation then it would need to be truly enormous, with a diameter of hundreds of kilometres; one might almost term such an object a minor planet. By comparison, a body the size of Halley's comet has a diameter of only about 12 kilometres, with most comets smaller even than this. However, we need not consider impacts of such rotation-stopping magnitude. An average-sized comet would be quite sufficient to disturb the position of the rotational axis by a fraction of a degree of latitude, and that is all that would be required to trigger geodetic changes. Even quite a small comet striking the Earth at a shallow trajectory could affect the rotation.

A freely rotating body, such as a spinning planet, cannot respond directly to an angular impulse in the way that a non-spinning body is able to do. Instead its axis would be forced to *precess*. The impulse would not produce a rotation in the direction of the impulse, but at right angles to it. The effect would be as shown in figure 4.2. Comparison may be made between a spinning planet and a spinning gyroscope, or top. A rapidly spinning gyroscope has the ability to resist any force that would tend to change the direction of its rotational axis. However, this must not be over-stated. The Earth's spin is very slow; it possesses a high angular momentum only due to its great mass. It must be considered as having rotational stability only over geological time, against slowly acting forces.

A further factor to consider is how the shock of the impact

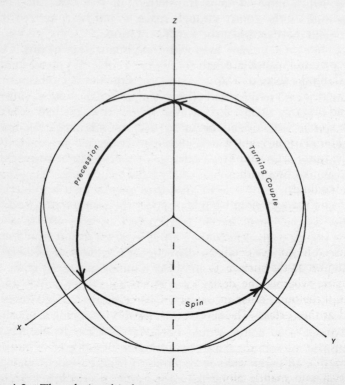

Fig. 4.2 The relationship between turning couple, precession and spin.

would be transmitted from the point of impact to the rest of the planet. The transfer of momentum resulting from the impulse is entirely localized at the point of impact. This is quite unlike the tidal effect of the Moon or the astronomical precession, which act upon every molecule of the Earth simultaneously. An impact would be more like an earthquake. The shock would be transmitted to the rest of the body of the planet, via the medium of seismic waves.

It should be apparent from everyday experience that an impulse cannot be transmitted through a liquid. This can be verified by a simple experiment: spin up a raw egg on a smooth surface and then momentarily stop it with your finger. The egg will begin to spin again as the retained momentum of the central yolk is transferred back to the shell. It is for similar reasons that the shear waves resulting from an earthquake cannot pass through the fluid outer core of the Earth. Any force that tended to apply a rotation to the surface of the Earth could not be directly transmitted to the deep core.[12]

The crust and mantle are not totally rigid and would be capable of absorbing the force of a small impact by deformation. However, if the impulse were to be sufficiently great then the entire outer crust and mantle would slip against the fluid outer core. This slippage would then continue until the viscous friction at the core–mantle boundary brought it to a halt. The overall effect would be to set the outer crust and mantle rotating about a different axis to the solid inner core, with a region of transition created within the intervening fluid.

This is only a very simple intuitive view of the phenomenon and in reality the effect would be a great deal more complicated. However such considerations may be left until the next chapter to be discussed in greater detail. Here we are only concerned with its manifestation at the surface and the geodetic effects would be just as dramatic whether the deep core is affected or not.[13] It is the rotation of the outer crust and mantle which largely determines the ellipsoid at the surface. The contribution of the inner core rotation is minimal.

This greatly reduces the scale of impact required to trigger a shift in the Earth's axis. Far less energy would be needed to rotate the outer crust and mantle alone than would be needed to apply a rotation to the entire mass of the Earth. Due to the high densities present in the core, it makes up about 31.5 per cent of the Earth's mass.

There is yet a further variable that must be taken into account. Comets may approach the vicinity of the Earth from any direction, not just the plane of the ecliptic, although bodies travelling in the same plane as the planets should be more common. They may be travelling in the same direction as the Earth's orbit, or retrograde. A random impact might occur at any point between the equator and the poles and at any angle. It could impact in the same direction as the spin, or against it. Consider the extreme cases of all these possibilities.

A near tangential impact could occur exactly parallel to the line of the equator, and in the same direction as the rotation. This would have the effect of speeding up the rotation (i.e. shortening the day) but no precession or wobble would occur. The effect can be visualized by a simple example: it is analogous to spinning up the wheel of an upturned bicycle with your hand. If the impact were to be against the spin then it would instead slow the rotation, thus lengthening the day. Once again, no precession would occur. The scale of this should not be exaggerated however; the length of day change resultant from a comet impact would be, at most, of the order of minutes.

The effect would be to set the outer Earth spinning temporarily at a slightly different rate to that of the inner core. Over a period of revolutions the rotations would then equalize. The outer crust and mantle would gradually transmit its momentum to the inner core via the medium of the fluid outer core, and vice versa; the outer core may be likened to a fluid 'clutch' acting to equalize the rotations. But if the inner and outer Earths were to rotate at different rates for any length of time, then their respective ellipsoids of revolution would also differ. If the outer crust and mantle were to spin more slowly, then the flatter ellipsoid of the core would exert pressure on the mantle at equatorial latitudes. Conversely if the crust and mantle were to spin more quickly, then the pressure would be exerted at high polar latitudes. The effect felt at the surface would depend on the violence of the change. Presumably up to a certain critical value, the mantle would be able to absorb the pressure. Above this value it would fracture at its weakest points: the mid-ocean ridges and earthquake zones.

Consider also the opposite extreme case: that of a near tangential impact occurring precisely at one of the poles. A comet approaching in a prograde orbit and impacting at the North Pole would be identical in effect to one approaching in a retrograde orbit hitting the South Pole. In this extreme, no direct change in the speed of rotation would occur. Instead, the rotation axis of the outer Earth would precess in a direction at right angles to the direction of the impact. The inner and outer Earths would then be set spinning about different axes, but at similar speeds. In this instance, the core would exert pressure on the mantle at only two zones on opposite sides of the Earth. Greatest pressure would be exerted at mid-latitudes, along the longitude of precession.

In reality, though, neither of the two extremes is very likely. An impact could occur at any point on the Earth's surface, from any direction and at any angle. The most likely result would be some combination of axial precession, change in the length of day, and some slight alteration to the orbital motion. The effect on the orbit may be ignored, as it would produce little noticeable effect for the small impacts under consideration here – although it might render our calendars inaccurate after a few hundred years. Indeed from a human point of view, a high-angle, crater-forming impact is quite the safest possible outcome. It is the near-tangential impact in the ocean of which we must beware!

At this point it is relevant to consider why the Earth has a rotation at all. It is usually considered to be primeval in origin, having formed with the Earth during its accretion.[14] If the Earth accreted from planetesimals travelling in predominantly prograde elliptical orbits around the Sun then the majority of collisions would have tended to give it a positive rotation, but there must also have been occasional impacts against the spin which would have tended to slow it down. We know that the Earth's rotation has slowed since its formation, but not primarily for this reason. During the Devonian Age, some 375 million years ago, fossil evidence indicates that the rotation was much faster at around 400 days per year.[15]

It should be appreciated that the process of accretion has never entirely ceased, but has merely slowed down. If impact events could determine the Earth's rotation during its formation then they would also affect it now. The laws of physics have not changed. There is a certain blindness among geologists and geophysicists regarding catastrophic phenomena. So long as they can be consigned to the remote past, or to other planets, then they are acceptable to science. It matters little whether collisions occur once per day or only once in 5,000 years. The propensity of any individual impact to disturb the rotation is precisely the same as it was all those millions of years ago when the Earth was born.

5

The Chandler Wobble

The discussion thus far has centred upon the physical structure and geodesy of the Earth, and the effect that a quite small comet impact might have upon them. It now becomes essential to examine the nature of the rotational axis itself in more detail. The layman's view of the rotation is to see it as a uniform motion about an axis drawn through the North and South Poles, rather like the fixed mounting of a geographer's globe. In reality, the mathematical treatment of the rotation is highly complex.

In order to describe the rotation fully, three axes must be defined. The first of these is the *geographic axis*, which is the easiest to describe as it is simply a line drawn between the two physical points on the Earth's surface that we wish to call the North and South Poles. These form the points of origin for the lines of latitude and longitude, which serve as a fixed reference frame for the purposes of mapping. They represent the points where the polar explorers plant their flags in the snow and remain constant however much the true poles of rotation may wander away from them.

The second axis that will be needed is the *axis of instantaneous rotation*. This is the line drawn through the Earth about which it is actually rotating at any instant. It may coincide with the geographical axis or it may wander away from it for some reason. The points where it cuts the Earth's surface are termed the *rotation poles*. It is also very close to the line along which the angular momentum vector acts; conventionally considered to be in a northerly direction. The two are so close together that for most purposes they may be considered as coincident. The direction of the angular momentum vector must remain constant unless the body of the Earth is disturbed by an external force. It may be visualized as an arrow pointing towards a distant point in space, currently close to the star Polaris.

The third axis is the *axis of figure*, sometimes also referred to as the *axis of maximum moment of inertia*. It can also be considered as the axis of symmetry of the Earth's spheroid and is determined by the distribution of mass within the body of the planet. If the Earth were a perfect sphere then it would have no axis of symmetry, but as soon as it began to rotate about some arbitrary axis, centrifugal force would redistribute mass towards the equator making it oblate; the arbitrary axis would then become the minor axis and the axis of figure of the ellipsoid.

Theoretically, the position of the axis of figure can never be precisely constant since every particle of the Earth's mass contributes towards it. Weather systems, ocean tides, the movements of animals and even humans as they drive around in their cars, all contribute towards the distribution of mass. Each tiny movement alters the mass distribution, and therefore the precise position of the axis of figure.

For everyday purposes, these three axes are so close together that they may be considered as coincident. The tiny polar motions that do exist amount to just a few metres on the ground. These small but measurable discrepancies are known as *latitude variations* and they occur because the axis of figure is not precisely coincident with the axis of rotation. The Earth's rotation does in fact exhibit a slight wobble; and the latitude variation at any point on the surface can be measured as the difference between the geographical latitude and the true astronomical latitude, as measured from the rotation axis.

For a freely rotating body, such as a planet, with unconstrained axes, there is only one perfectly stable state of rotation and that occurs when it rotates about its axis of figure. That is to say, when the axis of figure and the axis of rotation coincide. If, however, an internal redistribution of mass occurs such that the axis of figure is dragged away from the rotation axis, then an unstable condition is created. The rotation axis must then attempt to realign itself with the figure axis, but is unable to do so immediately as a consequence of the rotation. The pull between the two axes causes the axis of figure to precess about the axis of rotation describing an ever-decreasing circle, or spiral, until the two axes are once again coincident. The angle between the two axes is termed a *nutation*.

The mathematical theory of the Earth's free wobble was first described by the mathematician Euler in 1765, who calculated that

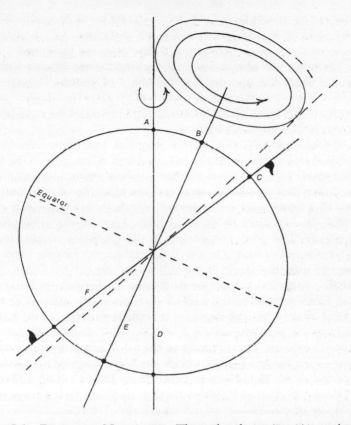

Fig. 5.1 EULERIAN NUTATION. The pole of rotation (A) marks the point at which the rotation axis (D) cuts the Earth's surface. The pole of figure (B) marks the point where the figure axis (E) cuts the surface. The geographical pole (C) – marked by the explorer's flag – is equivalent to the North Pole of all our maps. The geographic axis (F) is the only fixed axis. Normally all three are roughly coincident, but may wander apart. The axis of rotation precesses (i.e. describes a cone) about the axis of figure. As shown here, it would then describe an ever-decreasing spiral until the two axes again coincided.

the axis of figure should describe a complete circle about the rotation axis in a period of 305 days, or approximately 10 months. Throughout the nineteenth century many researchers searched for evidence of the Eulerian nutation, apparently without success. The reason, as we now know, is that Euler's theory only applies to a totally rigid body and it was not until 1892 that S.C. Chandler discovered the famous 'wobble' that has come to be named after him. Chandler was able to determine a slight polar motion with a period of about 428 days, or approximately 14 months, by analysis of latitude variations over a period of years. The fluidity and elasticity of the Earth's interior modify the period of the rigid body nutation to that actually observed.

The Chandler motion is highly irregular and unpredictable in amplitude and the track of the pole position is far from being the perfect spiral form predicted by theory. More recent investigations have shown that the oscillation is actually made up of two components. One component has a period of exactly a year, which can therefore be explained by seasonal movements of the atmosphere and oceans. The other component is the Chandler wobble itself which turns out to have a less well defined period varying between 13 and 15 months.

At this point it is important to distinguish between movements of the Earth relative to the axis of rotation and variations in the obliquity of the axis. The Chandler wobble is a motion of the Earth relative to the axis and occurs due to purely internal shifts in the rotational balance. The direction of the angular momentum vector in space remains unchanged throughout. Euler was able to calculate the period of the rigid body nutation from another quite different precessional cycle to which the Earth is subject, the *astronomical precession* or *precession of the equinoxes*. However, unlike the Chandler wobble, the astronomical precession is a 'forced' motion; a true change in the inclination of the axis, under the action of external gravitational influences.

The precession of the equinoxes is yet another consequence of the equatorial bulge and the fact that the rotation axis is tilted at an angle of 66½° to the plane of the Earth's orbit (the ecliptic plane). The Sun, Moon and planets exert a gravitational turning couple upon the equatorial bulge, which cause the axis of rotation to precess with a period of 26,000 years, about the normal to the plane of the ecliptic. The position of the North Pole of the heavens therefore describes a complete circle over this period. At present it lies near the star Polaris, which we call the Pole Star, but around 4,600 years ago it would have been near the brightest star in the constellation of Draco. The discovery of the precession of the equinoxes is attributed to Hipparchus in 126 BC, who noticed that the stars had all shifted from their positions on older star charts.

The Chandler wobble is an entirely different phenomenon. It is a free oscillation, representing a reaction to a temporary excitation of the axis of figure. Regardless of its cause, any free oscillation should decay away completely once the source of excitation is removed. The axis of figure should then realign itself with the axis of rotation. The motion should be fully damped over a period of about 20 years unless something excites it again. Sir Harold Jeffreys in *The Earth* estimates the theoretical damping period of the Chandler wobble to be about 23 years, but other recent estimates suggest 20–40 years.[1]

The fact that the Chandler wobble persists leads to the conclusion that there is a source of regular and random mass movements within the Earth, which excite the motion. There is no agreed consensus among geophysicists about the source of this excitation. Earthquakes deep within the mantle have been proposed, but they do not appear to be powerful enough to be the major cause.[2]

Another recently proposed theory is that the source of excitation is to be found in the coupling of the core to the mantle. If the inner core and the outer mantle rotate independently, coupled only by the viscosity of the fluid outer core, then some discrepancy in their respective axes of rotation is to be expected. It is also likely that the core–mantle boundary is not a perfect ellipsoid. A further possibility is that the viscous fluid of the outer core may be layered and uneven in its density. The only certainty seems to be that we really know much less about the internal structure of our planet than we like to think.

However, the lengthening of the free oscillation period is entirely explainable.[3] If the Earth were a truly rigid body of homogeneous composition, and if it were a perfect ellipsoid, then the period would indeed be 10 months as calculated by Euler. The introduction of a liquid core into the calculations shortens the predicted period by some 30 days; whereas if the mantle is assumed to be somewhat elastic the effect is to lengthen the period by about 120–30 days. The apparent variation of the Chandler period between 13 and 15 months demonstrates that neither property is constant in its effects.

Neither is this the only possible mode of free oscillation. Geophysicists model the rotating Earth as a spheroidal shell enclosing

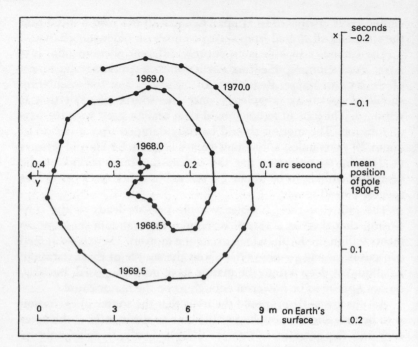

Fig. 5.2 The pole path from 1968 to 1970. The pole positions are given at intervals of 0.05 year. The X-axis is directed towards the Greenwich Meridian. The origin corresponds to the mean position of the pole for the years 1900–5 and the pole now appears to rotate about a mean position that has shifted a total of about 0.25 arc second in a direction about 90° west of the Greenwich Meridian.

Reproduced by courtesy of Irwin Copplestone Books Ltd.

an ideal fluid.[4] The equations suggest that a further motion should exist, known as the *nearly diurnal wobble*.[5] The name derives from the characteristics of the motion, which is a retrograde precession of the rotational axis over a period of 23 hours 53 minutes – or about 4 minutes less than the sidereal day. The study of this motion is in about the same state as that of the Chandler wobble during the nineteenth century, in that it has not yet been observed with any certainty. The complete theory suggests that the motion should occur along with a nutation of the axis in space, having a period of some 460 days. Some researchers claim to have found such a nutation with a period averaging 440 days.[6] The damping time for the oscillation is also uncertain, but recent estimates suggest that it may have a lifetime as long as 2,000–5,000 years – assuming that some viable mechanism is found to excite the motion in the first instance!

Other Earth models give other solutions, and yet more modes of oscillation. Models which allow for the inner core give an additional motion of period 86 minutes.[7] Tiny variations in the length of the day are also detectable, however these amount to just a few thousandths of a second per day. This is an interesting phenomenon as it implies that the oblateness of the Earth is not entirely constant either. If the Earth were to become slightly flatter then its speed of rotation should slow down. Conversely if it becomes rounder then it should speed up slightly. This is rather like the technique used by ice skaters to spin faster by folding their arms. Most of the observable variations are found to be seasonal, resulting from the heating of the atmosphere when the Sun is higher in the sky.

Recent research has shown that some changes in the length of the day are related to earthquakes.[8] Some appear to make the Earth spin more slowly, but by far the majority appear to make it spin faster. The overall result seems to be to make the Earth more compact. Projected into the past, this would imply that the Earth has until recently been somewhat more oblate than at present. Once again, the changes can be entirely explained by changes in the internal mass distribution and no external forces are required to act.

It is likely that all these theoretical oscillations would become evident in the aftermath of a comet impact. An impact is a far more substantial source of excitation than any of the earthquakes experienced today, and it may be expected that the Earth would literally ring like a bell. Any sizeable impact at sea would create a temporary 'hole' in the ocean. This alone would be sufficient to excite the axis of figure and the tsunami waves generated would propagate right round the planet adding to the disturbance. The amplitude of the modern Chandler wobble amounts to less than a single second of arc, but a comet impact in the ocean might produce a wobble of perhaps a degree, or even more depending on the scale of the catastrophe.

The period and the decay time of the Chandler wobble are both independent of its amplitude. The equations of motion are just as applicable to a nutation of 45° as to one of only a few arc seconds. It can therefore be assumed that a wobble triggered by an impact event would still exhibit a period of approximately 14 months and should be fully damped within about 20 years. It must be appreciated that this alone would not result in any permanent shift in the axis of rotation. If the excitation were entirely due to the movement of ocean water around the planet, without affecting the solid body, then ultimately the axes would simply settle back into their former positions.

However, it is easy to see how permanent deformation of the interior could occur, especially during the initial stages. Areas of the crust would find themselves temporarily above or below the equipotential surface and this would generate gigantic earthquakes as the body of the Earth attempted to realign itself with the geoid. Throughout the motion, the equipotential surface remains aligned to the rotation axis. The further the axis of figure strayed from the axis of rotation, the greater would be the strains generated in the crust. The result of these crustal movements would be to reposition the figure axis within the body of the Earth, and at the end of the episode of nutation the geographical location of the poles would be permanently modified.

From the viewpoint of an observer situated on the surface of the Earth, a period of axial wobble would be a very strange time indeed! The observer would have no sense of abnormal motion, any more than it is ever possible to detect that the Earth is rotating; but the sky above would appear to be doing strange things. The North Pole of the sky would not be stationary in its position near the Pole Star as it is now, but would appear to be describing an irregular spiral course about it, changing its position noticeably from day to day.

More importantly, the height of the Sun and Moon in the sky would be similarly affected. The seasonal variations that we experience in the climate are the direct consequence of the changes in the height of the Sun in the sky. Changes in the Sun's elevation due to any other cause would similarly influence the climate, producing unseasonable weather. The tiny latitude variations produced by the Chandler wobble would begin to have a marked influence on the climate if they were increased to the order of a whole degree or more.

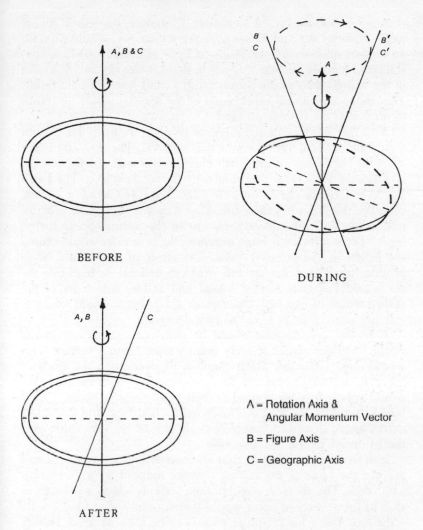

Fig. 5.3 THE MECHANISM OF A POLE SHIFT. Before the disturbance all three axes are coincident. After the impact, the figure axis (B) is displaced, but the rotation axis (A) is tied to the direction of the angular momentum. The ellipsoid of the solid Earth precesses with the figure axis while that of the ocean remains with the rotation axis. Eventually the solid Earth deforms and the rotation and figure axes settle down to a new stable position. The geographic axis remains unchanged.

A polar motion, say, of amplitude 5°, making the Sun 5° higher in the summer sky and 5° lower in the winter sky, would produce an abnormally hot summer, followed by an abnormally cold winter. If instead it made the Sun 5° lower in the summer sky and 5° higher in the winter, then a cool summer and a mild winter would result. This enhancement and suppression of the seasons would all return to normal as the wobble decayed.

A further unpleasant consequence of a significant polar motion would be periodic variations in the sea level. These would occur since the solid body of the Earth must precess with the figure axis, whereas the sea level is determined by the rotation axis. The Earth would experience significant *pole tides*. The tiny Chandler wobble of today also generates these tides, but they are only of the order of millimetres and subsequently are lost in the normal ocean turbulence.[9] For a sufficiently large nutation, the pole tides would exceed the height of the ordinary tides. The effect of this would be to produce longer beaches around world shorelines. At high tide the sea would penetrate further inland and at low tide more of the seabed would be exposed. Once again, tidal ranges would return to stability after 20 years as the wobble decayed.

A further consequence would be temporary variations in the vertical and horizontal at every point on the Earth's surface. This would most noticeably affect the flow of rivers, and the levels of lakes. Rivers might cease to flow, or even flow backwards. Lakes would appear to slosh around in their beds, perhaps bursting their banks to drown anything on the shoreline. The high and low water marks would describe a complete circle around the lake shore over the 14-month period of the wobble.

It must be stressed again that all these effects are transient and are not the same as the lasting changes induced by a permanent axial shift. The shortest possible time-scale in which a permanent shift of the axis could occur would therefore be about 15–20 years – the time taken for the polar motion to be fully damped. During that period, an increase in the magnitude and frequency of earthquakes and vulcanism could be expected. Thereafter, further major tectonic movements might occur at any time until total stability was restored.

Even this scenario only describes the outcome of a comparatively minor impact in the ocean. The preceding discussion has assumed that all the energy of the comet would be absorbed within the oceans. This is no more than an extension to the theory of the Chandler motion. There is also the possibility of the more violent disturbance which would result from an impact exerting an angular impulse on the solid shell of the Earth.

In the case of the polar motion, the external force only triggers an excitation of the figure axis. It is the subsequent realignment of the figure axis that causes a permanent shift in the position of the rotation axis. The inclination of the axis in space is unaffected by this. The total angular momentum vector continues to point in the same direction, and the motion should rather be considered as one of the Earth relative to it. An angular impulse would produce all of these effects, but in addition it would have the capacity to alter permanently the tilt of the axis to the ecliptic.

To visualize this a little more clearly, the Earth's rotational axis, along which the angular momentum vector acts, is inclined at an angle of 23½° to the normal to the plane of the ecliptic; that is to say, the *obliquity* of the axis is 23½°. It is this axial tilt which determines the annual seasons. As the Earth progresses in its orbit round the Sun, the axis continues to point in the same direction in space. When the northern hemisphere is tilted towards the Sun, then it experiences summer, whereas the southern hemisphere is experiencing winter. Half a year later, when the Earth is on the opposite side of the Sun, the positions are reversed. The precession of the equinoxes pulls the axis around in a complete cone over a period of 26,000 years, but does not change the obliquity, although this does vary slightly on a longer time-scale.[10] An impact of sufficient violence could modify the axial tilt and thus bring about a permanent change in the intensity of the seasons.

An impact exerting an angular impulse on the Earth's crust could rotate the outer shell (the crust and mantle) against the fluid core. Some turbulence would undoubtedly be introduced into the rotation of the fluid outer core, but very little of the impulse would be transferred to the solid inner core. The angular momentum of the core would remain virtually unaffected while that of the outer shell would be permanently altered. The outer shell of the Earth would be set to rotate about a different axis from that of the inner core.

A new phenomenon must then occur; one which is not evident at all on the Earth today. The two parts of the Earth would begin to exert a force upon each other through the medium of the fluid outer core. The crust and mantle would exert a force on the core,

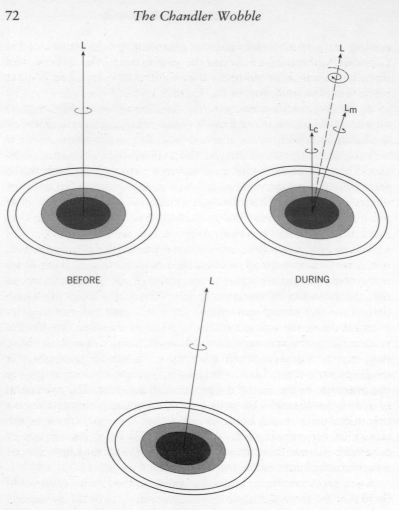

Fig. 5.4 AN ILLUSTRATION OF CORE–MANTLE PRECESSION. The Earth's total angular momentum is represented by the vector L; that of the crust and mantle alone by L_m and that of the core by L_c. An impact on the surface affects only L_m and the core rotation is unchanged. The misaligned axes must then precess about the new principal axis until the change of momentum is transmitted to the core. Only the outer motion is apparent at the surface and any free wobble relative to geography must then be superimposed upon this motion in space. (See figure 5.3.)

causing its axis to precess about the axis of the crust and mantle. Conversely, the core would exert a pull upon the outer crust and mantle, causing it to precess about the axis of the core. The net result would be an apparent motion about an intermediate principal axis, which must then maintain a fixed attitude in space. The two axes would precess about each other in an ever-decreasing spiral until they were once again aligned about the principal axis.

It is not immediately apparent what the period of this precession would be. The motion is not the same as the Chandler wobble, or the nearly diurnal wobble, which would be superimposed upon it. Neither is it possible here to say anything definite about how long the motion might persist. In the case of the Chandler wobble, it is the figure axis that precesses about the rotation axis. The core motion is an entirely different consideration. Once the free wobble is damped, the figure and rotation axes of the core and of the outer shell would once again coalesce. The core–mantle precession would then be a motion of the angular momenta of the outer shell and that of the core about each other.[11]

From the viewpoint of the hypothetical observer on the Earth's surface during this phase, the initial effects would differ from those discussed previously only in their scale. All the characteristics of the impact itself would be of increased magnitude, resulting in a much greater excitation of the figure axis, and therefore a nutation of greater amplitude. The intensity of the resulting earthquake and volcanic activity would be much greater, both because of the higher energy of the impact itself and because of the increased strains generated in the crust. Inundation of low-lying areas by the sea would also be more extensive.

Assuming that our observer survived both the impact and the flood that followed, he would find himself once again in a relatively stable world. After the 20-year wobble had decayed, the sea level world-wide would settle down again to a new stable shoreline and life could begin to return to normal. However, the core motion would continue. It is important to appreciate that the geographical displacement of the rotational poles and the sea level variations are very largely completed at the end of the nutation phase. The core–mantle precession would only affect the inclination of the rotation axis in space. This would manifest itself as a gradual adjustment of the axial tilt with inevitable consequences for the world's climate and seasons.

Our observer would notice a distinct change in the climate during his own lifetime, which would continue to affect his children. In the sky above he might notice the celestial pole describing an irregular spiral course about a fixed point in the sky. Ultimately, as the amplitude of the core–mantle precession became smaller, the apparent rotation of the sky would settle upon this point which would then become the new permanent pole of the sky. The position of the new pole of the heavens is determined in the instant after the impact. The new direction of the total angular momentum vector is then set and the inner and outer parts of the Earth can only precess about it.

So long as this oscillation persisted (for its lifetime is uncertain), it would continue to have an effect on seasonal weather patterns. For an observer at a point on the Earth's surface, it is not possible to distinguish between movements of the Earth relative to the axis and movements of the axis itself. All that is detectable is an apparent change in the motion of the Sun, Moon and stars in the sky above. Real changes in the obliquity have the same effect as latitude variations and would produce a similar pattern of enhanced and depressed seasonal variations.

A further factor to consider is the magnitude of the initial impulse exerted on the Earth. We are only concerned here with an event that might produce a sudden displacement of the axis of the outer shell through a small angle, amounting to a few degrees at most. If an initial displacement of the axis were to be of the order of, say, 5° along a line of longitude then the eventual displacement of the axis at the end of the precessional phase would amount to only perhaps 2° or 3° along the same line. That is to say, the obliquity might be increased or decreased by this margin. The same impact event might produce a shift in the geographical position of the rotation poles of less than a single degree. There should be no doubt that any such impact would be quite sufficient to trigger a world-wide catastrophe with permanent consequences for world sea levels.

There is a final consideration here. The most intense strains in the crust would be generated immediately after the impact. The discussion here has assumed that the body of the Earth would retain most of its rigidity during a period of axial wobble and would conform only gradually to the new geoid, via a smooth series of earthquakes, until the wobble was extinguished. There is also the possibility that the initial strains on the crust and mantle might be too great, resulting in the crust splitting open at its weakest points. The figure of the Earth would then be able to adjust more rapidly to the demands of the new dynamics. This would not affect the period or the decay time of the nutation, but would have the effect of reducing its amplitude much more quickly. The outcome would be rapidly to get rid of the worst symptoms of the catastrophe.

Any sudden adjustment of the Earth's figure, if it tended to make it either more or less oblate, must also affect the length of the day. Whatever else happens, angular momentum must always be conserved. If in the process of realigning its axes the Earth became more oblate, then it would have to rotate more slowly to conserve angular momentum. Should it become less oblate then its angular velocity would increase. A change in the length of the day is therefore to be expected as a further consequence of an impact event.

We now have a fairly complete, if rather qualitative, picture of how a comet strike in the ocean would affect the Earth. Of course there is much more geophysical detail that could be pursued but the present author makes no claim to be a geophysicist. This study is principally concerned with mythology and prehistory; these few general rules will suffice for that purpose and there is no need to compound an already complex subject still further. It may be worth while at this point to summarize precisely what this theory predicts for the aftermath of a comet impact. The signs may then be recognized as we encounter them in the physical and mythological record of the past.

1. Direct Memories of the Impact
   These may be recognized by references to sky gods, fiery dragons, snakes, or 'second suns' in the sky. These may come down to Earth and cause fire and destruction, or some other calamity.

2. Memories of the Immediate Aftermath
   During the 20-year period of rotational instability following an impact there would be an abnormal incidence of vulcanism and massive earthquakes, even in regions that do not normally experience them. Shorelines would be unstable. As well as memories of flooding there should be the opposite case of the sea retreating to expose the seabed.

3. Climatic Fluctuations
   During a period of nutation the weather patterns would be influenced by a combination of the annual seasons with those caused by the nutation. These would follow a regular cycle determined by the period of the nutation. Expect to see evidence of abnormal summer and winter weather, droughts and famines. Geodetic changes would follow the same cycle, affecting lake levels and the flow of rivers.

4. Permanent Sea Level and Climate Change
   It should be possible to detect a transition from one stable climatic and sea level regime to a new stable regime. Such evidence should be synchronous and world-wide.

5. Changes in the Length of the Day
   This would act either to increase or decrease the 'flattening' of the Earth, producing equal and opposite sea level changes above and below latitude 45°. The number of days in the year would change and during the transition it would be difficult to formulate a calendar. The Earth's magnetic field would also be affected.

The geophysical and astronomical theories proposed here are entirely credible and require only an extension of existing knowledge of the Chandler wobble. If one compares the present theory with the outlandish claims of Velikovsky and others, whereby the Earth is postulated to have exchanged orbits with Venus, or turned upside-down on its axis, then it will seem almost modest by comparison. All that is proposed here is a quite small excitation of the rotation axis caused by the strike of an average-sized comet.

Even so, if such a comet were to collide with the Earth today and increase the amplitude of the Chandler wobble by even a fraction of a degree, then no one should doubt that this would be a disaster of biblical proportions! If any such impact has occurred in recent prehistory then it will certainly be remembered in mythology and legend. Not only this, but the 'signature' of such an event should be discernible in the climatic record, in the record of sea level change, and in archaeological evidence, provided that one knows how to recognize it. The pattern of evidence will not be spectacular, or it would have been found long ago. It is to a search for this evidence that our attention must now turn.

6

The Evidence of Sea Level Variations

All around the coastlines of the world, evidence exists that variations of sea level have occurred relative to the land. Despite this, the recognition and study of sea level change is a recent science, with the former belief in the invariability of the oceans persisting well into the twentieth century.

The recognition that the level of the oceans could have varied in the past came with the growing evidence for the occurrence of past 'ice ages'. It became apparent that the polar ice caps had once extended into regions much further south than they do today. A logical extension of this realization was that much more water must formerly have been locked up in these ice caps; and, consequently, world sea levels must have been much lower at that time. Most modern research starts from this premise and this has grown into a comprehensive theory of glacio-eustatic control of sea level change.

The melting of the ice sheets, which covered most of northern Europe and America until 10,000 years ago, mark the end of the *Pleistocene* epoch and the beginning of the *Holocene* in which we live today. The prevailing view of the world's climate during the Holocene is that of a steadily warming climate up to about 5,000 years ago. Since this peak period of warmth, the climate has become somewhat cooler again. If the theories of eustatic control are correct then the melting of the glaciated areas should have led to a steady rise of sea level until 5,000 years ago, followed by a somewhat lesser decline up to the present day.

Eustatic changes should affect the world-wide sea level evenly and gradually. A rise or fall in, say, Europe or America during any particular era should also be discernible elsewhere in the world. However, such regular oscillations are seldom detectable around world coastlines and this leads to the conclusion that other forces must also be at work.[1] A eustatic rise in sea level might be masked at a particular geographical location by a compensating rise of the land, due to tectonic warping or isostasy. Researchers have therefore tended to restrict their investigations to areas of the crust that are considered to be stable, in order to rule out these effects.

If all the world's ice cover were to melt, it would probably raise the world sea level by about 60–70 metres. Estimates of the amount of ice locked up in past ice sheets set a limit of 80–150 metres for the amount which sea level was lowered during the ice ages. However, raised beach features are found at much greater heights at various places around the world. The eustatic lower limit is also exceeded in many places. Off the Hawaiian Islands, for example, a sequence of submerged shorelines has been detected down to a depth of 1,100 metres. The high beaches can usually be dated to the Pleistocene or even earlier; but oscillations during the Holocene are of a lower order than this. The published sea level curves generally agree on an average rise of sea level of about 35–40 metres between 10,000 and 5,000 years ago, with only a slight decline, if any, since that time.

Former sea levels can be detected at the shoreline by the observation of a number of features. The most obvious of these are the raised beach terraces and raised cliff features. The present-day seashore is observed to form beaches and erode cliffs by the incessant action of the tides. If the sea level should fall, or the land rise, for whatever reason, then the present beach would be left above the tidal reach where it would gradually turn into permanent dry land. The sea would then begin to cut cliffs at the new sea level. Such displaced beaches are the easiest features to spot, but in areas of soft sedimentation they erode rapidly. Evidence of falling sea level is also provided by the changing flow of rivers, which meander and widen as they approach the sea. If sea level falls, then rivers begin to cut down into their flood plain, forming a steeper and straighter valley.

Rises in sea level are rather less obvious, as the former beach features are drowned and subject to erosion by the sea; or, over a long period, covered by fresh sediments. The continuation of river channels can often be discerned on navigation charts, running out for many kilometres beneath the sea; clear evidence that when the channels were cut, the present day seabed must have been part of the land. Oscillations of the sea sometimes leave these formerly drowned areas above sea level again, where the sediments can be examined to give further evidence of past movements.

Sometimes, layers of organic matter such as peat and even whole tree trunks are found in the sedimentary layers. These are usually referred to as *submerged forests* although they by no means always consist of forest material alone. Submerged forests are found all over the world, often covered by only a thin layer of beach sand which may be periodically washed away. In other places a submerged forest layer may be covered by oceanic sediment such as clay or sand, with yet another younger forest or peat layer above it. Often, whole tree root systems remain in place, indicating that the trees actually grew in situ and were not simply washed in from elsewhere. They are thought to indicate inland regions, which were below sea level, but somehow protected from the sea by a coastal ridge. Once such a protective ridge is breached, sudden inundation by the sea would occur.

The dating of these displaced coastal features is not always easy, especially for the older sites. However, for those thought to be of Holocene age, it is possible to apply radiocarbon dating provided that some suitable organic matter can be found. On well-preserved raised beaches it may be possible to find seashells or the remains of some other sea creature that can be used for dating purposes. However, a beach could easily be contaminated by material from elsewhere and, in any case, the sample could date from any time during the lifetime of the beach. Layers of peat can give a more reliable date in the case of submerged features.

In most prevailing theories, changes of sea level are considered to take place gradually over centuries. Clearly, the erosion of cliffs requires thousands of years and implies that the sea level remained reasonably constant throughout that period. The cliffs and beaches now found inland imply a rapid change in the relative sea level from one stable height to another. If some gradual process of change were at work then we would expect to find evidence of intermediate beaches and cliffs formed during the transitional period. Usually, there is very little evidence to be found of such intermediate features.

Another enigma is that quite often raised beaches are found to be tilted. Perhaps the best examples are the famous raised beaches of Scotland, which used to be termed the '100-foot', '50-foot' and '25-foot' beaches. The highest beaches are thought to be the oldest, with the '100-foot' beach being of late glacial age, the others dating from the early Holocene.[2] All are discernible along the west coast of Scotland, and the higher beaches display a distinct tilt.

The tilting of these beaches is usually explained as the result of isostatic recovery since the Ice Age, when Scotland was depressed under the weight of a great ice sheet. These examples are far from unique. Around the world, the tilting of raised beaches is the norm rather than the exception. Around the shores of the Mediterranean Sea, a prominent series of older tilted beaches exists, dating from the Pleistocene. A similar series of ancient stepped and tilted beaches is to be found along the length of the Chilean coastline and in the Arctic. Such features cannot be explained by glacial-eustasy alone, as some flexing of the land must also have occurred. Eustasy alone would have produced a perfectly level series of raised beaches around the world, parallel to the Earth's curvature. However, the tilting of former shorelines is precisely what would be expected if the sea level variations were due to a change in the geodesy of the Earth. The greatest tilting would then occur at high latitudes where the flattening of the ellipsoid is at its greatest.

The submerged forests and peat beds offer an even greater argument in favour of more rapid changes of sea level. J. A. Steers remarks that all such peat and forest beds are very thin and must result from a sudden submergence beneath sea level, to be then rapidly covered up by protective sand deposits.[3] Any other scenario would allow the living matter to decompose in the normal way. The preservation of the beds must also imply that the extent of the sudden submergence was greater than the tidal range; otherwise the soft material should have been long eroded away by the waves.

The hypothesis adopted here is that geodetic effects, resultant from changes in the Earth's rotation, should be considered as the primary cause of past sea level variations. If this theory is correct then it should be possible to group the sea level evidence into distinct episodes, with long periods of relative stability between them. This is not to say that glacio-eustatic and isostatic effects do not also occur or that gradual change should be entirely ruled out. However these should be regarded as secondary effects resulting from the adjustment of the world to its new geoid.

Any theorist who would propose a geodetic cause for sea level change has an immediate problem. To prove the theory by sea level evidence alone, it is necessary to put together a complete picture of world-wide variations for a particular era; and the dating of that evidence must be accurate to the order of only tens of years. This is by no means easy, as the majority of published papers are local studies, often with little firm dating evidence.

A North American researcher, for example, might survey the coastline of North America and then extrapolate the conclusions to suggest correspondence with other world-wide evidence. An Australian or European researcher attempting to do the same might come to differing conclusions. It is not uncommon for one theorist to hold that sea level along a certain stretch of coastline was rising during a particular epoch, while another will suggest that it was falling! The more published evidence one studies, the more confusing the picture becomes.

Clearly, if sea level changes have a predominantly glacio-eustatic cause, then the findings from one continent should be repeated in every other part of the world. However, this argument is entirely invalid if the cause is geodetic. The pattern would then be one of correspondence occurring only on the opposite side of the world, with an equal and opposite effect prevailing at the mid-points. Although a number of papers and reference works do exist on the subject of geodetic sea level changes, it is unusual for field researchers to make reference to them in their published results. Their conclusions are inevitably biased towards the theories of glacial-eustasy and isostasy that appear in all the textbooks. So much of the existing fieldwork therefore cannot be used to formulate a geodetic hypothesis.

The radiocarbon dating method also has its limitations and published dates may only be considered as approximate. In some cases they are published with a degree of uncertainty of as much as 300 years either way. It would therefore be very difficult to identify a pole tide oscillation if this results from a free wobble that decays within a period of only 20 years. Many of the raised beach terraces identified around world shorelines may be nothing more than the upper limit of such temporary pole tides; as such they can tell us little about the stable regimes existing between the disturbances. To this must be added the additional complication that many of the most useful papers on the subject of sea level change were published before the tree ring calibration of dates was understood. An approximate correction therefore has to be made to find a calendar date.

The examination of sea level evidence within this chapter is made somewhat easier by the fact that the period of interest is clearly defined. We are interested in evidence of major world-wide sea level changes during the period 3300–2900 BC (or approximately 5000 BP) although it will also be necessary from time to time to make reference to both earlier and later fluctuations.

As one might expect, the greatest volume of published research material concerns the coasts of Europe. The Baltic Sea in particular has been subjected to extensive investigation, since it was the site of one of the major ice sheets of the last Ice Age. The region has undergone extensive isostatic uplift during the Holocene, which apparently still continues today. At various periods the Baltic has been both an enclosed freshwater lake and a fully open tidal sea.

At about 6000 BC the Baltic was a land-locked freshwater lake known as the Ancylus Lake.[4] Then by approximately 3500 BC marine conditions had returned and the Baltic was again a sea, referred to as the Littorina Sea. However, there is reason to believe that the conditions were somewhat more saline than today. During the Littorina transgression the entire Karelian Isthmus may also have been underwater. Certainly all the modern shores of the Baltic were transgressed and Lake Ladoga was joined to the sea. Scandinavia was an island with a continuous flow of fresh ocean water between the North Sea and the White Sea. The closing of this channel occurred some time around 3000 BC, leaving the Baltic Sea much as it is today.[5]

At the other end of the Baltic lies Denmark, a low-lying country which has been greatly influenced by human settlement. The works of Neolithic man abound throughout Jutland and the main islands.[6] Archaeologists use the term 'Funnel Beaker Culture' to describe the population of Denmark at this period, which was responsible for building the passage graves and dolmens commonly found there. The period normally ascribed to this culture dates from 4200 BC to about 3200 BC. Curiously, though, no evidence of occupation from this period is found on the nearby Baltic island of Bornholm, although there is ample evidence of later settlement.

To the west of this, dolmens and tombs of this age are now found beneath the sea in shallow inlets such as that at Kolding Fjord in east-central Jutland.[7] However, in north-east Jutland, coastal settlements from the same period are now to be found inland, only a few metres above the present shoreline. Before

3000 BC the north-eastern part of Jutland was apparently broken up into a number of small islands. A typical example of this is the Djursland peninsula, which is dissected by low-lying plains with a shallow covering of Littorina age marine sediments.[8] Denmark appears to occupy a pivotal position. To the west of Jutland, there is evidence of submergence since 3000 BC, while in the Baltic to the east all the evidence favours the emergence of land. A large area to the west of Jutland, taking in Heligoland and the Frisian Islands, has apparently subsided, with the loss of large parts of Schleswig recorded in medieval times.

Up to about 6000 BC, the whole of the southern part of the North Sea was a dry plain and the British Isles were linked to the Continent. But long before 3000 BC the Mid-Holocene rise of sea level had drowned the North Sea basin and separated Britain from the Continent. The shorelines of the North Sea then lay close to their present positions. This is confirmed by the work of Jelgersma in the Netherlands, who found that the apparent rise of sea level was extremely rapid after 6000 BC, but by 3000 BC had reached a level of about 5 metres below that of the present day.[9] Since then, Holland has continued to sink gradually. In the Thames estuary a similar picture emerges.[10] Peat deposits of this age are found at a depth of 8 metres with a steady apparent rise since that time. There is also some evidence of more recent metre-scale oscillations.

In the British Isles, it is the 25-foot beach of Scotland that has been termed the 'Neolithic Beach', as it is the only one of the raised beach sequences on which artefacts of this age are found. However, the beach is only evident in the northern half of Britain and may only be approximately dated to between 6000 and 3500 BC. By the later part of the fourth millennium BC, these raised beaches were already in existence. In the southern half of Britain all the evidence from this period points to submergence. Peat and submerged forest beds are found all around the shores of Britain and Ireland and those in Wales, Lancashire and the Severn estuary have been dated to approximately 3100 BC and 1750 BC. Oak wood from Mounts Bay, near Penzance, gave a date close to 2000 BC.[11] Forest beds are also to be found around the Orkney Islands, the Isles of Scilly, the Channel Islands, and along the north coast of France. Along the east coast of Britain, submerged forests of this age occur in the Humber estuary.

The general picture of submergence along the west coast of Europe is further reinforced by the archaeological evidence. The Brittany coast of France holds some of the earliest megalithic monuments known. The design and spiral decoration of the various chambered tombs show a strong cultural affinity with those found in Anglesey and in Ireland, all of which may be tentatively dated to the Middle Neolithic (c.4000–2500 BC).

At about 3700 BC the high-tide mark in this region was at or below the present low-tide mark and as a result many structures of this age now lie in the intertidal zone. A structure known as a *cromlech* is now to be found below the waters of the Gulf of Morbihan, off the small island of Er-Lannic. The site actually consists of two related circles, the northernmost being still visible at low tide.[12] At Kernic there is a small granite tomb or '*allée couverte*' which is exposed only at low tide.[13] Similar examples of submerged walls and tombs exist on the Isles of Scilly, the Channel Islands and in Ireland, although these are of uncertain date. At Rostellan, near Cork harbour, a Neolithic chambered grave is now to be found on a tidal estuary where it is almost submerged at high tide.[14]

The Mediterranean shores are usually considered a poor area for sea level research due to tectonic instability. The frequency of earthquakes and volcanic activity makes it rather pointless to draw conclusions from the heights of beach terraces. However at the eastern end of the Mediterranean, the Nile delta is comparatively free from tectonic movement. Dating of the deposits of the Nile valley show that the river reached its present level about 5,000 years ago and a stabilization in the height of the annual flood then took place.[15] In the modern delta, sediments of this age are now to be found 5–10 metres below the surface.

The ancient Egyptians kept regular measurements of the annual Nile floods, and some of these have survived on an inscription of the Fifth Dynasty, known as the Palermo Stone. It appears that during the First Dynasty (c.3100–3000 BC) the Nile floods were high and erratic by comparison with later records.[16] Unfortunately no true sea level information can be deduced from this, as all the measurements are relative to some unknown datum. Another tantalizing piece of evidence from this period is supplied by Herodotus, who tells us that in the time of Egypt's first king, Menes (or Min), the Nile delta was not yet in existence.[17]

the first man to rule Egypt was Min, in whose time the whole country, except the district around Thebes, was marsh, none of the land below Lake Moeris – seven days voyage up river from the sea – then showing above the water.

Herodotus was extremely interested in the Nile and the origin of the delta, remarking on it several times. His own observations and the information he gleaned from the priests, dating from about 450 BC, are deserving of note.[18]

I have observed for myself that Egypt at the Nile Delta projects into the sea beyond the coast on either side; I have seen shells on the hills and noticed how salt exudes from the soil to such an extent that it affects even the pyramids; I have noticed too, that the only hill where there is sand is the hill above Memphis.

Herodotus also has some interesting comments about the possibility of a high river level around 1600 BC which may indicate a higher sea level, or a climatic variation at that period. He records that in the reign of King Moeris, the Nile had to rise only about 4 metres before it flooded, whereas in his own day a rise of some 7 metres was required.

It was King Min, according to Herodotus, who built a dam to protect the city of Memphis from the floods. He diverted the river and built the city on the drained land. This evidence from Herodotus is precious and we have nothing else quite like it for any other part of the world. Plutarch likewise relates that Egypt used to be beneath the sea.[19] However, he cites mythology, saying that the Nile delta was first revealed in the age when Horus defeated the serpent god Set. An abundance of rains came and forced out the sea, revealing the fertile land. This age of Horus and Set may also be assigned to the First Dynasty, when all the kings included these gods within their title. After 3000 BC the sea level at the eastern end of the Mediterranean dropped, or the land rose, exposing the Nile delta and causing the river to cut deeper into its bed.

Evidence of rising land is also to be found throughout Greece and the Aegean. Here, many of the great seaports of the classical period, such as Miletus and Heraclea, now lie inland due to the silting up of their rivers.[20] The major river estuaries of Greece can be shown to have apparently silted up during only the last 5,000 years. Radiocarbon dating is available on sediments from the

Pamisos River valley in the south-western Peloponnese. Here deposits at 15.5 metres below sea level can be dated to a marine transgression which occurred between about 3710 and 3360 BC.[21] Since that time, the sea has retreated further out. But the record is difficult to interpret; later evidence suggests submergence along the Aegean coasts and the sea level curves indicate numerous reversals and standstills of the sea. Many Greek myths recall a time when the islands of the Aegean were 'floating'; and neither should we forget that curious reference by Plato to the forgotten geological disasters of Greece:[22] 'But afterwards there occurred violent earthquakes and floods; and in a single day and night of misfortune all your warlike men in a body sank into the earth . . .'

Further to the east, more indications of rising land are found where the rivers Tigris and Euphrates flow into the Persian Gulf. The flat plain of Mesopotamia is built up entirely of the sediments brought down from the surrounding mountains by the two great rivers. In this region lie the remains of some of the oldest known cities, with archaeological evidence dating back beyond 6000 BC. It has been calculated that the deposition of sediment where the rivers meet the sea is sufficient to raise the level of the delta by 60 centimetres per century.[23]

North of the modern city of Nasiriyah lie the ruins of the ancient civilizations of Sumer and Akkad. South of it no ancient sites are found, indicating that all of this land may have been uncovered by a relative fall in sea level and subsequently built up by deposition. Near Nasiriyah lie the remains of the Sumerian cities of Ur and Eridu. An inscription survives from the Third Dynasty of Ur (*c.*2100 BC), indicating that Eridu may once have been a seaport.[24] The inscription reads that Shulgi, a king of Ur, 'cared greatly for the city of Eridu, which was on the shore of the sea'.

The opinion of modern geologists is that the coastline of that time was near its modern position. The rivers Tigris and Euphrates are thought to be discharging their sediment into a slowly subsiding basin. According to this theory, Eridu lay on the shore of an inland lake, or arm of the river. But the belief that the seashore was formerly much further north than today is far from new. It is at least as old as the Roman geographer Pliny, who presumably got it from even earlier sources.[25] Why must we always consider our ancestors to have been either fools or liars? If King Shulgi said that he lived by the sea, then perhaps we should believe him!

To the east of a line drawn through Denmark, Italy and continuing down through Africa, the picture for 3000 BC is one of emergence. To the west, it is predominantly of submergence. If we continue across the Atlantic to examine the east coast of the North American continent then yet more submergence may be found. Along the east coast of the USA the evidence suggests an apparent down-warping of the continental shelf, resulting in a rise of some 3–17 metres since the Mid-Holocene.

In the shallow seas of the Bahamas, mangrove swamps, which only grow within the tidal range, are now found at a depth of 3 metres on the island of Bimini.[26] These have been dated to about 3210–3120 BC. Other evidence of submergence is present all along the coast of the United States. The delta of the Mississippi River consists of seven different lobes where the course of the river has changed during the last 5,000 years. Prior to that time, the Mississippi flowed into the sea much further out.

Submerged forests are found just off the coast of Maine and New Hampshire which can also be dated to the early third millennium BC.[27] Submerged peat of this age is also found off the Labrador coast. Shell middens dating from around 3300 BC are found 7 metres below high-water mark in Boston harbour.[28] Fairbridge notes evidence of this submergence from as far south as Punta Gorda in Venezuela where an Indian kitchen-midden found below sea level is of similar age.[29] The west coast of North America yields comparable evidence.[30] Off the coast of California, pottery at least 5,000 years old has been brought up by divers from submerged middens.

Only when we look as far west as Alaska does the picture begin to change again. The Bering Sea is shallow and in the recent past, a 'land bridge' has linked North America with Siberia. Submergence of this shallow plain was long complete by 3000 BC. As elsewhere in the world, the evidence indicates a eustatic rise of sea level up to 5,000 years ago, but since then it has remained within a few metres of its present level.

On the north-western coast of Alaska in the region around Cape Krusenstern, barrier bars are found, consisting of a series of beach ridges.[31] These ridges extend from about 3 metres below sea level to 3 metres above it. The oldest ridge, at only 2 metres high, has been dated to approximately 3800 BC. However, Alaska is a highly-active earthquake zone and there is evidence of minor oscillations of sea level all around the coast, to which it is difficult to attach any significance. Studies of the coastal peat bogs around Cook Inlet show that a high sea level occurred between 5,000 and 6,000 years ago and there is also evidence from the Aleutian Islands that the shallow pass separating Umnak Island from Anangula was first transgressed by the sea at around this time.[32]

As we progress south of the equator, down the chain of the Andes, we move back into a zone of emergence. Here, some of the most prominent raised beaches anywhere in the world are to be found. Charles Darwin first drew attention to the raised beaches of Patagonia and Chile during his famous voyage of the *Beagle*. The entire region has clearly been uplifted in recent geological time, leaving prominent terraces as high as 500 metres in some places. However, all these high beaches are of Pleistocene age and of little interest to the present discussion. The Andes are one of the world's youngest mountain chains and tectonic displacement is quite common. Following the Chilean earthquake of 1960, many coastal features were observed to have dropped as much as 1.5 metres below their former positions.[33]

Along the more stable Atlantic coast of Argentina, a raised beach near Comodoro Rivadavia at a height of 9 metres has been dated to around 4300 BC.[34] This same line of emerged beaches is discernible northwards as far as the Valdez peninsula and south as far as the Magellan Strait; a clear indicator that the entire Patagonian coastline has risen since that time. Further north, Brazilian sea level curves show a high sea level *c.*3000 BC of about 3.5–4.7 metres.[35] Near Rio de Janeiro, samples from a raised beach 4.8 metres high yielded a date of 3700 BC.[36]

Along the Chilean coast, a similar series of beach terraces occur at heights between 5 metres and 7 metres which have been tentatively dated to the same period. Between Carrizal Bajo and La Serena it forms a perfectly level terrace, as do the older beaches at 18 metres and 110 metres, strongly indicating that this area has been free from tectonic warping.[37] The beach can be correlated as far south as the latitude of Valparaiso, but southwards the lowest terrace is at about 10 metres near Valdivia and the bay of Hueicolla.[38]

In the southern hemisphere generally, there is very little continental coastline at a latitude comparable with that of Europe. The exception is to be found in the Antarctic Peninsula, the South

Shetland Islands and the island of South Georgia, but radiocarbon dating is difficult in these polar regions due to the scarcity of carbonaceous material. On South Georgia a beach at 6–7.2 metres has been approximately dated as forming 'later than 9,500 and earlier than 4,000 years ago' and peat overlaying a higher raised beach was dated to approximately 2000 BC, indicating that the beach cannot be younger than this.[39] On the South Shetland Islands, fresh beach terraces of Holocene age occur at 17–20 metres and 5–7.5 metres.[40]

The overall picture for Antarctica at this time is one of emergence. A beach at 13.5 metres in McMurdo Sound was dated to between 3700 and 3300 BC by a radiocarbon date from a seal carcase embedded within it, while a 23-metre terrace in the Windmill Islands has been dated at about 7,000 years old.[41, 42] It must be said, though, that evidence for submergence is not to be expected from Antarctica, as there are no forests or peat deposits to form submerged layers.

Emergence is also strongly evident in the far north of Arctic Canada, where a prominent series of raised beaches is found. The emergence of this region, in contrast to the submergence noted further south, is usually ascribed to the isostatic rebound of this formerly glaciated region. On Ellesmere Island, around Cape Storm, there is a sloping strand line, which rises from 16.5 metres at its eastern extremity to 22.5 metres at Cape Storm. The radiocarbon dates from driftwood found on this beach cluster around 3700–3100 BC.[43] Raised beaches in this region also show a north–south tilt. On Devon Island to the south, beaches of similar age are found at a height of 30 metres.[44] There is no evidence at all of submergence in the high Arctic, thus from both North and South Polar regions the pattern is one of emergence.

For Africa at this time, the evidence for sea level change is most notable by its absence. There is ample evidence for sea level changes in the past, but nothing to compare with the raised beaches of South America. In South Africa, a high sea level is suspected between 4900 BC and 0 BC, but no change is noted for the intervening years.[45] A date of approximately 4500 BC has been obtained on mangrove wood found exactly at sea level on the coast of Ghana.[46] Around the Ivory Coast, Nigeria and the Congo the sea level curves indicate a level below the present until 6,000 years ago and all the indications are that little variation has occurred along the coast of south-west Africa since that time.[47, 48] However, this does not hold further west. Around the coast of Senegal and Mauritania the history of sea level variation is much more confused and difficult to interpret.[49, 50]

The evidence from Australia and New Zealand for this time is once again contradictory. Recent research around Australian shores tends to stress the post-glacial sea level rise which culminated at about 4000 BC with a relative fall of about 2 metres postulated since that time.[51] The case for upper Holocene fluctuations is unproven and remains a subject of much dispute.

However, the earlier research of Fairbridge and others suggested many later oscillations. All along the west coast of Australia a prominent 'fresh' submerged beach platform has been noted by divers, at a depth of 3–4 metres below sea level, which has also been tentatively dated to about 5,000 years ago.[52] Near Fremantle, there is evidence that a large area of soft limestone coastline between Rottnest Island and the mainland has been eroded and submerged since 4000 BC.[53] To this must be added the testimony of researchers who have searched for, and failed to find, any Holocene raised terraces along the west coast of Australia.[54] Evidence of submergence in and around the Indian Ocean is found as far west as the island of Réunion, where sea level curves show 5,000-year-old deposits now at a depth of 5 metres.[55]

Additional evidence for the Australian coast is supplied by archaeology. All along the coast of New South Wales are found Aboriginal occupation sites or middens, containing seashells and other indicators of a coast-living culture.[56] All the known sites were first occupied within the last 5,000 years. Shallow, gently sloping, continental shelves exist all around the shores of Australia and the absence of older coastal settlements suggests that they have been drowned by the sea. Relict Aborigine cultures survive on offshore islands in the Great Barrier Reef, trapped there by the rising sea.[57]

A submerged forest near Wellington in Hutt Valley, New Zealand, is also prime evidence.[58] Dated at around 3200–3000 BC, it shows a good correspondence with the similar submerged forest deposits of this age in western Europe.

The Pacific coastline of Asia is a difficult area to assess as it is a strong earthquake zone, thus invalidating any firm conclusions that might otherwise be made about former sea levels. The large area occupied by the Asian land mass, too, is devoid of sea coasts, and evidence of changes in the geoid would have to be sought by other means, such as alterations in the flow and level of rivers.

The islands of Japan clearly illustrate the problem. The area around Tokyo bay is subject to frequent earthquakes and prominent terraces can be observed, which were formed by known earthquakes experienced in recent centuries. A sequence of much earlier Holocene terraces of this kind is evident all around the bay; the Mid-Holocene was a period of high sea levels, known as the Jomon transgression after the Neolithic culture found on the islands. Raised beach terraces of this age attain a height of 30 metres in some places and the regression from this high point is put at 3000–2000 BC.[59] Similar evidence of high sea level between 6,000 and 4,000 years ago is found along the nearby coast of Vietnam.[60]

One part of the Asian coast that is of enormous significance is the North China Plain and the delta of the Hwang Ho, or Yellow River. This is one of the few low-lying regions to be found along the entire east Asian coast and the only one of any size. The Hwang Ho is a remarkable river. For the last 725 kilometres of its journey to the sea it straggles across the North China Plain dropping an average of only 5 centimetres per 1.6 kilometres. The plain is so flat that the riverbed in many places has built up to as much as 9 metres above the surrounding land.

Near the oldest course of the river, the depth of the silt extends to as much as 150 metres. Mostly this consists of freshwater sediment, but the surface layer is of marine origin, as indicated by the abundant shells of sea creatures found on the surface, and in ancient times the Chi region of the North China Plain is recorded as a source of salt. In the recent geological past, much of the North China Plain has clearly been transgressed by a shallow sea and there are indications that this was the case before 3000 BC. The North China Plain is the cradle of Chinese culture, yet no sign of human occupation prior to 3000 BC has yet been found there.[61] All the evidence for early Neolithic occupation in China comes from the higher ground around the plain.

The earliest Neolithic farming community in China is the Yang-Shao culture. Prior to 3000 BC these people farmed the fertile loess of the upper Hwang Ho in Shansi and Honan provinces. In places, the river has cut down into the soft loess to form steep ravines and it is on the terraces of these ravines that evidence of agriculture has been found. Some sites are now many metres above the modern flood plain and it is difficult to see how these ancient farmers irrigated their fields unless the level of the river was far higher than it is today. Recent sea level research confirms that the highest sea levels along the China coast occurred between 7,000 and 5,000 years ago.[62]

This brief gazetteer from around the coastlines of the world is sufficient to indicate a distinct pattern in the coastal changes since 3000 BC. A pattern of correspondence in alternate quarter-spheres can be demonstrated, which is precisely the effect that would be produced by a shift in the position of the rotational axis. The pattern is clearest around the mid-latitudes where the effect of any length of day changes would be broadly neutral.

A 'line of neutrality' may be drawn right round the Earth along which there has been little or no sea level change. Passing through Norway, Denmark and Italy, it continues down through the centre of Africa until it reaches the ocean again east of the Cape of Good Hope. The line continues through Antarctica between Princess Martha Land and the Ross Ice Shelf, thence through the central Pacific Ocean to the east of New Zealand. Northwards it passes through the Hawaiian Islands and the Bering Strait, then back across the Arctic Ocean to Norway.

This line, and a second line roughly corresponding to the equator, divides the Earth into four quarter-spheres. In two opposite quarter-spheres the evidence is predominantly of submergence, or sinking land. In the other two quarter-spheres the evidence favours emergence, or rising land. The date at which the change occurred can be estimated with some precision from the radiocarbon dating of the submerged forests, while only approximate indicators can be gained from the raised beaches and other circumstantial pointers. A date close to 3100 BC is favoured by the sea level evidence.

The first quarter-sphere is in the northern hemisphere extending from western Europe and west Africa, the northern part of South America, all North America, except the extreme west of Alaska, and Hawaii. Within this quarter-sphere the evidence points to sea level rise.

The corresponding southern quarter-sphere of submergence extends from Western Samoa, New Zealand, Australia and Indonesia, west across the Indian Ocean to Madagascar and Mozambique. However, any correspondence with north-west Europe is

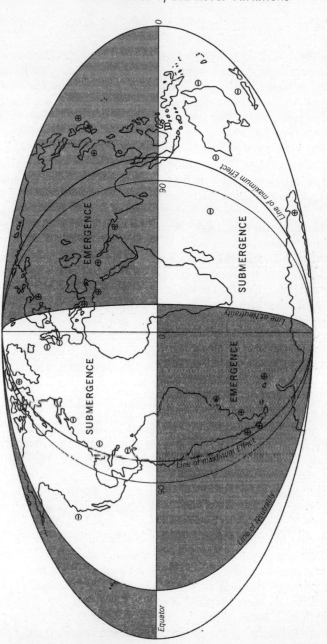

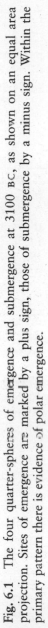

Fig. 6.1 The four quarter-spheres of emergence and submergence at 3100 BC, as shown on an equal area projection. Sites of emergence are marked by a plus sign, those of submergence by a minus sign. Within the primary pattern there is evidence of polar emergence.

difficult to prove as there are few southern coasts lying above 45° latitude.

The second quarter-sphere in the northern hemisphere is the predominantly land quarter-sphere extending from eastern Europe to the Bering Strait, including China, India, Arabia and the north-east part of Africa. Within this zone, the evidence indicates falling sea level, or rising land. The corresponding southern quarter-sphere of emergence extends from south-west Africa across the Atlantic to include South America and as far west as Polynesia.

The line of greatest effect would therefore run at 90° longitude from the proposed neutral line. It runs from Ellesmere Island, south through Quebec and Cape Hatteras, then on through Cuba, Colombia and Peru right down the eastern seaboard of South America. Passing close to the Antarctic Peninsula, it returns north again through the Indian Ocean west of Australia, through Sumatra, Burma, Mongolia and the Yenisei region of Siberia. To produce this geodetic effect requires a permanent displacement of the rotational poles along this line. In the case of the North Pole, a former position somewhat closer to Ellesmere Island is indicated.

The extent of the required pole shift is not easy to determine. It does not have to be very large to produce the effects discussed in this chapter, probably a shift of only a fraction of a degree of latitude would be quite sufficient. The greatest effects would be experienced at the mid-latitudes immediately after the disturbance. Maximum sea level rise is predicted off Nova Scotia and Newfoundland in the north; and in the Indian Ocean near Kerguelen Island. Conversely, maximum rise of land would have occurred in Mongolia and northern China while in the southern hemisphere it would have occurred in southern Chile and Patagonia. This fits the evidence extraordinarily well.

If there were no adjustment of the solid Earth to take into account, then it might be possible to estimate the extent of pole shift from the height of raised beaches alone. It would only be necessary to subtract the radius of the old ellipsoid from the modern geoid. Sadly the problem is not so simple; if we assume a 20-year transitional phase for the rotational poles to settle to a new stable position, then by the end of that period some adjustment of the land surface to the new ellipsoid is to be expected.

There should be evidence of submerged land emerging again slowly from the sea over the past 5,000 years. Similarly, land raised above the optimum geoid height can be expected to have sunk. By now this process of adjustment is virtually complete and the crust is again close to its optimum height relative to the ideal geoid. Not too much significance should therefore be read into the modern heights and depths of the dated evidence, only the pattern is significant. A best estimate should be obtainable by relying upon measurements taken from close to the line of neutrality, where strains on the crust have been at their minimum.

Other factors must also complicate attempts to determine the extent of any pole shift. This particular displacement of the axis is almost certainly not the only one to have occurred in geologically recent times. The lithosphere may also be responding to both earlier and more recent strains and this would disguise any geodetic pattern.[63] In particular, the formerly glaciated areas are still undergoing extensive uplift, which may be greater than any strains imposed by a more recent pole shift. The possibility of a change in the rate of rotation (i.e. the length of the day) must also be borne in mind, as this would further complicate the observed pattern, particularly in equatorial and polar regions. The evidence of emergence at polar latitudes argues strongly that an increase in the rate of rotation has occurred since 3100 BC.

The survival of such a clear pattern favouring a pole shift 5,000 years ago argues strongly that no event of comparable magnitude has occurred since that time. But the 5,000-year-old fluctuations discussed here are dwarfed by the sea level changes that occurred at the end of the Ice Age; and many later oscillations have also left their mark around the shorelines of the world.

The apparent emergence of tropical coastlines since about 1600 BC still needs to be satisfactorily explained. Space does not permit an examination of this problem here, but some instances have already been mentioned; such as the fluctuations of the Nile flood level described by Herodotus and the growth of the Tigris/ Euphrates delta. There was a similar emergence of the Indus delta during the third millennium BC where the remains of the coastal Harappan civilization now lie far inland.[64] The emergence of the Pacific coral islands may also have occurred only since 1600 BC.[65, 66] Other radiocarbon dates quoted by Fairbridge suggest a date of between 1500 and 1800 BC for this Pacific emergence.[67] A comparable regression at this period is also evident in east Africa,[68] and along the Brazilian and Peruvian coasts.[69, 70]

At the eastern end of the Mediterranean, there is clear archaeological evidence to support a rise in sea level during the Bronze Age. A rise of about a metre around the coast of Crete has submerged many ancient Minoan harbours dating from before 2100 BC.[71] The underwater archaeologist Nicholas Flemming investigated the ruins of a submerged coastal settlement called Elaphonisos (Pavlo Petrie) lying off the Greek coast, which he judged to be of Middle Helladic age (*c.*2000 BC).[72] He based his estimate on the discovery of cist graves typical of this period and the typical style of pottery discovered intact and rolling around on the sea floor – clearly indicating that this was no gradual submergence.

Further north, drowned forest deposits began to form again at around this time. As well as the deposits around the coasts of Britain there are examples from the North American coast; and many published sea level curves show an oscillation at around 1500–1600 BC.

These may well be clues that another, less violent disturbance of the Earth's rotation occurred around 1500–1600 BC. A pattern of tropical emergence would suggest that this time its effect was mainly to slow down the Earth's rotation, with only minimal permanent pole shift. Other variations in the record may perhaps be better explained by a long-period free oscillation of the axis of rotation. There may also have been other less significant impact events during the last 5,000 years; important though each of these may be in their own right, they lie beyond the scope of the present study.

Vertical movements of a few metres around the coasts of the world may not seem to be particularly 'catastrophic' in nature. It is only if they can be shown to be part of a world-wide pattern that they become significant. To date, few specialist researchers have shown any interest in a primarily geodetic cause for sea level change. The glacio-eustatic theory may have the weight of many textbooks heaped upon it, but it must remain unsatisfactory so long as it relies on random crustal movements to explain away evidence that refuses to fit in with its rules. Only the correct combination of geodetic factors can explain why one area of the world shows a falling sea level at the same time as another shows an apparent rise. Perhaps the scientists' fear of the biblical Flood will diminish somewhat with the realization that there was not a single flood, but many!

7

The Changing Climate

An important distinction must be made between a shift in the geographical position of the rotational poles and a change in the obliquity of the axis. While a pole shift would influence world-wide sea levels and shorelines it would not necessarily result in a permanent modification of the climate at any point on the Earth's surface. In the previous chapter it was concluded that a pole shift of less than a single degree of latitude would be sufficient to account for the pattern of sea level variations observed. However, even at its maximum extent, such a small displacement would not produce permanent climate changes any greater than those between, say, Paris and Brussels.

The differences in the weather experienced in the summer and winter seasons are the inevitable consequence of our planet's orbit around the Sun in combination with its axial tilt. Small variations in average temperature, rainfall and other determinants are to be expected from year to year, but these generally fall within the predictable average of weather patterns which we term the climate.

The Earth's axis is tilted at an angle of 23° 27' to the normal to the plane of the ecliptic. This results in a change in declination as the year progresses. At the June solstice the North Pole is tilted towards the Sun and the northern hemisphere experiences its summer. At the December solstice it is tilted away from the Sun as the southern hemisphere experiences summer. Midway between these two dates occur the equinoxes, at which the Sun's rays just penetrate tangentially to both the poles.

The most important single variable in the climate is the temperature. This is influenced by two main factors: the angle of incidence at which the Sun's rays strike the surface, and by how long the Sun remains above the horizon each day. The heat of the Sun's rays is reduced both by the thickness of the atmosphere through which they must pass and by the increased area of ground over which their effects are spread. The heating effect per unit area is at its maximum when the Sun is vertically overhead and at its minimum when it is on the horizon. The total heating effect resultant from the angle of incidence and the length of the daylight period is termed the *intensity of insolation*. A lower angle of incidence may be compensated by an increase in the number of daylight hours.

The Earth's axial tilt divides it neatly into three climatic zones. At the equator, the midday Sun never strays more than 23.5° from the vertical. At the June solstice, the midday Sun is vertically overhead at the Tropic of Cancer (23.5° North). At the December solstice, it is vertically overhead at the Tropic of Capricorn (23.5° South). Within this region lies the tropical or torrid zone.

At latitudes between 23.5° and 66.5° lie the northern and southern temperate zones. Within these regions, the Sun can never be vertically overhead but the intensity of insolation becomes increasingly seasonal with distance from the equator. The midday Sun is at its highest point during the summer solstice and at its lowest during the winter solstice. The number of daylight hours experienced also depends on the seasons. At a typical latitude of 50°, there are just over 16 hours of daylight at midsummer whereas only about 8 hours are experienced at midwinter. At 10° further north this effect is even more pronounced, with about 19 hours of sunlight at the summer solstice, but only 6 hours at midwinter.

At latitudes above 66.5° lie the polar or frigid zones. In the northern hemisphere this latitude is termed the Arctic Circle; in the

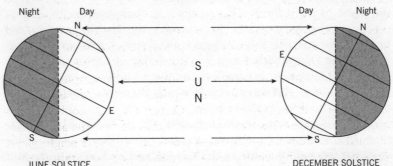

JUNE SOLSTICE   DECEMBER SOLSTICE

Fig. 7.1 The Solstices.

southern hemisphere the Antarctic Circle. Here, seasonality is taken to extremes. At the equinoxes both poles are just reached by the Sun's rays and the Sun appears to circuit the horizon. At 66.5° there is a day of 24 hours daylight at the summer solstice and 24 hours darkness at the winter solstice. At 79° there are 2 months of permanent daylight during summer and 2 months of winter darkness. For the 6 months of winter the Sun never rises at all at the poles, while during the summer 6 months of permanent daylight are experienced.

The net insolation effect of these seasonal variations increases to a maximum at latitude 43.5° – which is roughly the latitude of the Mediterranean. Up to this latitude, the angle of incidence and the duration of daylight reinforce each other. Beyond this limit, the increased daylight hours cannot compensate for the reduction in sunlight received.

It is this imbalance between the heat supplied to the equatorial and polar regions that lies at the heart of the world's weather system. At latitudes above 40° more heat is radiated away into space than is received from the Sun. Since the world as whole maintains an overall temperature balance, then the loss of heat from the polar regions must be compensated by a flow of heat from equatorial to polar regions. This transfer is accomplished by both the ocean currents and the atmospheric weather systems.

Other factors, too, combine to modulate the climate at various geographical locations. The unequal distribution of land and sea have their effect since the oceans tend to act as a heat store. In summer the interior of a continent will usually be warmer than the oceans at the same latitude. But in winter this is reversed and the continents are colder than the oceans; for example, the extremes of temperature experienced in central Siberia. Regions that experience such extreme seasonal swings are said to have a *continental* climate, while those moderated by proximity to the sea have a *maritime* climate. This can work both ways. Norway, for example, is spared from the bitter cold experienced elsewhere at the same latitude by the warmth of the Gulf Stream. Conversely, the cool Peruvian coastal current ameliorates the tropical climate of Chile and Peru.

Further factors influence the microclimate, such as height above sea level, prevailing winds, rainfall and the type of vegetation cover. But, ultimately, all these influences are subordinate to the basic parameters of climate determined by the insolation. The world's weather system, with its swirling air masses, may be chaotic and unpredictable, high and low extremes of temperature and rainfall may be experienced, but for any given location these average out and the extremes of the climate remain within a predictable band.

It is interesting at this point to estimate the effect on world climates of a permanent change in the obliquity of the ecliptic. Leave aside for the moment the problems of the transitional stage and conjecture a stable world, like our own, but with the tilt of the axis increased to, say, 26°.

The consequences of such a hypothetical situation would be a 'squeezing' of the temperate zones. The tropics would move to a higher latitude of 26°, increasing the range of the tropical zone. Tropical vegetation and animals would then be able to migrate north and south of their current ranges. However, the polar zones would also extend their range, the Arctic and Antarctic Circles would move down to a latitude of only 64°, bringing tundra conditions with them. Within the temperate zones, too, all intermediate zones of climate would be compressed. Only at the mid-latitudes of 45° North and South would there be little noticeable change.

Other climatic determinants would, of course, be unaffected by such a change. Continental interiors would still experience their comparative extremes, but the temperature range would change – probably for the worse. Regions sheltered by mountains would still be drier than their surroundings; and maritime influences would continue to exert an ameliorating effect on the coastal regions.

The most noticeable change would probably be in the predictability of the weather. Increased extremes of temperature in summer and winter would require a more vigorous atmospheric and oceanic circulation to transport the heat from the tropics to the poles. This would result in increased storminess, fierce winds and general unpredictability of the weather. Since the length of the year would be unchanged and the total surface insolation must be the same, then the only difference is that more energy would have to be transferred across the temperate zones during the same period.

Consider, too, the opposite scenario. What if the obliquity were to decrease to only about 20°? In this case the temperate zones would expand at the expense of both the tropical and polar zones. The tropics would move down to a latitude of 20°, compressing the tropical zone. The Arctic and Antarctic Circles would move higher, to a latitude of 70°.

In this scenario, temperate flora and fauna would be able to expand their ranges north and south of present limits. The variations between summer and winter insolation would also be reduced. Although continental regions would still experience seasonal extremes, the range of temperatures would be much more equable. From a purely human viewpoint the interiors of continents would become more habitable places, experiencing neither extreme cold in winter, nor extreme heat in summer.

The temperature gradient between the tropical and polar regions would be greatly reduced and consequently less heat would need to be transferred across the temperate zone. The whole weather system would be effectively 'turned down' and the weather patterns would become much more stable and predictable. Not only would seasonal temperature extremes be reduced, but severe storms would become less common, and the equinox winds less pronounced. This mild, gentle climate has all the characteristics of a paradise!

The ideal world for human habitation would be one with little or no 'weather' at all. If some future race of supermen should wish to engineer the perfect planet for human life to inhabit then they certainly would not design one with an axial tilt! On a planet without seasons there would be little or no heat flow and the weather system would be reduced to only the gentler circulations of atmosphere and oceans resultant from the rotation and Coriolis forces.

The opposite extreme of a world with its axis tipped over on its side like that of the planet Uranus is an awful prospect to consider. With each hemisphere alternating between constant tropical sunshine and polar darkness during the course of a year, the seasonal weather patterns, even at mid latitudes, would be of a horrifying intensity, probably far worse than anything we dare imagine.

However we need not consider either of these extremes in any great detail, for there is no reason to suspect that they are a model for anything that has happened on the Earth in recent millennia. But have there been smaller changes in the obliquity in the recent past? Is there any evidence of the changes in climate that such a model predicts? As was discussed in the previous chapter, there is strong evidence that a permanent shift of the rotational axis occurred around 3100 BC. It is inconceivable that an impact severe enough to cause such a shift would not have also affected the axial tilt.

The period around 3000 BC does indeed coincide with a time of major climatic change. But it is certainly not the only one to have occurred during the Holocene epoch. In recent decades, much evidence of Holocene climatic history has been accumulated from the study of ancient pollen (palynology). The sequence of changes in the vegetation cover has been derived from analysis of the pollen preserved in the layers of ancient peat bogs. Although pollen analysis alone cannot provide an absolute chronology, the occurrence of pollen from various species in the bog sediments can be used as an indicator of the major changes in the climate.

The technique works on the premise that plant species have in the past thrived in much the same type of climate as they inhabit today. This is a reasonable assumption. Provided that the proportions of the various species in a particular layer can be established, then the climate can be equated to that of a region where similar species occur today. If in one layer we find that deciduous trees were the dominant vegetation, then it can be assumed that the climate was temperate and wet. If the layer immediately above is dominated by grasses then this probably indicates a transition to a drier climate. If the layer above that contains predominantly evidence of coniferous forests, then this would indicate a move to colder conditions.

Using pollen analysis, it has been possible to define the various climatic changes of the Holocene as a sequence of 'pollen zones'. Much of the pioneering research was done in the 1920s and 1930s, but since that time the application of radiocarbon dating to the pollen samples has enabled a very precise chronology to be established for the development of the vegetation since the last Ice Age.

The pollen zones suggest a marked world-wide synchronicity of climate change. For north-west Europe, the Holocene climatic amelioration commences at about 8300–8000 BC, with the disappearance of the major European ice caps. Three major climatic zones span the period of increasing warmth up to 3000 BC. For the British Isles and the Atlantic province of Europe, the tundra conditions gave way to northern taiga vegetation dominated by birch and pine forests. The interval between about 7500 and 5500 BC is known as the *Boreal* period. This is the era when the North Sea was dry and Britain was linked to continental Europe. Pines predominate in samples of this age dredged from the submerged forest deposits of the North Sea.

A very pronounced transition occurred at about 5500 BC. The end of the Boreal period is marked by increased dryness and a lowering of lake levels. The warmer *Atlantic* period then begins, so called due to the maritime nature of the climate. From this point onwards, pine declines in the pollen record and its place is taken by mixed forests of oak, elm and lime. High forest became established over most of the British Isles and western Europe as pine retreated to the higher ground.

The Atlantic period, between approximately 5500 and 3000 BC, represents the Climatic Optimum for Europe. Taking all the evidence into account, it would appear that the Boreal–Atlantic transition represents a change from a climatic regime more continental in character than that experienced in north-west Europe today to one in which maritime influence was even more pronounced than today. During the Boreal period, summer temperatures in northwest Europe were probably a degree or so warmer on average than at present, with the winters cooler by a similar margin. By contrast, the Atlantic period seems to have been more equable, with both summer and winter temperatures averaging 1–2°C above their present-day equivalents.[1] The lush afforestation would also imply an average rainfall some 10–15 per cent higher.

At about 3000 BC this all came to an end. A sharp decline in the occurrence of elm and lime in the pollen record marks the transition to the *Sub-Boreal* period. A phenomenon known as the *elm decline* has been a hotly debated subject over the years, but there is little real agreement either as to its cause or its precise dating.[2] Since this period is also characterized by the first appearance of cultivated crops in the pollen record, the elm decline is usually ascribed to the effects of human coppicing and clearance of the forests. Throughout Europe, the elm decline commences around 4000 BC, with an apparent recovery after about 3340 BC. It is noticeable that in Scandinavia the collapse of Neolithic farming in the far north occurs shortly after the resurgence of elm in the pollen record.[3, 4]

The Sub-Boreal is again characterized by an increased seasonality, not too different from that of today. However, increasingly there is evidence of deforestation and agriculture, which confuses attempts to infer climatic change from pollen spectra alone. Increasing dryness and the spread of steppe grassland conditions in eastern Europe are characteristic of this period.[5]

There is evidence of a further move to cooler, wetter conditions during the first millennium BC; but unlike the earlier periods there is no sharp boundary to mark the change. A date of about 500 BC is assigned to this transition to the *Sub-Atlantic* period, in which we live today. Minor fluctuations of the climate have continued right up to the present century, but there is nothing to compare with the sharp transitions at the close of the Boreal and Atlantic periods.

In Europe, the Atlantic period up to about 3000 BC is characterized by the spread of mixed oak forests, with elm and lime found far to the north of their present ranges.[6] Elm is a tree of the wet lowlands, yet in Britain and Ireland it was able to extend its range to altitudes as high as 750 metres.[7] The lime, or linden, tree similarly requires moist conditions. It is highly intolerant of temperature extremes and has a very short growing season at the northern limit of its range. Today, neither species will grow readily north of the English Midlands, but in the Atlantic period their range extended far into Scotland. Lime was the dominant species in Denmark and southern Scandinavia during this period and the range of both elm and lime extended far north into Sweden.

Contrast this with the fortunes of the beech tree. Beech is the dominant forest tree of central Europe, thriving on drier soils and more tolerant of the temperature extremes of continental Europe.[8] Although it was undoubtedly present in the British Isles and the Atlantic coastal province during Boreal times, it then declines in the pollen record throughout Europe during the Atlantic period, only to rise again after the elm decline, along with an increase in hornbeam and spruce. Beech did not become prominent again in the forests of southern England until Roman times. Taken together with the elm record, this gives a strong clue to the nature of the climate during the Atlantic period.

Pointers to the climate of Europe during Atlantic times need not come solely from the vegetational record. Animal life too can tell us something. In Denmark, the remains of pond turtles can be found dating from both Boreal and Atlantic times.[9] These creatures are temperature-sensitive and can only survive where the climate is sufficiently warm to incubate their eggs. Today the northern limit of their range is defined by the 20°C July isotherm across France, Germany and eastern Europe. This suggests a consistent summer temperature in Denmark 1–2°C higher than today. In Hungary, changes in the range of forest molluscs indicate that during the Atlantic period the European forest advanced eastwards.[10] After 3000 BC drier conditions returned.

The Climatic Optimum is also evident further east in Siberia.[11] Here it is usually dated from about 6500 BC to 2500 BC and there is no equivalent of the wet Atlantic phase noted in Europe. During this period the coniferous taiga forests extended much further north of present limits. Remains of birch and alder are found in fossil peat bogs at the mouth of the River Yenisei, which can be dated to around 3300 BC. Forests of larch, pine and birch were abundant in the Kara Sea region – 250 kilometres further north than today. Tree lines were higher in mountainous areas and many species such as oak and the Siberian elm were able to migrate north of Lake Baikal. Oak is no longer present at all in Siberia and its presence prior to 3000 BC is surely indicative of a climate with a more genial temperature range.

In North America, the post-glacial warm period is known as the Hypsithermal. Remnants of the North American ice cap survived in Labrador and Keewatin until about 6,000 years ago, when they shrank back to leave only the small remnant on Baffin Island.[12] Forests of spruce and larch spread into the formerly glaciated areas. In the valley of the Mackenzie River they were able to penetrate 110 kilometres beyond their present northern limit.[13]

Although the New World floras are not directly comparable with the European species, a similar sequence of pollen zones has been defined.[14, 15] Between 5500 BC and 3000 BC, the deciduous oak-hickory forests now found in southern Wisconsin were able to penetrate north of the Great Lakes, where now mainly spruce and pine are found. In New England, a decline of pine at this time is compensated by a rise in the occurrence of oak and hemlock, the latter being a species which is generally favoured by cool wet conditions. After 3000 BC a return to a drier climate is indicated by an increased presence of beech in the pollen record.

A search for similar evidence in the southern hemisphere is difficult due to the absence of land at comparable latitudes. There is no southern taiga belt, as this latitude is occupied by the Antarctic Ocean. However such evidence as there is from the southern tip of South America tells a similar tale: trees now found only much further north were flourishing in Tierra del Fuego, Patagonia and even on the Falkland Islands.[16, 17] Evidence for the Climatic Optimum in South America is also supported by a shrinkage of the Patagonian glaciers and a higher snow-line at this time.

New Zealand, at a comparable latitude, also exhibits vegetational changes at this period. The flora of New Zealand is quite unique and difficult to compare with other regions; however the pollen record suggests that the spread of the podocarp pine forests reached their maximum extent at this time.[18] Their stumps are found beneath peat and gravel in areas which are now too dry to support such forests. Evidence of climatic correlations from New Zealand is of particular value since, unlike Europe, vegetational changes cannot be attributed to human deforestation.

Further indications of climatic change after 3000 BC are to be found too at lower temperate latitudes. Today, the hot deserts of the world occur between latitudes of roughly 15° and 30°, but this has not always been so. Not only did temperate conditions extend their range northwards into Europe during the Climatic Optimum, but they also pushed southwards into the Sahara.

The earliest indications that the Sahara is a fairly recent desert come from Herodotus.[19] His descriptions of the Libyan tribes at about 450 BC, around the beginning of the Sub-Atlantic period, give us an insight into what the climate of north Africa was like at that time. It is clear that by 500 BC the Sahara was already a desert. Herodotus describes the great belt of sand extending inland from Egypt to the Straits of Gibraltar, but it seems that the Mediterranean coastal region was deeper and far more habitable than we know today. Wild animals were abundant and several tribes lived in the interior. The Garamantes hunted in four-horse chariots, and the Atlantes and the Atarantes farmed the land around the oases. The latter, according to Herodotus, cursed the Sun each day for burning themselves and their land.

That the Sahara was formerly a green and habitable land is attested to by the remarkable rock paintings found at Tassili N'Ajjer in the central Hoggar Mountains of Algeria. These depict a landscape vastly different from today, with palm trees, giraffes, elephants and men hunting antelope of various kinds. All these animals require plentiful supplies of water, indicating that at the time the rock paintings were made the climate was cooler and more humid. Other paintings depict a pastoral people herding their flocks of goats, sheep and cattle. Radiocarbon dating of charcoal from

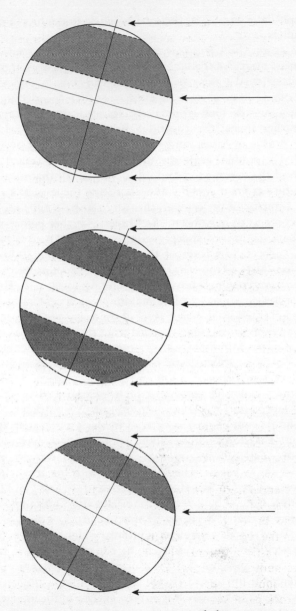

Fig. 7.2 The expansion and contraction of the temperate zones as determined by the obliquity of the ecliptic.

camp-fires dates the era of these pastoralists to the fourth and early third millennia BC.[20]

Once again, the trend towards desert conditions seems only to have set in after 3000 BC. Until then, areas such as the Hoggar highlands enjoyed a pleasant Mediterranean climate. Pollen samples from about 3500 BC show temperate trees such as alder and walnut growing alongside such tropical species as acacia and myrtle.[21] In much earlier times, the central Sahara was submerged beneath shallow seas and lakes into which most of the region's rivers drained. The gradual evaporation of these inland seas is the origin of much of the desert sand and salt deposits. All that now remains of these former great seas is Lake Chad; and the level of Lake Chad is itself a mirror of the temperature and rainfall of the region. The lake level seems to have been 35–40 metres higher before 3000 BC, after which it dropped sharply to a level 15–20 metres below the present.[22] The falling level of the Nile floods after 3000 BC may also be indicative of the trend towards desert conditions.

Other desert regions show corresponding variations. The Negev Desert of Israel also received its maximum Holocene rainfall at this time, as indicated by the high level of the Dead Sea.[23] Further west in Iran, analysis of the pollen record from the shallow Lake Zeribar in the Zagros Mountains also points to a cooler and wetter climate.[24] The southward spread of oak reached its maximum in this part of Iran between 4000 and 3000 BC, where it appears to have formed extensive forests. A high lake level at this time also suggests more rainfall and less evaporation. Yet further to the east, water buffalo and elephants thrived in the Thar Desert region of India and Pakistan.[25] Since 3000 BC the region has undergone progressive desiccation and was already a desert by the time Alexander the Great marched through it with his army. In China, too, forests existed in Sinkiang, in the area of today's Gobi Desert.[26]

In South Africa, by contrast, the Climatic Optimum seems to have been a period of dryness.[27] The podocarp forests were temporarily replaced by dry scrub conditions, which reverted to forest when wetter conditions returned. In equatorial Africa, however, there is little to indicate that the climate during Atlantic times was any different from today, except at high altitude. Pollen profiles from the Sacred Lake, which is almost exactly at the equator, show changes in the composition of the rain forests at the Atlantic/Sub-Boreal boundary.[28]

In China and eastern Asia, the temperate zone lies further south than in Europe due to the combination of continental climatic conditions and the cold ocean currents which prevail down the Asian coast. Archaeological excavations at Banpo near Sian reveal that at the time of the Yang-Shao culture (*c.*4000–3000 BC) water deer, tapirs and bamboo rats were hunted as part of the daily diet of the people.[29] These subtropical animals are no longer to be found this far north, indicating that the climate was warmer and rainfall perhaps higher prior to 3000 BC. However, the Yang-Shao people also cultivated millet and vegetables, but apparently not rice. Millet will tolerate drier and more extreme climates than rice, which will not grow much outside the tropics, as it requires a long, hot growing season. This may be an indicator that 5,000 years ago the tropical zone did not extend as far north as it does today.

The Chinese scientist Chu Ko-Chen calculates that the range of bamboo has also retreated south since the time of the Yang-Shao culture by as much as 3° of latitude.[30] This would indicate that winter temperatures were perhaps 5°C warmer than today and the yearly average 2°C warmer. Along the nearby Japanese coast the range of warm water molluscs retreated some 6°C further south at about 3000 BC, indicative of a temperature up to 5°C higher than today and synchronous with a local fall in sea level.[31]

Further indications of climate change are to be found in South America. Here, the cool Peru Current determines the climate along the Peruvian coast. The cool ocean reduces evaporation and rainfall to such an extent that the Peruvian coast is a perfectly dry desert. Despite this, the air itself is so humid that it produces a climate far cooler than is experienced elsewhere at such latitudes. These cool desert conditions prevail as far north as Manta in Ecuador, almost, in fact, to the equator. Here the cold current turns west towards the Galapagos Islands where its cool waters are responsible for the remarkable diversity of animal life. The Ecuador coast further north is a total contrast, with rain forests and mangroves extending right down to the sea.

The coastal desert of southern Ecuador is known to have developed very recently. Prior to about 1000 BC, the mangrove forests covered the entire coast south of Manta as far as the Gulf of Guayaquil.[32] Their maximum southern extent seems to have occurred at about 5000 BC, when they extended as far as Talara in Peru, some 3° of latitude further south. These changes imply

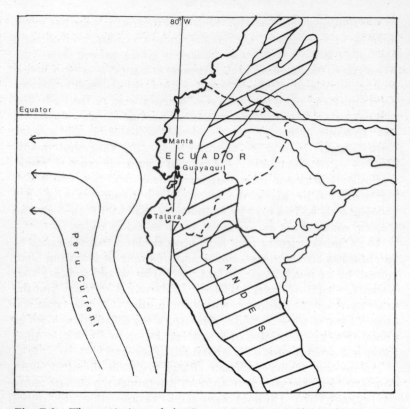

Fig. 7.3 The variation of the Peruvian Current along the coast of Ecuador. Today, mangrove forests are only found north of Manta, but 7,000 years ago they extended as far south as Talara.

variations in the nature of the ocean current, allowing the tropical rainfall to move further south. Since the equator effectively divides the ocean circulations into two hemispheres, the changing range of the mangroves may be telling us something about its former position.

A distinction must also be made between permanent climate change, and the various fluctuations of climate which have undoubtedly occurred over the past 5,000 years. The examples discussed so far are primarily indicators of the stable regimes prevailing before and after 3000 BC. Other evidence points to shorter periods of climatic instability, as is manifested by such factors as the advance and retreat of glaciers, fluctuations in lake levels and the growth rings of trees.

The advance and retreat of mountain glaciers is evident in many places and a significant neoglaciation occurred at the Atlantic/Sub-Boreal transition. In Europe, the transition is marked by an advance of the Alpine glaciers, and a retreat of the tree-line down the slopes. Near Salzburg, at an altitude of 1,500 metres, a brief cold spell is marked by the spread of juniper heath, replacing elm, hazel and oak, which had grown to those heights during the Atlantic phase.[33] After a very short interval, forests of fir trees replaced the juniper heath. This is one of many correspondences that can be found linking the elm decline to a sharp cold spell at the end of the Atlantic phase. In the Harz Mountains of southern Germany, the sharp change in the composition of the forests at the higher altitude has again been dated to the close of the fourth millennium BC.[34]

Further evidence of glacier resurgence at this period is to be found in Norway. At Glomfjord in Norland, peat overridden by an advancing glacier has been dated close to 3300 BC.[35] Deposits overridden by a glacier cannot give a precise date for the climate change, as surface material could be eroded away or pushed down the slopes. However, the neoglacial advance cannot be older than the deposits beneath the terminal moraine. Tree stumps shorn off by an advancing glacier are good candidates for dating, but can only be considered approximate. Evidence of the Atlantic/Sub-Boreal and later neoglacial advances are evident throughout Norway, but none has subsequently reached the limits achieved at the end of the Atlantic phase.[36]

A readvance occurred in North America too at this time. All the major ice caps and mountain glaciers of the continent shrank back during the Hypsithermal, but a prominent readvance then followed. The Barnes Ice Cap on Baffin Island began to expand at a little before 3000 BC and throughout the length of the Rocky Mountains glaciers advanced, overriding trees which had grown up the slopes.[37]

A typical example occurred in Washington State where a tree stump sliced off by the advancing end-moraine of the South Cascade Glacier is dated to approximately 3400 BC.[38] Another moraine on Crows Nest Mountain, British Columbia, is similarly datable to about 3500 BC.[39] In Alaska, most of the evidence from this period is now hidden beneath existing glaciers, but similar dates have been obtained from moraines in the area of Cook Inlet.[40] Since the trees could already have been dead when the glaciers reached them, the climate change which triggered the readvance must be dated slightly later: towards the end of the fourth millennium BC.

Most investigators agree that the readvance marks the end of the warm period in North America; but the advance seems to have continued, with evidence that more recent advances have overridden and destroyed most of the older terminal moraines. Some North American glaciers appear to have reached their maximum extent only as recently as the sixteenth century AD, or even more recently in some cases.[41]

Evidence from the southern hemisphere shows an interesting pattern of correspondence. The readvance of mountain glaciers in New Zealand seems to have occurred only during the last 3,000 years.[42] The remains of any earlier advances, if they ever existed, have been destroyed by more recent advances. However, in South America there is again correspondence. In the Andes the San Rafael Glacier began to advance after 3000 BC, reaching its maximum advance around 2500 BC.[43] This date comes from the bottom sediments of a pond that formed on the terminal moraine. Subsequently, pollen samples indicate a return to the warm, dry conditions that had prevailed during the Climatic Optimum.

Many glaciers in southern Patagonia appear to have achieved their maximum post-glacial extent between 3000 and 2000 BC. Evidence of two more recent advances show them to be of a lesser order.[44] This is the very opposite of the situation noted in North America and New Zealand. Comprehensive studies by Heusser in 1960 and 1961, in the Laguna San Rafael area of southern Chile, led him to conclude that the maximum extent of glaciation in the area was about 5,000 years old, following a period during the Climatic Optimum when the glacier was smaller than it is today.[45, 46]

It is important to note any correspondence between glaciation and sea level changes, as the cause of glacier surges may also be geodetic. In the absence of climatic factors, the tree-line and the permanent snow-line are simply heights above sea level. If the sea level rises or falls (for whatever reason) then the tree- and snow-lines must follow it up or down by a similar margin. Various attempts to show correspondence between glaciation and the eustatic sea level curves have met with little success.

The overall pattern of neoglaciation is complex; there is some evidence here to suggest a geodetic cause, but this is greatly complicated by other climatic factors. However, the pattern of long-term climate change since 3000 BC does not correspond to such a pattern. If climate change at the Atlantic/Sub-Boreal transition were attributable to a migration of the rotational poles then we would expect to see evidence of correspondence in alternate quarter-spheres; but this is not observed. Instead the evidence suggests that during the Atlantic phase the temperate zones expanded parallel to the equator, while the equatorial regions themselves underwent very little change. This pattern would appear to indicate that during Atlantic times the obliquity of the Earth's axis was somewhat less than it is today.

The extent of this change can be roughly estimated. The northward movement of the permanent tree-line in the northern hemisphere is about 3° of latitude. In China, the northern limit of bamboo has retreated south by a similar amount. However, in western Europe the range of frost-sensitive trees has moved south by about 5° and the northward spread of the Sahara Desert would appear to have been rather more than this. A crude estimate would be that the axial tilt has increased by some 3–4° since the Atlantic/Sub-Boreal transition and that the obliquity during Atlantic times was therefore only about 20°.

A change to the axial tilt alone, without any pole shift, would have affected the equatorial regions very little. Neither should it have affected the east–west ocean currents that prevail at the equator. Any such variation must therefore be taken as an indication of a shift in the position of the rotational axis rather than the tilt. The northward movement of the coastal desert in southern Ecuador by some 3° of latitude since 5000 BC sets a limit to how much this displacement has been and it must be concluded that the pole shift at the end of the Atlantic period was at most 1–2°. This is rather more than the sea level variations would indicate, but the direction of the proposed pole shift is entirely consistent with the pattern previously derived from the sea level evidence.

Any attempt to derive a precise date for the Atlantic/Sub-Boreal transition presents problems. The Atlantic period is conventionally dated between about 5500 BC and 3000 BC, but the extent to which these represent 'round figures' is uncertain. The dates suggested for neoglacial advances are too vague to be of much help. The vegetational response would not be immediate either; trees can survive for hundreds of years and adult trees would continue to release pollen even into an unfavourable environment. Young trees would then fail to grow up to replace the older generation, which might linger on for perhaps a further century.

It would clearly be quite impossible to survey all the available evidence of climatic change in a short chapter and the foregoing should be regarded as only a representative sample. Attention here has concentrated on the most significant transformations in the Holocene climate, in particular the situation around 3000 BC. Changes in the climate are often ascribed to the effects of a reconfiguration of the weather system. Various astronomical factors affect the Earth's orbit and axial tilt over thousands of years, altering the pattern of insolation. The suggestion is that the weather system can periodically flip from one stable regime to another. But it is difficult to see how this could account for such momentous changes occurring within little more than a human lifetime.

The effects of massive volcanic eruptions have also been advanced as a possible trigger for such changes in the climate. The great eruptions of Tambora (1815) and Krakatoa (1883) ejected clouds of dust and ash into the upper atmosphere, blocking the sunlight and resulting in noticeable cooling. Following the Tambora eruption the year 1816 came to be known as 'the year without a summer'. Could volcanic eruptions be the cause of the cold spell noted at the Atlantic/Sub-Boreal transition?

Indications that there may be such a link with volcanic activity have come from another dating technique: dendrochronology. Variations in the thickness of the annual growth rings of trees reflect the favourability of the climate during the growing season. In a year of good rainfall and sunlight a tree will put on a wider growth ring than in a bad year. These growth rings can then be used as climatic indicators. The rings can also be dated very precisely, simply by counting back the annual rings from the present day. Provided that an unbroken sequence of rings can be correlated from trees of different age, then a precise chronology can be derived. Moreover, a tree ring chronology can then be used to verify the accuracy of carbon-14 dates.

An analogous series of annual layers has been obtained by taking cores from the polar ice caps. The layers within the ice-core can be similarly counted back from the present day to give a continuous chronology and clues to the climate at the time the snow was falling. Within each annual layer the level of atmospheric acidity can be determined. Atmospheric acidity is known to increase following some volcanic eruptions due to the profuse quantities of sulphates ejected into the upper atmosphere.[47]

When the climatic history obtained from Greenland ice-cores is compared with that obtained from the growth rings of Irish bog oaks, a remarkable correspondence is found.[48] Seasons of low tree growth are found to coincide with the peaks of acidity associated with volcanic eruptions. Narrow growth rings occur when the summer growing season is curtailed, and in exceptionally poor years the spring growth may also be reduced.[49] The chronology obtained from the Irish bog oaks suggests that exceptionally low growth years occurred around 1153 BC, 3199 BC and 4377 BC. These correlate closely with periods of high acidity dated to 1100 BC, 3250 BC and 4400 BC.[50] Around 1150 BC a distinct 20-year period of abnormally thin growth rings is noted in the Irish bog oaks. Other periods of low growth within the last 5,000 years occurred between 1628 BC and 1626 BC. The former event has been suggested as the effects of the dust veil thrown up by the Santorini volcanic eruption.[51, 52]

Tree ring dates must by definition correspond to calendar years. It is tempting to suggest, therefore, that the Atlantic/Sub-Boreal transition occurred at the 3199 BC event as the result of a massive volcanic eruption; but this would be an over-simplification. The question then has to be asked why similar abrupt transitions did not occur after all the other volcanic eruptions in prehistory. Certainly they may be advanced as a cause of some fluctuations in the climate during prehistory, but it is difficult to see how they could possibly be the cause of the sea level variations occurring at around the same time.

Moreover, there is no indication that the volcanic activity around 3199 BC was any more severe than that which occurred at the other acidity peaks. If the 1628 BC event may indeed be equated with the Santorini eruption then it must be noted that it was a comparatively modest outburst by comparison with Tambora. The Tambora eruption is usually assigned a volcanic explosivity index (VEI) of 7, whereas Santorini is believed to have rated only 6 on the same scale – about the same as Krakatoa.[53] Tambora ejected more than twice as much ash as has been estimated for Santorini. The Tambora explosion caused some strange weather (such as snow in India) and a few poor summers, but nothing more dramatic than that. There has not been a permanent climate change since 1815, or any measurable effect on world sea levels.

It would appear, then, that the volcanic activity and the climate changes around 3100 BC must be seen as only evidence of a much wider malaise. That malaise should rather be viewed as the aftermath of an impact event, the resultant wobbling of the Earth on its axis, and an inexorable change in the axial tilt.

8

Memories of the Flood

As we look back in time we reach the point where recorded history ends and myth and legend begin. This vast expanse of time, about which we know so little, is so often simply lumped together into the period called 'prehistory'. Since we have so little information, it is easy to be drawn into the error of supposing that nothing of importance happened before historical times. Shadowy groups of people lived out their short, primitive lives uneventfully and, occasionally, they left their own remains and bits of pottery for the archaeologists to find. Sometimes this meagre archaeological evidence is the only record we have of ancient peoples. In fact, each thousand years of prehistory must have been as eventful and as rich in detail as the last thousand. In each generation there were kings and queens, wars and politics!

The historical period does not commence at the same time for all cultures. Thanks to missionary zeal very little is known about pre-Columbian America. Of Africa and Australia we know almost nothing. For most of Europe, history begins only with the Roman annals, which may take us back to the early centuries BC. Only from Greece and Rome do we have records that go back to about 600 BC. Without Herodotus, father of history, we would know even less. The Chinese historical period extends back to about 1500 BC, with the beginning of the Shang Dynasty. Only for Egypt and, to a lesser degree, Mesopotamia and the biblical lands do we have a chronology extending back anywhere near 3000 BC.

Of the time before the historical period, mythology, legends and garbled folk tales are all we have to go on. Some are undoubtedly based upon a core of truth, preserved verbally from generation to generation by pre-literate societies. Modern archaeology shows little respect for mythology and legend. Whenever legend disagrees with the archaeologists' conclusions then it is always the legend that is discarded! Even if one is tempted to believe the stories, without a chronology we can have no idea when the events occurred, or even their proper sequence.

One common theme runs through the mythologies of peoples as far removed as Eskimos and Australian Aborigines, and that is the legend of a great flood. As has been previously discussed, the secondary effects of even a modest comet impact would be felt world-wide. It would be remarkable indeed if such a cataclysmic event, and the resulting effects on the Earth's rotation, were not to be remembered in legend. It therefore should not surprise us that flood and deluge legends are so common.

There are indications that more than one catastrophic flood has occurred during prehistory. Some of these may be just memories of local flooding and it is vital not to confuse these with the memories of the Great Flood. The most vivid, and least garbled, stories will usually be the most recent, but the distinction between earlier and later events may become confused. Recall the words of the Egyptian priest in the *Timaeus*: 'You [Greeks] remember a single deluge only, but there were many previous ones.'[1]

Interesting though these lesser events may be in their own right, they are not the subject of primary interest to this discussion. Neither is there space here to give them the attention they deserve. However, their effects must be ruled out in any investigation of the legends of the world and some discussion of them is unavoidable. Evidence has already been offered that permanent sea level changes occurred around 3100 BC and 1650 BC, with evidence of massive volcanic episodes occurring as recently as 1150 BC.

Any review of flood legends must surely commence with the biblical account. Noah's flood is probably the most widely known of all the stories of the Old Testament.[2] The Judaeo–Christian tradition portrays the Flood as God's punishment for the wickedness of man. Noah and his family are chosen as the only people worthy to be saved and God warns them that he is about to destroy the world. Noah is instructed to build an Ark, into which he takes his entire family, and one male and female of every living creature.

The biblical Flood is a deluge. That is to say, the waters come from above in the form of rain, which persists for 40 days and 40 nights. When the rain ceases, the land is covered by water for a further 40 days before the Ark comes to rest on the mountains of Ararat. Even the high mountain tops are submerged in the Flood and not until another 150 days pass does the water begin to recede. Noah was 600 years old when the Flood came; it began on the 17th day of the 2nd month and the world did not become dry again until the first day of his 601st year. Noah's flood is often rationalized as no more than a memory of a local flood which devastated Mesopotamia and the Levant in very ancient times. However, Genesis is quite specific that the Flood affected the entire world.

The biblical Flood is representative of beliefs widely held by Middle Eastern peoples. There is sound evidence to suggest that the story is of Sumerian origin, preserved through the beliefs of the later Babylonians. A very similar flood legend is found in the Babylonian *Epic of Gilgamesh*. The story is preserved on a series of tablets excavated from the Library of Assurbanipal, among the ruins of Nineveh.[3] Composed in about 2000 BC, it must predate any written source for the biblical Flood. Gilgamesh is believed to have been an early king of Uruk, whose name has become associated with a number of old Sumerian legends. The epic details the journey of Gilgamesh to the Land of the Dead to visit his ancestor Utnapishtim. He finds him within a mountain at the world's end; and he tells Gilgamesh a story about the time of the great deluge.

Many years ago, the gods of Shuruppak on the Euphrates sent a flood against the city and its inhabitants as punishment for their sins. But Ea warned Utnapishtim who together with his family began to build a ship. It was two hundred feet long, by two hundred feet wide, by two hundred feet high. When the people asked what he was doing, Utnapishtim told them that Enlil had come to hate all men, and that he, Utnapishtim, planned to change allegiance to Ea and to dwell with him in his underwater kingdom. He loaded his Ark with food, drink, all his treasures, cattle and sheep. Finally he took all his family safely inside.

Then the terrible storm came, and the gods themselves were so frightened that they hid for safety in the remote heaven of Anu; but after only six days and nights, the wind died down and the rain ceased.

On the seventh day Utnapishtim opened a window and wept with joy to see the sun shining. At this time, the Ark came to rest on the summit of a mountain. Utnapishtim released a dove and a swallow, but both returned as the Ark was the only place they could find rest; but a raven released later did not return and he knew that the waters were going down. So they left the Ark, together with all their animals and made sacrifice to the gods.

The similarity of the Babylonian story to the flood of Noah is immediately apparent, even down to the details of the birds released, although the rest of the Gilgamesh epic has little biblical parallel. But the flood itself lasts for a mere 7 days, suggesting that the estimates of the duration of the storm, here and elsewhere, are unreliable.

It is safe to assume that the story was already old when it was included in the Gilgamesh epic. It therefore cannot relate to any event more recent than 2000 BC. Less complete, but older versions of the Flood legend have also been discovered. In one of these, from Nippur, the hero was named not Utnapishtim, but Ziusudra. Now this is important, for Sumerian king lists are also known which list a dynasty of 'rulers before the Flood'.[4] The last of the semi-mythical rulers of Shuruppak is named Ubartutu and one of the fragmentary Flood legends also mentions him – as the father of Ziusudra. It would seem that Ziusudra-Utnapishtim must be regarded as a real historical character.

After the Flood, the king lists tell us that 'kingship was sent down again from on high' and the first dynasty of Kish then commences. Not until King Enmebaragesi, the twenty-second ruler of this dynasty, is there archaeological proof of the authenticity of the king list. Two inscriptions naming this king have been found and it would appear that he reigned in about 2700 BC.[5] Counting back the reigns before him, an approximate date of 3000 BC has been suggested for the start of the dynasty – provided that the incredibly long reigns assigned to each king are ignored. Gilgamesh himself is unverified by archaeology, but appears to have reigned at about 2600 BC.

Once again the years just before 3000 BC appear significant and the origin of the Sumerian flood legends can be dated to approximately this period. Archaeological evidence would also appear to support at least a local flood in Mesopotamia at this time. In the course of excavations at Ur between 1929 and 1934, the archaeologist Sir Leonard Wooley discovered a deep layer of silt beneath the ruins of the great Sumerian city.[6] Telling his workmen to dig deeper, fully 2 metres of silt had to be excavated before artefacts began to be found again. Recognizing this immediately as possible evidence of the Flood, Wooley ordered wider excavations to confirm that the flood deposits did indeed cover the whole site. Below it were three more levels of human occupation.

At Ur, the flood deposit is thick, up to 3 metres in places. Microscopic analysis shows that it was deposited in fresh water, and the composition indicates that it came from higher up the valley of the Euphrates. This particular flood was not caused by an overflow of the sea, but was a river flood. The 'flood' layer has also been found at other Sumerian cities, but is not nearly so prominent. It does not occur at all at Eridu only a few kilometres away, but thin layers are also found at Lagash, Uruk and even Shuruppak, where Ziusudra and Utnapıshtım reigned.

The flood at Ur can be dated from the archaeological layers.[7] It occurs below the layers of the Early Dynastic I period, dated to after 3000 BC. Below it are remains from the Neolithic Ubaid culture, which is ascribed a date between 4500 and 3500 BC. The flood layers elsewhere are later, occurring between 3000 and 2800 BC. This disparity of dates would support an alternative hypothesis: that the flood deposits are the result of the rivers Tigris and Euphrates drastically changing their courses and overflowing their banks, inundating first one region then another.

It is difficult to see how this archaeological confirmation could support the idea of a flood assailing even the highest mountain tops. Certainly mankind was not all but wiped out at this time as the flood legends suggest; although there may indeed have been a cultural break. Possibly this represents a far more ancient flood tradition which has become attached to genuine historical kings and characters reigning at the time of the later Mesopotamian flood.

The Greek legend of the flood of Deucalion also seems to have originated in this way. It follows the same basic theme. Zeus determines to destroy the world with a great flood, but Prometheus, the father of Deucalion, somehow knows that the flood is imminent and warns his son to build and provision a ship. When the flood comes Deucalion and his wife Pyrrha drift upon the waters for 9 days before they are finally washed ashore on Mount Parnassus.

But the rest of mankind perish in the flood and so they consult the Oracle at Themis, to ask how the world might be repopulated. The reply is that they must throw over their shoulders the bones of their mother! Guessing that this is a riddle they assume this refers to Gaea – Mother Earth. They each instead throw stones over their shoulder. The stones that Deucalion throws became men; those thrown by Pyrrha become women; and so the world is repopulated.

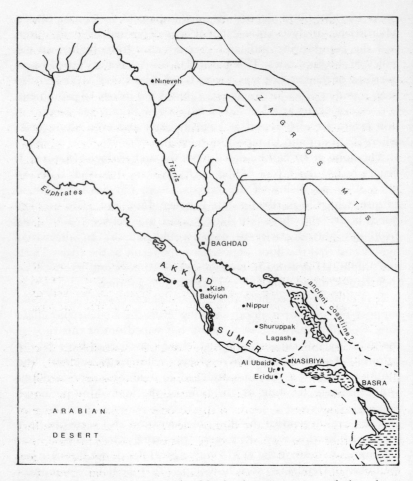

Fig. 8.1 Ancient Sumer and Akkad, showing some of the places mentioned in the text.

Whether the flood of Deucalion is inspired by the Mesopotamian story we cannot know, but there are clear similarities. Plato clearly regarded Deucalion's flood as only the most recent of many such occurrences. That he was not alone in this view is evident from the surviving fragments of Manetho. In his Egyptian king list, during the Eighteenth Dynasty (New Kingdom) we find the following remark regarding the sixth king of the dynasty.[8] 'The sixth, Mis-phragmuthosis, for 26 years: in his reign the flood of Deucalion's time occurred.' If Manetho's chronology can be trusted, this would date Deucalion and a lesser flood event of some kind to the years around 1500 BC. Possibly another memory of this later flood is to be found in the events surrounding the biblical exodus, for it too must be regarded as a memory of a flood event.[9] The crossing of the Red Sea by the Israelites, during their flight from Egypt, is shrouded in religious imagery. Faced with certain destruction at the hands of the pursuing Egyptians, Moses smites the sea with his rod, at which the waters part, allowing the Israelites to walk across the dry bed of the sea in safety.

As Josephus records: 'the sea went out of its own place and left dry land.'[10] When Pharaoh and his army attempt to follow along the same path, the sea returns to engulf them:

> As soon therefore as the whole Egyptian army was within it, the sea flowed to its own place, and came down with a torrent raised by storms of wind, and encompassed the Egyptians. Showers of rain also came down from the sky and dreadful thunders and lightening, with flashes of fire.[11]

In the rather sober description of Josephus, it is possible to discern many similarities between the exodus and the Great Flood. The difference is one of degree only. The sea level appears to oscillate about its natural height; this time retreating and returning rather than flooding over the land, to the accompaniment of a deluge of rain. This is not the place to discuss the events of the exodus; suffice it to say that however hard we try it is not possible to assign it a date as early as 3000 BC. The exodus story is unsupported by any archaeological evidence, but is usually assigned a date some time after 1700 BC.

It is often said that there are no Egyptian references to the Flood, but a closer examination will show that this is simply not true! It is to be expected that minor floods would not be remembered in a country where a flood of the Nile was an annual event. Of course, the legend of Atlantis could be regarded as an Egyptian memory of the Great Flood, but there is only circumstantial evidence that it has an authentic Egyptian origin.

Other clues come from sources more positively connected with Egypt. The historian Manetho (according to later chroniclers) placed the Flood immediately prior to Menes. There is also the previously noted reference by Josephus to the god Thoth (Hermes) inscribing records on the Siriadic Columns, at 'a time before the Flood'.[12] Plutarch narrates a myth describing the emergence of the Nile delta, after a deluge of rain had forced out the sea.[13] Plutarch is quite clear that this was a genuine Egyptian tradition, which he assigns to the age of Horus and Set. Yet further indications of the Flood may also be extant within Egyptian Book of the Dead papyri.[14]

Many commentators have noted an apparent absence of flood traditions from the African continent. Indeed, it is difficult to find anything other than naïve myths in African tribal mythology. Myths speak of a great serpent coiled around the Earth to support it. When he becomes hungry and eats his own tail, the world will sink into the sea!

Elsewhere, in Europe to the north, the Scandinavian races also recall calamitous events in their mythology. The myths of the Vikings have been preserved for us so excellently in the Icelandic Eddas; in one epic poem, called the *Voluspa*, we hear of the time of Ragnarok and the destruction of the gods.[15] Ragnarok is a prophecy of how the world will end. In another myth, we hear how the god Odin destroyed a frightful monster, the Serpent of Midgard, casting it into the ocean where it lies coiled around the centre of the world. At Ragnarok, the Midgard Serpent will rise again from the depths of the sea to attack the world. The sea will rise to overflow the land and only Loki, the son of a giant, will escape from the flood in the great ship *Naglfar* with its crew of giants. All the gods and men will be destroyed, and the serpent with them; but this is just the end of one cycle of the world. A new world, as green and fruitful as the old, will emerge from the waves and the sons of the gods will inherit it.

The gods lived in a land called Asgard in which lay a great plain called Vigred, described as 'one hundred miles square'. According to Snorri, there were twelve gods and thirteen goddesses in Asgard. They lived in great palaces and halls roofed over with silver and gold.

There were giants in Asgard too. At the beginning of the world the giants, who were skilled craftsmen, built a great wall to encircle it and keep out the enemies of the gods. At Ragnarok, the great destruction will be preceded by many portents, there will be untold suffering and people will commit evil acts of violence and incest. Men will fight each other in wars and the rule of the gods will break down. The giants will come in ships to storm Asgard and destroy it. In the end, the gods and the giants will meet on the great plain of Vigred for a final battle, before the world sinks slowly into the sea.

As if all this were not bad enough, the end of the world will also be preceded by another great calamity, the Fimbulvetr, or 'great winter'. This great winter will last for three years and be accompanied by huge earthquakes that will send the mountains crashing down. There will be a darkening of the Sun, as the great wolf Fenrir attempts to devour it, and the Moon and stars will tumble from the sky.

There is a clear association in the Nordic myths between astronomical phenomena and the destruction of the world. Here the flood is no mere legend, but has become absorbed into the mythology. The gods are located on the Earth and it is the monsters that are to be found roaming the sky. The flood is quite clearly caused by an overflow of the sea, rather than a deluge, and intensely cold winters replace the torrents of rain remembered further to the south.

Other northern peoples, such as the Eskimos of northern Canada, similarly recall a flood by the sea, which came on so fast that only a few people could save themselves by lashing together their canoes to make a raft.[16] The Eskimos of Alaska also remember this flood, when only those who fled to the highest mountains were saved. In Greenland, the first missionaries found an even more surprising story.[17] The Eskimos there recalled a time when the Earth tilted over and all men were drowned in the sea. They cited the occurrence of the bones of fish and whales on the high mountains as evidence of this.

The Pawnee Indians of North America also tell a flood legend with a familiar theme.[18] They believed that when the end of the world was at hand, they would be able to predict it by careful study of the stars. One day, the South Star would approach the place of the North Star and then flood and destruction would follow. They believed that their god Tirawa had once made a race of giants. When these giants became too powerful and corrupt, he determined to destroy them and sent storms and rain from out of the north-west. The flood waters rose and the race of giants were all drowned.

It is worth while to examine these Pawnee legends in a little more detail, for they are significant. They believed that on the day of destruction the Sun would first grow dark, much darker than in an eclipse, and the Moon would grow pale. Sometimes the South Star was allowed to leave its proper place in 'the dance of the stars' and look upon the North Star to see that it was in its proper place.[19] The South Star would then move back to its own place and the dance of the stars would continue. At the time of destruction, the skies would move, the stars would come to Earth and the Pawnee too would become stars.

The Creek Indians also have a flood story.[20] In their version, it is a dog who warns his master that a flood is imminent and tells him to make a raft. When the flood comes, the man sees the mountains break open and terrible monsters are unleashed. But the rising water drowns them. All people perish except the man and his dog. The man is saved only when he reluctantly throws his dog into the waters to placate them, upon which they begin to subside, taking only 7 days to dry out completely. The man then returns to the place where he formerly lived, to discover the spirits of his tribe waiting for him. This legend seems to recall both a volcanic eruption and a simultaneous flood. Many variations of the flood legend are to be found among the North American Indians, but these examples will suffice, as all are very similar.

On the opposite side of the world the Australian Aborigines remember a flood.[21] They celebrate it not only by stories handed down from generation to generation, but in their rock paintings. The legends contain extraordinary detail. The paintings of the Warumungu of northern Australia tell of the great rock snake Wollunqua, who emerged out of the sea from the direction of Timor. He transformed the landscape, making the rivers meander and the mountains shake as he passed overhead. He pulled the wind and waters of the flood behind him and formed the broad, irregular channels at the mouth of the Ord and Victoria rivers.

In south Australia, too, there is a legend associated with the Murray River.[22] Here it was the ancestral hero Ngurunderi who pursued the first great fish across the sky. As the fish swished his tail, he splashed water over the land, flooding and broadening the Murray River estuary.

Another legend about Ngurunderi tells of the time when his two wives ran away and he had to chase after them.[23] He caught up with the two women as they waded across the shallows to Kanga-roo Island and in his anger he determined to punish them. He commanded the sea to rise. Obediently, the waters rose and the two women were drowned as the sea drove them back to the shore. Ngurunderi turned their bodies to stone, and now they form the two rocks off Cape Jarvis known as the Two Sisters. This was how Kangaroo Island was formed, and it remains sacred to the Aborigi-nes as a place where the spirits of their ancestors dwell. This legend is well supported by science too. Kangaroo Island was certainly joined to the mainland 10,000 years ago, and it is thought that the sea reached its present height there between 5,000 and 7,000 years ago.[24] The legends recall a time when it was possible to walk to Kangaroo Island from the mainland.

Many other Aborigine traditions recall the rising of the sea around the shores of Australia. Away from the coast, the flood is remembered rather differently in legends of the time when the lakes dried up and became salty. The story is told of a powerful medicine man named Gumuduk, who lived in the hills.[25] Thanks to the power of his magic bone, the hill people were prosperous and happy. He called the rain in its proper season, to ensure that food was always plentiful. He made the trees blossom and the animals multiply.

The jealous tribe from the plains below kidnapped the medicine man and stole his magic bone, thinking that they too could prosper. But the medicine man escaped and buried his bone in the ground. He cast a terrible spell, declaring that wherever he trod upon the plain, salt water would rise from the ground. The waters over-flowed the plain, salting up the rivers and lakes. When eventually the water dried up, it left the once fertile plain as a dry and useless desert, where neither man nor animal could live.

This is a remarkable legend indeed, perhaps the most useful of all the Australian stories, for not only does it recall the flood, but also dates the event as concurrent with a permanent change in the climate. The Aborigine legends once again describe an overflow of the sea rather than a deluge. The waters do not go down again and the permanent rise of the sea is remembered by the changes it caused around the Australian coastline.

Legends from South America do not disappoint us either. An example from Brazil follows a familiar theme.[26] In the course of a fight between the two mythical brothers Ariconte and Tamendonare, one of them stamped his foot in anger, shaking the ground. At this a huge fountain gushed up, as high as the clouds, higher than the mountains. It flowed and flowed until the whole world was submerged in water. The two brothers and their wives ran to the highest mountain and were able save themselves by clinging to trees and eating the fruit. All mankind was destroyed in the flood except these four, from whom two separate tribes are descended, the Tupinambas and the Tominus. The legend of the Caryans of Amazonia is very similar.[27] Again the heroes save themselves by climbing a high mountain, but this time the flood is explained as originating from bottle gourds of water that are dropped on the ground!

In the Andes Mountains of Chile, the Araucanians remember a flood from which only a few of the tribe escaped.[28] A great earthquake and volcanic eruptions are said to have been the cause of the flood. The survivors escaped by climbing a high mountain called Thegtheg, which had three peaks and was reputedly able to float on water. The tribe still fear earthquakes and rush to the mountains whenever an earthquake occurs. As a further precaution, they take along a wooden bowl, to protect their heads should the mountain float on the waters and rise too close to the Sun.

The climbing of mountains to escape the flood is a very common theme in South American flood legends. There is little mention of escape by boat or of deluges. The water comes from below or from the sea. But there is also a new factor here. Sometimes the mountains themselves can float or rise above the flood. In the version of the Canarians of Ecuador this theme occurs again.[29] They relate that two brothers escaped the rising waters by climbing a high mountain called Huaca-ynan. But as the waters rose, the mountain too grew higher, ensuring that the two brothers remained always above the flood. Later, the waters retreated allowing the brothers to come down again into the valley.

This theme of land rising, as distinct from water retreating, is also prominent in the mythology of the Finno-Ugrians. This broad grouping of peoples includes the Finns, Estonians, Lapps and other races occupying the Arctic fringes of Europe and Siberia.

References to the flood are found within the Finnish epic *Kalevala* ('The Land of Heroes'), where the emphasis falls rather upon the time when the land first emerged out of the sea.[30] One poem recalls how the people grew crops on the fertile new land:

> Do you remember the time
>> when the seas were ploughed
>> were ploughed up,
>> were sown
> when the rocks beat together
> when the cairns were first piled up
> when the waves gave way to land?

The flood is also recalled in the tale of Väinämöinen's wound, where the torrents of blood flowing from the knee of the wounded hero form a river, which inundates the land. Väinämöinen goes in search of someone who can heal his wounds, but an old man mocks him, saying that greater floods than this have been reversed, when rivers ceased to flow, and in the aftermath new land emerged from the sea.[31]

> Bays were formed in rocky headlands,
> Tongues of land were linked together

Another fascinating story concerns the theft of the Sun and Moon. The god Jumala fashions a new moon from a spark of fire; but the careless goddess of the air lets the fire drop and unleashes chaos on the Earth.[32] The fire falls into the Lake of Alue, causing it to burst its banks:

> Three times in the nights of summer,
> Nine times in the nights of autumn,
>
> Rose the lake the height of fir-trees,
> Roaring rose above the lake banks
> . . .
> Thus retired the lake of Alue,
> And fell back from all its margins,
> Sinking to its former level
> in a single night of summer.

Folk memories of the disappearance, or some other abnormality, of the Sun and Moon are most prominent in those parts of the world where flood legends are weak. It is perhaps to be expected that the Pacific island societies would have legends about floods by the sea, but the flood legends are not nearly so common, nor so richly entertaining, as those that describe how the islands were 'fished up' from the ocean. Indeed many Pacific islands have no recognizable flood legend at all; others are naïve and must obviously refer to localized memories of recent tidal waves.

Only in Hawaii and Samoa do we find legends of the time the world was destroyed by water and re-created. In most island cosmogonies, the sea is regarded as eternal, and little attempt is made to explain its origin. Originally there were no islands, only a single god or gods who roamed the sky above; but throughout Oceania there exist many different explanations of how the islands were first created out of the ocean.

Prominent in all the Polynesian myths of creation, and also to a lesser extent in Melanesia, is the figure of Maui, the trickster god. About twenty different stories exist describing the exploits of this demigod, which vary a little from island to island. Most notably he fished up the very islands on which they lived.

In one version, from the Tuamotu Archipelago, he and his brothers go fishing among the dangerous reefs.[33] His brothers are wary of his trickery, and not pleased when he leads them out of sight of the land to cast their fishing lines. They fish all day but catch nothing. Eventually, his brothers all drop off to sleep leaving Maui fishing alone. He catches a huge fish and struggles with it, but the noise as it breaks the surface wakes his brothers. 'Oh Maui! Oh Maui!' they cry, 'that's not a fish, it's an island!' The fish struggles so hard that its tail breaks off, leaving only the head above water. He had fished up the island of Havaiki! In similar fashion, the Hawaiians and the Maoris of New Zealand trace the origin of their islands to Maui's fishing expertise. Sometimes he created whole archipelagos when the island broke up as he pulled it from the water.

Some of Maui's other tricks are also worthy of note. He is said to have starved his own grandmother to death so that he could use her jawbone for his magic.[34] Next, he trapped the Sun in a noose as it rose one day. Using the magic jawbone, he beat the Sun to make it move more slowly across the sky. In other versions he is said to have bound the Sun with rope made from the sacred hairs of his mother's head.[35]

The legends also speculate as to why Maui should wish to slow down the Sun. On Arawa it was to give the people more time to tend their gardens. On many other islands it was said to be so that there would be more time for the women to make Tapa cloth and to do the cooking, or to give more time for the men to build canoes.[36] In the Society Islands, the reason is to give the priests more time to build temples. Sometimes it is explained another way. When Maui was born the world was still in a state of chaos and disorder.[37] The sky was closer to the Earth, so close that it pressed down on the trees. At that time the Sun travelled too quickly and there was no time for cooking and making canoes. Maui raised the skies, slowed down the Sun, controlled the wind and set the stars in orderly motion.

In the many legends of Maui, it is possible to discern many of the elements elsewhere found attached to flood legends. The references to the slowing down, or speeding up of the Sun need not be taken too literally. It seems to be only the daylight hours that are extended – not the nights! What we have described here is the first experience, by a tropical people, of the seasonal shortening and lengthening of the days and nights. People who live in temperate latitudes are well accustomed to the seasons and would probably place less emphasis on the phenomenon. Near the equator, the days and nights remain roughly equal, at 12 hours each, throughout the year. Any departure from this, for a society confined to the same small island for generations, would be certain to cause alarm. These myths clearly recall some kind of change in the Earth's rotation and axial tilt.

The descriptions of Maui himself are equally enigmatic. Sometimes he takes human form, as we have seen, but his actions are those of a god. He is said to have been abandoned by his mother and raised by his father and grandparents.[38] He grew into an ugly youth, who eagerly learned all the tricks that his divine relatives could teach him, until his powers were greater even than theirs. He is portrayed as a clown and an embarrassment to the other gods, who jealously mocked and feared his actions. But in the myths of some islands, he is clearly not human at all. In Tahiti, he was said to have eight heads and to reflect a light as bright as the Sun![39] The last in the stories of the Maui Cycle describes the death of Maui as an attempt to gain immortality for all mankind. He fails and is cast into the sea by the other gods who have grown tired of his tricks. There, he enters the body of the goddess of the underworld (or is swallowed by her). Unable to break free from her, he dies.

To interpret the origin of the Maui legends, it is essential to appreciate something of the history of the Pacific peoples. The dispersal of the Austronesian peoples from their ancestral home in

southern China, Formosa and the Philippines is now well understood from archaeological and linguistic evidence.[40] The dispersal
into Indonesia began before 3000 BC, from which the ancestral
Polynesians had colonized islands as far west as Fiji by about 1500
BC. Permanent settlement of Micronesia began only after 1000 BC.
The later dispersal of the Polynesians into the Pacific began only
after AD 500, eventually reaching Hawaii and New Zealand.

The similarity of the Polynesian myths suggests that they have
diverged from a common ancestral story. Maui, as a fisher of
islands, is also known throughout Melanesia. In Micronesia, the
fisher of islands is known as Motikitik, and the duties of raising the
sky and snaring the Sun are shared with other gods.[41] This argues
strongly that the myths of island creation are older than the
colonization of the islands. Indeed they must date from as early as
the third millennium BC when the ancestors of the Pacific races
lived in the islands off south-east Asia.

Continuing with the east coast of Asia, the historical period of
Japan is surprisingly short and the origin of the Japanese people
themselves obscure. The written sources for most of their early
mythology date from as recently as AD 720 and the earliest semi-
legendary emperor is thought to have reigned in about 660 BC.
Before that time, the age of the gods begins and in Japanese
mythology we find a rich series of images describing the creation of
land from the sea. Even the creation myths follow this theme. The
god Izanagi stirred the ocean with his spear and the drops that fell
from its tip congealed to form islands.[42] Another myth describes
how a bridge once linked Earth and heaven. But one day when the
gods were all sleeping, it collapsed into the sea. Its remains formed
the long isthmus of Honshu west of Kyoto.

Many myths describe Susano the storm god and Amaterasu, the
Sun goddess. The name Susano can be translated as meaning 'swift
and impetuous deity'.[43] These two gods were eternally at war with
each other, and one day Susano let loose his horses in the home of
Amaterasu. They trampled her rice fields and destroyed her property. In retaliation the Sun goddess hid herself away in a cave, so
that the whole world became dark.[44] All the lesser gods and
goddesses came together on the dried-up bed of a river to discuss
what could be done to persuade her to come out again. They sang
and danced outside the cave to tempt her out. At length, she
emerged to see what all the noise was about and the gods captured

her image in the first mirror. Since then the world has always had normal days and nights, and in memory of this a mirror forms part of the imperial regalia of Japan.

Susano is said to have taken the Izumo Peninsula, on the north coast of Honshu, as his province.[45] His grandson Oh-kuni-nushi – 'the Great Land Master' – was not satisfied with his province and wanted to make it larger. He changed the coastline to its present shape by dragging the offshore islands and parts of Korea towards him with ropes, which he slung around the mountains. When all these were joined together, they made the peninsula in the north of Izumo.

This quaint little story does not have any overtones of catastrophe associated with it, as one might expect from such a volcanic island as Japan. It is a fact that Japanese earthquakes do tend to elevate the land. In Tokyo bay, for example, earthquakes in 1703 and 1923 have created raised shorelines; and older platforms are evident all around the bay.[46] But earthquake, catastrophe and flood do not figure prominently in Japanese mythology.

Apart from Egypt and Mesopotamia, the historical period of China is one of the longest in the world. It extends back to the start of the Shang Dynasty, which the Chinese legendary chronology puts at 1766 BC. But myth and history overlap in China. The mythical past is said to have been first collated and recorded in about 820 BC. Towards the end of the Chou Dynasty, the teachings of Confucius began to affect the style of the myths and legends, and they become much more formalized.

The rigid political ideology of Confucian historians required that China should always have been subject to a single all-powerful sovereign. We therefore see the past represented as a unified Chinese empire ruled over by a succession of mythical dynasties; each emperor controlling a well-organized civil service which ordered both the state and the cosmos to his will. The Chinese myths offer yet another opportunity to estimate the date of the Flood.

Towards the end of the reign of the Empress Nu Wa, or Nu-uang, there lived a feudal prince whose name was Kung Kung. His duties were to administer punishment and to keep the law.[47] But he became over-ambitious and sought to take power for himself, for which he has come to be known as 'the first rebel'. He is said to have tried to use the influence of water to overcome the power of wood, under which Nu Wa reigned. He was defeated in battle and

in anger he struck his head against the Imperfect Mountain Pu-
chou Shan, which supports the sky. One version of the legend
states:

> In ancient times Kung Kung strove with Chuan Hsu for the empire.
> Angered, he smote the Unrotating Mountain,
> Heaven's pillars broke, the bonds with earth were ruptured,
> Heaven leaned over to the north-west;
> Hence the sun, moon, stars and planets were shifted,
> And earth became empty in the south-east.[48]

Chinese cosmology visualized the world as an inverted, square-
cornered bowl, which was either described as the back of a great
tortoise, or as simply floating upon the ocean. The sky above it was
viewed as another inverted bowl, this time circular, which rested
upon and rotated about a great mountain. In another version of the
legend, the Empress Nu Wa sought the influence of fire to defeat
the influence of water.[49] She forced Kung Kung to flee towards the
west, where he came to the mountain that supports the sky.
Climbing to the top, he found the eight pillars which support the
vault of heaven. In his despair he seized one of the columns and
shook it violently; the pillar collapsed, bringing down a corner of
the sky. It landed on the southern slope of the mountain, devastating it completely. As a consequence, the heavens were tilted lower
in the north-west and rivers began to flow in the opposite direction!

Thereafter the mountain was called the Imperfect Mountain, Pu-
chou Shan. Through the hole in the sky, violent rain and wind-
storms descended, flooding the land of Chi. Legend has it that Nu
Wa melted stones of five different colours and used them to repair
the breach in the heavens. She cut off the feet of the celestial tortoise
to stop it moving, the flooding waters ceased and the land of Chi
was saved.

The land of Chi, where the early legendary rulers of China
reigned, is usually identified with the region around the mouth of
the Yellow River. The Chinese chronology of mythical rulers places
the reign of Nu Wa after the long reign of her brother Fu-hsi who
supposedly reigned between 2953 BC and 2838 BC.[50] The mythical
credentials of Fu-hsi are established by his many achievements,
which include the invention of the calendar, fishing and the breed-
ing of silkworms. As occurs in the earliest king lists of Egypt and
Mesopotamia, the mythical rulers are assigned incredibly long

reigns. Nu Wa is said to have lived to the age of 143 years and is remembered in China as the Patron Deity of Go-betweens or arrangers of marriage.

The legendary chronology begins in 2953 BC with a series of mythical rulers until 2357 BC. These are followed by the two 'patriarchs', Yao and Shun. The first ruler of the legendary Hsia Dynasty, Yu, ascended the throne in 2205 BC and his descendants ruled until 1766 BC when the Shang Dynasty commences.[51] The Shang Dynasty too was thought to be legendary until the discovery towards the end of the nineteenth century of the so-called 'oracle bone' inscriptions; and the authenticity of the Shang Dynasty is now well established.

The accuracy of the Chinese legendary chronology cannot be entirely trusted. As early as the second century BC, the historian Ssu-ma Chien refused to trust the dates in the king lists before 841 BC.[52] Many documents give differing accounts of the legendary period, which question the orthodox chronology accepted by the Confucian historians. We can therefore only regard the Chinese king lists as a useful guideline.

Official Chinese history was recorded in the *Shu*, or *Book of History*, known as *Shu Ching* since the time of the Han Dynasty and first translated into English in the nineteenth century by James Legge. Within it we find many references to floods and the attempts of various administrators to cope with their disastrous effects. The history opens in the time of the patriarch Yao, where we find him instructing the brothers Hsi and brothers Ho to 'calculate and delineate the movements and appearances of the Sun, the Moon, the stars and the zodiacal houses'.[53] These brothers are clearly astronomers, as they set out to measure 'the exact limit of the shadow' to determine midsummer and midwinter day. They establish a calendar year of 366 days and demarcate the four seasons.[54] 'Thereafter,' declares the sovereign Yao, 'the various officers being regulated in accordance with this, all the work of the seasons will be fully performed.'

In true Confucian style, the heavens are set to order upon the instructions of the all-powerful sovereign. The flood, too, is seen as all the fault of an aberrant minister.[55]

Huan Tou said, 'Oh! The merits of the Minister of Works have just been displayed on a wide scale.'

The Sovereign said, 'Alas! when all is quiet, he talks; but when employed, his actions turn out differently. He is respectful only in appearance. See! the floods assail the heavens!'

The Sovereign said, 'Oh! Chief of the Four Mountains, the waters of the inundation are destructive in their overflow. In their vastness they embrace the hills and overtop great heights, threatening the heavens with their floods. The lower people groan and murmur! Is there a capable man to whom I can assign the correction of this calamity?'

The task of controlling the floodwaters is left to his appointed successors Shun and Yu. The sovereign and his ministers labour for many years to control the flood. We hear that the rivers are channelled to the sea, lakes are formed and marshes are drained. Assisted by the able forester Yi, woodlands are burned and paths made through them for men. The land is divided into nine provinces. At length, the sovereign Yu declares that, 'The earth has been reduced to order and the influences of heaven produce their complete effect.'[56]

If we accept the Chinese chronology at face value, then this period of disastrous floods in China is dated between 2357 and 2205 BC. Floods in the Yellow River region are common and the rivers are known to have changed course many times in the recent past, with drastic effect; but the flooding during the third millennium BC seems to have been particularly devastating. In the later documents of the Hsia Dynasty, we hear how the nine branches of the Hwang Ho were made to keep their proper channels.

This early part of the *Shu Ching* is now believed to be a later forgery, based on the mythology prevailing during later dynasties. Beneath the Confucian straitjacket, the patriarchs Yao and Shun and their able civil servants may be discerned as mythical figures. Their actions in controlling and shaping the landscape have more in common with the acts of a demiurge, such as Heracles or Maui, than any human industry. It is quite likely that China was not subject to any central authority during the early part of the third millennium BC and that, as with flood legends elsewhere, the details have become attached to prominent characters contemporary with the events.

Flood and catastrophe continued to shape the destiny of China. The legendary Hsia Dynasty founded by Yu lasted for 439 years and also came to an end amidst catastrophe and confusion. *Shu*

Ching records that the last of the Hsia rulers, Chieh, was a tyrant who oppressed the people. Later historians regarded him as the very definition of evil. He neglected government and frittered his time away in evil vices. In 1766 BC the oppression of Chieh led one of his provincial governors T'ang to rise against him. James Legge described the events of this time and the outcome of the struggle as follows.[57]

> There could be no doubt as to the result. Heaven and earth combined with men to show their detestation of the tyrant. Two suns fought in the sky. The earth shook. Mountains were moved from their strong foundations. Rivers were dried up. Chieh was routed and fled south to Ch'ao. There he was kept a prisoner until his death three years after.

This memory of 'two suns' fighting in the sky is another strong candidate for comet imagery. Compare it with a well-known British legend from Geoffrey of Monmouth's *History of the Kings of Britain*.[58]

> As he lay lulled in sleep he saw a bear flying through the air. At the growling of the bear every shore quaked. Arthur also saw a terrifying dragon flying in from the west and lighting up the countryside with the glare of its eyes. When these two met they began a remarkable fight. The dragon which I have described attacked the bear time and time again, burning it with its fiery breath and finally hurling its scorched body down to the ground.

These two references from opposite sides of the world might easily be describing the same comet fall; but in China the sighting is attached to a firm chronology dating it to the early second millennium BC.

As the all-powerful ruler, Chieh seems to have been held to account for cosmic catastrophes beyond his control. With T'ang, the historical Shang Dynasty commences and the semi-legendary history of China begins to fall into line with archaeological evidence. It is perhaps to be expected that the later Shang rulers would justify the rebellious acts of T'ang by reviling Chieh, attributing the natural calamities of his reign to a judgement of his evil and incompetence; but hidden in all this is a memory of a further geological catastrophe, dated by the Chinese chronology to 1766 BC.

These three episodes of flood and catastrophe in Chinese history, dated at 2953 BC, 2357 BC and 1766 BC concur remarkably well with the episodes of volcanic activity and low tree growth noted previously, and dated at 3199 BC, 2345 BC and 1628 BC.[59] However, it is the earliest, concerning the exploits of the rebel Kung Kung, which should be correlated with western myths of the Great Flood.

For all its faults, the legendary chronology of China is the only one that has preserved a definite account of three separate episodes of flood and catastrophe. Unlike elsewhere, the very existence of a chronology and written records has prevented memories of similar experiences from becoming amalgamated into a single legend. Irish mythology also speaks of three floods but the associated chronology is lost.

Even in the small sample of flood legends described here it is possible to identify a pattern. From one source or another it is possible to find descriptions of most of the expected features of an impact event. We find monsters, dragons, serpents and powerful demigods in the sky. Sometimes these come down to Earth where they die. Sometimes they shake the mountains and are the cause of the flood. There are the references to the permanent shift of the sky above. Memories of the time when the Earth wobbled on its axis and the seasons and the length of the day were altered. The changing climate is remembered. In addition, we find not only memories of land deluged beneath the waters of the flood, but also accounts of the creation of land, the rising of mountains, and of rivers changing their courses.

There is the same geographical pattern of correspondence in alternate quarter-spheres, as was noted from the physical evidence. While memories of a flood are universal, the legends differ in their structure. Mostly they describe a flood that persists for many days before going down again, but sometimes the flood does not recede and land is permanently submerged. This occurs in the Australian Aborigine myths, and also along the Atlantic coast of Europe, where Welsh and Breton legends describe lost cities beneath the sea.

Elsewhere, the memories of a flood are of secondary importance and the legends mainly describe rising land and the protracted struggles with river floods. Again the pattern corresponds. The flood stories of the Finns recall only emergent land and the rounding-off of the coastline, as the goddess Luonnotar completed the work of creation. Legends from South America describe the rising of the mountains; and in China and the Western Pacific descriptions of the flood take second place to the effects of land rising. This is most evident in the legends describing the appearance of islands out of the ocean, but also in the struggles of the Chinese to confine and channel the rivers on the North China Plain. The effects of the proposed later catastrophes must have been comparatively slight, as the memories of them have not disturbed this pattern of correspondence. Only the African continent seems to have escaped lightly and there is the predicted scarcity of true flood legends from that source.

Myths and legends are a singularly imprecise tool with which to probe the past. They are subject to individual interpretation and can only be used to support other evidence where it exists. However, once we have the key that unlocks their secrets, they may be viewed in a whole new light. There will always be those who will dismiss the traditions of our forebears as mere nonsense. So long as this attitude persists we ignore a wealth of valuable evidence about the past. Those who survived times of great adversity have passed on to us the evidence of their own eyes. They can scarcely be blamed for the way their incredulous descendants have trivialized and distorted the things they saw.

9

Parallel Trends in Ancient Cultures

History begins in Egypt. The unification of the Two Lands at about 3100 BC marks the boundary of recorded history before which we cannot look with any certainty. Precisely why the great civilization of the Nile valley should emerge at just this era has always been something of an enigma. It is all too easy to overlook how very ancient Egyptian civilization is. It is more than twice as old as the Roman Empire, twice as ancient as the earliest history of Greece, and older by 1,500 years than the earliest verifiable history of China. Nearby Mesopotamia is the only rival of Egypt for antiquity, but the Mesopotamian chronology is much less reliable and not so well confirmed by archaeology.

The Egyptian chronology became the yardstick used to measure the age of archaeological finds elsewhere in the Near East. Until the advent of carbon-14 dating, cross-dating against the established Egyptian chronology was the only method available to date any ancient site. Sir Flinders Petrie used it in the late nineteenth century to date the ruins of Mycenae, where he found imported Egyptian pottery that could be correlated with similar finds in Egypt. Once a reliable chronology for Egypt was established then it could be used to date any nearby culture in which Egyptian artefacts could be identified.

The argument could be taken a stage further. Once other cultures in the Near East were dated in this way, then their own artefacts could similarly be used for cross-dating sites further away from Egypt. In this way, a whole series of prehistoric cultures throughout Europe were assigned an approximate era. Archaeology embraced cross dating and put its trust in those few specialists able to interpret the Egyptian hieroglyphs. Cross-dating was able to produce fairly accurate correspondences for the Aegean and Anatolia, where direct imports from Egypt could be found; but the method broke down further away from the eastern Mediterranean where no direct links could be established.

Moreover, since it was customary to look back ultimately towards correlation with Egypt to date any archaeological discovery, the idea somehow grew up that all forms of culture and innovation could be traced to an origin in Egypt or Mesopotamia. This concept, known as *diffusionism*, considered settled agriculture and civilization to have originated somewhere within the 'Fertile Crescent' in an event that was termed the 'Neolithic Revolution'. This was the original germ of culture whence it was supposed that cultural advances gradually filtered to barbarian Europe and beyond.

The application of radiocarbon dating techniques to archaeological finds during the 1950s offered the first truly independent check on accepted chronologies. All living matter contains carbon, but in addition to the stable isotopes, carbon-12 and carbon-13, a small proportion exists in the form of the radioactive carbon-14 isotope. During its lifetime a living organism will absorb carbon-14 from the atmosphere, but after death no further absorption can occur. All carbon-14 must ultimately decay to nitrogen-14 at a steady rate and the proportion remaining in a piece of dead tissue acts as a 'clock' which can be used to determine its age.

Carbon-14 has a half-life of about 5,600 years. That is to say, over this period half the carbon-14 in the sample will have decayed. After 11,200 years half as much again will have decayed, and so on, until the proportion eventually becomes too small to detect. Since radioactive decay occurs at a constant rate, the level of the isotope in the atmosphere represents an equilibrium between the rate of decay and the rate of production. It is known to originate in the upper atmosphere where cosmic ray neutrons interact with atmospheric nitrogen, converting it into carbon-14, which quickly oxidizes and finds its way into the food chain. This much is certain. Rather less certain is the amount of radiocarbon present in the atmosphere at the time the creature died.

In the absence of any evidence to the contrary, scientists assumed that the rate of carbon-14 production had not changed in the last few thousand years. The immediate results were good. The method could be tested against samples of known age, such as the growth rings of giant sequoia trees, which could be counted back to about 900 BC. It seemed at first that the assumption of constant radiocarbon production in the past was fully justified.

The world of archaeology was initially slow to accept the new method of dating. The Egyptologists in particular remained satisfied with the chronology they had. Why should they adopt a technique that had a margin of error attached to it, which was greater than that of their trusted king list? There was a tendency to publish radiocarbon dates only if they agreed with their theories. However, as more radiocarbon dates became available from older Egyptian sites, it became clear that there were glaring inconsistencies between dates obtained by radiocarbon and those derived from the king list. Even allowing for the known uncertainties in both methods, it became apparent that something was wrong.

Back to about 1000 BC, radiocarbon dates closely support the expected historical dating. But beyond this point the results appear to be 'too young'. The margin of error then increases steadily. An artefact which should be dated to about 2500 BC in 'calendar' years would yield a radiocarbon age of only about 2000 BC – a discrepancy of some 500 years. At 3000 BC, the margin of error increases to about 700 years.

The Egyptologists justifiably refused to accept that their chronology could be in error by such a huge margin. They insisted that there had to be a flaw in the radiocarbon dating method. If it yielded results that were too young, then possibly this was an indication that there was more carbon-14 in the atmosphere prior to 1000 BC. But how could this be proved? To appreciate why the Egyptologists were so confident of their chronology, it is essential to understand a little about its derivation.

In about 280 BC, Manetho, an Egyptian priest, wrote a short history of his native land. He wrote in Greek; and if all of his work survived today it would certainly be among the most important of historical documents. Sadly only fragments survive in the quotations of later authors, but most of the king list can be reconstituted. Manetho was the first to group the kings into thirty dynasties, which agree quite well with those accepted today. Manetho's chronology is invaluable as he had access to Egyptian source documents that have not survived.

Five other king lists have now been found. The oldest of these, the Palermo Stone, dates from the Fifth Dynasty of the Old Kingdom (*c.*2400 BC) and is a crucial document. It may even hold the names of several kings from before the unification of Egypt by the legendary Menes, the first king of Manetho's Dynasty I. A later document, the Turin Royal Canon, is now only a fragmentary papyrus. In its original form, it held a complete list of kings back to the beginning of Dynasty I. Although the earliest period is incomplete, it gives a total of 955 years between the beginning of the First and the end of the Eighth Dynasties, as well as listing mythical pre-dynastic rulers. Other sources, the Karnak Tablet (c.1450 BC), the Saqqara Tablet (c.1250 BC) and the Abydos Tablet (c.1300 BC), all list kings back to the First Dynasty and are generally supportive of Manetho.

In order to use such a king list as a chronology, it is necessary to count back the reigns of each king from a fixed reference point which can be precisely tied to our modern calendar. The older this reference point is, the more accurate the chronology becomes. Now there are references in Egyptian inscriptions and papyri that deal with calendrical and astronomical events that can be precisely dated. If these can be associated with the reign of a king, then they can be used as the required fixed reference point. Fortunately, the Egyptian calendar is sufficiently well understood and a number of such correlations are known.

The later Egyptians employed a civil calendar of 365 days with three seasons: inundation, planting and harvest. Each season contained 4 months of exactly 30 days.[1] At the beginning of each new year, 5 epagomenal days were added to complete the 365-day cycle. Since this is a quarter-day short of the precise period of the orbit, this means that the starting point of the civil calendar year must have wandered through the seasons, losing a whole day every 4 years, and correcting itself only every 1,460 (4 × 365) years.

Controversy centres around whether the Egyptians ever corrected their calendar to stop this wandering of the seasons. There is every reason to believe that they did not. The later Ptolemaic pharaohs swore an oath never to change the days and months of the calendar.[2] Traditionally, the start of the year was associated with the heliacal rising of the star Sirius, which the Egyptians called Sothis; but the rising of Sirius can only have actually coincided with the new year in 4 out of every 1,460 years.[3] This long cycle of the calendar is termed the Sothic Cycle.

The assumption that the civil calendar was never corrected during the entire period of its usage is critical to the establishment of a chronology. The heliacal rising of Sothis (i.e. when the star rose just before dawn) symbolically coincided with the onset of the

Nile flood, or inundation season. This leads to the assumption that the two events, the heliacal rising of Sothis and the first day of the civil calendar, must have coincided when the calendar was first devised. By the merest chance, the Roman writer Censorinus recorded that just such an event occurred in the year AD 139. We may therefore postulate that the calendar was first devised an exact multiple of Sothic Cycles prior to that date, in either 1322 BC, 2782 BC or 4242 BC.[4]

A number of references to the Sothic calendar have been preserved in Egyptian documents. They range from the Decree of Canopus in the reign of Ptolemy III to the earliest known source, the Illahun Papyrus (*c.*1872 BC) which is usually ascribed to the reign of Senuseret III.[5, 6] The document does not mention the name of a king, however other papyri from the same temple refer to the death of Senuseret II. These few calendar dates provide fixed points for the chronology from which it is possible to count back the reigns. Doing so, we arrive at an approximate date of between 3100 BC and 2950 BC for the reign of Menes and the Unification.[7]

The Egyptian Chronology

Period	Approx. Dates BC
Archaic Period (Dyn. I–II)	3110–2686
Old Kingdom (Dyn. II–VI)	2686–2181
First Intermediate Period (Dyn. VII–X)	2181–2040
Middle Kingdom (Dyn. XI–XII)	2040–1782
Second Intermediate Period (Dyn. XIII–XVII)	1782–1570
New Kingdom (Dyn. XVIII–XX)	1570–1070
Third Intermediate Period (Dyn. XXI–XXIV)	1070–715
Late Period (Dyn. XXV–XXX)	715–343

The chronology is generally accepted as accurate to within 25 years for the first and second millennia BC and is probably out by no more than 100 years for the third millennium.[8] Certainly the Egyptologists were right to reject the results of uncalibrated radiocarbon dating, which suggested that the First Dynasty should be brought forward to around 2400 BC.

A further clue to the time-scale of Egyptian chronology comes from the Sothic Cycle itself. The civil calendar was well established by 1321 BC and so its date of origin must presumably fall one or more cycles earlier. It is now generally accepted that 4242 BC is far too early, and that the calendar must have been devised around 2781 BC. Another observation by Herodotus may be relevant here.[9]

> They (the Egyptian priests) declare that three hundred and forty generations separate the first king of Egypt from the last I have mentioned – the priest of Hephaestus – and that there was a king and a high priest corresponding to each generation. Now to reckon three generations as a hundred years, three hundred generations make ten thousand years, and the remaining forty-one generations make 1340 years more; thus one gets a total of 11,340 years, during the whole of which time, they say, no god ever assumed mortal form; nothing of the sort occurred either under the former or under the later kings. They did say, however that four times within this period the sun changed his usual position, twice rising where he normally sets, and twice setting where he normally rises. They assured me that Egypt was quite unaffected by this: the harvests, and the produce of the river were the same as usual, and there was no change in the incidence of disease or death.

Can any significance be attached to these curious remarks of Herodotus? He seems to imply that twice during the existence of the Egyptian state the Earth changed its direction of rotation; at one time rotating west to east, at another rotating east to west! However there is no need to resort to such a drastic interpretation.

It may well be that this describes the wandering of the calendar through the Sothic Cycle. Herodotus, who well appreciated the workings of the Egyptian civil calendar, may have misunderstood what his hosts were trying to tell him. More likely, the priests themselves did not fully understand the phenomenon they were describing. If the reference does indeed allude to two complete Sothic Cycles before the time of Herodotus, then it would date the era when the Egyptians themselves believed their religious institutions were founded to about 3370 BC.

Another important factor to note here is the fabulous antiquity which Herodotus calculates for the Egyptian state, based on the information he received from the priests of Hephaestus. We cannot be sure whether the religious institutions began at the same time as the First Dynasty. All the indications we have suggest that much of Egyptian religious belief is very ancient indeed and dates from the pre-dynastic era. Whether the religious institutions date from 3100 BC or 3370 BC is not important; what this does tell us is that during the era when Herodotus and Solon visited Egypt the priestly caste harboured a grossly inflated view of the antiquity of their state.

If the Egyptian chronology was indeed to be regarded as reasonably accurate, then the anomalous radiocarbon dates had to be rejected. It seemed that the radiocarbon 'clock', which was so reliable back to 1000 BC, could not be extended any further into the past. Fortunately, the credibility of the technique was restored thanks to a method of calibration that became available during the 1960s.

The application of dendrochronology to check the accuracy of radiocarbon dating had been used since the earliest days. The difficulty had been to find a continuous tree ring chronology that would stretch back beyond 1000 BC. The answer came in the form of the remarkable bristlecone pine tree. Living specimens more than 4,000 years old have been found in the mountains of California and Nevada.[10] The oldest known tree is believed to be about 4,900 years of age. Even older dead trees have been discovered which provide a continuous series of annual rings extending back beyond 5000 BC. This was just the check that was needed for the radiocarbon chronology and, with a suitable correction factor, radiocarbon dates once again fell into line with the Egyptian chronology. Moreover, with modern methods of calibration it is now possible to perform the exercise in reverse, resulting in close confirmation of the long-accepted Egyptian king list.

As yet there has been no satisfactory explanation for the discrepancy in older radiocarbon dates. Since the rate of radioactive decay is constant it implies that there was more carbon-14 present in the atmosphere before 1000 BC than there is today. Moreover, it would also seem to imply that there was a steady decline in the level of carbon-14 between 5000 and 1000 BC. The accepted explanation for this phenomenon is that it results from a variation in the strength of the Earth's magnetic shielding.[11] The strength of the magnetic field is known to have varied throughout geological time. Since only the magnetic field protects us from the full force of cosmic radiation, any variation in its strength would surely affect the rate of carbon-14 production. A higher level of carbon-14 in the atmosphere would therefore indicate a weaker magnetic field, allowing greater penetration of cosmic rays.

Very little is known for certain about how the magnetic field of the Earth originates, but, once again, it is probably all tied up with the rotation. Short-term fluctuations in the field are known to result from the unpredictable occurrence of solar flares, but these cannot explain a persistent long-term change. Probably the best explanation for the magnetic field is that it originates from a 'dynamo' effect, due to the rotation of the fluid nickel–iron core deep within the Earth. As with any other rotating electromagnetic apparatus, if the speed of rotation varies, then the strength of the resulting magnetic field varies in proportion. If the magnetic field was weaker prior to 1000 BC, this might be giving us a clue that the Earth's rotation was slower. It is quite in accord with the theory that an increase in the rate of rotation was in progress up to about 1000 BC.

It is worth while examining this possibility for a moment. This is certainly a factor which the Egyptologists did not take into consideration when they worked out the historical date system for Egypt. It is always assumed that the rotation of the Earth has been virtually constant for aeons and that our present-day calendar can be simply projected as far back into the past as we wish to go. If the length of the day has indeed been modified by an impact event, then this comfortable supposition must be challenged.

It is unlikely that an impact event would be sufficiently violent to affect measurably the orbit of the Earth (the year) and so we can rely on it as a measure of time. Less certain however, is the number of days (i.e. rotations) occurring within the year. If we standardize the year as 365 modern days, then a chronology counted back in 'days' of a different length would begin to drift from one counted back in years – such as a tree-ring chronology. Think hard about this, for it is not credible to propose that the Earth's rotation has changed without this also having some effect upon calendars and chronologies.

If indeed we accept the Egyptian chronology then we may also rely on what the history of Egypt can tell us about the past. History may begin around 3100 BC, but Egypt itself is older. The archaeological evidence suggests the existence of a settled culture in the Nile valley as far back as 5200 BC.[12] Some of the oldest remains are to be found in the Fayum Depression around the shores of the ancient Lake Moeris. This period of some 2,000 years is often referred to as the pre-dynastic period, after analogy with Manetho. The record suggests a steady evolution throughout this period towards a society that is recognizably the forerunner of dynastic Egypt. Many late pre-dynastic burials are known and the Egyptologists have great difficulty in distinguishing them from early dynastic sites.[13]

At around 3500 BC the older chalcolithic cultures of the upper Nile were influenced by a new wave of immigrants bringing with them a style of art and pottery characteristic of Mesopotamia at this period.[14] Egyptologists refer to this transition as the beginning of the Gerzean, or Naqada II epoch (*c.*3500–3100 BC). The newcomers appear to have been of predominantly Mediterranean racial type, of diminutive stature and with narrow skulls, who rapidly merged with the indigenous African inhabitants.[15] The Egyptian language shows both Semitic and native north African influences. Even the earliest inscriptions are intelligible to the specialist; its formative period must therefore predate historical times.

However, some Egyptologists have suggested that the pre-dynastic population of Lower Egypt was quite different. Skeletal remains found in the Fayum and at Merimda in the delta show many anthropological similarities with those found along the neighbouring Mediterranean coast. These people we know were a pale-skinned race with blue eyes and reddish hair whom the Greeks referred to as 'Libyans', the Egyptians themselves as 'Libu'. Whenever we find the northern Egyptians depicted on the earliest slate palettes (such as the well-known palette of Narmer) they are shown as bearded men with a style of dress typically found in later descriptions of the Libu.[16]

The climate of north Africa was also very different in pre-dynastic times and comparisons with later Egypt may not be entirely valid. The Sahara and the Mediterranean coast to the west would then have been a grassy savannah supporting a dispersed population of nomadic herdsmen and their flocks. It is known that these early Egyptians grew barley and emmer wheat, and herded sheep and goats; but it must not be assumed that they were totally dependent on the annual flood at this early period.[17]

Religion too suggests a strong cultural continuity between pre-dynastic and later Egypt. The cemeteries and tombs excavated at Naqada indicate the kind of belief in the afterlife which is also found in the later Pyramid Age. Of the gods worshipped by the later Egyptians, the falcon emblem of Horus occurs as a common decoration on shrines and pottery. So too does the 'crossed arrows' emblem of the goddess Neit, indicating the great antiquity of her cult.[18] One other indication of continuity deserves mention. In the

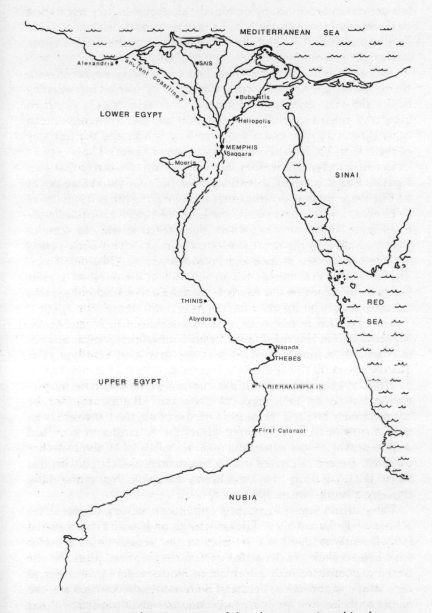

Fig. 9.1 EGYPT – showing some of the places mentioned in the text.

late pre-dynastic tombs at Naqada, the characteristic representation of the human form occurs for the first time, with the upper body depicted as front view and the lower limbs in profile.[19] This ritual style of art persisted right to the end of Pharaonic Egypt.

The unification of Upper and Lower Egypt is an event with strong foundations in Egyptian tradition. In the period immediately before the First Dynasty, the country was subject to a northern king who ruled in the delta region and along the Mediterranean coast (Lower Egypt), and a southern king who ruled the territory of the Nile as far as the First Cataract (Upper Egypt).

Unfortunately, archaeology cannot conclusively verify that two separate kingdoms existed at this period, but why should we doubt it? There are some indications that the Lower Egyptian capital was at Pe (Buto) in the delta, while the kings of Upper Egypt probably ruled from Heirakonpolis, where the later dynastic era temples were dedicated to the royal falcon god Horus.[20] This early period of division is often termed the Protodynastic (*c.*3200–3050 BC). The weight of evidence points to the violent conquest of a non-Egyptian kingdom in the north by a more recognizably Egyptian culture from Upper Egypt.

The traditional unifier of the Two Lands was King Menes. Manetho makes him the founder of his First Dynasty, while Herodotus records a king named Min as the first king of Egypt. The Turin Canon and Abydos king lists both identify a king called Meni as the first king. However doubt continues as to whether Menes was a real person or a mythical character. All these sources are comparatively late and the oldest king list of all, the Palermo Stone, does not mention him by name. Here, the first ruler of a unified state bears the Horus name Aha and the names of all the kings are different. Recent calibrated dating of artefacts associated with this Horus-Aha confirms the established chronology for the First Dynasty, placing him at 3023 BC.[21]

The Palermo Stone, found in a royal tomb at Naqada, preserves a little of Egyptian historical knowledge as it was known in the Fifth Dynasty (*c.*2400 BC). Its fragmentary record holds a list of what appear to be pre-dynastic kings on the first line, while the rest of the document records information about events in the reign of each king – including the height of the annual inundation. Only the names of the earliest kings are recorded, presumably indicating that little else was known about them. They are accompanied by only the symbol of the northern crown, indicating that they were rulers of Lower Egypt. Even as far back as the Old Kingdom, it would appear that the Egyptians were uncertain of their history prior to the First Dynasty.

By the time of the Nineteenth Dynasty when the Turin Canon was written, these early kings had been elevated to the status of demigods, with a complex mythology attached to them. Both the Turin Canon and the chronicle of Manetho commence with dynasties of gods and demigods who ruled immediately prior to the mortal kings. The so-called 'old chronicle' included these divine kings in a long chronology of 36,525 years in an apparent attempt to emphasize the antiquity of Egypt. This figure is precisely twenty-five Sothic Cycles (25 × 1,461 years).

The Sun's reign	33,000
The dynasty of gods	984
The dynasty of demigods	217
The dynasties of kings	2,324
Total (25 × 1,461)	36,525

We cannot really be certain that Menes and his unification of the Two Lands occurred at the beginning of the First Dynasty. It may have been a pre-dynastic event. No definite artefact has been found bearing the name of Menes, however Egyptologists tend to identify him with a king called Narmer, who has a definite place in the archaeological record. This king is depicted on the Narmer Palette from Hierakonpolis, which apparently commemorates the victory of a southern king over a king of the delta.[22] He is shown beating a captive with a mace, above which is an inscription translated as 'Horus brings prisoners of Lower Egypt'. The king is depicted wearing the double crown of a unified Egypt.

Egyptologists could debate endlessly as to whether Narmer, or Aha, or someone else corresponds to the unifier Menes. Until further evidence turns up there must remain doubt about the real date of his reign. The identification is of importance here if we are to attempt a calendar dating for the character of Min, as described by Herodotus. He, you will recall, traditionally reigned at a time when the Nile delta was not yet formed and the mouth of the Nile was actually an estuary. He also founded the city of Memphis, undertaking great earthworks to protect it from the effects of the 'inundation'. If the delta did not exist as such before the First Dynasty (as Herodotus seems to suggest), then some of our ideas of what constituted Lower Egypt would have to be revised.

It can hardly be coincidence that Menes should be concerned with protecting the city from devastating floods at a period when neighbouring Mesopotamia was also in the grip of a great flood catastrophe. Jacobsen in his treatment of the Sumerian king lists also derived a date of 3100–3000 BC for the beginning of the Mesopotamian chronology. Admittedly, he accomplished this only by ignoring the 'antediluvian' section and by substituting average reign lengths of 20–30 years for the fabulously long reigns quoted in the text.[23] This, taken with the archaeological confirmation of the Mesopotamian flood and the struggles of the Chinese with the Hwang-Ho, lead to the conclusion that the combating of floods and the channelling of rivers was a major preoccupation of kings during the early third millennium BC.

Manetho's chronicle also holds several more pointers to a picture of continuing geological upheaval during the Archaic dynasties (c.3100–2600 BC). In the reign of Eunephes, fourth king of Dynasty I, we hear that a 'great famine' seized Egypt, and in the reign of King Mempses, many 'portents' and a 'pestilence'.[24] In the reign of Bochos, the first king of Dynasty II, Manetho records that 'a great chasm opened at Bubastis and many perished'.[25]

The Third Dynasty also seems to have begun under unusual circumstances. In the reign of Necherophes the Libyan subjects revolted against Egypt, but surrendered when the Moon 'waxed beyond reckoning'.[26] Evidently this was a very bad portent. Precisely what is intended by 'waxing' in this context is unclear. It is usual to refer to the waxing and waning of the Moon in the context of the increase and decrease in brightness of the lunar disc as it passes through its phases. Here it may represent a glitch in the Earth's rotation, causing it to rise higher than expected in the sky, or to rise earlier than expected. Another version of Manetho describes the Moon as 'waxing unseasonably', which may indicate a failure of the calendar.

We must not dismiss these remarks as if they were mere mythical nonsense. It is a paradox that Manetho, whose chronology was for so long at the very crux of archaeology, should be completely ignored when he describes something that sounds like mythology!

Another indicator of geological and climatic change in early Egypt is evident in the height of the annual Nile flood, as recorded on the Palermo Stone. The American astronomer Dr Barbara Bell investigated these flood annals.[27] They show a marked decline in the height of the annual floods between the reign of King Djer (*c.*3050 BC), the second king of Dynasty I, and the Fifth Dynasty. Unfortunately, no heights are recorded for the reign of Horus-Aha.

The measurements tell us nothing about the true height of the river above sea level, but the range of variation is comparable with recent experience. They show that the highest levels consistently occurred during Dynasty I, with the greatest variation occurring during the reign of King Den. This king may well correspond to Manetho's Eunephes, in whose reign a great famine occurred. Since the Nile floods are directly related to the amount of rainfall occurring at its source in east Africa, they are yet another indicator of permanent climatic change around 3000 BC.

If the time of the unification is indeed contemporary with a great world-wide conflagration, which may be associated with the legends of the Great Flood, then why was Egypt apparently so little affected by it? The Egyptians continued as a race and as a state, with their religion and culture intact. Large numbers of people clearly survived and remained in the valley of the Nile to build a great civilization. This need not preclude a time of great hardship and a temporary decline in the population. There is plenty of evidence that such 'dark ages' occurred later in Egypt's history and it is entirely possible that another occurred immediately before historical records begin.

It may be that the unification represents the recovery following a recession, lasting for a generation or more. Possibly the earliest kings on the Palermo Stone represent rulers during this dark age. Lost civilization was reborn again in Egypt first, precisely because more of its people survived. Its annual floods were the one certainty in an otherwise uncertain world. Its prosperity would have attracted other survivors, both from the east and from the drying Sahara.

Other parts of the world were not so lucky. There are indications that the years just before 3000 BC mark a watershed in most cultures. In nearby Mesopotamia, not only is there evidence of the Flood, but also indications of a cultural break. As in Egypt, there is sound evidence of a thriving culture throughout the fourth millennium BC. Archaeologists classify the closing 500 years of the millennium into the Uruk period (*c.*3500–3100 BC) and the Jemdat Nasr period (*c.*3100–3000 BC).[28] At Jemdat Nasr, near Baghdad, a new style of pottery and architecture suddenly appears around 3100 BC which may indicate an influx of new population elements. Jemdat Nasr cylinder seals are also found in late pre-dynastic Egyptian tombs, indicating contact at this period.

The remains of the city of Uruk are an impressive testament to the achievements of these early Mesopotamians. It is here that the earliest known cuneiform writing is found on clay tablets. These early forms of pictographic writing are thought to have influenced the development of Egyptian hieroglyphs.

The development of writing is a further crucial pointer to when we should date the beginnings of the Egyptian state. In the *Timaeus*, the priest is boastful to Solon that historical records survived in Egypt when the population in Greece to the north was decimated and had forgotten its past.[29] He claimed that an accurate history had been written down and preserved in their temples in the most ancient times. We therefore cannot realistically date it much before the first proven occurrence of writing in Egypt. Archaeology would suggest that this occurred just before 3000 BC when the first traces of an already evolved style of hieroglyphics are found on the slate palettes from Heirakonpolis.[30]

Of Greece to the north, very little is known of what was happening at this early period. Pollen zonation comparable with northern Europe is found, with signs of a less pronounced transition to a cooler, wetter climate occurring at about 3000 BC. Deforestation of the Peloponnese had occurred well before the Bronze Age and the Neolithic is the only era which fits the lush landscape described by Plato. The remains of a Neolithic house and an abundance of pottery have been excavated from the south slope of the Acropolis, some of which may be as old as 5000 BC.[31] However, much of the Neolithic of mainland Greece remains uncertain.

The historical period of Greece is very short and everything prior to the classical period has decayed into legend. The works of Homer, dating from about 800 BC, describe events which probably took place in the Mycenean period, before 1100 BC. They had no knowledge of the former existence of the flourishing civilization of Crete, which disappeared after about 1400 BC, although they recalled many aspects of it in their extensive mythology. Of the Greek 'dark ages', hinted at by Plato, the most recent occurred between 1100 and 800 BC, but archaeology suggests that there were many earlier cultural breaks.

From the early third millennium BC, traces of a sophisticated bronze-using culture are found on the Greek mainland, which the archaeologists term Early Helladic.[32] Its decline after about 2100 BC is enigmatic. At one time it was seen as the consequence of the first wave of invaders from the north, bringing with them the Indo-European language which forms the basis of classical and modern Greek. Philologists deduce from the structure of Greek that the indigenous inhabitants spoke a non-Indo-European language, as many of its words survive in modern Greek, particularly those associated with the sea.[33]

It is reasonably certain that before 3000 BC Greece was occupied by a non-Indo-European race, with narrow skulls and short stature. Greek-speaking Dorian invaders later established settlements at sites such as Mycenae and Tyrins. These were a much taller race who established a lasting political dominance. By the classical era the two peoples were racially and linguistically well mixed, but the aboriginal race was still remembered. The classical writers called them Pelasgians. The Athenians and the Ionians claimed descent from them and the Arcadians claimed Pelasgus as their first king.[34]

Much of the chronology of the Aegean world and Anatolia remains problematical. The earliest fortress at Troy, near the entrance to the Dardanelles, has been dated as contemporary with Protodynastic Egypt.[35] The site seems to have been destroyed many times during the earliest phase, known as Troy I, before it was devastated by a great fire.[36] Up to 5 metres of debris from Troy I are now to be found at the lowest levels of the site, in which occur objects of copper, together with stone tools.

At some later time, estimated at about 2800 BC, the site was reconstructed on a much grander scale over the top of the burned ruins of Troy I. Once again, it is evident that the walls were rebuilt several times, presumably after destruction by earthquake or assault, before being again destroyed by fire at about 2300 BC. Gold ornaments and jewellery found at this level are indicative that the population had no time to evacuate, and that the site was probably not looted. This period corresponds closely with the close of Early Helladic culture in mainland Greece and the dark age of the First Intermediate period in Egypt. The destruction of the period is evident elsewhere along the Aegean coast of Turkey.[37] Burning and depopulation is found at literally hundreds of sites. Many villages were destroyed at this time and never again occupied.

Rebuilding and destruction at Troy continues again and again right up to the time of Homer's Trojan Wars and provide some indication of the repeated destructions and dark ages spoken of by Plato. Once again the period of greatest instability in this geologically active region can be placed during the early third millennium BC.

It would not be possible to examine here all the evidence that exists world-wide for a pronounced cultural break in the years around 3000 BC. However, some of the more important clues merit examination. Western Europe and the Atlantic coast are of obvious significance. Before the radiocarbon dating revolution, diffusionists considered the megalithic societies of western Europe to be late, degenerate forms of the civilizations of the east. The unbiased evidence of radiocarbon dates shows that many of the greatest megalithic monuments are older than the pyramids. The construction of Avebury in Britain is contemporary with the First Dynasty of Egypt; and the earliest phase of construction at Stonehenge predates the Great Pyramid. From Spain to Scandinavia there exist tombs and monuments which can be dated to as early as 5000 BC.

Two regions, Britain and Denmark, may be taken as good indicators of cultural break. Denmark in particular shows some of the earliest evidence of farming communities found anywhere in northern Europe. From about 4200 BC, pollen analysis indicates that the virgin forest was gradually cleared and the incidence of cereal pollen increases.[38] The first Danish megalithic monuments, dolmens and passage graves were constructed towards the end of the fourth millennium BC and the growth of population indicates a flourishing agricultural community. Forest clearance reached its peak in Denmark at about 3200 BC.

Pollen evidence then tells a puzzling story. A short period of intensive farming is then followed by an apparent abandonment of the fields.[39] Natural vegetation then reappears temporarily, and there is evidence interpreted as cattle grazing on the abandoned land, before the full reassertion of the natural forest. After 3000 BC, new settlements begin to appear around the modern coastline, and there is evidence of a mainly pastoral type of farming. In Denmark, the Late Neolithic period begins at about 2800 BC, at which time the earliest evidence of renewed tomb building is found: the so-called 'single grave' culture.

In Britain, too, the prehistorian Aubrey Burl notes an apparent megalithic dark age.[40] Between 3100 and 2850 BC, the forest regenerated after Neolithic clearance, and there is an apparent dearth of datable archaeological finds from this period. The last of the long barrows of southern England were constructed around 3100 BC. There then follows a break in monument building until the later stone circle period, when smaller round barrows replace the long barrows and there is an obvious decline in the number of burials. In southern England this dark age corresponds closely to the resurgence of elm in the pollen record.

Britain is a much larger and more topographically diverse country than Denmark and evidence of early agriculture is restricted to clearings in the forest. A number of clearings are known to predate the elm decline, particularly in Cumbria, Somerset and East Anglia, most of which later reverted to forest again.[41] Another notable phenomenon is the increase in evidence of coastal settlement.[42] Few artefacts more than 5,000 years old are found around the modern shoreline. This is remarkable for an island population which could be expected to favour the coast. It is also noteworthy that an increase in coastal settlement sites has been found, at around the same period, on the opposite side of the world – in Australia!

The period following 3000 BC also marks the beginning of an age of great migrations. In Europe and Asia the expansion of the Indo-European races took place, of which the southward drift of the Dorian invaders into Greece is but one example. All the nations of modern Europe, with the exception of the Basques and the Finno-Ugric peoples of the north, speak languages that have evolved from a single ancestral group. But looking back to the earliest classical period it is clear that there were many non-Indo-European groups living in western Europe, such as the Iberians and possibly also the Etruscans. Looking further back to the Neolithic all the signs suggest a non-Indo-European society in western Europe.

The first signs of this drift of tribes out of central Eurasia occurs at about the time Troy I was destroyed, when there is evidence of cultural change. An Indo-European language may have been first introduced into Anatolia around this time.[43] After 2300 BC, we find the intrusion of northern barbarians, the 'Gutian Horde', into Mesopotamia; and the rise of the Hittites in central Anatolia.[44] By the middle of the first millennium BC, Celts, Germans and other

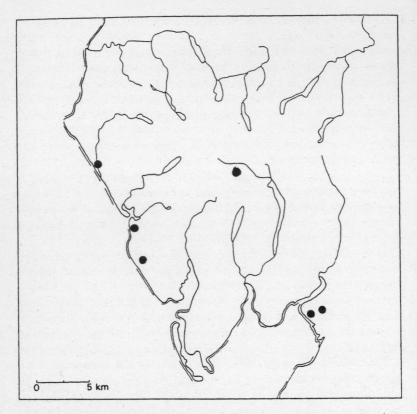

Fig. 9.2 The location of pre-Elm Decline clearings in Cumbria (Bradley 1978).
Reproduced by permission of International Thomson Publishing.

recognizably Indo-European groups were well established in Europe, where they appear to have both displaced and absorbed the indigenous population of Old Europe.

Racial and linguistic comparisons would suggest that the Indo-European homeland lay in the temperate steppe grasslands of central Asia, or in Europe north of the Black Sea.[45] The explanation usually advanced for their southward and westward expansion is that they were reacting to a gradual worsening of the climate.

Many other population movements commenced around this time. In North America, philologists trace the spread of the Eskimos

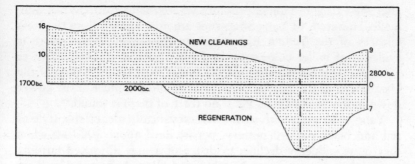

Fig. 9.3 The chronological distribution of new and abandoned clearings 2800–1700 BC. Based on data from Bradley (1977).
Reproduced by permission of International Thomson Publishing.

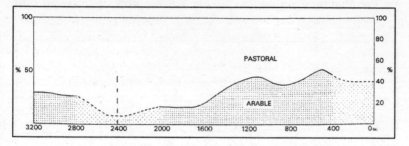

Fig. 9.4 The arable/pastoral ratio in dated clearance horizons, plotted on a 200-year moving average. Dates were originally plotted at two standard deviations (Bradley 1977).
Reproduced by permission of International Thomson Publishing.

from Alaska to as far west as Greenland.[46] Similarly, the races of south-east Asia and the Pacific islands can be traced back to a common homeland in southern China and the Philippines.[47] All these dispersals began only after 3000 BC.

Perhaps one of the best cultural markers is to be found in northern China. Chronology in China was always difficult to interpret, for there was no question of cross-dating it with other cultures. The advent of carbon-14 dates enables China, too, to be correlated with the west, but the Chinese legendary chronology remains unreconciled with the archaeological evidence. The earliest Neolithic culture identified in China is known as the Yang-Shao, after the village in Honan province where the first discoveries were made. Hundreds of Yang-Shao sites are now known from the loess terraces of the Yellow River and its tributaries, where there is evidence of millet cultivation and silk spinning from as early as 5000 BC. The known sites are all found high up the valley of the Hwang Ho in the provinces of Honan, Shensi and Kansu. Lower down in the North China Plain no trace of them is found.[48]

Yang-Shao sites, with their characteristically identifiable style of red and black painted pottery, persist until about 3000 BC when they quite suddenly decline; evidence of a new advanced farming society then appears in the North China Plain. As Joseph Needham put it: 'the apparently empty land begins to support a large and busy population.'[49]

Archaeologists call this new culture the Lung-Shan, after the site on the Shantung peninsula. All the known sites lie on small hills

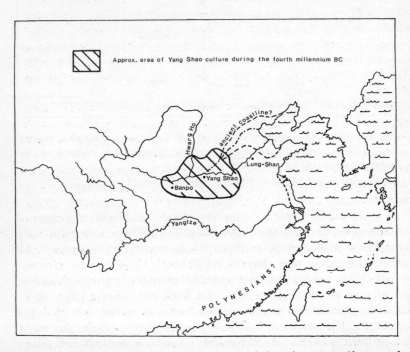

Fig. 9.5 The approximate areas covered by the Yang-Shao and Lung-Shan cultures of northern China.

above the plain, where they were protected from the unpredictable river floods. The settlements of the Lung-Shan culture are found overlaying those of the earlier Yang-Shao only in Honan province, where cultural comparisons can be made. Although pottery styles differ, the funerary customs are identical, which would argue against the theory that the Lung-Shan people were an invading race. It seems that prior to 3000 BC the Chinese simply did not inhabit the plain of northern China. Only on the higher ground of Shantung is there evidence of early occupation. Why should the Chinese choose precisely this period to come down from the hills?

Correspondence may also be found over on the other side of the world, in Peru. Here, along the Pacific coast, the earliest evidence of occupation is placed at about 3200 BC.[50] Some thirty coastal village sites are known, all of which were definitely established after this date, but before 2500 BC; the villagers made extensive use of whalebone in the construction of their houses and for making tools. Once again one must ask why evidence of coastal colonization only commences at this date? It has been estimated that the coastal population at this period was as high as 100,000 people, all making a living from the sea in one of the driest desert regions in the world. Prior to 3200 BC there is little evidence of any coastal occupation at all.

No doubt further arguments of this kind could be advanced to support the hypothesis of a cultural break or 'dark age' just before 3000 BC. The terms 'after about 3000 BC' or 'around 3000 BC' are often used loosely in the archaeological literature (as indeed they are here). Many authors treat the millennium boundary as a convenient reference frame, and it is important to guard against the introduction of an artificial cultural horizon where none really exists.

The historical record suggests that as one culture declines another rises. But when cultures world-wide go into abrupt decline at more or less the same era, then we have a right to suspect that some other force must have been at work. It would be almost impossible to prove conclusively that breaks of culture in prehistory are due to anything more than the usual cycle of growth and collapse. Only if they can be shown to be concurrent would they constitute evidence of a world-wide geological catastrophe. Perhaps a little more progress may be made by combining the archaeological evidence with clues from other disciplines, particularly with mythology.

10

The Calendar Confusion

A calendar, in its simplest and most practical form, is both a chart of the passage of time, and a means of predicting and scheduling the various cyclical phenomena of nature. For the earliest societies, a knowledge of the seasons and the ability to predict them was a matter of basic survival. The nomad must know the proper season to migrate with his animals, the farmer needs to know when to plant, and the fisherman must understand the tides and the weather. The period since 3000 BC takes in the formative stages of the world's oldest known calendars. If there have indeed been changes in the rotation of the Earth during these ancient times, then we should expect to see some evidence of it in their construction.

To devise a workable calendar requires an appreciation of both astronomy and of mathematics. It should not surprise us, therefore, that these are among the oldest of the sciences. Each of the great civilizations of the ancient world developed their own systems of counting and cosmology and in their calendars we see the embodiment of this knowledge for a practical purpose. The beginnings of our modern calendars and mathematical systems can, in many cases, be traced back to these very ancient origins.

The division of the day into 24 equal periods or 'hours' is of Egyptian origin. The further subdivision of time into 60 minutes and 60 seconds is a direct heritage from the sexagenary cycles used by the Babylonians. We still divide the circle into 360 degrees, in the manner used by the Sumerians, and these angles too are further subdivided into 60 minutes and 60 seconds. The use of these sexagenary cycles is known from very early cuneiform inscriptions.

The Babylonians also devised a system of counting in units of 60. In cuneiform notation the symbols for 1 and 60 were identical. These were simply repeated to make numbers up to 9, with a different symbol being employed for 10. The symbols were then repeated in combination to make all the numbers up to 59. For larger numbers, units of 60-squared and even 60-cubed were later introduced. This counting system was used for all types of weights and measures; and there was even a notation for fractions based on the number 60. While it is immediately apparent why the number 10 should be chosen as a base for counting, the reason for choosing such a cumbersome unit as 60 is rather less clear.

The earliest calendar used in Mesopotamia was a lunar calendar, based on alternating months of 29 and 30 days.[1] There were apparently no strict rules to the alternation of the 29- and 30-day months, which were determined by direct observation of the new Moon. The year was a rather vague period, roughly equivalent to 12 lunar months and little importance seems to have been attached to it during the earliest period. The sexagenary cycle also found its way into the calendar. In addition to weeks of 7 days based upon the phases of the Moon, a 'week' of 5 days is also known from the merchant colony of Kanesh in Anatolia. Here, the month was divided up into 6 weeks of 5 days each.[2] The origin of this 5-day week was probably an attempt to reconcile the lunar calendar with the sexagenary system. The Babylonians divided the day into 12 'double hour' periods, thus a 5-day week was a period of 60 'double hours'.

Up to about 2000 BC, there was little uniformity between the calendars and festivals of the Sumerian city states.[3] During the reign of Hammurabi, the calendar was standardized and from this time onwards the period of the year was fixed at 365 days. Prior to this time, the year had been only a loose affair, based on the passage of 12 lunar months, but since this adds up to only 354 days, the calendar would soon have wandered through the seasons unless a correction was applied to it.

It is known that the Babylonians did correct their calendar to keep the festivals in line with their proper season. After an arbitrary succession of lunar months of 29 or 30 days, they would notice that the calendar was wandering out of line with the seasonal festivals. To remedy this, they inserted either an extra intercalary month, or increased the length of an existing month. Inscriptions survive from the reign of Hammurabi recording just such an occurrence.[4] In later times, the intercalary month was inserted every second or third year and, significantly, it was not until as late as

747 BC that the Babylonians first standardized the insertion of 7 intercalary months over a period of 19 years.[5]

It would be a mistake to suppose that the Babylonians were incapable of devising an accurate calendar. To generations of Mesopotamian farmers, it must have been a necessity to predict the seasons accurately. Possibly there was another reason for their failure. Perhaps the cycle of the seasons was not then the regular and predictable phenomenon that we experience today. Any suggestion that the Babylonians were incapable of handling the mathematics or observation required must be immediately dismissed, if we consider their other achievements in astronomy and algebra. At least as early as 1800 BC, they were accurately charting eclipses and the movements of Venus.[6]

This irregular lunar calendar is quite useless as the basis for a historical chronology, but then that was never its purpose. The calendar devices were intended to serve purely short-term needs. At first, each year was named after an event that occurred in it and quite often each city state gave it a different name. Looking back on such a calendar after only a few generations, it would prove very difficult to keep the events of history in their proper sequence. Even the later Babylonians themselves were quite unable to make sense of their own past, as is evident from the confusion of their early king lists.

The Chinese also employed a sexagenary cycle within their calendars, but its use outside the calendar was more restricted than in Mesopotamia. The occurrence of 60-day cycles in both countries from an early period has led to suggestions that it was the result of early cultural contact; but the later Chinese did not use anything like the system of sexagesimal fractions devised in Mesopotamia. Neither did they divide the circle into 360 degrees. Instead, their circle was divided into 365¼ parts, clearly showing that it was calendrical in origin.[7]

A sexagenary day count is known to have been in use in China from at least as early as the Shang Dynasty (after 1520 BC), where it is found on the 'oracle bone' inscriptions.[8] In the earliest inscriptions, the characters used to represent the numbers were used strictly as a day count, but from about the first century BC they were used to denote the years. The Shang Chinese also operated both a lunar and a solar calendar of great accuracy. They knew that the period of the year was close to 365 days. As early as

1384 BC, they were aware of the 19-year Metonic Cycle and were able to reconcile the lunar and solar calendars.[9] Very little is known about the Chinese calendar prior to the Shang Dynasty. Later tradition spoke of a 'Hsia calendar' as a distinct entity, but nothing survives to tell us of its workings.[10]

Perhaps the earliest indications of Chinese calendrical knowledge come from the *Shu Ching*.[11] Here, at a supposed date of 2357 BC, we find the mythical brothers Hsi and brothers Ho determining the length of the year by measurement of the extremes of the shadow; and, significantly, they arrived at a period of 366 days for the year. Are we to assume that the brothers were incompetent astronomers, or did they actually measure it correctly? *Shu Ching* contains many inexplicable references to the calendar. At a later time, we hear that these mythical brothers were put to death for their failure to predict an eclipse. This suggests that, perhaps, most eclipses were predictable but sometimes they refused to occur at the expected time. This too points to some irregularity in the Earth's rotation.

By far the most interesting of all the ancient calendars is that of the Mayan civilization of Central America. In general, the civilizations of the Americas are all too recent to offer any clues about events 5,000 years ago. However there is every reason to believe that the Mayan calendar may be of ancient origin.

The classic Maya civilization reached its height only as recently as AD 250. The sudden abandonment of their great cities in the Yucatan remains as obscure as their origins. Of the few codices that survived deliberate destruction at the hands of the Spanish conquistadors the most important is undoubtedly the Dresden Codex. Scholars have painstakingly deciphered about a third of all the Maya glyphs, revealing it as a remarkable calendar cycle, recording solar eclipses and the cycles of Venus.

There is no evidence to suggest that the Mayan calendar was in use before 200 BC, but by the classic period it had already been perfected. The Maya left no known texts on the subject of mathematics or observational astronomy. Their system of counting also seems to have been already fully evolved and was a vigesimal system, based on multiples of the base 20. There is no trace of a sexagesimal unit, but significantly, any phenomenon of nature which can be counted in units of 60 could be just as easily counted in 20s.

From its earliest conception, the Mayan calendar seems to have been intended for the purpose of charting and predicting long periods of time. In this respect it differs from all the other ancient calendars. The Mayan year consisted of 365 days divided into 18 'months' of 20 days duration.[12] Since this would make a year of only 360 days (called the 'tun'), 5 additional days were added to the calendar, known as 'days of evil omen'. In addition, the Maya maintained two other day counts, the 260-day 'tzolkin' cycle, used for religious purposes, and a lunar calendar. The tzolkin was generated by the meshing together of two smaller cycles of 20 and 13 days. The lunar calendar ran concurrently with the 365-day year and the tzolkin. The two were never allowed to become out of step and great importance was attached to the meshing of the tzolkin and the 365-day 'vague' year.

The Maya were also fascinated by the synodic period of the planet Venus: the period between the appearance of the planet at a particular position in the sky, and its next return to that point.[13] This period they calculated at 584 days, which is very close to the true period of 583.92 days. They combined this with the 365-day year into a long cycle of 2,920 days, which is precisely 8×365 and 5×584 days. The Venus cycle too was further meshed with the tzolkin to form a 'great cycle' of 37,960 days (146×260 and 104×365).

In addition to these cycles, there was the Long Count, which was used to give a system of dates rather like the centuries and decades of our modern calendar. It is these dates that are found in the codices. With the exception of the tun they are a system of progressively larger multiples of 20.

20 kins	= 1 uinal	= 20 days
18 uinals	= 1 tun	= 360 days
20 tuns	= 1 katun	= 7,200 days
20 katuns	= 1 baktun	= 144,000 days
20 baktuns	= 1 pictun	= 2,880,000 days
etc. . .		

Although some very large spans of time, involving millions of years, are known from mythological codices, most dates encountered in inscriptions contain no units larger than baktuns.[14] The dates were always quoted in baktuns, along with their equivalent date on the 260-day tzolkin cycle. The zero point of the calendar was therefore a day in the not too distant past. Just as our modern calendar dates are numbered from the birth of Christ, so the zero point of the Mayan calendar marked some significant event in their history or religion.

It was the German philologist Ernst Forstemann who in 1887 first calculated the zero point, from his studies of the Dresden Codex.[15] It is not difficult to correlate the modern calendar with that of the Maya, as the 260-day cycle is still used today by the Maya Indians.[16] There exist, too, many records of the rising of Venus from Mayan sources, which can be used as fixed reference points. The zero point of the Mayan calendar can be precisely calculated as 10 August 3113 BC on the Gregorian calendar.[17]

By now, the significance of this date should be immediately apparent. Its importance to the Maya themselves, 3,000 years before the classic period, has been the subject of much debate. The Maya themselves were in no doubt what it meant. They believed in the cyclical nature of time and that all events repeated themselves over and over again.[18] The Maya therefore had no difficulty in perceiving the passage of millions of years. According to their mythology the world had been previously destroyed four times only to be reborn again. They believed that we presently live in the fifth creation, and the start date of their calendar corresponded to the date of the most recent 'rebirth' of the world.

Any suggestion that the Mayan calendar might have been in use as long ago as 3000 BC tends to be dismissed. The development of a calendar requires no great civilization or technology; it only requires that a continuous day-count of some kind should be maintained over a long period, together with a religious recording of the movements of the Sun and Moon. The calendar cycles themselves may have been devised much later, after hundreds of years of data had accumulated. Certainly, too, the Maya envisaged dates older than the starting point of their calendar, equivalent to our own dates BC. But before 3113 BC they counted back only in multiples of 360-day years.[19] The Maya apparently believed that before this date the 365-day year did not apply!

The development of the Egyptian calendars can also be traced from a very early date. The civil calendar was briefly described in the previous chapter, but this was probably not the first calendar to be used in Egypt. Like their Mesopotamian neighbours, it is believed that they originally employed a lunar calendar. The cycle of their year was inevitably conditioned by the annual flooding of the Nile. The three seasons of inundation, sowing and harvest must have ruled from an early date and it would have been essential to tie any calendar to this rhythm.

Much of modern theory regarding the earliest Egyptian calendars is based upon very little evidence. The civil calendar may be viewed as their solution to the problem of reconciling the lunar month with the solar year. Unlike the Mesopotamians, who rigorously observed the Moon and alternated 29- and 30-day months, the Egyptians early on standardized a month of 30 days, making a lunar year of 360 days rather than 354 days. Each month was split into 'weeks' of 10 days each. To bring the 360-day period up to the true length of the year, the five additional days, which the Greeks called epagomenal days (or the epact), were added.[20] These days were celebrated as the birthdays of the five principal gods of Egypt.

The accepted date of about 2800 BC for the establishment of the civil calendar is purely theoretical.[21] It is not directly confirmed by any contemporary evidence from Egypt. The earliest records, from the Old Kingdom and the famous Illahun papyrus, all show the existence of a lunar calendar, with festivals celebrated according to alternating 29- and 30-day months.[22, 23] From the surviving evidence and the way that the lunar calendar operated in later times, it is possible to suggest how this early lunar calendar worked.

Originally, the true length of the year would have been estimated from observation of the heliacal rising of Sirius.[24] Assuming the period between each rising to have been 365 days, there would have been a discrepancy of 11 days between this and the lunar year. Whenever the rising of Sirius occurred within the last 11 days of the opening month of the year, it became instead an intercalary month and the new year was lengthened to one of 13 months. Thus, the rising of Sirius was retained as the marker of the new year. An ivory label discovered by Petrie in the First Dynasty tombs at Abydos confirms this with the inscription, 'Sothis, the opener of the year; the inundation'.[25]

For this connection to be made in the minds of the Egyptians, the origin of the calendar must date from a period when the rising of Sirius naturally coincided with the onset of the Nile floods. Although the actual rising ultimately failed to coincide with the flood season, this connection was never forgotten throughout

Egyptian history. This is thought to have been the case around 2800 BC when the civil calendar was devised, with its standardized months of 30 days. To complicate matters still further, the lunar and civil calendar months soon became out of step. A second lunar calendar was therefore devised which was adjusted to the civil calendar rather than the rising of Sirius.[26] All three of these calendars remained in use right up until Roman times.

The importance of the foregoing discussion is to establish the era at which the Egyptians first settled upon 365 days as the period of their year. The occurrence of 60-day cycles in both China and Mesopotamia is remarkable, as is the likelihood that in the earliest period they believed the length of the year to be only 360 days. The calendars of Central America also exhibit a 360-day year and there are indications that in the earliest period the Egyptians also held this belief.

There are two highly respected sources which might indicate an early Egyptian belief in a 360-day year. The first of these is Manetho.[27] He remarks that in the reign of King Saites, who has been identified with the Fifteenth Dynasty King Sharek (c.1652–1636 BC) 12 hours were added to the month to make it 30 days long. At the same time, 6 days were added to the year.

The addition of 6 days would have made a year of 366 days, but the reference is clearly describing the establishment of the civil calendar. Since experts are convinced that the calendar was in full swing long before this date, Manetho tends to be ignored. In any case he is only referring to the addition of extra days to the calendar, rather than to the true year. The possibility that the Egyptians operated a hopelessly inaccurate calendar prior to this time cannot be ruled out.

The second clue is given in the myth of Osiris. There is no complete version of this myth from Egypt itself, and the only authority that we have for it is the Greek author Plutarch in his essay *Isis and Osiris*.[28] The myth explains the origin of the birthday feasts of the gods, which were held on the 5 days of the epact. The Greeks equated the Egyptian goddess Nut, wife of the Sun god Re, with their own goddess Rhea; and the Earth god Geb with their own Cronus. Plutarch relates that Rhea was coveted by Cronus and returned his affection. Re discovered their affair and placed a curse upon his wife, decreeing that she should never bear a child on a day in any month, or in any year.

Rhea called upon Hermes (Thoth), who was responsible for the calendar, to help her. Hermes devised a way around the curse. He played a game of draughts with the Moon god and won. For his prize, he took away a seventieth part of each of her periods of light, which he used to create 5 extra days. The new days did not belong to any year or to any month and so Re's curse was circumvented. Rhea gave birth to each of her children on these 5 days. On the first day was born Osiris, lord of all the Earth. On the second Horus, followed by Set, Isis and Nephthys on the remaining days.

This is a remarkable little story, for it implies that the Egyptians believed the length of the year to have been only 360 days prior to the intervention of Thoth. The implications of this would be that the number of days in the year changed from 360 to 365 during the formative stages of the Egyptian calendar.[29] Once again we should not ignore mythology just because what it describes seems too incredible to believe. It is important to remember that the Egyptians had no concept of the Earth's orbit around the Sun. Such an effect could only be produced if the period of the day was changing, rather than the year.

Neither would this in itself contradict any current theories about the workings of the Egyptian calendars. The civil calendar may indeed have been in existence before 1650 BC, but it may have been used, at first, without the epact. The only effect upon a lunar calendar would be the number of days required in the intercalary month, or, alternatively, the frequency of its insertion. The changing length of the day would also explain why the Mesopotamians were unable to reconcile the lunar and solar years until a comparatively late period.

We must return to the question posed at the beginning of this chapter: what is the origin of the sexagenary cycle and the 360-day year? Neither interval reflects any currently extant natural cycle. They are neither lunar nor solar in origin. All the more remarkable then, that they should occur world-wide! It is possible that the cause of the coincidence could be early cultural contact, but any suggestion of early Egyptian voyagers to the New World is now out of favour. It is possible that there was early cultural exchange between Egypt and Mesopotamia, but the ideas of the Ultra-Diffusionists, who even derived Chinese culture from Egypt, were never taken seriously by the Chinese themselves.

You cannot have it both ways! If each of these nations developed their own calendar independently then we are faced with the reality that not only did they all derive an incorrect period for the year, but that they were all in error by the same margin. The belief in a 360-day year is evident world-wide in the early development of calendars.

However, there is a phenomenon of nature that could explain the origin of the sexagenary cycle. In chapter 5, the various effects associated with variations in the Earth's rotation were discussed. In the immediate aftermath of a comet impact, the Earth's rotation could be expected to develop a wobble. Moreover, if the impact were of sufficient violence, it could result in the displacement of the rotational axes of the inner and outer parts of the planet. Could these wobbling and precessional motions lie behind the unexplained calendrical devices?

First, consider the effect of a significant latitude variation upon the annual seasons. This was briefly touched upon in earlier chapters, but we must now look in rather more detail at the effect that a latitude variation, or a real variation in the axial tilt, would have upon the cycle of the seasons. The modern Chandler wobble is imperceptibly small and has no discernible effect on the seasons. But consider what would happen if the amplitude of the nutation were to be significantly increased as a result of an impact disturbance. Since the period of the Chandler wobble is independent of its amplitude, we may safely assume that any nutation large enough to have seasonal effects would exhibit a similar period. The period of today's Chandler wobble lies between 13 and 15 months, or about 420 days.

A further possibility to be considered here is the postulated core–mantle precession. As a result of a tangential encounter with a comet, the rotational axis of the Earth's outer crust and mantle might be displaced from that of the core. As a consequence, the two rotations would be forced to precess about their mid-point, until they were once again able to realign themselves. The period of this motion and the time taken for total realignment of the axes to occur is uncertain. However, it is possible that the modern polar motion is itself partly explainable by the coupling of the core to the mantle and may be composed of many free oscillation components in addition to the Chandler wobble. If so, then the period of the precession may also fall within this 13–15-month band.[30]

At the surface of the Earth, an observer would be able to distinguish only the motion of the lithosphere about the common axis. This would be apparent to an astronomer as a spiralling motion of the whole sky about a central point. This point would ultimately become the new permanent pole of the sky as the axes realigned. The observer would be unable to distinguish between a latitude variation and a true precession by observing the sky alone; however, only a free wobble would be accompanied by other unpleasant effects, such as inundation by the sea.

A precessional motion would act either to suppress or enhance the seasons by causing a real variation in the tilt of the Earth's axis to the ecliptic. An enhanced Chandler wobble would cause the same apparent effect due to latitude variation. In both cases, the outcome is either to increase or decrease the height of the Sun in the sky during any given season, thus altering the intensity of insolation at every latitude. The consequences of this may best be demonstrated by the use of a harmonic analysis.

Figure 10.1 illustrates the effect of combining a nutation of period 14 months with the Earth's annual 'tilt' seasons. If the axis were not tilted at all with respect to the ecliptic, then the nutation would produce seasons of its own, with the 'summers' and 'winters' separated by intervals of 14 months. However in reality the Earth's axis is tilted and the nutation must be combined with the orbit to give the true composite effect. The example starts with the 'tilt' seasons and the 'nutation' seasons reinforcing each other. This would cause an enhanced summer, followed by an enhanced winter. At midsummer, in this example, the noonday Sun would appear higher in the sky as a consequence of the nutation; at midwinter it would be lower.

However, after a period of some 3½ years this situation would be reversed. The 12-month 'tilt' seasons and the 14-month 'nutation' seasons instead oppose each other, resulting in a suppressed summer and a suppressed winter. At midsummer the noonday Sun would be lower in the sky as a consequence of the nutation. At midwinter it would rise higher. After a period of 7 years the 12-month and 14-month seasons move back into phase, and the cycle of enhanced and suppressed seasons can be seen to repeat itself at 7-year intervals. There is no suggestion that a motion as great as that illustrated has occurred within recent prehistory, but even a nutation as small as half a degree would markedly affect the

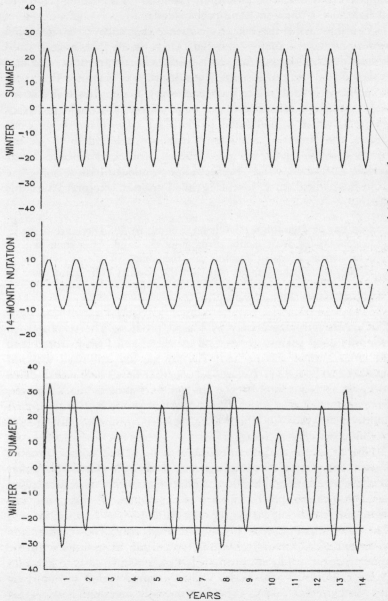

Fig. 10.1 The combination of a 14-month nutation with the normal 12-month seasons.

climate and it would be absolutely essential for a farming society to include such a phenomenon in the calendar.

You may ask if there is any evidence that such 7-year seasonal variations have actually occurred. There is, in fact, a very well-known description of a time of 7-year seasonal variations, and that is the biblical story of Joseph. The story is so well known that there is surely no need to relate it in its entirety. Rather less well known is an analogous reference to a 7-year period of drought in Mesopotamia, which is contained in the *Epic of Gilgamesh*. In both stories, the famine is predicted and stores are laid in to see the people through the hard times.[31] There is, too, a reference to 7-year periods of 'lashing winds' preserved in an ancient Irish saga.[32]

In the biblical story, Joseph is called upon to interpret Pharaoh's dreams.[33]

> God has let Pharaoh see what he is going to do. There are to be seven years of great plenty throughout the land. After them will come seven years of famine; all the years of plenty will be forgotten, and the famine will ruin the country. The good years will not be remembered in the land because of the famine that follows; for it will be very severe.

The events unfold precisely as Joseph predicts. The surplus corn from the good years was 'beyond measure' and Joseph stored it in the cities until it was needed. The famine that followed was not restricted to Egypt, for Genesis tells us that the 'whole world' came to Egypt to buy Joseph's corn. In some versions of the Koran the story is related slightly differently. After the 7 bad years comes another good year, in which the people enjoy surplus and time to celebrate with the exchange of gifts.

Now it is not the intention here to delve too deeply into the Joseph story, beyond its implications for the calendar. It is another of those interesting side-alleys which there is no time to explore here. Other than the coincidence of the number 7, there seems to be no immediate similarity between these biblical happenings and the 7-year seasonal cycle postulated previously. The combination of an enhanced Chandler wobble of period 14 months with the annual seasons could not produce Joseph's famine. Instead it would produce only a 7-year cycle, with 3½ 'good' years followed by 3½ 'bad' years. Joseph's famine actually requires a repeating 14-year cycle.

To reproduce the 7 good years and 7 bad years of the Joseph story, it is necessary to try something different. The duration of the cycle gives us the clue. After the 7 bad years, there should follow a further period of 7 good years; but there is no mention of this in Genesis. This would suggest that Joseph's famine can be explained by the Chandler motion which could be expected to be fully damped within less than 20 years. It is also likely in the immediate aftermath of an impact event, or a major earthquake deep within the Earth, that the outer core might become temporarily more fluid in its behaviour; and theory predicts that this would shorten the period of the motion to only about 13 months.[34]

The combination of a 13-month nutation period with the tilt seasons is shown in figure 10.2. This does indeed produce the required cycle of 14 years, during which the normal seasons are alternately enhanced for 7 years, and then suppressed for 7 years. A further consideration is that the amplitude of the nutation would be continuously decreasing throughout the episode, and the seasonal abnormalities would be far greater in the first 7 years than in the second. This can be seen more clearly in figure 10.3, which illustrates the effect of a wobble decaying exponentially over about 20 years.

There are two further considerations here. First, there is absolutely no reason why the cycle should commence at the equinox as illustrated here. The event that triggers the wobble could occur at any time during the year. It was fortuitous for the Egyptians that the 7 good years occurred first; it could just as easily have been the 7 bad years, in which case Egypt might not have survived. Possibly one or two 'bad' years occurred before the 7 good years, which might explain why the biblical pharaoh so readily handed power over to Joseph!

Second, we should consider precisely what would constitute 'good' or 'bad' years in an Egyptian context. For Joseph to store up so much grain from the good years can only imply that these were years of high inundation, when a greater area was flooded on the banks of the Nile. The annual inundation occurs as the direct result of summer monsoon rainfall over east Africa.[35] This would imply that the 'good' years correspond with periods of enhanced seasonality, whereas the 'bad' years occurred when the seasons were suppressed. This would correspond to the situation illustrated in figure 10.3.

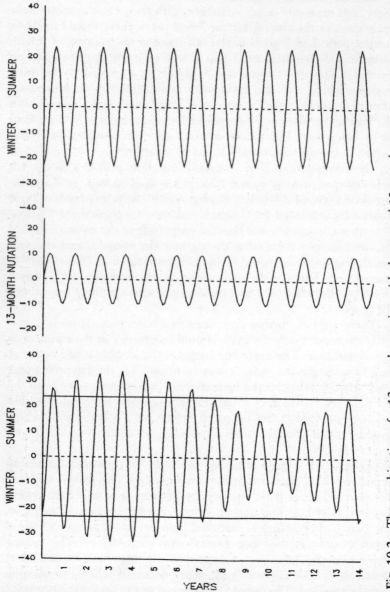

Fig. 10.2 The combination of a 13-month nutation with the normal 12-month seasons.

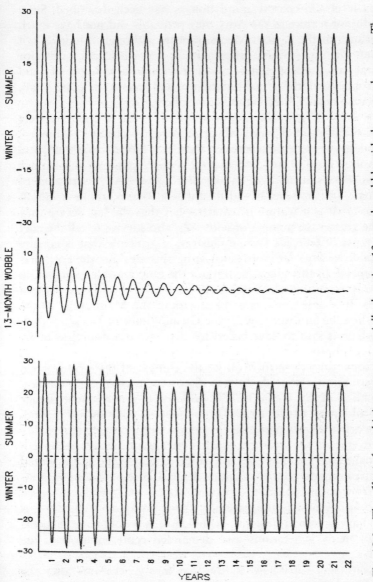

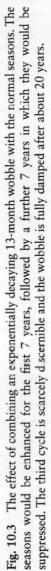

Fig. 10.3 The effect of combining an exponentially decaying 13-month wobble with the normal seasons. The seasons would be enhanced for the first 7 years, followed by a further 7 years in which they would be suppressed. The third cycle is scarcely discernible and the wobble is fully damped after about 20 years.

Any such period of instability should also produce variations in the sea level and coastal inundation as has been described. Since these do not feature in the story they probably did not have much significance in the eastern Mediterranean, although this need not rule out their occurrence elsewhere in the world. In order for seasonal variations of climate to occur without a widespread flood catastrophe, then the actual nutation would have to be quite small, in this case mainly affecting the atmosphere.

The story of Joseph's famine seems to recall a comparatively benign nutation of the axis which occurred, according to biblical chronology, at some time between the Great Flood (*c.*3100 BC) and the exodus (*c.*1650 BC) and may also correspond to the earliest Chinese floods mentioned in the *Shu Ching*. An inscription of Ptolemaic age on Sehel Island describes a 7-year famine at about 2600 BC.[36] It is a feature of catastrophes that the less severe they are, the greater the number of witnesses who survive to tell the tale! The events of Joseph's famine illustrate a principle that is equally applicable to other far more devastating episodes that the Earth has experienced. In this phenomenon lies the only feasible explanation for many strange occurrences that we find related in myths and legends. It is able to explain the stories in the Maui cycle, of the time when the Sun went away; the Great Winter of Norse mythology, which is said to have lasted for 3 years; and doubtless many other inexplicable references found in mythology.

At some time close to 3100 BC the climate of the whole world was permanently altered. As was discussed in chapter 7, the best explanation of this would be if it were due to a permanent change in the obliquity of the axis. Throughout the Sub-Boreal period, particularly the early part, there is evidence of increased seasonality and extremes in the weather, which were absent during the preceding Atlantic period. For such a change to occur, the Earth would first have to undergo the transitional phase of core–mantle precession. During this phase, the pattern of seasonal variation would follow the 7-year repeating cycle as shown in figure 10.1. But this would have been no transient phenomenon. It would have persisted through many generations and demanded representation in the calendar.

To our ancestors, born in the first few generations after the Great Flood, the seasons would therefore have appeared subject to both a 1-year and a 7-year cycle. They would have inherited a tradition that the cycle of the year – the interval between any season and its next recurrence – was 360 days. In time, they would have noted the regular interval between the Long Seasons and found it to be very close to 2,520 days (7 × 360). They may even have measured the period of the nutation by direct observation. This they would have observed to be very close to a 420-day cycle. The origin of the sexagenary cycles then becomes apparent, for 360 is precisely 6 × 60 whereas 420 is precisely 7 × 60. It therefore represents the largest unit of time that could be used to count both seasonal cycles.

The application of the sexagenary cycle in both China and Mesopotamia can therefore be seen as the obvious solution to the problem of the calendar. Normal seasons would recur every 6 × 60 days, whereas the Long Seasons would repeat every 7 × 6 × 60 days. In the Egyptian civil calendar the same problem was solved by using 2 × 30-day 'months', and in the Mayan calendar by 3 × 20-day cycles. The very existence of these calendrical devices is strong circumstantial evidence that a change in the axial tilt has occurred, and that the postulated core–mantle precession was a real phenomenon during the third millennium BC. This may perhaps explain why the Egyptians needed a separate lunar calendar, and why they never attempted to correct the wandering civil calendar. The fixed 30-day 'months' were non-lunar in origin and were never intended to track the cycle of the Moon.

The 30- and 60-day periods are unlikely to have tracked the precessional motions precisely. When the civil calendar was first devised, it was probably good enough to predict adequately the Long Seasons. However, ultimately it would have become inaccurate, both because the period of the precession was never precisely 420 days and because the length of the day was itself gradually evolving throughout this period. By the time the 5 epagomenal days were inserted, the original purpose of the calendar may have been long since forgotten.

During the early stages of core–mantle precession, during, say, the first 50 years after a major impact event, the irregular rotation of the sky above would have been a very obvious phenomenon. On any starry night, our ancestors could have observed the sky in its nightly rotation about the celestial pole. If they were patient astronomers, they would have noticed that over a period of some 14 months the celestial pole itself was describing a complete circle in the sky. A little more patient observation would reveal that this circle was becoming smaller with each circuit and would ultimately converge towards a central point. It was in fact a spiral. The sky above their heads would have been a perfect calendar for all to see. It would therefore be possible to devise a simple 'spiral calendar' rather like that shown in figure 10.4.

The passage of a year could be determined, as the Egyptians did, by noting the heliacal rising of an equatorial star. Over the same period, the pole of the sky would be observed to perform only 6/7ths of its circuit, and would not complete its circuit until a

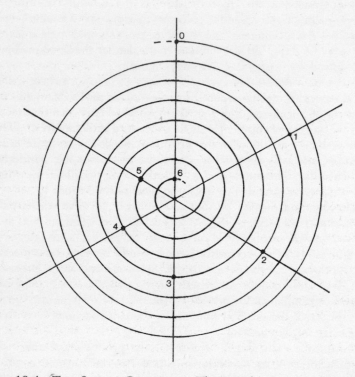

Fig. 10.4 The Spiral Calendar. The 360-day year is split into six sexagenary cycles. As the rotational pole of the sky spirals in towards the new celestial pole it performs one circuit every seven sexagenary cycles. Every 7 years the rotational pole describes approximately six circuits.

further 60 days had elapsed. Only after 7 years had passed would the celestial pole return to the same position, with respect to the four cardinal points, from which it had started. Initially, it would not have been too difficult to devise an accurate calendar by direct observation of the sky.

Neither should it surprise us that the spiral figures so prominently world-wide during the third millennium BC. It is found inscribed on megalithic monuments, such as Newgrange in Ireland, which have an undoubted calendrical purpose. In Britain, spiral markings may be found associated with many stone circles. A three-and-a-half turn spiral is found at the stone circle of Long Meg and her Daughters in Cumbria. On the Isle of Man a similar spiral of three and a half turns is carved on an unspectacular monument known as the Spiral Stone, and there are other examples. There may even be examples of spiral calendars surviving from this period.

One such object was found in the First Dynasty Egyptian tombs at Saqqara. This object, which the Egyptologist W.B. Emery described as a 'board game', takes the form of a circular board on which is marked the crude design of a coiled serpent.[37] Along the body of the serpent are numerous marks and notches, the significance of which is not immediately apparent. Accompanying the board were a number of small stone 'counters', which would have been used as markers. It is highly pertinent that the object should date from this period around 3000 BC and also that the serpent should be coiled in precisely seven turns.

Another similar object, which may also be a form of spiral calendar, is the well-known Phaistos Disk. This object, discovered in excavations at Phaistos on the island of Crete, dates from the early second millennium BC.[38] On a disc of fired clay are inscribed a series of glyphs in an as yet undeciphered script. On both sides of the disc the glyphs run from the outer edge in a spiral of three and a half turns into the centre. There is nothing to prove its use as a calendar but it is one further coincidence to add to the list. Possibly in this case a counter was moved around the spiral from the outside to the centre. The calendar could then simply be turned over to track the second 3½ year period of the 7-year cycle.

The structure of the earliest calendars gives strong support to the theory that a change in the axial tilt has occurred. If the postulated core–mantle precession was in progress during the third millennium

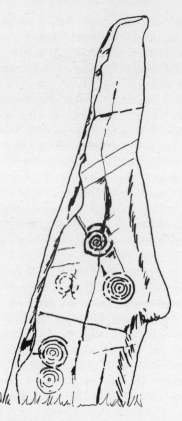

Fig. 10.5 The three-and-a-half turn spiral on the Long Meg standing stone. Below it are cup and ring marks.
Drawing by the author.

BC, then it can only have been as a result of a powerful external disturbance of the Earth's rotation. This event, according to the many clues presented in the preceding chapters, occurred at a date close to 3100 BC. Prior to that date, as the Mayans knew, the rules of our modern calendar did not apply. Before the impact disturbance, the seasons were far less extreme and it may be that very little emphasis was placed upon the year as a unit of time.

All the great civilizations of the ancient world tended to exaggerate time in their oldest records and legends. The earliest Babylonian

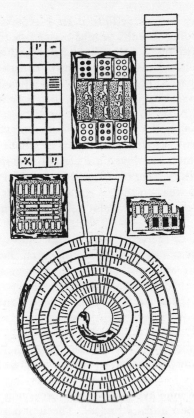

Fig. 10.6 Walter Emery's 'gaming board' from the First Dynasty tomb of Hesy at Saqqara. Could this be a spiral calendar? (W.B. Emery 1961)
Reproduced by courtesy of Penguin Books.

king lists, for example, give a period of 1,200 years for one of the earliest kings of Kish after the Flood. Before the Flood it seems that kings lived even longer![39] Here reign lengths of 28,000 and 36,000 years are recorded. Of course, we may be certain that no human being ever lived this long. It is little wonder that the earliest kings came to be thought of as immortal gods.

These incredible reigns only make sense if they were not measured in years at all, but in some shorter time span. The antediluvian reigns become just about credible if they are assumed to be day counts, whereas lunar months would better suit the later reigns. It is difficult to read much into the figures and they are usually ignored by the archaeologists in attempts to construct a chronology.

In the earliest part of the Bible, too, which has clear associations with Mesopotamia, we find incredible longevity ascribed to some of the patriarchs. Noah is said to have lived for a remarkable 950 years and Methuselah, the longest of all, for 969 years.[40, 41] His age reduces to a more reasonable life span of about 80 years if one assumes that the units employed are actually the months of a lunar calendar. To attain the age of 80 must have been a great rarity in ancient times and well worthy of remark. All this suggests that in the earliest times the year was relatively unimportant as a measure of time.

To us the cycle of the year, as it swings from summer to winter and back again to summer, is an obvious and inescapable part of our lives; but this may not always have been so. The climatic evidence suggests that the axial tilt was formerly much less and at the mid-latitudes the seasons may have been scarcely distinguishable. The year would have had little relevance to the common man and only an astronomer would notice the annual cycle of the stars.

For perhaps a millennium following the impact, the year would have seemed an unreliable period, varying between 360 and 366 days as the Earth's rate of rotation gradually increased. The most obvious period of time available as an unvarying standard would have been the Moon and its phases. The unreliable period of the year not only explains the early preference for lunar rather than solar calendars, but also the importance attached to the synodic period of Venus. This is evident from both the Mayan calendar and the observations of the Old Babylonians. The motion of the Moon would be scarcely affected by any gyrations of the Earth and the orbit of Venus not at all. It could therefore be used as an absolute check on the calendar cycle over long periods. The use of the Venus cycle again reveals the high standard of astronomy attained by our ancestors. It is quite wrong to look upon our forebears as if they were simpletons, incapable of measuring the true length of the year. If they did not employ the year as a measure of time then it must either have been too unreliable, or it simply was not important to the routine of life.

It would seem that there is a wide range of evidence available,

The submerged forest at Borth, near Aberystwyth; one of many such submerged peat beds around British and Irish coasts. Dating from around 5,000 years ago, such features cannot occur by gradual encroachment of the sea, but must result from a rapid inundation that was greater than the tidal range.

Courtesy of The Photolibrary Wales. Photographer Jeremy Moore.

A view from the top of Mount Snowdon. On a clear day, the Isle of Man may be seen in the distance, across the Irish Sea. The summit of both Snowdon and Snaefell on the Isle of Man, can today be reached by a comfortable narrow-gauge train ride. However, the visitor is more likely to find their summits shrouded in mist.

Courtesy of The Photolibrary Wales. Photographer Jeremy Moore.

The Neolithic passage grave at Kernic, Brittany; one of a number of Neolithic monuments lying on modern beaches and regularly submerged at high tide.
Courtesy of Aubrey Burl.

Les Pierre Plats. Another Brittany tomb now lying close to the modern beach. Such monuments, dating from the Early to Middle Neolithic periods, must originally have been built some distance inland.

Courtesy of Aubrey Burl.

The Court Cairn at Cashtal yn Ard on the Isle of Man. An example of a class of Neolithic monument passage tombs throughout Ireland, Scotland and Wales; indicative of a common culture province throughout the British Isles during Middle Neolithic times, before about 3100 BC.
Collections/Lawrence Englesberg

The Court Cairn at Cairn Holly, Dumfries & Galloway; one of the best preserved examples of the crescent-shaped forecourt typical of this class of tomb.
www.doughoughton.com

Neolithic field walls excavated from peat in Co. Mayo, western Ireland. Many such field walls are observed to run right up to court tombs, showing that they date from the same era.
David Lyons Photography.

Spiral carvings at the Knowth passage grave, Boyne Valley, Ireland. The Boyne Valley tombs are believed to date from just after 3100 BC.
Anthony Weir/Fortean Picture Library

The three-leaved spiral carved on the walls of the Newgrange passage grave. At mid-winter sunrise, the carving is briefly illuminated by a beam of sunlight.
Anthony Weir/Fortean Picture Library

The stone circle of Long Meg and her Daughters in Cumbria, northern England. One of the earliest of the stone circles, it dates from some time around 3000 BC. The Long Meg stone carries a prominent spiral carving, which the present author believes to represent the motion of the Celestial Pole as the Earth wobbled on its axis.

Courtesy of Aubrey Burl.

Sunset at Callanish, a late stone circle on the Isle of Lewis. Alignments at Callanish and elsewhere are believed to mark the seasonal rising and setting points of the sun and moon on the horizon. If the Earth were wobbling on its axis then these rising and setting points would oscillate to the north and south over a 7-year cycle.

drawn from an examination of sea level changes, climate, mythology, history and chronology, to support the hypothesis of a catastrophic impact occurring towards the end of the fourth millennium BC. The biblical Flood, the destruction of Atlantis and a whole host of other flood legends may be seen as different views of this same event. Plato's assertion that it was only one of many catastrophes suffered by the Earth is also seen to be supported by a number of other sources.

The greatest single weakness of Plato's story has always been the remote era in which he placed his Atlantis. Its supposed destruction was placed at some 9,000 years before Solon's day. In view of the calendar confusion of the third millennium BC, the error in Plato's chronology becomes a little more understandable. The Egyptians of Solon's day appear to have had a very sound idea of their history as far back as Menes, as is shown by the surviving king lists. Before this date, they believed in a series of mythological dynasties spanning an immense period of time.

The chronology from which the date of Atlantis was derived was not a king list, but a priest list; probably that of the priests of Sais. It is likely that in its earliest entries the term of each priest was measured in shorter units such as the month, or the day, leading to fabulously long terms, analogous to Manetho's dynasties of demigods. When the Saite priest related the story of the lost island to Solon, he would naturally have included part of this mythological time-scale within his estimate of its antiquity. The most important chronological detail within the Atlantis story therefore remains the assertion that it was concurrent with the earliest period of the Egyptian state.

The shift in the rotation axis that occurred at this time is unlikely to have been much different from a whole host of others that preceded it even earlier in prehistory. Some factors should be common to each and every shift of the axis. Each would be accompanied by permanent sea level changes, inundation of the land, and a 20-year transitional period. The rotation of the Earth would oscillate in a number of free modes, the manifestation of which should produce other longer-term periodic fluctuations in the climate. Permanent changes in the climate will be associated with much longer periods of transition in which the rhythm of the 7-year Long Seasons may at times become dominant over the annual seasons.

Recent studies also suggest that the desert locust, a creature so prominent in times of biblical calamity, also exhibits a preference to swarm at 7-year intervals![42] No doubt there are other adaptations to the Earth's rotational rhythms to be found elsewhere in the natural world. Such an adaptation as this within an archaic insect species like the locust, unchanged in the fossil record for many millions of years, must suggest that the 7-year seasons are a fundamental and ancient rhythm of the Earth.

11

The World of the
Fourth Millennium BC

Sufficient evidence has now been presented to enable the recent history of the Earth's rotation to be understood. Particular attention must focus upon the events of 5,000 years ago, at the beginning of recorded history; around that time a pattern of evidence, drawn from various sources, suggests that a major impact event took place which was to affect the course of human development profoundly. By a close examination of this event it is possible to reconstruct what the world was like during the preceding era. The theory and evidence presented so far require a leap of imagination that many people will never be prepared to make, but the reconstruction that follows is merely a logical extrapolation of them. It must be stressed, therefore, that this chapter is largely a presentation of theory based upon the evidence already offered. To visualize fully the sea level changes suggested requires an appreciation of the Earth as a sphere (or rather that it is not quite a sphere) and the assistance of a geographer's globe may be found useful in this.

Attention has so far focused upon the likely dating of the impact event. We must now move on to consider precisely where a large area of land could have been lost to the sea, together with the nature of the impact event that triggered the changes in the Earth's rotation. Before attempting this, however, it is useful to summarize the various strands of evidence upon which the dating of the impact event is based.

The Atlantic/Sub-Boreal Transition	3300–2900 BC
Sea Level Changes	3200–3000 BC
Neoglaciation	3300–3000 BC
The Mesopotamian Flood	3100–2800 BC
Greenland Ice Cap High Acidity Event	3250 BC
Irish Bog Oaks Low Growth Event	3199 BC

| Egyptian Chronology (Protodynastic) | 3200–3050 BC |
| Mayan Calendar Day Zero | 10 August 3113 BC |

There are so many uncertainties in all these dates that the true date might lie anywhere within a band 3300–3000 BC; however, the probability that they are all recording one and the same event is high indeed.[1] For the purposes of further practical discussion here, a loose date of 3100 BC is good enough. Before this date evidence suggests that the world was very different from the one we inhabit today. The length of the day was some 20 minutes longer and consequently only 360 of them made a year. The climate of the Atlantic period, at least at temperate latitudes, was far more genial than today, without seasonal extremes in the weather. The map of the world would have had an unfamiliar look about it, with many islands that do not exist today.

There is no need to go back further than about 5500 BC. This date closes the Boreal climatic period, ushering in the warmer Atlantic period which marks the Holocene Climatic Optimum. The nature of the climate changes at the Boreal/Atlantic transition suggest that these too were the result of an impact event, similar to that which was to occur around 3100 BC. We need not look too deeply into this event, but it may be postulated that the outcome was a shift of the rotational axis, followed by a decrease in the obliquity of the ecliptic. The world then settled into a more equable climatic regime which was to last throughout the Atlantic period.

The warm period was to last for only some two and a half millennia before the stability of the Earth's rotation was shattered once more. The impact was of sufficient violence to cause the rotational axis of the crust and mantle to become separated from that of the core. The two axes then began to spiral about each other as they tried to realign, in the phenomenon here referred to as core–mantle precession.

Of more immediate significance, a wobble developed as the axis of rotation was displaced from the axis of figure. The most serious consequences of this occurred in the immediate aftermath of the impact, when the axis of rotation would have experienced its maximum displacement from the figure axis. Not only would this have produced inundating floods as the sea spilled over the land, but it would have placed intolerable strains on the crust. The crust would have been torn open at its weakest points, the mid-ocean ridges, as the Earth was forced to adjust its figure to the new dynamics. Massive volcanic and earthquake activity would have been triggered, covering the Earth in a veil of dust and ash. The geodesy of the whole planet was permanently altered during a 20-year period of instability.

Although the shift of the axis and the resultant sea level changes were completed during this short period, the core motion would have continued. Indeed there is good reason to suggest that this motion continued throughout the whole of the succeeding Sub-Boreal period. From 3100 BC to about 800 BC, the axial tilt continued to oscillate between about 20° and 26° before settling to its modern value. Over the same period, the rate of rotation was steadily increasing from its former rate of 360 days in the year towards the modern 365¼ days in the year. The greatest variation would have been experienced within the first few hundred years, between about 3100 and 2800 BC. Indeed the rhythm of the 7-year seasons may be the cause of the increased seasonal variation that is so characteristic of the Sub-Boreal period. A gradual shortening of the day during the Sub-Boreal can also offer a plausible explanation for the observed decrease in atmospheric carbon-14 over the same period.

Plato himself gives us a further clue in the *Timaeus*. In its entirety, it is a work of theology and philosophy embodying many of the ideas of the Greeks on the physical world and its origins. To the Greeks – and Plato was no exception – the Earth was regarded as the living body of Gaea (Mother Earth). In the *Timaeus* he describes the motions of the Earth and the heavens around it. In an obscure passage, which has puzzled many translators, he explains the wandering of the planets and the rotation of the fixed stars.[2]

> This is the origin of the fixed stars, which are living beings divine and eternal and remain always rotating in the same place and the same sense; the origin of the planets and their variations, of course, we have already described. And the earth our foster-mother, winding as she does about the axis of the universe, he devised to be guardian and maker of night and day, and first and oldest of the gods born within the heaven.

In addition to the wandering of the planets and the apparent rotation of the fixed stars, he perceives another motion of the Earth itself. This motion, conveyed by some translators as 'winding', by others as 'oscillation' or 'rotation', is difficult to explain by any conventional theory. Perhaps he is describing here the nearly diurnal wobble or the postulated core–mantle precession (for the former cannot occur without the latter). It must be remembered that climatic evidence places the Sub-Boreal/Sub-Atlantic transition at about 500 BC and it is possible that some vestige of the motion survived until the classical period.

There is also evidence to suggest three further episodes of instability during the Sub-Boreal period. Whether these were also caused by impacts, or whether they represent the effect of other free oscillation modes, is debatable. During the period when the rotation was slowly adjusting, the interior would have remained unstable. Both the frequency and severity of earthquakes would have been far greater than we experience today. Even a quite minor disturbance could have triggered further jumps in the position of the axis.

The first of these episodes occurred around 2300 BC. This is marked by the dark age of the First Intermediate Period in Egyptian history and the widespread destruction in the Aegean at this time. The story of Joseph's famine, the Monster of the Aegis, Phaeton, and the early Chinese floods may all be dated at about this period. It coincides with a low growth year in the tree ring chronology at 2345 BC.

The next disturbance is also signalled by a low growth year at 1628 BC and the eruption of Thera (Santorini), which is thought to have brought the Cretan civilization to an end. Other writers have dated the biblical exodus and Deucalion's flood to this time. It seems to have been much more severe than the previous episode, with evidence of widespread sea level changes. The emergence of some tropical coasts at this period is perhaps indicative of a slight slowing down of the rotation and it may be at this time that the number of days in the year changed from 366 to its modern value of 365¼. It corresponds to the Second Intermediate Period in Egypt and the downfall of the Hsia Dynasty in China.

A further climatic disturbance occurred around 1150 BC. It correlates with the Third Intermediate Period in Egypt and the beginning of the last dark age in Greece. At around this time, the empire of the Hittites suddenly collapsed and we hear of the invasion of Egypt by an alliance of 'sea-peoples' from the north. After this, the world seems to have settled down to the more stable conditions that we enjoy today. For although other oscillations in the climate can be discerned, they are nowhere near as severe as these earlier dark ages.[3]

The Sub-Boreal seems to have been a time of almost continuous geological and climatic change, punctuated by episodes of catastrophe. Although each of these episodes of upheaval is of immense importance for the history of the human race, there is unfortunately insufficient space to dwell further on them here. They seem to have been little more than setbacks in the recovery of mankind from the far greater disaster of 3100 BC and serve to disguise the true extent of the changes occurring at that time.

In chapter 6 the evidence of sea level changes was advanced in support of the theory that a shift has occurred in the position of the axis of rotation. A pattern was demonstrated of correspondence in alternate quarter-spheres, indicating that the position of the North Pole has moved from a former position rather closer to Ellesmere Island. This resulted in a change to the geodesy of the Earth which would have had its greatest effects along a line of longitude running through Quebec down to the Andes. In Europe, a 'line of neutrality' was established passing through Denmark, Italy and down through Africa. To the west of this line there is evidence of submergence at 3100 BC. To the east of it, the indications are of emergence, or rising land.

The area of greatest interest here must be the Atlantic Ocean and the west coast of Europe. Before attempting a reconstruction of the coastline before the sea level changes occurred, the extent of the pole shift must be estimated. There is no easy way to do this, but an examination of sea level changes close to the neutral line may give some clues.

Immediately after the proposed impact event, during the 20-year transitional phase, sea level and shorelines would have been subject to pole tides. At any particular locality, the sea would have appeared to oscillate over a 7-year cycle, at times retreating to expose the seabed, at other times flooding over the land. After the damping of the wobble some coastal areas and islands were left permanently submerged, while elsewhere the former seabed was permanently exposed. The compliance of the sea to the instantaneous geoid is immediate, but adjustment of the land surface would take a little longer to occur. In some places it may not have adjusted at all. As we have seen, the curvature of each of the continental land masses is ancient and has probably changed little over millions of years. Most of the adjustment of the geoid must therefore have occurred in the thinner crust of the ocean floor.

The structure of the deep ocean floor, with its spreading ridges and transform faults, could not be better designed to adjust to changes in the Earth's rotation; for nothing in nature exists without reason. The ocean bed could absorb most of the adjustment required, leaving the continental land masses either to rise, fall or tilt as independent blocks. Within a continent little change would occur relative to other parts of the same continent, while they would each rise, fall or tilt relative to each other.

The coast of Europe lies at the western edge of the largest stable land mass on Earth. The geodetic changes proposed for 3100 BC would have resulted in a relative 'tilting' of this entire land mass about the proposed neutral line. To the east as far as the Pacific, the land was elevated, while to the west the edge of the continent dipped down into the ocean. Perhaps the best way to visualize this is to imagine that this entire stable land mass has retained most of its curvature, while the adjustment of the sea to the geoid has occurred around it. Total adjustment of the solid crust is not to be expected and, 5,000 years on, this has left us with the raised and submerged beach features that we find today.

Now a shift of the pole would cause its maximum change in sea level, or difference in radius of the old and the new ellipsoids, at latitude 45°. Here a change in latitude of 1° would cause a difference of as much as 373 metres. The latitude is extremely important in any such estimate. The same 1° shift would cause a change in sea level of only about 6.5 metres at the poles or a similar amount near the equator. At the latitude of Denmark, a 1° shift would raise the sea level by about 355 metres along the line of maximum effect, equivalent to a rise of some 40 metres at the Greenwich Meridian.

This geodetic model predicts that there should be some evidence in the sea level record of 'tilting' between the coast of Denmark and the west of Ireland. A review of some of the available evidence shows that over the past 5,000 years emergence of about 2.5 metres is evident along the Baltic coast of Denmark. Along the west coast of Jutland the submergence is estimated at about 3 metres. Progressing further west the submergence increases to 5 metres along the Dutch coast, and in the Thames estuary it is about 8 metres. A simple ratio of figures (8/40) would therefore suggest that the extent of pole shift 5,000 years ago was only of the order of a fifth, or at most a third of a degree of latitude.

To this must be added a further note of caution. In chapter 7, the vegetational changes along the coast of Peru were advanced in support of a change in the position of the equator at this time by as much as a whole degree of latitude. The South American coast lies close to the postulated line of maximum geodetic effect and so this should be a good indicator of the extent of pole shift. A 1° shift probably represents the upper limit for the amount of pole shift at 3100 BC, as anything greater would not be consistent with the sea level evidence; to accept a movement as great as this would imply that the Earth's crust must be far more pliable than is generally believed. It would require that the adjustment of the ellipsoid has been both more drastic and more rapid than is otherwise proposed here.

No doubt other estimates of this kind could be attempted, but there remain so many factors that could complicate the data. The above calculations are based on nothing more complex than ellipse geometry and rely solely upon the difference in radius of the Earth's ellipsoid, for a change of 1° of latitude. No allowance is made here for changes in the flattening of the ellipsoid. However, it does help to give a sense of the magnitude of change under consideration. Compared with the vast scale of the Earth these are very modest changes indeed.

To this must be added the effects of a possible increase in the rate of rotation since 3100 BC. If the interpretation given here is valid, this at first increased to perhaps 366 days per year and has subsequently slowed down again slightly. The outcome of this would be to create a flatter ellipsoid. Once again, if the adjustment of the crust has lagged behind that of the oceans, this would lead to submergence at latitudes below 45° with emergence at high latitudes. This is further confirmed by the existence of 5,000-year-old raised beach features in the Arctic, showing that the polar regions have only partially adjusted.

Further complication is caused by the likely addition of a true eustatic rise in the world sea level over this same period. An increase in the tilt of the axis would also increase the summer temperatures at high latitudes, leading to melting of polar ice. Again, we know that this has occurred. All the northern ice sheets have retreated during the last 5,000 years; the total extent of melting is uncertain, but its overall effect would be to raise the sea level uniformly all over the Earth. This would mask the effect of a faster rotation by drowning any raised beach features, except at high polar latitudes.

There is yet further complexity to add. At least three other minor oscillations since 3100 BC have been postulated. Any of these might have resulted in lesser shifts in the position of the rotational poles. Each event would produce its own pattern of sea level change with correspondence in alternate quarter-spheres, the extent of which has only been touched upon here. These might add or subtract from the local sea level predicted by the model and all that can be said with any conviction is that they have not been large enough to destroy the overall pattern of the 5,000-year event. To this must also be added the possibility of other movements within the crust, or even within the core, which would have purely local effects upon the geoid.

The impacting body, which caused all this damage 5,000 years ago, was probably a comet of about average size. The nature of the pole shift demands that it struck the Earth a near-tangential blow; most of the nucleus then bounced off into space again with its orbit radically altered.[4] Remnants of this object may have remained in the vicinity of the Earth's orbit, only to strike it again at a later date. A comet head consists largely of water ice and frozen volatiles. These would simply vaporize on impact leaving little trace today.

A precession of the axis from the direction of Ellesmere Island to its current position demands an impact in a direction at right angles to this. This is parallel to the same great circle of longitude as the proposed line of neutrality drawn around the Earth, passing through Denmark. The comet could have approached the Earth from any direction to strike along this line, but as the majority of comets orbit close to the plane of the ecliptic this would favour a strike near one of the poles. Since Chinese mythology has preserved a sighting of this comet (the monster Kung Kung), this would further suggest that the most likely track of the comet was over the Bering Strait, to strike in the Arctic Ocean. If one wishes to find evidence of a 5,000-year-old impact, this would be the logical place to look.

Moving on to what the world was like before the catastrophe, it is possible to use these theoretical arguments to reconstruct the former coastlines of Europe and the Atlantic. Some assumptions must first be made as to the extent of the sea level changes. In the

reconstruction that follows, allowance has been made for the effects
of a pole shift of about a third of a degree. To this has been added
a further allowance for the effect of increased flattening due to a
faster rotation, plus a glacial eustatic rise due to polar melting. All
the other possible variables have been excluded.

Figure 11.1 illustrates a section through the northern hemisphere
at about the 10°W meridian, which runs roughly parallel to the
west coast of the Iberian Peninsula and of Ireland. The first curve
shows the shape of the ellipsoid before any changes. The second
curve shows the geodetic effect of a pole shift alone; this creates a
maximum rise at 45°N, decreasing towards the North Pole and the
equator. The third curve shows the effect of an increased equatorial
bulge. This adds to the sea level further below 45°N but reduces it
at higher latitudes. The fourth curve shows the situation following
a eustatic rise and is equivalent to the modern sea level. The overall
result is to raise the sea level, except at very high latitudes (the
small shaded area), where raised beaches are to be expected.

Figure 11.2 shows a similar section taken along the proposed
neutral line at about 10°E. Here the effect of the pole shift is zero

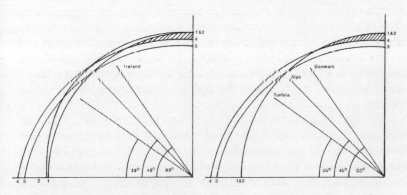

Fig. 11.1 A section through the   **Fig. 11.2** A section through the
northern hemisphere at 10° West.   northern hemisphere at 10° East.

Curve 1: shows the sea level before 3100 BC.
Curve 2: shows the sea level adjusted for a pole shift.
Curve 3: shows the increase in oblateness due to a faster rotation.
Curve 4: shows the effect of a general eustatic rise.

The shaded region indicates polar emergence.

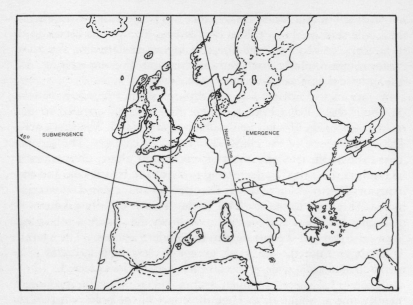

Fig. 11.3   A reconstruction of the European coastline as it may have looked before 3100 BC.

and curve two is identical to curve one. Falling sea level is predicted at the latitude of Scandinavia, with a rise at the latitude of the Mediterranean Sea. Based upon these broad assumptions, figure 11.3 then gives an outline of the former coastline suggested by this model.

The first thing to strike the eye is not how much the coastline changes, but how little! The model predicts that the greatest sea level rise should have occurred along the coasts of Portugal and west Africa where the pole shift and increase in the equatorial bulge reinforce each other. However, Iberia and Africa lie on different continental plates and are therefore free to adjust independently to the geoid. The continental shelf drops away sharply to 200 metres all along these coasts and a change of sea level would have little effect upon the overall shape of the shoreline.

It is unlikely that the Straits of Gibraltar were closed, but they may formerly have been much narrower. Even if the sea level were to drop 200 metres, a passage to the Mediterranean would remain open. Within the Mediterranean itself, the model predicts a rise in sea level due to the gradual flattening of the Earth as the length of the day shortened. This should have resulted in a slow drowning of the shores of the Mediterranean between 3100 BC and about 800 BC, with the greatest effects occurring in the early centuries. Again, here the coastline drops away steeply to great depth, except along the coast of Tunisia and between Malta and Sicily. Here there is ample scope for a shallow shelf of land to have been drowned, in the area where the classical writers placed the marsh Tritonis.[5]

In the eastern Mediterranean and the Aegean we are into an area where little overall change is predicted. In this region, the theory predicts that the fall in sea level resultant from the pole shift would have been slowly cancelled out by a gradual rise of the sea since that time. A number of islands may have been exposed in the Aegean, only to be submerged again over the following 1,500 years. This may account for some of the legends of 'floating islands' found in Greek mythology. In the Mediterranean tectonic movements complicate the pattern of sea level change and the greatest danger to man comes from earthquakes and volcanoes. Again we see the privileged position of Egypt. Close to the neutral line, it suffered comparatively little from the shift in the axis of rotation.

In the Atlantic Ocean itself, there are no great land masses that might be exposed if the sea level were to be lowered by, say, 50 metres. There are, however, a number of small volcanic islands, and several seamounts which at present have only a shallow covering of water. Out in the middle of the Atlantic lie the Azores, the location favoured by Donnelly as the remains of his 'sunken continent'. Around this archipelago lie a number of shallow sea-mounts, such as the Princess Alice Bank, which is now only about 30 metres below sea level. Some of these may have been low-lying islands before 3000 BC, but even a sea level drop of over 300 metres would not create a single land mass here!

Off the Moroccan coast lie the Canary Islands. A lowered sea level here would certainly enlarge each of the islands and it is possible that Lanzarote and Fuerteventura may have been linked as a single island. But the ocean around each island is deep and a similar deep channel separates this volcanic island chain from the mainland of Africa. Further north, the Madeira Islands may have been similarly enlarged, and towards the coast of Portugal a number of other seamounts only just fail to break the surface.

The best candidates for submerged islands are the Ormond Seamount, now just 23 metres below sea level and the Gettysburg Seamount at 35 metres depth. Other neighbouring seamounts probably lie too deep to have been exposed as islands but there are other peaks on the Iberian continental shelf which may have been above water. All these seamounts lie opposite the Straits of Gibraltar, but at most they can have been just tiny islands. In the whole of the vast Atlantic there are no other obvious locations for submerged islands. The only other seamount lying at a depth of less than 200 metres is the Milne Bank, some 800 kilometres north-west of the Azores. Bermuda too is the summit of a seamount surrounded by deep ocean.

On the opposite side of the Atlantic, a shallow continental shelf lies off the east coast of North America. The Gulf of Maine and Georges Bank are particularly shallow and a large shelf lies off Nova Scotia. Parts of the Grand Bank off Newfoundland are also very shallow and may also have been exposed. Further south lie the Bahama Islands, where the Great Bahama Bank surrounding Andros Island is notoriously shallow. The theory predicts that this too was dry land until 5,000 years ago.

In the whole of the North Atlantic there is realistically only one location where a significant area of land could have been submerged. The largest area of shallow continental shelf lies off the north-west coast of Europe, surrounding the British Isles and it is here where the theory predicts that the most far-reaching sea level changes have occurred. The extent of submergence should be at its minimum towards the north and east, with maximum submergence occurring towards the south and west of the shelf. The 45° line of latitude runs through France to the south of the Brittany peninsula and it is here on the Rochebonne Plateau that the theory predicts the deepest submergence.

Commencing at the coast of Jutland, the model suggests only a few metres of submergence and minimal submergence around the fjords of Norway, where further north another neutral line is encountered at about the latitude of the Arctic Circle. Moving south and westwards, along the coast of Holland and France, steadily increasing submergence is predicted. At the Strait of Dover a reduction in sea level of about 8–10 metres is indicated, which would still leave Britain as an island. Today, the deepest parts of the strait are over 30 metres deep. But moving westwards, the

theory predicts submergence along the north-west coast of France
to have been as much as 30 metres around the Normandy peninsula, rising to perhaps 50 metres at Ushant and the Rochebonne
Plateau. Much of the coast drops away steeply to beyond these
depths, but between Brittany and Normandy a low-lying triangle
of land may have linked Jersey to the mainland.

Across the north-west of Britain and Ireland run a series of
geological faults associated with the ancient Caledonian mountain
chain. Notable examples of these are the Great Glen fault in
Scotland, the Highland Boundary fault, the Southern Uplands fault
and further south, the Dinorwic Fault, which is marked by the line
of the Menai Strait. Although these are all ancient fault lines, which
have not been tectonically active for many millions of years, they
still represent lines of weakness along which the crust could fold in
the event of abnormal stress; even today occasional tremors occur
along these fault lines. All this makes the former coastlines around
the British Isles very difficult to determine.

In the North Sea, a reduction of 8–10 metres would not be
sufficient to expose the Dogger Bank, but the former existence of a
few small islands in the North Sea cannot be ruled out, as the soft
sediments would have suffered rapid erosion. A similar loss of low-
lying land is known to have occurred around Heligoland and the
Frisian Islands. The east coast of Britain is still subject to rapid
erosion today, and it is likely that the shallow seabed around the
Wash was formerly exposed; however, much of the north-east coast
of Britain would have changed little. It is only when we arrive as
far north as the Orkney and Shetland Islands that substantial
changes to the coastline are indicated. The Orkneys lie as far west
as the Channel Islands; although this far north much less submergence is predicted this would still be enough to link the Orkney
Islands to the mainland.

Down the west coast of Scotland and Ireland, if it is assumed
that no folding has taken place along the many ancient fault lines,
the predicted submergence steadily increases again towards the
south-western extremity of the continental shelf. As may be seen
from figure 11.3, the depth of submergence increases from about
30 metres at Cape Wrath to perhaps 50 metres at the south-western
extremity of Ireland. These changes are of great significance. Not
only do most of the islands of the Inner Hebrides become linked to
the Scottish mainland, but also many new islands appear on the

map. The Outer Hebrides are linked as a single large island, but remain separated from the mainland by a deep channel. By far the most significant feature indicated is a land-bridge linking the north of Ireland with Scotland.

Between Malin Head and Islay, the seabed currently lies at depths of only 30–40 metres. This may well have been exposed, perhaps as a low-lying tidal isthmus of land. Further east, however, the North Channel is deep and a narrower strait would have separated Scotland from the Antrim coast. The whole of the shallow Firth of Clyde would have been exposed as a flat plain. However, to the west of Ireland the seabed drops away sharply and the effect is little more than to smooth off the features of the existing coastline.

Geographers often remark that the south-western coastlines of both Britain and Ireland have a rather 'drowned' look about them. In Ireland, Galway Bay, the River Shannon, Dingle Bay and Bantry Bay are obvious examples of drowned valleys. In south-west Britain, Falmouth Bay and Milford Haven may be similarly advanced. Submergence around these south-western extremities may have been as much as 40–50 metres. Along the south coast of England, the pattern is similar to that proposed for northern France. Large flat areas would be exposed south of the Isle of Wight and in Lyme Bay, but further west around the coasts of Cornwall a lowering of the sea by as much as 50 metres would have significant effects. Mounts Bay would be exposed, and off the north coast of Penwith a sizeable plain would be created, where today the Cape Cornwall bank lies at a depth of just 21 metres. The Isles of Scilly would merge as a single island, but remain separated from the mainland by a shallow channel.

It is between Britain and Ireland, in the Irish Sea and around the Welsh coast, that the most significant change of all is predicted. A lowering of sea level ranging from about 30 metres in the North Channel, increasing to about 50 metres at Land's End, would significantly reduce the extent of the Irish Sea. Between north Cornwall, Lundy Island and west Wales, the Bristol Channel would be exposed as a triangular plain; and similarly, the whole of Cardigan Bay is shallow and would be exposed as a flat plain between Strumble Head and the Lleyn Peninsula. Shallow banks also lie off the east coast of Ireland; these too may have been exposed and the River Liffey would turn at a sharp right angle to run south in a channel parallel to the modern coast.

The western Irish Sea and the North Channel are deep, but on the British side of that sea between Anglesey, the Isle of Man and south-west Scotland the sea is shallow. To give a sense of how shallow the Irish Sea is here, it is equivalent to about the height of a mature tree. A drop of only 35–40 metres would be sufficient to expose the entire eastern Irish Sea as a low-lying rectangular plain. The Irish Sea would be reduced to a long narrow inlet of the ocean, cut off from the Atlantic in the north but with an open channel to the south. Within this much reduced Irish Sea, midway between what is now Anglesey and the Isle of Man, a small island would be exposed.

This reconstruction of the former sea level around Britain and the coasts of Europe is markedly different from the conventional view. Theories based entirely upon a glacio-eustatic rise of the sea since the Ice Age favour the separation of Britain from the European mainland about 8,000 years ago, with the separation of Britain from Ireland occurring at around the same time.

The limitation of purely eustatic theories of sea level change is that they cannot produce a tilted strand line. Evidence from peat deposits of Boreal age from the bed of the North Sea dictate that the Irish Sea bed should have been similarly exposed at that period. However eustatic theories demand that if the North Sea basin was flooded in later Atlantic times then the Irish Sea must also have stood at a comparable level. A theory of sea level change based upon a variable geoid is able to overcome this obstacle; it is then perfectly plausible for the basin of the Irish Sea to be dry at the same time as that of the North Sea is flooded. The problem of the former coastlines around the British Isles can then be examined with a fresh insight.

12

Beneath the Irish Sea

We now arrive at the end of a long chain of theory and circumstantial evidence, each step logically derived from the meagre clues available from various disciplines. Individually, each piece of the puzzle is open to a different interpretation; but together they add up to a highly consistent pattern. The hypothesis that the Earth's axis has shifted is able to produce a map of the former shorelines around Britain and Ireland which bears a remarkable resemblance to Plato's description of his lost island. If this superficial resemblance were all the evidence available then it might be acceptable to pass off even this as a coincidence, but there remains plenty more evidence to present and more coincidences yet!

The suggestion that the British Isles should be equated with Plato's lost land may at first seem a little unlikely. The main reason for this is that we are preconditioned to the idea of Atlantis as a 'lost continent' situated in the middle of the Atlantic Ocean. In fact Plato never actually said this. The idea is no older than Ignatius Donnelly. Now that modern oceanography has largely discredited the sunken continent hypothesis, the entire subject of Atlantis tends to be discredited along with it. But Plato's story is only one of many strands of evidence pointing to a Neolithic submergence of land along the Atlantic coast.

The resemblance of the submerged shelf around the British Isles to Plato's description of the lost island should be apparent from a glance at figure 11.3. The geodetic hypothesis suggests that submergence has been greatest in the south and west. On this reconstruction, Britain remains cut off from the Continent by a narrow strait and it becomes part of a much larger island including all of Ireland and much additional land. Right at the centre of that island there is a flat rectangular plain where broad river estuaries flow across what is now the bed of the eastern Irish Sea. Where those rivers meet the much-reduced Irish Sea, another small island is exposed lying right at the geographical centre of the main island. In a moment we shall examine how closely this island fits Plato's description of the central island of Atlantis. First, however, it is worth while investigating a little of the geomorphology of the Irish Sea and the modern shores around it.

The basin of the western Irish Sea and the North Channel is a deep and ancient rift, formed many millions of years ago when Europe and North America drifted apart. During most of the recent Ice Age the Irish Sea floor was covered by an ice cap, which extended far down into the Celtic Sea and the English Channel. The removal of the ice left behind deep deposits of glacial till. Recent oil and gas exploration reveals that these soft deposits are as much as 30 metres deep in the centre of the basin and deeper still in places. Soft glacial till is subject to rapid erosion and strong currents continue to alter the topography of the sea floor.

Current theories of when the Irish Sea basin was flooded, and the link between Britain and Ireland severed, centre upon the raised beaches found around Scottish coasts. The so-called 50-foot beach is thought to date from a cold period at the end of the last glaciation and is noted as far south as Islay and the Galloway peninsula. It has been destroyed in places by the younger 25-foot beach, upon which several dugout canoes have been found. Neither beach can be traced south of Lancashire; but corresponding beaches do occur in Northern Ireland, particularly around Rathlin Island. These beaches are often cited as evidence that the rise of the sea had cut off Ireland from Britain at least as long ago as the Boreal period.[1]

At Ringneill Quay in County Down, archaeological excavation has revealed estuarine clay deposited before 6400 BC, at a height of some 2.5 metres above modern sea level.[2] At some later time, this clay was cut away by the sea and evidence of Neolithic artefacts is found above it, together with the bones of domesticated animals. Radiocarbon dates from this occupation assign it to the Atlantic pollen zone at about 4400 BC. The site was subsequently covered again by some 2 metres of raised beach deposits at some time before 2000 BC. This gives a fairly typical sequence: illustrating a high sea level during Boreal times, followed by a regression below modern sea level during the Atlantic period; and finally a rise to modern levels.

There is a good deal of evidence to suggest that the first separation of Britain from Ireland did indeed occur during the Boreal period. A subsequent regression of the sea below modern levels is also generally accepted and older literature speaks freely of a 'submerged forest period'. An abundance of peat deposits and submerged forests of Atlantic age occur all around the coasts of Ireland and western Britain; and scores of Neolithic implements are found scattered about the older raised beaches. It is here suggested that the sea may indeed have been at a high level during the Boreal, but at the Boreal/Atlantic transition (c.5500 BC) the geoid changes were sufficient once more to reveal the bed of the eastern Irish Sea.

In Ireland, submerged forest deposits are found around Wexford, Wicklow, Dundalk Bay and in Belfast Lough.[3] In Lough Foyle there is a forest bed lying beneath a beach bar, which has been dated to 5005 BC; and again in Dublin Bay, shingle covers a kitchen-midden site dated at 3300 BC.[4, 5] From elsewhere in Ireland there is much evidence to suggest that the coast was below its present level during Atlantic times. At low tide submerged peat is visible at Strand Hill, County Sligo.[6] Beneath a light covering of sand, peat of Atlantic age is found in which the pollen assemblages would indicate the presence of elm and hazel forests.

The deposits on the western coast of Britain are rather better known, particularly in the Severn estuary and Cardigan Bay. However, the published papers rest heavily upon a base of glacio-eustatic and isostatic theory. The submerged forests of the intertidal zone were investigated by Godwin in the 1940s and more recently by D.M. Churchill.[7, 8] The latter was able to conclude, from peats laid down in early Atlantic times, that a distinct tilting of the crust must have taken place since that time, between Holland and the west of Britain. Churchill investigated the peat layer at several points around southern Britain and the Netherlands. These included Lochar Moss on the Solway Firth, Silverdale Moss on the Lancashire coast, Westward Ho in north Devon, Tilbury and Willemstad, Holland. Dated samples taken from the base of the peat deposits all suggest the early Atlantic as the approximate era when growth of peat began.

The basis of Churchill's argument was that all the peats he surveyed rested upon a base of marine deposits. This he took as an indication that either a fall of sea level, or a rise of land, occurred in the early Atlantic, and freshwater peat, or even forests then grew up on the same site. Churchill was looking for evidence of isostatic warping, but tilting of the crust can be just as easily explained by an alternative geodetic hypothesis.

Radiocarbon dating from the peat and forest beds can offer a fairly reliable date for the subsequent submergence event. Peats of Atlantic age are found in Bridgwater Bay and the Somerset Levels. Here, there is evidence to suggest that at about 5000 BC peat deposits now found beneath the beach near Stolford were forming below a freshwater pond.[9] Similar evidence comes from the south Wales coast near Port Talbot where peat deposits have been dated to c.4200 BC.[10] Evidently the seashore of that time lay somewhere further out than today.

Along the coast of Cardigan Bay, at the mouth of the Dovey around Borth and Ynyslas, fallen trunks and tree stumps still in the position of growth lie beneath only a thin covering of sand and are frequently exposed at low tide. In a recent dendrochronological study, samples of oak wood from the Ynyslas exposure showed the trees to date from throughout the Atlantic pollen zone.[11] Here and at other places around the coast the trees appear to have been killed by salt water within 50 years of 4500 BP (c.3300–3100 BC).[12] Unfortunately there is every reason to believe that mature oak trees could survive for many years with their roots immersed in a tidal sea; and the date of the outermost growth ring would therefore not necessarily indicate the date of submergence.

The forest beds at Ynyslas and further down the coast at Clarach were investigated in detail by J.A. Taylor. He gives dates from Clarach and Ynyslas which suggest that the forests were rapidly overwhelmed by the sea at some time before 3000 BC. Taylor also studied the orientation of the fallen trees at Ynyslas; he discovered a strong tendency for the fallen trunks to align along a south-west to north-east axis, which he suggests is due to a rapid collapse under severe tide or wind conditions.[13]

In north-west England it is the older research of R. Kay-Gresswell which fits best with the present hypothesis.[14, 15, 16] He identified a wave-cut notch at about +5.8 metres running through the low-lying countryside of south-west Lancashire and the Fylde, which he termed the *Hillhouse coast*. He attributed this to a post-glacial marine transgression of Boreal age and equated it with the 25-foot beach of Scotland. Kay-Gresswell envisaged that the Hill-house coast marked the furthest eastward penetration of the sea during the Holocene, after which it receded far below modern levels during Neolithic times.

Submerged forest deposits underlie most of the Lancashire coastal strip west of the Hillhouse 'cliff' and from time to time these have lain exposed on the modern beach between Formby and the Wirral. Most of the prominent exposures noted by older sources have now been washed away, but it is recorded that here too the fallen trunks showed a preferred south-west to north-east alignment. The pollen spectra of the forest beds are described as typically Atlantic, the trees themselves being mainly oak and silver birch.

The more recent research of Tooley and Shennan contradicts Kay-Gresswell's pre-radiocarbon hypothesis of a submerged forest era, favouring a more conservative series of metre-scale oscillations around the modern shore.[17, 18, 19] The Hillhouse coast is dismissed as a fiction on the grounds that it would require a mechanism by which storm waves could rise some 6 metres above the norm. However, it is possible that the Hillhouse 'cliff' merely records the upper limit of a pole-tide oscillation of Boreal/Atlantic age and as such would have been very short lived.

Around the south-west coast of Scotland there is a similar story to be told. In the Solway Firth and Wigtown Bay, the Boreal transgression is marked by the presence of marine clay deposits extending several kilometres inland from the present coast. The estuaries of the Rivers Cree and Nith then extended much further inland. The sea subsequently receded from its maximum and in the Lochar Gulf peat deposits are found above the estuarine clay.[20] Within this peat layer there is evidence of elm regeneration and clearance suggesting Neolithic pastoral farming.

A temporary period of freshwater conditions is also suggested.[21] Near the village of Racks, 3 metres of silt overlays the peat deposits, implying deposition within a freshwater pond. Nearby, on the coast between Southerness and the village of Caulkerbush, there is again evidence to suggest that swampy marsh conditions occupied the site of the present coast. At a later date this marsh was filled in by wind-blown sand dunes.[22] The sequence in Wigtown Bay also suggests a period of freshwater conditions, before the deposition of peat commences again at about 2700 BC. This evidence again suggests a temporary regression of the sea.

As with evidence from elsewhere in the world, a eustatic or

isostatic cause is usually advanced to explain these variations. While the eustatic theories are entirely rejected here in favour of a primarily geodetic cause, there is still much in the published evidence to support a regression of the sea during the Atlantic period, followed by a rapid rise to modern levels after 3000 BC. But evidence gathered at the modern shoreline will not tell us whether the sea level rolled back only a few metres beyond the present shore or whether the fall was much more dramatic.

There are a few other clues. Submerged forest deposits have also been found in Pentewan Valley, Cornwall during the course of tin mining work.[23] Stumps of trees were found at a depth of 15 metres beneath marine sediments, however no dating evidence is to hand and such deep deposits are usually assumed to be of interglacial age. In Cardigan Bay, sonar mapping of the seabed has revealed a possible submerged cliff at a depth of 33 metres.[24] In the Irish Sea, similar fossil cliffs have been postulated at the 40-metre and 27-metre lines. Again these are assumed to be of late glacial age. On the floor of the Firth of Clyde, another possible submerged shoreline is found to the north-west and south-east of Ailsa Craig, at 46 metres below modern sea level.[25] There is absolutely nothing to prove the age of these sunken cliff features.

The submerged forests found close to the modern shoreline testify to the occurrence of a rapid transgression of the sea at the close of the Atlantic period. The theory advanced here is that the sea level was lowered geodetically by as much as 30–50 metres at the Boreal/Atlantic transition (*c.*5500 BC), revealing much of the Irish Sea bed. At the Atlantic/Sub-Boreal transition (*c.*3100 BC) the sea claimed back what it had given. There was thus a period of perhaps two millennia during which the eastern Irish Sea was a dry plain. There is probably nothing at all unique about this process. The shelf to the west of the British Isles has been submerged and revealed on countless occasions throughout geological time and in many places today the sea is re-cutting into ancient cliffs.

The seabed shelves only gently away from the north-west coast of England, reaching a depth of 30 metres by about 24 kilometres out. A distinct ridge runs from Ramsey Bay on the Isle of Man south-eastwards to the Fylde coast, which at its maximum depth is only 23 metres. This ridge divides the geologically distinct northern and southern basins. The Isle of Man is similar in composition to Cumbria, but north of it lies the Solway Firth Basin and to the south the Manx-Furness Basin; an almost perfectly flat surface, which drops only a further 20 metres in the remaining 48 kilometres to the edge of the basin.

A sea level drop of about 35–40 metres is all that would be required to expose the floor of the eastern Irish Sea. A further drop to, say, 65 metres would make little difference to the overall shape of the shoreline created. Somewhere between these limits, an irregular concave shoreline would be created starting from a point west of Holyhead, to a point south-west of the Calf of Man. The shoreline would then continue more or less directly north to a point only a few miles from the Mull of Galloway, then continuing on beyond Ailsa Craig to the Mull of Kintyre. To the west of this shoreline, between Anglesey and the Isle of Man, there would also be a small low-lying triangular island, of about the same area as the Isle of Man.

Running roughly parallel to the north Wales coast, a submerged river channel can be discerned in the sea floor. This is a prominent feature on the charts, which has been referred to as a 'glacial meltwater channel'. This is really no more than the continuation of the River Dee through the Welsh Channel, into which the Rivers Conway, Mersey and Ribble would all ultimately flow during an era of lowered sea level. The river would form a broad estuary flowing to the north-east of Anglesey. North of the Manx-Furness Ridge, the rivers emanating from Cumbria would all flow to the north of the Isle of Man to join the rivers which drain into the Solway Firth. Here, however, the topography suggests a former landscape dominated by lakes and kettle-holes.

The exception is the River Lune, which emanates from Morecambe Bay via the Lune Deep. No clear channel can be discerned on the charts for it to flow either north or south. Fluviomarine deposits may have buried its former channel, but current topography suggests that it would have to follow a meandering route to the south of the Isle of Man, from which many lesser streams would flow to join it.

At the edge of the Manx-Furness Basin, the sea floor drops away to depths greater than 60 metres, but further west it rises again to another flat plateau at a depth averaging about 40 metres. Any lowered sea level between about 40 and 60 metres would leave this plateau exposed as an island. The island so created would then lie directly opposite the river estuaries emanating from the plain.

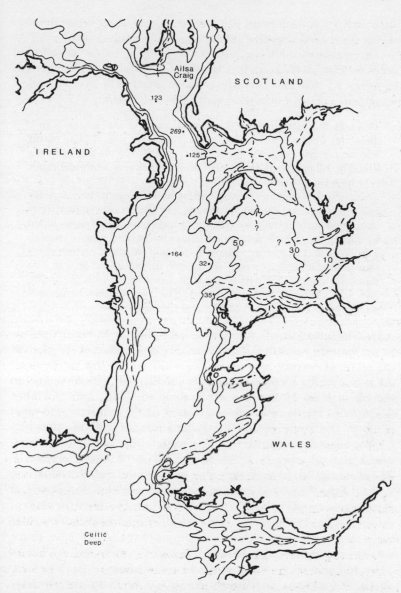

Fig. 12.1 The 10-, 30- and 50-metre submarine contours around the Irish Sea. The major submerged river channels are shown as dotted lines. Based on UK Admiralty charts 2, 1121, 1826 & 1411.

Although the plateau is for the most part level, there is one point at which the seabed rises to a peak at only 32 metres depth.

The similarity of these submarine features to the description given by Plato is striking. It is worth while looking again at certain elements of this and, in doing so, to exercise a little harmless imagination. First, his basic description of the island.

> Towards the sea, halfway down the length of the whole island, there was a plain which is said to have been the fairest of all plains and very fertile. Near the plain again, and also in the centre of the island at a distance of about fifty stadia, there was a mountain not very high on any side.
>
> . . . The whole country was said by him (Solon) to be very lofty and precipitous on the side of the sea, but the country immediately about and surrounding the city was a level plain, itself surrounded by mountains which descended towards the sea; it was smooth and even, and of oblong shape, extending in one direction three thousand stadia, but across the centre of the island it was two thousand stadia. This part of the island looked towards the south, and was sheltered from the north. The surrounding mountains were celebrated for their number and size and beauty.

A little imagination will allow this description to be transposed on to the features beneath the Irish Sea. The description of the plain at the centre of Atlantis fits remarkably well, and the low mountain at the centre of the island corresponds equally well with Snae Fell on the Isle of Man. However, there is some ambiguity here in Plato's description. He describes the mountain at the centre of the great plain as the home of the Earth-born Evenor and his daughter Cleito; but a little further on he transfers this hill to the central island and describes how Poseidon built fortifications around it. The royal citadel, he says, was also built around this central island.

As for the shape and dimensions of the central plain, those that Plato gives are rather large to fit the Irish Sea. However the ratio of the sides (3:2) is a good fit. This could be applied equally well to the rectangle made by the modern shores of the Irish Sea, or to the smaller rectangle of the Manx-Furness Basin between the Isle of Man and the Welsh coast. One Greek stadium is equivalent to about 185 metres. The dimensions given by Plato are therefore equivalent to about 555 by 370 kilometres, which more closely approximate to the dimensions of the British Isles as a whole. It is just conceivable that a mistranslation of units has occurred at some time during the life of the story, which has preserved the ratio but not the scale.

The coastline of Atlantis was said to rise steeply away from the sea on all sides, except near the central plain. As we have seen, a lowered sea level around the British Isles would leave steeply shelving coasts around the south of England, Ireland and most of

Fig. 12.2 The lowered shorelines around the British Isles as they may have looked between about 5500 BC and 3100 BC. Is this a map of Atlantis? Note the large rectangular plain at the centre and the small central island, open to the south as Plato described.

Scotland. The central plain was also said to be surrounded by mountains which came right down to the sea. The Irish Sea is enclosed on three sides by ranges of hills, from the Southern Uplands through the Pennines down to the Welsh mountains. Only in Cumbria and Snowdonia can they correctly be termed mountains. However, it is clear that the mountains described by Plato were not especially high, as they were said to be covered by dense forests. These mountains also held many lakes and human settlements. There were, and still are, many lakes in Wales, Cumbria, Scotland and the north of Ireland.

The description of the irrigation works on the great plain add further points of similarity.

> It was naturally for the most part rectangular and oblong, and where falling out of the straight line had been made regular by the surrounding ditch. The depth, and width, and length of this ditch were incredible, and gave the impression that a work of such extent, in addition to so many others, could never have been artificial. Nevertheless I must say what I was told. It was excavated to the depth of a hundred feet, and its breadth was a stadium everywhere; it carried round the whole of the plain, and was ten thousand stadia in length. It received the streams which came down from the mountains, and winding round the plain and meeting at the city, was there let off into the sea.

If we neglect for the moment the scale of the human labour involved in all this, the impression is one of a perfectly flat plain across which rivers were scarcely able to flow at all. The Manx-Furness Basin has only a very gentle slope, but if we allow for an east–west tilt to have taken place then even this disappears. The rectangle between the Isle of Man, Cumbria and north Wales then fits quite well with Plato's description, with the river channels skirting the edge of the plain just as he maintains. He asserts that some of the artificial channels were as much as 30 metres deep in places. These dimensions are not at all out of scale with the topography of the Irish Sea floor. Channels of this depth would have been more than sufficient to link the water tables north and south of the Manx-Furness Ridge.

Plato says that at the point where these rivers and channels met the sea lay the central island on which the great city was situated. On a hill at the centre of this island was the acropolis on which the royal palace was built. The story of how the god Poseidon encircled the hill with three rings of water reads like a piece of pure mythology. Plato describes the waterways as perfect circles and narrates how, at a later time, a canal was cut to the outermost ring, turning it into a harbour.

It is not clear from the description whether the central island was a natural or a wholly man-made feature. The mythological tale about Poseidon suggests a creation story to explain the existence of a series of natural islets within the river delta. There is a feature on the Irish Sea floor, which fits the description of the central island, and that is the triangular plateau previously described. A lowering of the sea level by some 40–50 metres in this area would create a largely flat island about 40 kilometres long by 20 kilometres wide. On the western side of this island, facing the plain, would be a hill of some 20 metres height. The survival of such a steep-sided feature on the seabed suggests that it consists of solid rock and if we ignore the requirement for perfectly circular channels, it is about the right size for the central island and acropolis described by Plato. The island would also be situated in the open sea, facing south, or with a route south to the Atlantic Ocean, just as Plato suggests.

The scale of the engineering works with which the Atlantians are credited are only feasible if the canals were cut into soft sediments. Indeed the only place where Plato clearly describes the excavation of hard rock is the quarry beneath the central acropolis. The irrigation works become far more credible if the excavated material was only soft sand and gravel, such as exists on the Irish Sea floor.[26]

Further useful clues are offered by the construction of the houses of Atlantis.

> The stone that was used in the work, they quarried from underneath the centre island, and from underneath the zones, on the outer as well as the inner side. One kind was white, another black, and a third red, and as they quarried, they at the same time hollowed out docks double within, having roofs formed out of the native rock.

This tells us something about the geology of the island. Clearly these are not grey volcanic rocks, but sedimentary rocks of a continental type. Indeed vulcanism is nowhere mentioned in the narratives, which is damning for any theory that would site it on

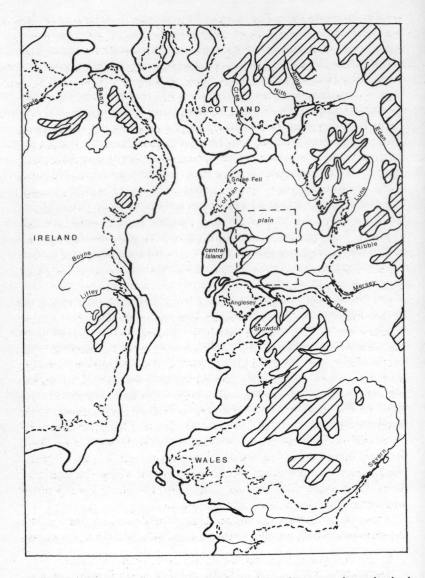

Fig. 12.3 The shorelines of the Irish Sea as they may have looked during Atlantic times. The present day shoreline is shown by the dotted line. Note the presence of the small central island opposite the central plain.

one of the Mid-Atlantic islands. Once again, the geology of the Irish Sea fits very well with this picture. Around Anglesey and beneath Caernarvon Bay a sequence of sandstones, mudstones and pebble beds is found, known as the *Red Measures*.[27] Shallow cores taken from the Manx-Furness Basin also reveal evidence of red Triassic mudstones and sandstones. Most notably, red sandstone outcrops around Peel on the Isle of Man.

White chalk is common throughout southern England and also outcrops in Northern Ireland. Seismic surveys over the southern Irish Sea and St George's Channel have revealed the existence of a thick layer of Upper Cretaceous chalk, which may extend further north.[28] Another reason why the reference to white rock rings true is the association of chalk with flint mining. Flint usually occurs in association with chalk and was extensively mined in Britain during the Neolithic period, as at Grimes Graves in Norfolk. The period before 3100 BC falls squarely within the British Neolithic. Quarrying for flint is perfectly plausible as is the use of the excavated rock as a building material.

The Red Measures overlay a seam of coal which has been mined in Anglesey.[29] Coal is also thought to underlie much of the Manx-Furness Basin. The Cheshire Basin is an onshore continuation of the Manx-Furness Basin and coal is mined on either side of it, in north Wales and Lancashire. But coal seems an unlikely building material. A far more likely candidate here is slate. The region between Snowdonia and the sea is one of the few sources of slate anywhere in Europe and is known to have been quarried since ancient times. Slate is also found on the Isle of Man, and in seabed cores taken off the south-east of the Isle of Man.[30] Neither are these the only candidates. Pebbles of white quartz and a kind of black marble dominate the beach shingle near Port St Mary on the Isle of Man. With more difficulty one may also find black slate pebbles and occasional pieces of red Peel sandstone.

There is a further geological clue available, and that is the mysterious orichalcum. Plato refers to this substance in three places.

In the first place, they dug out of the earth whatever was to be found there, solid as well as fusile, and that which is now only a name and was then something more than a name, orichalcum, was dug out of the earth in many parts of the island, being more precious in those days than anything except gold.

. . . Some of their buildings were simple, but in others they put together different stones, varying the colour to please the eye, and to be a natural source of delight. The entire circuit of the wall, which went round the outermost zone, they covered with a coating of brass, and the circuit of the next wall they coated with tin, and the third, which encompassed the citadel, flashed with the red light of orichalcum.

. . . In the interior of the temple the roof was of ivory, curiously wrought everywhere with gold and silver and orichalcum; and all the other parts, the walls and pillars and floor, they coated with orichalcum.

No one is quite sure what this substance orichalcum was; some have suggested that it was amber, but the etymology suggests that it means 'mountain copper'. We can see that it was red and lustrous and since it was used in the same way as the other metals mentioned, it was probably also a metal. Though considered more precious than anything except gold, it must have been locally abundant, for it was used to coat large areas of the palace, interior and exterior, in a display of unparalleled opulence.

The substance which fits this description best is red gold, a naturally occurring alloy of copper and gold. The addition of copper in any quantity gives gold a reddish tinge, whereas alloyed with silver it becomes whiter. It must be remembered that the Atlantis legend is of Egyptian origin. Most of the gold known to the Egyptians was white gold, from the upper Nile, and it is understandable that they should consider red gold to be such a rarity.[31]

Gold was mined extensively in the nineteenth century from the Welsh mountains around Dolgellau. Most of the seams are now worked out but although operated principally for the extraction of gold, the same mines also yielded copper in commercial quantities. Near Amlwch on Anglesey, copper has been worked since ancient times. Stone hammers have been found at Parys Mountain which are loosely assigned a 'Bronze Age' date.[32] In the eighteenth century, Parys Mine was the largest single producer of copper in the whole of Europe. Copper ores are found throughout Wales and in Carmarthen, where they are associated with lead and zinc.

Plato also states that an entire wall around the palace was coated with tin. This metal was a great rarity in the ancient world. The Phoenicians are known to have made long voyages to Cornwall and the Isles of Scilly, precisely because they were one of the few sources of the ore known in Europe. Wherever Atlantis may have been, it is probable that the Atlantians also obtained their tin from this source. Plato does mention that the twin brother of Atlas was given to rule over a land called Eumelus, or Gadeirus. This, we are told, was at that extremity of Atlantis which faced towards the Pillars of Heracles. This may be a reference to the south-west peninsula, which, as the only source of tin, would have assumed great political importance.

The Irish Sea and the regions around it may therefore be seen to fit all the geological requirements of the Atlantis myth. All the metals mentioned are available from local sources including those required to make alloys, such as bronze and brass. Indeed Plato tells us that all their needs were met within the island itself.

The island is also said to have been a rich source of wood for carpentry, which the Atlantians floated down from the mountains via the various rivers and canals. Plato tells us quite clearly that the Atlantians ruthlessly exploited their forest resource. The British Isles are known to have been covered by dense primary forests throughout most of the warm Atlantic period; and this is also the era at which the first evidence of forest clearance is evident in the pollen record. Today much of northern Scotland is barren and devoid of natural tree cover, but during the Climatic Optimum the tree-line was higher and forests grew right up to the western and northern shores. Pine trees grew in the Cairngorms to well above today's limits and as far north as the Orkney and Shetland Islands.

Further south in Britain and Ireland, the vegetation was dominated by mixed oak forests with elm and lime. Today, the remains of these trees are found beneath the upland peat bogs, which began to form at about the time of the elm decline. From the determinations at Red Moss, Lancashire, the elm decline commences at about 3050 BC, or about 4000 BC, where it is associated with the pollen of plants which grow best on cleared and open ground.[33] The elm decline clearly begins during the Atlantic period and notwithstanding the work of the elm bark beetle has been ascribed to the effects of Neolithic 'slash and burn' agriculture.[34] The clear-cutting of forest leads to a rise in the level of the water table, and in the water-logged ground the forests cannot regenerate.[35] In appropriate conditions, the formation of peat will then commence.

The climate of Atlantis, as described by Plato, was clearly of a mild and Mediterranean type. While we must remember that this is the only climate that Plato ever experienced, we have no alternative but to take his description at face value.

> Twice in the year they gathered the fruits of the earth – in winter having the benefit of the rains of heaven, and in summer the water which the land supplied, when they introduced streams from the canals.
>   ... There was an abundance of wood for the carpenter's work, and sufficient maintenance for tame and wild animals. Moreover, there were a great number of elephants in the island; for as there was provision for all other sorts of animals, both for those which live in lakes and marshes and rivers, and also for those which live in mountains and on plains, so there was for the animal which is the largest and most voracious of all. Also whatever fragrant things there now are in the earth, whether roots, or herbage, or woods, or essences which distil from fruit and flower, grew and thrived in that land; also the fruit which admits of cultivation, both the dry sort, which is given us for nourishment and any other which we use for food – we call them by the common name of pulse, and the fruits having a hard rind, affording drinks and meats and ointments, and good store of chestnuts and the like, which furnish pleasure and amusement, and are fruits which spoil with keeping, and the pleasant kinds of dessert, with which we console ourselves after dinner, when we are tired of eating – all these that sacred island which then beheld the light of the sun, brought forth fair and wondrous and in infinite abundance.

The island did not experience cold winters and the climate described is clearly maritime and temperate in nature. Indeed the winters were so mild that they would allow the production of a second crop. The summers were apparently drier, as irrigation was necessary. We are not told precisely which crops they cultivated, but we can be certain that they cultivated fruit trees. Plato goes to inordinate lengths to describe these fruits, but it is still not easy to distinguish any particular variety. Fruit cultivation demands a warm, wet and equable climate such as is today found only in southern Europe. In Britain and Ireland today, the right conditions for fruit growing are only found in the southern and western regions, but citrus fruits and other southern species cannot be grown.

In the context of the theories advanced here, we may now consider a much more northerly location for Atlantis. If the obliquity was indeed less than today, then this would allow warm temperate conditions to spread much further north and the climate at the latitude of Britain and Ireland would be far more equable. There is no precise equivalent of this climate anywhere in the world today and it is rather as if we were to combine the winter temperatures of northern Spain with the summer temperatures of southern Norway. Surrounded by a warm ocean, this would give conditions no more extreme than those between a warm spring day and a cool autumn day, yet without the unpredictable swings that characterize the modern British weather. It must be stressed again that this all fits very well with the British climate during the fourth millennium BC, as derived from pollen evidence.

Perhaps the closest approximation to this today is the climate of the Isles of Scilly, or of south-east Ireland. In this part of Ireland today, a number of plant species survive which are otherwise confined to the Iberian Peninsula. The origin of this Lusitanian element in the Irish flora is enigmatic; possibly these species were far more widespread in the warm Atlantic climate.[36]

Of course, all this is merely a pattern of circumstantial evidence; and by itself cannot conclusively prove anything. By following the strict rules of the hypothesis so far presented; the evidence points towards the continental shelf around the British Isles as the best place to seek hard evidence of a submerged Neolithic civilization. In addition, a whole host of other myths and legends have survived which may also be explainable by a Neolithic submergence. We must now take a much closer look at these; and at what was going on in western Europe and the British Isles during the Neolithic age.

13

The Land of Youth

Little is known of the history of Britain before Roman times. A few tantalizing glimpses may exist in the writings of Greek and Roman authors, but really nothing on which to build history. There are no king lists, no chronology, and few events to which a positive date can be attached. For Ireland too, which was never troubled by Rome, history only really commences with the early Christian Church. Before this we have myth and legend in abundance – the so-called 'Celtic' mythologies of the Welsh and the Irish. At least 3,000 years separate the extant versions of Celtic legend from the events of 3100 BC. One thing is certain: if any memories of that era do lie hidden within indigenous British and Irish legends then we may be sure that they have very little to do with Celts.

The Celts first make their appearance as a historical entity in the early Greek histories, the name itself deriving from a Greek *Keltoi*.[1] Current theories see them as one of the Indo-European groups which intruded into central Europe from the east. By about 500 BC they were first noted as a powerful nation in Europe north of the Alps. In later centuries they expanded southwards into France, Spain, Italy and Illyria where their movements are historically attested; but their arrival in the British Isles is deduced only from archaeological and linguistic evidence. That Celtic-speaking people did settle in Britain and Ireland cannot be doubted, but neither the Irish nor the Welsh ever referred to themselves as Celts. Today Welsh, Irish and their derivatives are the only surviving Celtic languages.

The continental Celts appear to have reached the height of their power at around the time Alexander the Great set out on his wars against the Persian Empire. Before leaving Greece, he is said to have struck an alliance with the Celts to secure his northern flank. In promising their alliance, the Celtic ambassadors gave him their assurance:[2] 'If we fulfil not our engagement may the sky falling upon us crush us, may the earth opening swallow us up, may the sea overflowing its borders drown us.' When asked what thing they feared most of all, the ambassadors replied, 'We fear no one. There is only one thing that we fear, which is that the heavens may fall upon us . . .' Very similar fears are voiced in some versions of a seventh-century Irish saga called *The Cattle-Raid of Cooley*.[3] As early as the fourth century BC then, we see evidence of a common heritage between Ireland and the continental Celts. One wonders what events could have left such fears in the Celtic mind! Is it not pertinent to ask why a race of supposedly central European origin should so fear inundation by the sea? This part of their mythology at least must have originated along the Atlantic coast, where some very similar fears seem to have found their way into Geoffrey of Monmouth's *History of the Kings of Britain*. Geoffrey devotes an entire chapter to the so-called Prophecies of Merlin, a series of garbled and enigmatic astrological predictions.[4]

> The Moon's chariot shall run amok in the Zodiac and the Pleiades will burst into tears. None of these will return to the duty expected of it. Ariadne will shut its door and be hidden within its enclosing cloud banks.
> In the twinkling of an eye the seas shall rise up and the arena of the winds shall be opened once again. The winds shall do battle together with a blast of ill-omen, making their din reverberate from one constellation to another.

Geoffrey's book of somewhat dubious history contains a number of these interesting mythological references, which may be attributed to Celtic and even pre-Celtic sources.

There is no precise method to date the arrival of Celtic-speaking people in the British Isles, but the fact remains that all the indigenous mythology of Britain and Ireland has come down to us via the Celtic languages. It is therefore quite impossible to determine how much of it is really derived from the aboriginal inhabitants. These people are known only from archaeology: they are the Megalith Builders, the Neolithic and Bronze Age inhabitants of western Europe. It is suspected that these aborigines were not Indo-Europeans and that they spoke a non-Indo-European language, but there is little real evidence to prove this other than a few strange place names and some early literary references to the language of the

Picts. Despite this, there is every reason to believe that much of so-called Celtic mythology preserves pre-Celtic concepts.

By comparison with the classical mythologies of Greece and Rome, all the written sources of Celtic mythology are quite recent. The great works of Hesiod and Homer, which serve as the source for much of Greek mythology, can be shown to have stabilized in written form at least as early as 700 BC. We therefore know with some certainty that the world they describe belongs to a much earlier time. By contrast, the earliest Irish manuscripts date from no earlier than AD 700 and the Welsh stories can only be traced back to early medieval sources. Still other concepts only make their first known appearance in the Latin pseudo-histories of Nennius and Geoffrey of Monmouth. No source predates Christian influence and these late, and often unreliable documents serve to disguise the true antiquity of the material they contain.

The use of writing seems to have been a late arrival in Britain and Ireland. Julius Caesar records that the continental Celts used the Greek alphabet for their commercial transactions, but history and theology was the responsibility of the druids. They would not permit their teachings to be written down and so their accumulated wisdom had to be transmitted orally. The students of druidism underwent a protracted period of training during which they were made to learn many long verses by heart. We may presume that all of Celtic history was preserved in this way, passed on as oral tradition from one generation to the next.

So long as the doctrine of the druids held sway within a stable Celtic society, then we may envisage that the traditions were accurately preserved, perhaps even word for word, with various checks in place to prevent errors and loss of detail. The druids must surely have required a chronology of some kind, but it has not survived. It may only have been when their doctrine fell apart that the oral history degenerated into myth and legend. While we cannot be sure how old druidism is, we can at least trace its decline fairly accurately. It began with the suppression of the cult in Roman Gaul under Tiberius and culminated in the ruthless slaughter, by Sueto-nius, of the British druids in Anglesey. We may never know how much ancient British history was lost that day.

Far more of the Celtic and pre-Celtic past survives in Irish mythology. Here too we know that there were druids, for they feature in many of the Irish sagas. There is good reason to suppose that the Irish druids performed a similar function in Irish society to that of the druids in Gaul. It is known that they persisted for a while alongside the Christian Church and when Ireland was converted rapidly to Christianity the Church adapted pagan festivals and beliefs for its own purposes. Christianity brought with it Church Latin and writing; and the old stories began to be written down for the first time.

A mythological history of Ireland has been preserved, known as the *Book of Invasions*. It survives only as a number of fragments collected together from other Irish sagas and manuscripts long since lost. Some of its material was apparently known to Nennius in the ninth century and this lends it a degree of authenticity. It describes the races that have invaded and settled in Ireland before the coming of the modern Irish.

There is no Celtic creation myth except the Christian one. Ireland seems always to have existed and is referred to as *Eriu* or *Erin*. According to the *Book of Invasions* the first settlers were the tribe of Partholon, fleeing from the Flood. He is said to have come from the west, across the Atlantic, but in those days Ireland was quite a different place. There were just nine rivers in Ireland, three lakes and only one plain, called the Old Plain. Partholon and his people made many new clearings in the forest and fought to hold Ireland against a people called the Fomorians who were apparently already living there; this is the first mention of the Fomorians, who figure prominently elsewhere in Irish legend. Partholon and his tribe were eventually wiped out by a terrible plague, leaving Ireland deserted again for 30 years.

The next arrivals were the tribe of Nemed. We are told that they came from Greece, via Scythia and the Northern Ocean, which is presumably a reference to the Baltic or the North Sea. There then follows the first of the Irish flood legends. While Nemed and his thirty-four ships were wandering the ocean, they sighted a golden tower on the sea. When the tide was in ebb, the tower appeared above it, but when the tide rose it submerged the tower. They set course for the tower in the hope of plunder, but in their greed for gold they failed to notice that the sea was rising about them. The great waves took their ships and all but a few of the Nemedians were drowned. For a year and a half the survivors wandered on the sea until they reached Ireland where, according to the legend, their descendants still live today. There they built fortresses and cleared twelve plains, but still they were dogged by geological catastrophe:[5]

> Four lake-bursts over Ireland in the time of Nemed; Loch Calin Ui Niallan, Loch Munremur of Sliab Guaire, Loch Dairbrech, and Loch Ainninn in Meath. At the end of nine years after their coming to Erin, these last two lakes burst forth.

This catalogue of lake-bursts is curious, for such things do not occur very often in the normal course of events. When four such overflowings occur in the space of 9 years, then we may be sure that something highly unusual is happening to the world. The overflowing of lakes is precisely what would be expected if the local geodesy of the land was unstable. We should therefore not be surprised to note that the later Celts venerated lakes, propitiating them with regular offerings of gold and treasure.

The Nemedians suffered great oppression from the Fomorians. Nemed won three battles against them but his people were weakened. After his death from plague, the Fomorians returned. Their chief, Conann, built a tower on Tory Island, off the north-west coast of Donegal, from which he ruled over the people. His oppression was harsh, for he exacted from the Nemedians a tribute each year of two-thirds of their corn, their milk and their children. Ultimately this burden became too great to bear and they rose against the Fomorians.

The *Book of Invasions* describes at great length how the sons and grandsons of Nemed led the people. They demanded of Conann a 3-year respite from their taxes, or else they were resolved to resist. Conann granted this period of grace, but the Nemedians knew that eventually they would have to fight. They then sent messengers back to their homeland, which we are again told was in Greece! Before the 3 years were up, the king of Greece, who was related to Nemed by marriage, set out for Ireland with a great army and many druids and druidesses. The Greeks released strange 'venomous animals' (possibly snakes or scorpions) which were able to penetrate the walls of Conann's tower. The Fomorians were driven out and forced to fight. All, including Conann himself, were slain and their tower burned to the ground.

There then follows the second of the Irish flood references. No sooner were the dead of the battle buried than ships appeared carrying a further host of Fomorians, coming to reinforce Conann.

The weakened Nemedians resolved to hold the harbour and a pitched battle raged.[6]

> Such was the intensity of the fighting . . . that they did not perceive the gigantic wave of the tide filling-up on every side about them, for there was not any heed in their minds but for their battle feats alone; so that the majority were drowned and annihilated.

Only a single ship of the Fomorians survived together with thirty of the Nemedians. The survivors feared a return of the Fomorians, and began squabbling among themselves. They resolved to divide into three bands: one remained in Ireland, where they again fell subject to the Fomorians; another led by Briton Mael took refuge in Scotland – from which, according to the Irish, comes the name of Britain; and the third group returned to Greece.

To digress for a moment from the *Book of Invasions*, it is informative to examine these Fomorians in a little more detail. They are prominent elsewhere in Irish legend as a race of raiding pirates.[7] In one of the mythological tales, Elotha, a prince of the Fomorians, is described as a handsome golden-haired man; this is in stark contrast to descriptions of them elsewhere as ugly giants. In later literature the Fomorians became synonymous with raiders from Norway, who lived in the northern regions of ice and darkness. Indeed the Irish word *fomhoraigh* may mean a 'giant' or a 'pirate' and the Fomorians are sometimes represented as giants, as for example in 'Clochan na bh Fomhoraigh' – the Giant's Causeway. Analysed etymologically, the earliest sense of the word seems to imply 'men from under the sea'.[8] Though usually taken to imply that they are a purely mythical race, it is easy to see how such a name could originate. They were people who came from a place that now lies beneath the sea.

The *Book of Invasions* then describes Ireland as a 'desert' for a further period of 200 years. The descendants of the Nemedians then returned from Greece calling themselves the Firbolgs, a name which means 'men of the bags'. After a short interval, they were conquered by the Tuatha De Danann, or 'people of the goddess Danu'. These, it seems, were yet another branch of the Nemedians, returning to their old home.

After a battle at North Moytura, the Danaans drove the Firbolgs out of Ireland, whence we are told that they took refuge among the Fomorians in the islands of Arran, Islay, Rathlin and Man. The

Danaans then ruled Ireland for an indeterminate period. They suffered from weak kingship and this allowed their old enemies the Fomorians to return again and oppress them with their taxes; for the Fomorians seem never to have left the vicinity of Ireland. The struggles of the Danaans with the Fomorians are too long and complex to detail here; ultimately the Fomorians were defeated at the second battle of North Moytura and we hear no more of them in Irish legend. Early Irish literature portrays the Tuatha De Danann as a heroic and beautiful race; it is only under the influence of the Christian Church that they seem to degenerate into the mischievous Sidhe (pronounced 'Shee'), or 'faery folk'.

The final invaders were the Milesians. They are popularly identified with the Iron Age Celts who are considered to be the ancestors of the modern Scots and Irish; with their arrival we approach more closely to historical times. The body of Irish literature concerns the history of the Milesians themselves and clearly deals with events occurring shortly before the Christian period. At the earliest the sagas must be regarded as taking place in the Iron Age, whereas the Tuatha De Danann and the Fomorians were regarded, even by the early annalists, as ancient.

In the Irish sagas, the Danaans, as the former inhabitants of Ireland, become confused with the inhabitants of the Celtic 'Otherworld'. In many sagas, the heroes pass with ease between the real world and this mysterious place. It can be recognized under a number of names and guises. At one time it may be known as the 'Land of the Dead' or alternatively as the 'Land of the Living'. At other times it may be the 'Land of Many Colours', the 'Promised Land' or the 'Delightful Plain'. Perhaps the best known of all its many names is Tir na n Og – the 'Land of Youth'.

The Celts certainly believed in the rebirth of the soul. The Happy Otherworld was the place where they were reborn after death, to live among the gods. It should not be confused with the Christian heaven, for it is a much older concept. Douglas Hyde in his *Literary History of Ireland* states that he recorded some sixty different folk tales about the Otherworld, directly from the mouths of Irish peasants, during the latter half of the nineteenth century.[9] In the majority of the stories, it was viewed as a pleasant land located somewhere beneath the sea, but in others it was to be found beneath the hills or entered via the ancient burial mounds. It was believed that on the night of the Celtic feast of Samhain (31 October

– 1 November), the Otherworld was revealed and the dead souls could be seen once more. The festival of Hallowe'en is a direct survival from this pagan belief.

Some of the other names of the Otherworld are highly revealing. It is also the 'Land of Summer', for there is no winter in the Otherworld! It was also a great plain as is revealed by its name Mag Mell (the 'Plain of Happiness') or Mag Da Cheo (the 'Plain of the Two Mists'). But by far the most revealing name of all is Tir fo Thuinn, which means 'Land under the Wave'.

There is no need to trace back all these various references to the Otherworld, but a few of the best known stories merit a closer examination. Perhaps one of the most striking references occurs within a poem of the Finn Cycle, the story of *Oisin in the Land of Youth*. Although the surviving version dates only from the eighteenth century, it is clearly much older, having been passed on orally over the centuries. The hero Oisin (pronounced 'Ussheen'), son of Finn, can be dated to the early centuries AD.

The story begins with Oisin and Finn hunting on the shores of Loch Lena where they encounter a beautiful girl, riding upon a white horse. She announces that she is Niam of the Golden Hair, daughter of the king of the Land of Youth. She tells Oisin that she was drawn to him and begs him to return with her to the Land of Youth. Oisin is besotted by her and accepts the invitation willingly. Niam describes the Land of Youth to him thus.[10]

> Delightful is the land beyond all dreams,
> Fairer than aught thine eyes have seen.
> There all the year the fruit is on the tree
> And all year the bloom is on the flower.

So Oisin mounts the white horse behind Niam and they ride away. Eventually they reach the sea and the horse rides on over the waves until Ireland is left far behind them. Riding through a mist, they arrive in the Land of Youth.

Oisin's adventures in the Land of Youth are described at length, but after what seems to him to be a stay of a mere 3 weeks, he begins to long for home. Promising to return to her, he borrows Niam's white horse; but she warns him that when he reaches Ireland he must not dismount from the horse, nor ever touch the ground!

So Oisin sets off over the sea, riding back the way he had come and eventually arrives at his old homeland. Reaching his father's fort, he calls out for Finn and for the friends he knew, but they are all gone. He travels the length and breadth of Ireland in search of them, until finally he reaches Glanismole, near Dublin. There he meets up with some workmen who are trying to move a great boulder. To them he appears as a faery visitation – much taller and stronger than any of the men of Ireland. He helps them to shift the stone, but in doing so he slips from the saddle. Instantly, the horse vanishes and Oisin is transformed. Now he has become a weak and withered old man! When the people ask his name he tells them that he is Oisin, son of Finn mac Cumhail. They laugh aloud, for Finn and all his sons have been dead for hundreds of years.

In this delightful poem, which can scarcely be done justice to here, the nature of the Otherworld is clearly revealed. It is visited briefly in other early Irish sagas, such as *The Wooing of Etain* and *The Wasting Sickness of Cu Chulainn*. It also recurs in a number of later stories, where it is more clearly revealed as a land not beyond, but *under* the sea.

In a story dating from the eighth century called *Ruadh in the Land Under the Wave*, we hear of King Ruadh of Munster who is sailing around Scotland to meet the Norwegians.[11] All at once, his fleet of ships becomes stuck fast, unable to move in mid-ocean. They presume that something must be holding them fast from below and King Ruadh himself is chosen to go down and discover the cause. He dives into the sea and immediately finds himself in a great plain beneath the sea. There he finds nine lovely women who confess it was they who had stopped his ships, in order to lure him down.

Another short story by an unknown fourteenth-century author is called *The Air Ship*. Here the description almost resembles science fiction.[12] One day, while the monks of Clonmacnoise are meeting in their church, they sight a ship sailing through the sky above them as if it were on the sea! It drops anchor and the priests take hold of it. A man dives from the ship and swims down through the air, as if he were swimming through water. They grasp him and pull him down too. 'For God's sake let me go,' he pleads, 'for you are drowning me.' Then he swims away back to the ship carrying his anchor. One wonders what could have inspired such an odd tale? Here we see the Otherworld concept and the real world transposed, revealing the Otherworld as beneath the sea, but merely an ordinary world like our own.

The idea of the Otherworld as a great flowery plain with golden castles, inhabited by beautiful people, is seen again in *The Wooing of Etain*. This time the faery messenger from the Otherworld is a golden-haired man with sparkling grey eyes, adorned with gold and silver and riding upon a horse. The Plain of Ireland, we are told, beautiful though it may be, is but a desert compared to the Great Plain![13] An even more striking portrayal is to be found within one of the adventures of Cormac.[14]

A great mist was brought upon them in the midst of the plain, and Cormac found himself alone. There was a large fortress in the midst of the plain with a wall of bronze around it. In the fortress was a house of white silver, and it was half-thatched with the wings of white birds . . .

Then he saw another royal stronghold, and another wall of bronze around it. There were four palaces therein. He entered the fortress and saw the vast palace with its beams of bronze, its wattling of silver, and its thatch of the wings of white birds. Then he saw in the enclosure a shining fountain, with five streams flowing out of it, and the hosts in turn drinking its water.

Here we are told that there were at least two royal castles on the Great Plain. One was a fortress in the centre of the plain while elsewhere was another, much larger and containing the royal apartments. There are many parallels here with Plato's description of the palace of Atlantis, even down to the fountains within the palace. Once again Cormac encounters a lovely golden-haired girl, seemingly typical of the inhabitants of the Otherworld.

There is another branch of Irish literature, known as the Echtrae, or 'voyages'. They are usually regarded as tales of early voyages out into the Atlantic. From *The Book of the Dun Cow* dated about AD 1100, comes *The Voyage of Maeldun*. The voyage itself is pure fantasy, and seems only to serve as a vehicle for describing the existence of many fabulous places. Maeldun and his crew visit a succession of islands. Among them are an island inhabited by ants the size of horses, another where giant cattle are found, and many more. Hidden among them is yet another memory of the Irish Otherworld. One of the islands they encounter is an undersea island! They chance upon a sea as thin as mist which will not support the weight of their boat. As they look below they see a wonderful land with many roofed fortresses and herds of grazing cattle. Fearful that they might be drawn downwards, they sail on.

Of more significance is the *Voyage of Bran*, which dates from no later than the seventh century. It includes a poem written in a very archaic form of Irish which is said to have been first written down in ogham script by the hero of the story, Bran mac Febail himself. A mysterious woman appears in the house of Bran one day, while he is entertaining many kings and princes. All the doors are firmly locked and those inside have no idea where she came from, thus once again establishing her as a messenger from the Otherworld. She sings to them a poem describing the mysteries and wonders of 'The Pleasant Plain'.

The poem tells of a distant isle 'around which sea horses glisten'. The trees are eternally in blossom. There on a delightful plain, chariot races and boat races are held. There are bright colours everywhere, music in the air, and the sun shines.[15]

> Golden chariots on the sea plain
> Rising with the tide to the sun
> Chariots of silver in the plain of sports
> and of unblemished bronze

The last few verses of the poem are an invitation for Bran to visit the Land of Women, whereupon the strange female visitor vanishes again. Intrigued, Bran and his crew of twenty-seven depart across the sea in search of the Land of Women. After just 2 days and nights at sea, they encounter a strange man riding across the sea in a chariot. He is Manannan mac Lir, the Irish god of the sea, and he sings to Bran another poem, the twenty-eight verses of which provide the finest description of the Otherworld in the whole of Irish literature.[16]

> Bran deems it a marvellous beauty
> in his coracle across the clear sea:
> While to me in my chariot from afar
> it is a flowery plain on which he rows about.
>
> That which is a clear sea
> For the prowed skiff in which Bran is,
> That is a happy plain with a profusion of flowers
> to me from the chariot of two wheels.

Bran sees
the number of waves beating across the clear sea:
I myself see in Mag Mon
Rosy-coloured flowers without fault.

Sea-horses glisten in summer
As far as Bran has stretched his glance:
Rivers pour forth a stream of honey
in the land of Manannan son of Lir.

The meaning of these few verses could not be more clear. What seems to Bran to be only the sea on which he sails, to Manannan is Mag Mell, the Pleasant Plain. In the rest of the poem he taunts Bran that there are so many wondrous things that he cannot see. He cannot see the flowery plain, nor the many horses, nor the happy people. He cannot see that his boat is floating over an orchard of fruit trees!

In the final verse, Bran is invited to sail on to the Land of Women, which he will reach before sunset. Evidently this is not a part of the undersea world, but a real place that lies beyond. Bran sails on and eventually reaches an island. It turns out to be the Island of Merriment, where the inhabitants laugh and shout as he tries to land. They continue their journey and finally arrive at the Land of Women. They stay there for what seems like a year, enjoying the hospitality. The food does not diminish and there is a bed for every man.

One of the crew wishes to return home and Bran is persuaded to leave. He is warned by the women that he must not set foot on the soil of Ireland. When they arrive, the man who wished to go home is put ashore, but instantly he crumbles to dust as if he has been dead for many years! Bran and his friends remain on the ship and they converse with the crowd who have assembled on the shore. To them the *Voyage of Bran* is just one of the ancient stories they have learned from their fathers! Bran bids them farewell and sails off, never to be seen again.

This final theme is the same as that in the adventures of Oisin. Not only is the Pleasant Plain to be sought beneath the sea, but it also belongs to the past! One cannot visit it without travelling back in time and then there is no return; but there are many clues in the *Voyage of Bran* to tell us both when and where this place was.

Manannan mac Lir is one of the most important figures in Celtic mythology. His name means 'Manannan Son of the Sea', or son of the sea god Ler. In Irish legend, as we have seen, he is remembered as the Lord of the Sea, beneath which lay the Land of Youth. He was certainly one of the gods known to the Tuatha De Danann, for he is mentioned in the *Book of Invasions*. Lugh Lamfada, who led the Danaans against the Fomorians at the second battle of North Moytura, was said to have dwelt in the 'Land of the Living' throughout his boyhood. When he was old enough, he returned to become king. He brought back many magical gifts, among them Manannan's boat which would go wherever a man wished, his magical horse which could walk on water, and a terrible sword, which would cut through any armour.

Manannan is associated with the Otherworld again in the story of *The Wasting Sickness of Cu Chulainn*. In this story, it is the deserted wife of Manannan who falls in love with the warrior hero Cu Chulainn. Manannan is the ruler of an island kingdom within the Otherworld, which has been usurped by his queen. This may be in part historical, for elsewhere his name is strongly associated with the Isle of Man.

The Isle of Man (Welsh = *Manau*, Irish = *Manann*) traditionally takes its name from Manannan and the mist that frequently veils the island is 'Manannan's Cloak'. In Irish tales, he takes on the aspect of a demigod, who is able to visit the Otherworld as though it were just a part of his realm. However, in Manx tradition he appears in more sober guise as the first ruler of the Isle of Man. He was a great navigator and magician and is said to be buried in one of the many 'giant's graves' on the Isle of Man. He appears as an important figure in Welsh legend too, where he is known as Manawyddan son of Llyr. He loses his associations with the sea, but his Goidelic origins are confirmed by the retention of his father's name in the Irish genitive form. Here, then, we have a positive link between the Isle of Man and the lost plain beneath the sea.

Manannan is also recalled within a ninth- or tenth-century document known as *Cormac's Glossary*. By this late period the true meaning of Irish legend had long been lost, but Manannan as a historical figure was well remembered:[17]

[He was] a celebrated merchant who was in the Isle of Man. He was the best pilot in the west of Europe. He used to know by studying the heavens the period which would be the fine weather and the bad weather, and when each of these two times would change.

Another Irish manuscript, *The Yellow Book of Lecan*, describes him in similar vein.[18] Here we are told that he was also a druid, who employed science to observe the sky; and also that he traded between Erin, Alban and Manann.

By applying a little, admittedly circular, logic, it is possible to estimate the era in which Manannan must have lived. The date of the Neolithic flood catastrophe has been established here by a number of methods. Arguments have also been put forward which would suggest that the Isle of Man did not exist as an island before 3100 BC but was a part of the mainland, surrounded by a flat plain. Logically therefore, Manannan cannot be older than his island.

Manannan seems to have been no mere weather forecaster, but a druid who understood astronomy. His ability to predict the best season for sailing is a clue that he lived in the era when the climate was ruled by the rhythm of the 7-year seasons. Manannan, with his ability to navigate by the stars, must have stumbled upon the secret of predicting the Long Seasons and their effect on the weather.

We may therefore place Manannan somewhere in the period between 3100 BC and 1000 BC. His legendary status as the first king of Man would suggest an early date. The Irish legends suggest that the earliest inhabitants of the Isle of Man were the Fomorians, with whom a number of the Firbolgs later sought refuge. According to Nennius: 'Bolg with his people held the Isle of Man, and other islands about.' Manannan himself may therefore have been a Fomorian. The sequence of the *Book of Invasions* may then be used to attempt a closer dating of Manannan's era.

The Flood is fixed within the Irish legendary chronology by the experiences of Partholon and the tribe of Nemed. The reference made to the golden tower on the sea is the clue here. Since it is clear that a tower could scarcely have been constructed on the seabed, it must be assumed that it was originally built on dry land which subsequently became inundated. We are told that the tidal range alternately exposed and covered this tower. Clearly this is not a reference to the tides experienced today, for any structure that could be submerged by the modern tidal range would scarcely merit being called a tower at all! This must be a memory of the far

greater fluctuations that would be experienced if the Earth's rotation was wobbling; there is no other way to produce such an effect.
It would date the migration of the Nemedians to the 20-year period
following an impact event; but which one?

Even after the Nemedians settled in Ireland, the land continued
to be affected by gradual changes in geodesy. The many 'lake-
bursts' recorded in the *Book of Invasions* indicate a local tilting of
the crust. The settlement of the Nemedians lasted for two generations, followed by 200 years when Ireland was supposedly
deserted. The Firbolgs then colonized Ireland, only to be forced to
take refuge in the islands by the invasion of the Tuatha De Danann.
Manannan mac Lir may therefore be tentatively dated to some 300
years after the Flood, or about 2800 BC. By his time, as the legends
indicate, the Otherworld plain was already lost beneath the sea.

The dating of the Flood in Irish mythology may also be
attempted by another route. In one of the romance sagas, *The
Wooing of Etain*, there is a curious reference to two 7-year periods
of abnormally windy weather. The story is highly complex and rich
in detail. It reads like a garbled semi-historical narrative incorporat-
ing a number of related stories and themes, and really needs to be
read in its entirety. It commences in the time of a famous king of
the Tuatha De Danann known as the Dagda, and his son Oengus
Macc Oc. Ostensibly the story revolves around Etain, a princess of
Ulster, born of the faery mounds, and with hair the colour of red
gold. Etain is courted by Mider of the Tuatha De, but his wife
Fuamnach is jealous and employs her druid magic to transform the
beautiful Etain into a fly!

In an attempt to keep Mider and Etain apart, Fuamnach brings
on fierce winds which blow the fly away. For 7 years there is no
place where the poor fly, who is really the Princess Etain, can alight
to rest. Eventually the 7 years are up and the fly comes to rest again
on the tunic of Macc Oc at Bruig na Boinde. But Fuamnach
summons up 7 more years of wind to blow the fly away once more.

The fairy palace of Bruig na Boinde is traditionally equated with
the Newgrange mound on the River Boyne. Since this monument
has been securely dated by the archaeologists to about 3100 BC, the
events in the legend of Etain cannot be older than its construction.

The reference to a 7-year seasonal cycle is also too great a
coincidence to be ignored. It is possible that it is a coded reference
to the same period of climatic upheaval as is remembered in the

biblical story of Joseph. The arguments for placing this event at a later episode of rotational instability have already been examined; the best guess date would be at some time around 2300 BC. However, the story of Etain is set unequivocally within the era of the Tuatha De Danann and the Firbolgs are remembered within it too. It may therefore be assumed that the Danaans were already settled in Ireland well before this date. This fits quite well within the chronology previously established from the *Book of Invasions*, suggesting a date of about 2800 BC for their arrival in Ireland. It is almost as if the references to the strong winds were deliberately woven into the story in order to preserve its era.

The *Book of Invasions* claims that all these legendary early settlers came from 'Greece'. The Nemedians, the Firbolgs and the Tuatha De Danann all apparently started out from there. Geoffrey of Monmouth, in his *History of the Kings of Britain*, tells of the settlement of Britain by Brutus and his Trojans. Although Geoffrey's book has long since ceased to be taken seriously as a historical document, it contains many fundamental parallels with the Irish legendary history. Britain, we are told, was also a desert, populated by only 'a few giants' before the arrival of Brutus.

It is interesting at this point to consider the possibility that the Tuatha De Danann may be the same Greek race whom Homer referred to as Danaoi. He refers to the Greeks of the Mycenean period as *Achaioi*, *Argeioi* and *Danaoi*. It has been proposed that the name Danaoi or Danaans derives from an Indo-European root word meaning 'water' or 'river'.[19] This root is found in a whole spate of river names throughout Europe and beyond. In Greece, it is to be found in the River *Eridanus*. Further north, in the Indo-European heartland of Scythia, we find the Rivers Dnieper (*Danapris*) and Danube (*Danubius*). Archaeologists now recognize the Danaoi as a pre-Greek, Indo-European tribe which intruded into Greece during the third millennium BC.[20]

No clear references exist in classical literature to support an Aegean origin for an element of the British or Irish population, but really this is not to be expected. The chronology derived here from the Irish legends points to an association not with the later Mycenean and Dorian Greeks, but with the earlier pre-Greek inhabitants of the Aegean, the Pelasgians, the Cretans or the Trojans.

A reference to the three floods of Ireland is found in an Irish place-name legend, the legend of Tonn Clidna or 'Cleena's Wave'.

This small bay on the coast of County Cork is said to be named after the Princess Clidna, who had the misfortune to be lying asleep in a boat just as the Flood struck. We are told that she came from 'the Pleasant Plain of the Land of Promise'. In their translation, Tom Peate Cross and Clark Harris Slover described one version of the legend:[21]

> This is the time at which the illimitable seaburst arose and spread throughout the regions of the present world. Because there were at that season Erin's three great floods, namely Clidna's flood and Ladru's and Baile's; but not in the same hour did they arise: Ladru's flood was the middle one. The flood pressed on and divided throughout the Land of Erin till it caught the boat and the damsel asleep on the beach. So there she was drowned, Clidna the Shapely, Genann's daughter, from whom 'Tonn Clidna' ['Clidna's wave'] is named.

The form of this tale is not unlike that of a Welsh triad. Quite what is intended by the reference to three floods is not at all clear. This enigmatic tale seems to suggest that Erin was divided in two by the first of the three floods. Was the name first applied to a much larger island which formerly included the whole of Britain and Ireland, or at least to the western part of it? Three great floods are similarly recalled in the Gaelic folklore of the Outer Hebrides, as is the time when the Hebrides were linked together as a single island.[22]

Neither can it be a coincidence that the former link between the north of Ireland and Scotland is remembered in legend. The Giant's Causeway, a promontory of rectangular basalt columns between Portrush and Ballycastle on the Antrim coast, has a famous legend associated with it. The Irish name means 'The Stepping Stones of the Fomorians'. The local folklore recalls it as the start of a road built by the giants between Ireland and Scotland, where similar basalt rock formations are found on the island of Staffa. There is no doubt that the stones are entirely natural.

A complementary legend comes from the island of Islay, which takes its name from the Princess Ila.[23] She is said to have walked across to the island from Ireland on stepping stones that formed in the sea as she walked. The unfortunate lady later drowned while bathing and her grave is said to be marked by a standing stone near Ardbeg. It is indeed remarkable that legends of a land-bridge between Britain and Ireland should persist here, in the only place where the seabed is shallow enough for one to have existed. There are no comparable legends to be found where the strait is at its narrowest, between Galloway and the Ards Peninsula. The association with the Fomorians also reinforces the early dating of this land-bridge.

Possibly, then, it would be a mistake to differentiate too strongly between the Irish and British populations at this early period. Although the equivalent British legendary history is not so well preserved, it is entirely possible that these same tribal groups settled in Britain too.[24] Britain is an obvious stopping-off point on any migration between the Continent and Ireland and it is quite likely that we also glimpse a little of early Britain within these Irish stories.

Wherever the various invading groups originated they encountered an indigenous population in their new homeland: the people referred to as Fomorians. It is from these survivors of the time before the Flood that the legends of the Otherworld most probably derive. We already have some information about these aborigines. They were clearly not a single homogeneous race, but a complex mixture of races, including some who are referred to as giants.

From the various Irish Otherworld sagas it is possible to discern a ruling class who lived in the great castles and palaces. They were of tall stature, at least taller and more robust than the Irish. They seem to have possessed grey eyes and golden yellow hair. Perhaps they were one and the same with the Fomorians who are sometimes also described this way, but the stories are somewhat contradictory.

In their folklore and mythology, the Irish have preserved a glimpse of the Neolithic world. They recall an age when the seasons were kinder and life was much easier; a land of eternal springtime where trees and flowers bloomed and crops grew in the fields all the year round. Again this fits best with what we know about the climate of the fourth millennium BC. In the various memories of the Otherworld, they recall a great plain, lost beneath the sea. At other times this same place is also discernible as the Land of the Dead. There is, too, a memory of the three great floods of Ireland and of the 'illimitable seaburst' that divided Ireland from Britain. These may be correlated with the flood legends from other parts of the world, to yield further clues to the date when these momentous events occurred.

14

Sunken Cities – Lost Lands

When the early Anglo-Saxon invaders arrived in Britain in the sixth century, they conquered and absorbed a Romano-British population that had already lost its own history. Further north, the Scots, invading from Ireland, steadily drove the indigenous Picts and Caledonians into the north-east corner of the island, before eventually absorbing them within the kingdom of Scotland. The earliest Scottish history looks to Ireland for its inspiration and the origin of the Picts and Caledonians is utterly obscure. Their myths and legends are lost to us, but we do know that they called their country Alban, or Albion: the ancient name of Britain.

Only the Welsh have preserved something of the remotest British past. While we should be thankful for what we have, the nature of the Welsh legends is so intangible as to frustrate all attempts to make historical sense of them. The pre-Roman language spoken in southern Britain was Brythonic, a Celtic language ancestral to modern Welsh; and much of the amorphous material that survived the Roman suppression of druidism was preserved in poetry and prose by the earliest Welsh bards. These traditions were passed on orally from generation to generation as Brythonic evolved into Welsh, to be finally written down in a stable form in medieval Wales.

The period between the abandonment of Britain by the Romans in AD 410 and the establishment of the English kingdoms is a dark age in British history. The history of the next few centuries is almost a blank and little more is known about this period than about pre-Roman times. The most important historical source from this era is undoubtedly the Welshman who is usually known by his Latin name of Nennius. His *Historia Brittonum* is not only a valuable source of contemporary history, but can also tell us much about the poor state of historical knowledge surviving at the end of the eighth century. He informs us modestly that he 'made a heap' of everything he could find about history. The Britons, he tells us, 'had no skill, and set down no record in books'.

Nennius criticized most of the Welsh historians of his own day for leaving the subject even more obscure than they had found it! Sadly none of the works he criticizes have survived for us to compare and his sources are largely unknown. In the pages of Nennius, we find both the earliest references to the Irish *Book of Invasions* and the first reference to King Arthur, to whom he ascribes a sixth century date. Upon this dearth of real historical knowledge, the later romantic tales of King Arthur were to bloom.

In the twelfth century, Geoffrey of Monmouth drew upon Welsh and Breton sources, possibly including Nennius, for his *History of the Kings of Britain*. As he wrote in Latin, Geoffrey's work found a wide audience in England and France, which seized upon his work to fill the historical vacuum. While no one has ever suggested that Geoffrey invented the whole thing, sadly much of his 'history' simply does not agree with other sources and has to be rejected. But many of the legends he relates were clearly borrowed from contemporary Celtic sources; including the so-called *Prophecies of Merlin*, which hold a rather interesting reference to a time of famine, drought and fluctuating sea levels:[1]

> The sea over which men sail to Gaul shall be contracted to a narrow channel. A man on any one of the two shores will be audible to a man on the other, and the land-mass of the island will grow greater.
> The secrets of the creatures who live under the sea shall be revealed and Gaul will tremble for fear.

Much of the later Arthurian literature that followed Geoffrey must be regarded as mere fiction. The true written sources of Welsh (and indeed British) legend are to be found within the surviving medieval manuscripts. The oldest of these, the *Black Book of Carmarthen*, dating from about 1170–1230, contains a wealth of ancient poetry. The oldest version of the Welsh prose stories, *The Mabinogion*, is found in the *Red Book of Hergest* (*c*.1400) and the incomplete *White Book of Rhydderch* (*c*.1325). The two other prime sources are the *Book of Taliesin* (*c*.1250) and the *Book of Aneurin* (*c*.1250). These preserve the poems of these two bards, whom Nennius tells us were actively composing poetry during the sixth century. A further useful source of history and legend are the enigmatic Welsh triads.

Although it is difficult to find historical sequence in the Welsh legends, there is at least plenty of material to work on. For the purposes of the present discussion, it is of more importance to seek out the many references to floods and catastrophic events that lie embedded within the Welsh sources. Here, too, we find plenty of timeless references to the Celtic Otherworld within the stories of *The Mabinogion*. In the many local folk tales from around Wales, legends abound of sunken cities and lost lands around the British coast and of cities drowned beneath the Welsh lakes.

There are several such local legends, and many conflicting versions of each. One of the best known is the legend of Llys Helig in Conway Bay. The story goes that the rocks of Llys Helig, opposite Penmaenmawr, mark the site of the lost palace of Helig ap Glannog. Helig's palace formerly stood in a most fertile and fruitful valley and he and his family are said to have taken shelter on the hill above Penmaenmawr to escape a sudden inundation by the sea. However, there is no doubt that the rocks of Llys Helig are entirely natural and the immediate source of the legend can be traced back no further than a few paragraphs in a local survey, written about the year 1620.

Another legendary lost palace is said to lie beneath the waters of Caernarvon Bay. This is Caer Aranrhod, said to be the castle of that name mentioned in the mabinogi of *Math the son of Mathonwy*. The localization of the legendary palace in Conway Bay was investigated by F.J. North, who concluded that the modern form of the legend could be traced to a mistake made in a map of Wales published in 1568.[2]

Further south in Cardigan Bay, we find the more substantial legends of a lost land, known as Cantre'r Gwaelod, or 'the Lowland Hundred'. The story has a complex history, but in its essence it describes the sudden inundation of a triangle of land that formerly existed between the Lleyn Peninsula and the Cardiganshire coast around Aberystwyth. In the popular versions of the legend, the submerged pebble ridge known as Sarn Badrig is said to be the remains of a causeway which formerly extended right down to the lost land. But again there is no doubt that Sarn Badrig and the neighbouring Sarn y bwch and Sarn Cynvelyn further south are entirely natural features. The name itself is significant as it refers to the old Welsh unit of land, a cantref or hundred, representing an area of about 460 square kilometres.[3] This represents nowhere near as much submerged land as the extant versions of the legend would suggest.

According to the popular form of the legend, Cantre'r Gwaelod was a fertile plain, lying below sea level, which was protected from the sea only by a huge embankment of earth. It is said to have contained sixteen cities and must therefore have been a substantial tract of land. The lord of the Cantref was Gwyddno Garanhir and the keeper of the embankment was named Seithenin. One evening after a great feast, Seithenin lay in a drunken stupor and neglected to close the sluice gates. The sea burst through; Cantre'r Gwaelod was lost for ever beneath the sea and only a few inhabitants survived to tell the tale. The church bells, it is said, may still be heard whenever the sea is calm.

The roots of the Cantre'r Gwaelod legend do seem to be genuinely old, although the references are confusing and do not agree with the popular form of the legend. In Welsh legend, names and characters survive well, sequence and consistency of detail do not! Gwyddno and Seithenin are mentioned in this context in a poem in the thirteenth century *Black Book of Carmarthen*. Seithenin is compelled to look upon the fury of the sea, which has covered Gwyddno's Plain. The poem blames not Seithenin, but a maiden named Mererid (or Margaret) for the inundation, having 'let it loose after feasting'. Seithenin is recalled as a somewhat dull-witted individual and he is celebrated in a triad as one of The Three Arrant Drunkards of the Island of Britain.

This singularly Welsh catastrophe is popularly thought to have occurred during the sixth century AD, but there is little evidence in favour of this. Everything of importance in Welsh and Arthurian legend has come to be ascribed to this dark period by more recent authors. The contemporary historical sources, Gildas and Nennius, make no mention either of the lost land in Cardigan Bay, nor of Llys Helig, or of any other serious flood catastrophe. Neither is there any physical confirmation that the coastline of Wales has altered since Roman times. It must be remembered that the conquest of Anglesey by Suetonius is recorded by Tacitus and it is clear that the Romans had to cross the Menai Straits in order to take the island.[4] The true inspiration behind all these legends must be regarded as far older than the sixth century.

There is another important British flood legend: that of the lost land of Lyonesse. Cornish tradition relates that a rich and fertile land once existed between Land's End and the Isles of Scilly. Lyonesse was said to be densely populated, with great cities and 140 churches, and the Seven Stones rocks off Land's End are said to mark the site of a large city.[5] When the sea suddenly rose up and overwhelmed Lyonesse, only one man, Trevilian, was able to escape by fleeing to dry land on a swift horse ahead of the waves. Recent theorists have attempted to rationalize Lyonesse as a reference to the Isles of Scilly where there is clear evidence of submergence since Neolithic times. Submerged walls and field boundaries are discernible in the shallow waters between the islands at low tide.

One other legend of this type must also be included, and that comes from across the Channel in Brittany. Thought to be derived from a popular Breton ballad, it is associated with Pointe du Raz, near Quimper. There, a city called Ker-Is is said to have been lost to a sudden inundation of the sea in retribution for the sins of its inhabitants. Ker-Is had become so prosperous from its sea-borne trade that its inhabitants divided out their corn with silver measures.

The legend bears a strong similarity to the Welsh and Cornish versions. The ruler of Ker-Is was King Grallon. His daughter Dahut was persuaded by her devious lover to steal the keys of the sluice gates that held back the sea. The keys were then used by the enemies of Ker-Is to open the sluices and flood the city; but just as the waves were about to overwhelm his palace, Grallon and his daughter mounted a swift horse and were able to escape. As they fled, the ghost of St Gwenole appeared before them and compelled Grallon to cast the devil (his daughter) into the sea. There are elements here of both the Cantre'r Gwaelod and Lyonesse legends. The city is drowned by the opening of sluices and the hero escapes just in time on horseback. This suggests a common origin for all the stories which dates to before the time when settlers from Cornwall arrived in Brittany.[6]

Recollections of these ancient inundations are also found in a triad, the Exeter Triad, which unlike the others is unknown from any Welsh source. It is preserved only by its Latin translation in a manuscript currently housed in the library of Exeter Cathedral: the thirteenth-century *Chronica de Wallia*.[7]

These are the kingdoms which the sea destroyed: The kingdom of Teithi Hen, son of Gwynnan, king of Kaerrihog. That kingdom was called at the time the Realm of Teithi Hen; it was between St. David's and Ireland. No one escaped from it, neither men nor animals, except Teithi Hen alone with his horse; afterwards for all the days of his life he was weak from fear.

The second kingdom was that of Helig son of Glannog, it was between Cardigan and Bardsey, and as far as St. Davids. That land was very good, fertile and level, and it was called Maes Maichgen; it lay from the mouth [of the Ystwyth?] to Llyn, and up to Aberdovey.

The sea destroyed a third kingdom: the kingdom of Rhedfoe son of Rheged.

As demonstrably the oldest surviving source of the legend, the Exeter Triad deserves to be treated with some respect. But the confusion in the early British sources is apparent. Here, it is Teithi Hen who escapes on his horse, and his kingdom lies not at the tip of Brittany, nor the Cornish peninsula, but off St David's Head in Carmarthen. The second kingdom, in Cardigan Bay, is recognizable as Cantre'r Gwaelod but is ruled by that same Helig whose palace was supposedly lost in Conway Bay! The location of the lost kingdom of Rhedfoe must remain a mystery. We are given no insight as to when these catastrophes occurred or whether they should all be regarded as contemporaneous events.

The sources of all these Welsh legends were thoroughly investigated by F.J. North in his book *Sunken Cities* and his conclusions are generally accepted here. He concludes that while the immediate sources for the Welsh legends are comparatively recent, the degree of divergence within them suggests that their true inspiration is ancient.

As has been discussed in earlier chapters, the physical evidence from around the coasts of Britain points to submergence during Neolithic times. The submerged forest deposits along the Welsh coast suggest that sudden drowning took place at only two periods: around 3100 BC and possibly again around 1600 BC.[8] There is no evidence of coastal changes at a more recent period. If the legends of Cantre'r Gwaelod are indeed based on a real flood catastrophe then we can only conclude that it occurred at one or other of these periods. It may be that the legend in its modern form is a composite containing aspects of both an earlier and a later submergence.

Although Cantre'r Gwaelod is undeniably a flood legend, it is not of the same order as the memories of the Great Flood. There are other myths from Welsh sources that fill this role. There is good cause to believe that the Britons possessed their own version of the flood of Noah, long before the arrival of the Christian religion, and evidence of this is found in the triads. Witness the triad of the Three Awful Events of the Island of Britain:[9]

> First, the bursting of the lake of waters, and the overwhelming of the face of all lands; so that all mankind were drowned, excepting Dwyvan and Dwyvach, who escaped in a naked vessel (without sails) and of them the Island of Britain was re-peopled.
> The second was the consternation of the tempestuous fire, when the earth split asunder, to Annwn (the lower region) and the greatest part of all living was consumed.
> The third was the scorching summer, when the woods and plants were set on fire, by the intense heat of the Sun, and multitudes of men, and beasts and kinds of birds, and reptiles, and trees and plants were irrecoverably lost.

It must be said of the Welsh triads that some scholars doubt their authenticity.[10] Edward Williams (Iolo Morganwg), who collated them for the *Myvyrian Archaiology* in 1801, stands accused of inventing a whole series of mythological triads including the one above. He claimed that they were taken from a document of 1601 which reproduced the twelfth-century *Book of Caradoc*. Sadly this cannot be substantiated, but Iolo deserves to be given the benefit of the doubt.

The triads may represent a memory technique employed by the druids to preserve oral history by committing facts to memory in groups of three. Many of the themes recalled in the triads are then further explained within the prose stories of the mabinogi. Another reason for suspecting later contamination is the apparent presence of Christian influence, as in the triad of the Three Chief Master Works of the Island of Britain.[11]

> The ship of Nevydd Nav Neivon, which carried in it a male and female of all living, when the lake of waters burst forth;
> The drawing of the avanc to land out of the lake by the branching oxen of Hu Gadarn, so that the lake burst no more;
> And the stones of Gwyddon Ganhebon, on which were read the arts and sciences of the world.

Understandably, Nevydd has long been equated with the biblical Noah and he may also be equivalent to the Irish Nemed; but we cannot know how old the triad really is. In that previously quoted, the survivor of the Flood is Dwyvan (or Dylan), who has been similarly equated with the Greek Deucalion.

Another triad tells how, after the Flood, Hu Gadarn brought the Cymry to the island of Britain from Asia Minor, where they formerly inhabited the regions around the Bosporus.[12] By analogy with the flood legends elsewhere, we must place this legendary migration of the Cymry to some time early in the third millennium BC.

However, there are some uniquely British features in the triads which give them a degree of authenticity. The Flood is seen as merely the bursting of a great lake, the Lake of Waters (Llynn Llion), namely the ocean. It is easy to see how this belief originated, as the overflowing of lakes and wells is a common feature of both Welsh and Irish folklore. This must be seen as an indication that the Welsh flood legends are genuinely ancient. They must have originated at a period when lesser lake-bursts were a commonplace occurrence. The Cymry may have held a cosmology belief which modelled the Flood as merely a much larger manifestation of the lake-bursts with which they were familiar.

The terms 'Welsh' and 'British' must be considered largely synonymous before the arrival of the English invaders. The British people are predominantly of Celtic and pre-Celtic stock and the Brythonic language was spoken throughout Britain before and during Roman times, as far north as the Forth–Clyde line. The legends preserved through the medium of Welsh literature should not therefore be seen as of interest only to the Welsh. They represent the beliefs held throughout Britain during the most ancient times.

According to Julius Caesar, whose commentaries give us our earliest insight into pre-Roman Britain, the tribes of southern Britain were the descendants of Belgic invaders who had arrived there only a few centuries before his own time.[13] Importantly, he tells us that the interior of the island was inhabited by tribes who claimed, on the strength of their own oral tradition, to be aboriginal. This is clearly at odds with the Welsh triads, which recall the ancient immigration of the Cymry into Britain. It may indicate that at least a part of the British population preserved traditions dating from a much earlier time. There is no legend which recognizably records the arrival of the continental Celts in Britain. The Britons clearly did not consider themselves to be of central European origin and never called themselves Celts. Before the adoption of Brythonic, whenever that may have been, the inhabitants of Britain spoke a non-Celtic, possibly even non-Indo-European language, which may have survived in the north of Scotland as late as the Pictish period. Little is known of this language except a few indecipherable ogham inscriptions on the early Pictish symbol stones.

The identification of these aboriginal tribes is problematic. One is tempted to equate them with the non-Celtic Caledonians whom Agricola encountered in Scotland, north of the Forth–Clyde line.[14] But the Mythological Triads describe the Caledonians as just another invading race.[15] Originally there were three related tribes in Britain, of which the Cymry were one. Of the aborigines, perhaps the only glimpse we have comes from the Albanic Duan, a document attached to some versions of Nennius, which describes the people of northern Britain.[16]

> O, all ye learned of Alban,
> Ye well-skilled host of yellow hair
> What was the first invasion?
> Is it known to you?
> which took the land of Alban?

We have few other clues about the physical appearance and organization of the pre-Roman tribes of Britain and clearly much could have changed over the preceding 3,000 years. One example, though, is the Iceni tribe who inhabited East Anglia, and their famous queen Boudicca. The revolt of the Iceni against the Roman occupation is well documented. Boudicca is described by Dio Cassius as very tall with long fair or reddish hair, much as Tacitus later described the 'sandy-haired' Caledonians.[17, 18] This is revealing, for red or auburn hair is not characteristic of Indo-European peoples. Tacitus cites the claim of Boudicca to be descended from 'mighty men' and her further assertion that 'We British are accustomed to women commanders.'[19] One may also cite the example of Cartimandua, queen of the northern tribe, the Brigantes, at the time of the Roman conquest as evidence that women played an equal role in the political life of the northern British tribes.[20]

It is significant that stories in the Welsh *Mabinogion* refer to the

British Isles as 'the Three Islands of the Mighty'. Rhys considered this to be a British Celtic translation of the name Pict or Pecht in the sense of 'mighty warrior'. Boudicca is therefore virtually telling us that she was descended from the aboriginal stock.[21]

In addition, there is Caesar's claim that the British customs included polygamous marriages, with wives being shared between groups of ten or twelve men.[22] In such a society, paternity would have been quite impossible to determine, and it would be similarly unworkable to operate a custom of inheritance through the male line. Later writers do not confirm the occurrence of this polygamous practice within the Roman province. We do know, however, that the custom of royal succession through the female line survived in the north right up to the end of the Pictish kingdom.[23] It may be that Caesar's remark was applicable only to the tribes of the north and not to the Belgic tribes in the south. These matrilineal inheritance customs must be regarded as yet a further relic of pre-Celtic society.

In this context, it is again significant to note the Irish traditions of a 'Land of Women' located somewhere across the sea. It is mentioned in the *Voyage of Bran* and is often regarded as a part of the Otherworld. Another Irish saga, *The Wooing of Emer*, tells how the hero Cu Chulainn was sent abroad to Alban in his youth to be taught the arts of war by various female instructresses.

The reference to Alban in this context implies the Pictish kingdom in northern Britain. The Irish seem to have originally applied the name Albu to the whole of Britain, but later it was reserved only for the northern part, still later to Pictland alone. The survival of a matriarchal society there into historical times is a further piece of useful evidence. If the legendary Land of Women may be equated with northern Britain then it reinforces the earlier identification of the Irish Sea region as the location of the Celtic Otherworld.

In considering the aboriginal inhabitants of Britain, mention must also be made of the mythical 'giants'. If we ignore the many exaggerated giant legends that abound, then we must face the possibility that these giants represent a real race of men. The Irish Fomorii are sometimes described as ugly giants who came to Ireland in ships, and a saga of the Irish Mythological Cycle describes three hideous Manx giants.[24] Geoffrey of Monmouth relates the legend that Brutus and his Trojans were offered the Island of Albion (i.e. Britain) by the goddess Diana. It is described as 'an island in the sea, formerly occupied by giants. Now it lies empty and ready for your people.'

The Otherworld in Welsh myth may generally be recognized under the name Annwn. It is not always the happy place that it seems to be in the Irish sagas but there are still many similarities to be found. In Bardic philosophy, which claims to be the inheritor of the ancient tradition, Annwn is the Land of the Dead, a kind of pagan heaven to which dead souls retire. In later literature, the name survived, to be equated with Hades, perhaps following Roman influence, but none of the surviving Welsh sources actually depicts Annwn in this gloomy fashion. Usually it is closer to the Irish model of a timeless paradise, and is regularly visited by the hero figures of legend.

Perhaps the example that best shows the darker aspect of Annwn is a poem attributed to the bard Taliesin, called *The Spoils of Annwn*. The poem is difficult to interpret, but seems to describe a journey into Annwn by the hero Arthur and his men, which goes disastrously wrong. The object of the exercise is to retrieve (or steal) a magic cauldron belonging to the ruler of Annwn. This cauldron, or grail, is a familiar concept throughout Welsh and Arthurian literature and was evidently of immense religious and symbolic value. In Irish legend it may be equated to the Cauldron of the Dagda and in the later medieval grail legends it masquerades as a Christian relic!

The cauldron lies hidden somewhere in a fortress within Annwn. We are told that Arthur and three shiploads of the men of Britain made the journey there, but only seven men returned. The structure of the poem reveals that the fortress was known by a number of names. These are Caer Siddi, 'the Fairy Fortress'; Caer Fedwid, 'Fortress of the Mead-feast'; Caer Pedryfan, 'the Intractable Fortress'; and finally Caer Wydr, 'the Glass Fortress'. We are not told whether Arthur succeeded in his quest, but we must assume that he did, as the cauldron reappears in many other stories.

The reference to a glass fortress is significant, for Nennius also mentions it in his version of the Irish *Book of Invasions*. The story according to Nennius is recognizably the same as the Irish story of Nemed. In the Irish version, the Nemedians sight a golden tower in the midst of the sea and seek plunder; but according to Nennius the tower was of glass, not gold, and he associates the experience not with the Nemedians, but with the later Milesians. He also has their point of origin as Spain rather than Greece; indeed he brings all the Irish invaders over from Spain.

The similarities within these stories are striking. In the Irish version, the Nemedians raid the tower in pursuit of gold, but all except a few are drowned. In *The Spoils of Annwn* the heroes take ship in search of a golden cauldron and only seven escape drowning. Does the Welsh poem recall the same legendary feat as the Irish story of Nemed? It may be significant that Plato also describes a cauldron, or bowl in his narratives, within his description of the religious ceremonies of the royal house. The bowl was used by the kings of Atlantis during their gatherings, to hold the mixture of wine and blood from the sacrificial bull. Was this perhaps the 'mead-feast' alluded to in the Welsh poem?

A possible variant of the same adventure is recalled in the second branch of *The Mabinogion*, within the story of *Branwen the Daughter of Llyr*. However in this version, it is Ireland which rather hazily replaces Annwn as the location of the cauldron. It was the property of Bran the Blessed, king of all Britain, who claimed to have received it from a man who had brought it over from Ireland. He in turn had obtained it from a yellow-haired man of giant stature (clearly establishing him as an Otherworld figure) who lived near a lake called the Lake of the Cauldron. The cauldron is given to Matholwch, king of Ireland, as part of his dowry on the occasion of his marriage to Branwen, the daughter of Bran.

Later in the story, the men of Britain (here called the Island of the Mighty) learn that Branwen is being mistreated by her new husband and they mount an expedition to Ireland to rescue her. To cut a long story short, the cauldron is smashed into four pieces during a battle and although the Britons are victorious, only seven are left alive to return home. We are given their names, and among them is none other than Manawyddan, the Welsh equivalent of Manannan mac Lir.

The cauldron is named the Cauldron of Rebirth. It has the power that any soldier who is slain in battle may be reborn if his body is cast into it. There are similar references to the cauldron in other Welsh stories such as that in the mabinogi of *Manawyddan Son of Llyr*. In this tale, a tall fortress suddenly appears, we are told, 'where no fortress had been before', a sign that the castle is really a part of the Otherworld. Within the empty fortress Manawyddan discovers the cauldron:[25]

What he did see, as if in the middle of the fortress, was a fountain with marble stone around it, and a golden bowl fastened to four chains, the bowl set over a marble slab and the chains extending upwards so that he could see no end to them.

There is an interesting convergence of legends here. A very similar scene is also recalled in the story of *The Lady of the Fountain*. It is surely stretching coincidence too far if these legends do not recall the same scene as Plato's narrative. In all these stories we find a fountain, a bowl and a pillar of stone, all situated within a fortress.

It would be far too onerous a task to pursue all the points of interest within the stories of the mabinogi, but a few of the more crucial points must be examined, as they are too important to leave out. One should not look for much consistency within the Welsh tales, for they are all garbled and full of logical paradoxes. It is generally agreed that their subject matter is at least partly historical and very ancient. The stories were built around real events, places and characters, presumably for the purpose of preserving them.

Annwn is unquestionably the same place as the Irish Otherworld, for it has the same timeless quality and is populated by the same tall, golden-haired race. Unlike the Irish Otherworld, Annwn does not lie beneath the sea, but seems to be merely an extension of the land area of Wales! The heroes simply ride into it on horseback, or else they wander into it imperceptibly. One moment the characters of the mabinogi are in a recognizable part of Britain, the next we discover that they have strayed into the Otherworld. The geography of the stories is strange and unreal.

In the first branch of *The Mabinogion*, *Pwyll, Lord of Dyfed*, the hero of this particular tale, meets Arawn, a king of Annwn, while out hunting one day. His dogs are beaten to the quarry by a pack of strange white hounds with red ears. Pwyll drives them away and sets his own dogs upon the stag, but Arawn appears and rebukes him. To make amends for his discourtesy, Pwyll is persuaded to change places with Arawn for a year and a day and return to Annwn in his place. There he will have to fight with Havgan, a king of a neighbouring part of Annwn, who is threatening Arawn's land. He must kill him with a single blow, for a second blow will revive him stronger than ever. In return for this service, Arawn promises Pwyll the loveliest woman he has ever seen, to be his wife. Pwyll agrees and returns to Annwn in the guise of Arawn, while Arawn poses as Pwyll. The names of Arawn and Annwn may be preserved in the modern place-names Arran and Annan, both of which border the Irish Sea.

For a year and a day, Pwyll lives as Arawn. He fights and kills Havgan and unites the two kingdoms of Annwn, before exchanging places again. Thereafter Pwyll and Arawn remain friends, and, as promised, the beautiful Rhiannon is sent to be his wife. She comes to him wearing garments of gold and mounted upon a white horse. That she is an Otherworldly figure can scarcely be doubted, for later in the story she bears him a son, Pryderi. His hair is golden yellow and he grows so quickly that by the age of two he is as big as a child of six!

The coincidence of geography is revealed again in the story of Branwen, which was mentioned above in connection with the cauldron. Here is found one of the most important of all the geographical clues hidden within the mabinogi. When Matholwch comes to ask for Branwen as his bride, he sails across to Britain from the south of Ireland with his fleet of thirteen ships. Later he sails back to Ireland with his bride Branwen, leaving from the Menai Straits. However, later still, when Bran mounts his expedition to Ireland to rescue her he apparently has no need of ships, he simply walks across to Ireland! Many translators, both into English and into modern Welsh, have had difficulty with this passage and so it is useful to look at more than one version of it:

> Bendigeidfran and the host of which we spoke sailed towards Ireland, and in those days the deep water was not wide. He went by wading. There were but two rivers, the Lli and the Archan were they called, but thereafter the deep water grew wider when the deep overflowed the kingdoms.[26]

or alternatively:

> Bran and the host we spoke of set sail for Ireland, and since the sea was not deep he waded through. At that time there were only two rivers, Lli and Archan, but thereafter the sea widened and overflowed the kingdoms.[27]

and finally:

> Bendigeid Vran, with the host of which we spoke, sailed towards Ireland, and it was not far across the sea, and he came to shoal

water. It was but by two rivers; the Lli and the Archan were they called; and the nations covered the sea.[28]

It seems that some ancient bard has faithfully recorded the story as he was told it, even though he could not understand how it was possible to walk across to Ireland. It seems that at one time Ireland was only separated from Britain by two rivers, which Bran had to cross by wading. This fits well with the reconstruction of the lowered sea level around Britain and Ireland previously discussed, in which it may be seen that there would indeed be only two rivers of any size separating Britain from Ireland. One is the deep channel forming the extension of the Clyde, running down the eastern side of the Mull of Kintyre; and the other is the extension of the rivers which flow from Lough Foyle in Northern Ireland. The Lli would presumably refer to the Clyde, while the Archan is the other river; this is consistent with the order that the rivers are crossed.

This passage has been seen as a reference to Cantre'r Gwaelod by some commentators, but in the context of this book it is far more important than that. There are two possible ways to interpret the story. The first is that all the events described are taking place within the Otherworld, at a time before the sea flooded the low-lying plains (i.e. before 3100 BC in this context). The other interpretation is that Bran has temporarily strayed into the Otherworld in order to walk over to Ireland. The intended audience would have understood that in the time of the Otherworld, or Annwn, it would have been perfectly possible to walk to Ireland from Britain. In the opinion of the present author, the four branches of *The Mabinogion*, when they do not stray into the Otherworld, mostly recall events and characters of the third millennium BC.

Elsewhere the Welsh Otherworld may be seen to follow the Irish model and this is nowhere more clearly seen than in the romantic tale of *The Lady of the Fountain*. The story bears the stamp of later medieval Arthurian influence, but the Celtic themes within it are familiar. The introductory part of the tale describes the adventures of Kynon, a knight of King Arthur's court who rides off 'across deserts', to the furthest parts of the world, until he reaches the loveliest valley in the entire world. Kynon describes his journey to Owain.[29]

And at length it chanced that I came to the fairest valley in the world, wherein were trees of equal growth; and a river ran through

the valley, and a path was by the side of the river. And I followed
the path until mid-day, and continued my journey along the
remainder of the valley until the evening; and at the extremity of a
plain I came to a large and lustrous castle, at the foot of which
was a torrent. And I approached the castle, and there I beheld two
youths with yellow curling hair, each with a frontlet of gold upon
his head, and clad in a garment of yellow satin, and they had gold
clasps upon their insteps.

Kynon presses on into the castle and there he discovers an older
man, the lord of the castle, and twenty-four of the loveliest women
in the world. According to Kynon, the least lovely of them was
more beautiful than Arthur's wife Gwenhwyfar! He stays to eat
and asks the man where he might find a knight who would be his
match in combat. The lord of the castle directs him to a wood
where he will find a black man, a giant, with only one eye and only
one leg, who will direct him to what he seeks. The next day he sets
off again and finds the strange giant who directs him onward.[30]

'Take a path at the head of the clearing,' he said, 'and climb until
you reach the summit; there you will see a vale like a great valley,
and in the middle a great tree with branches greener than the
greenest fir. Beneath that tree is a fountain, and beside the fountain
a great stone, and on the stone a silver bowl, and a silver chain so
that bowl and stone cannot be separated.'

The giant tells him to fill the bowl with water and throw it over the
stone, whereupon a great storm will arise and blow all the leaves
from the tree. When the storm clears, a black knight will come to
him riding upon a black horse. Kynon does all of this, and the rider
appears as expected. They fight, but Kynon is no match for the
knight and is thrown from his horse; he is left to return in shame
to Arthur's court where he tells his story.

The remainder of the tale is fascinating, but scarcely relevant, as
it describes how Owain goes off in search of this wondrous place,
and how Arthur rides to his rescue. Although it is a late composition, it is clearly based on earlier Celtic memories of the Otherworld. The cauldron is powerfully present, as is the stylized
description of the shining castle in a land of eternal summer. But
two new details are forthcoming. The yellow hair of the Otherworld race is described as 'curly' and there is a significant detail in
the description of the Otherworld. The trees are described as being

all of equal height. Why is this detail included unless it has some significance? The only forest where all the trees are of the same height is a planted forest, or perhaps a fruit orchard. Could this be a description of an orchard preserved by a people who had no word in their language for such a thing?

A word at this point about the Arthurian legends. There is no reason to believe that King Arthur is an Otherworld figure despite his frequent association with it. He appears to be a much later hero figure who is used in the stories as a central character, and around whom the theme of a visit to the Otherworld is woven. The Arthurian legends also provide us with another view of the Celtic Otherworld. When Arthur was mortally wounded after the battle of Camlan, legend has it that he was carried off to the misty Isle of Avalon for his wounds to be tended. There he lives on, to await Britain's greatest hour of need. This most fascinating of all British legends is surely a reference to the Otherworld in its alternative guise as the Land of the Dead and as such is almost certainly a pre-Christian paradise. The etymology of the name *Insula Avalonia* has been interpreted by some as 'Island of Apples' or perhaps 'Island of Apple-trees' from a Gaulish *Avallo*, Irish *Abhall*, or Welsh *afal*.[31]

As for the previously discussed 7-year rhythms in the climate, there are few clear references within the British sources. These have been employed elsewhere as useful dating indicators but they are of little assistance in establishing an era for the Welsh material. Irish sources offer numerous references to a 7-year unit. In a saga of the mythological cycle, *The Second Battle of Mag Tured*, the visiting poet Cairbre (the son of Etain) begs to be allowed to stay until the end of 7 years. The son of the Fomorian Elotha in the same story is said to have attained a growth of 14 years by the time he was 7, and is perhaps the same person as the Welsh Pryderi.

Counting in units of 7 is similarly discernible within *The Mabinogion*. There is a reference in *Branwen* to 7 years of feasting, which may allude to the climate. In the same tale seven men are left in charge of the island of Britain and only seven returned with Bran from Ireland. They then remained for 7 years at Harlech. Elsewhere, seven men returned with Arthur to Annwn; and in *The Dream of Rhonabwy*, Arthur's messenger remained for 7 years in Scotland after the battle of Camlan.

Firmer indications of a 7-year unit are offered by the religious calendar of the early Celtic Church, which Bede tells us was of pagan origin.[32] The Celtic Christians employed an 84-year cycle which sometimes led them to calculate an erroneous date for the Easter festival. Eighty-four years is approximately equal to 1,039 lunar months. While not as accurate as a lunar calendar based on a 19-year cycle, an 84-year cycle does have the advantage that it is also a multiple of 7; and so could reconcile a 7-year rhythm with both the solar year and the lunar month.

Of the many views we have of the Welsh Otherworld, the most revealing of all is the remarkable *The Dream of Maxen*. It is clearly a later story than the four branches of the mabinogi, as is revealed by its lucidity and content. It cannot have been composed earlier than its principal character: Maxen, emperor of Rome. Maxen is a further example of a composite character, a historical figure caught in the very process of becoming a figure of legend. By an analysis of his historical origins we may see something of the way that such characters as Arthur and Manawyddan have taken on their present forms.

The name of Maxen seems to represent the Roman Emperor Maxentius (AD 306–12) but the story itself is based upon the life of Magnus Maximus. As a Spaniard serving with the Roman army in Britain, he was proclaimed emperor by his own soldiers in AD 383. He denuded Britain of its defences and led his army off to the Continent where, for a time, he ruled over most of Gaul, Spain and northern Italy. Ultimately however, he was captured and executed by Theodosius in AD 388. His escapade really marks the end of the Roman Empire in Britain.

To the Britons, Magnus seems to have become something of a folk-hero. His brief reign in Europe must have awakened memories of past glories, for, like Arthur, Manawyddan and Pwyll, he was used as the central figure in a fictitious visit to the Celtic Otherworld. Possibly the core of the tale is much older, with Maxen merely replacing some earlier hero figure in order to add popular interest. The historical truth about Maxen is not really important, for any powerful figure would suffice to fill the role. The story itself is short but unsatisfactory to the modern reader, for it drags on into an anticlimax, beyond the point where it should properly end; but within *The Dream of Maxen* is preserved a most marvellous description of the Otherworld.

The Emperor Maxen is out hunting one day, 'by the bank of the river that flows towards Rome'. But the Sun is hot and he lies down to rest while his soldiers stand guard about him. Soon he falls asleep.[33]

And he saw a dream. And this is the dream that he saw. He was journeying along the valley of the river towards its source; and he came to the highest mountain in the world. And he thought that the mountain was as high as the sky; and when he came over the mountain, it seemed to him that he went through the fairest and most level regions that man ever yet beheld, on the other side of the mountain. And he saw large and mighty rivers descending from the mountain to the sea, and towards the mouth of the rivers he proceeded. And as he journeyed thus, he came to the mouth of the largest river ever seen. And he beheld a great city at the entrance of the river, and a vast castle in the city, and he saw many high towers of various colours in the castle. And he saw a fleet at the mouth of the river, the largest ever seen. And he saw one ship among the fleet; larger was it by far, and fairer than all the others. Of such part of the ship as he could see above the water, one plank was gilded and the other silvered over. He saw a bridge of bone of the whale from the ship to the land, and he thought he went along the bridge and came into the ship. And a sail was hoisted on the ship and along the sea and the ocean was it borne. Then it seemed that he came to the fairest island in the whole world, and he traversed the island from sea to sea, even to the furthest shore of the island. Valleys he saw, and steeps, and rocks of wondrous height, and rugged precipices. Never yet saw he the like. And thence he beheld an island in the sea, facing this rugged land. And between him and this island was a country of which the plain was as large as the sea, the mountain as vast as the wood. And from the mountain he saw a river that flowed through the land and fell into the sea. And at the mouth of the river he beheld a castle, the fairest that man ever saw, and the gate of the castle was open, and he went into the castle.

And in the castle he saw a fair hall, of which the roof seemed to be all gold, the walls of the hall seemed to be entirely of glittering precious gems, the doors all seemed to be of gold. Golden seats he saw in the hall, and silver tables. And on a seat opposite to him, he beheld two auburn-haired youths playing at chess. He saw a silver board for the chess, and golden pieces thereon. The garments of the youths were of jet-black satin, and chaplets of ruddy gold bound their hair, whereupon were sparkling jewels of great price, rubies, and gems, alternately with imperial stones. Buskins of new cordovan leather on their feet fastened by slides of red gold.

And beside a pillar in the hall, he saw a hoary-headed man, in a chair of ivory, with the figures of two eagles of ruddy gold thereon. Bracelets of gold were upon his arms, and many rings were on his hands, and a golden torque about his neck; and his hair was bound with a golden diadem. He was of powerful aspect. A chess-board of gold was before him, and a rod of gold, and a steel file in his hand. And he was carving out chess-men.

And he saw a maiden sitting before him in a chair of ruddy gold. Not more easy than to gaze upon the sun when brightest, was it to look upon her by reason of her beauty. A vest of white silk was upon the maiden, with clasps of red gold at the breast; and a surcoat of gold tissue upon her, and a frontlet of red gold upon her head, and rubies and gems were in the frontlet, alternating with pearls and imperial stones. And a girdle of ruddy gold was around her. She was the fairest sight that man ever beheld.

Maxen is awoken from his dream and sadly returns to Rome. Thereafter, he cannot sleep without remembering the maiden he has dreamed of. He sends out messengers to search for her, but a year later they return, no wiser than when they set out. He returns to the riverbank where he had his dream. He tells his messengers to head towards the source of the river, westwards. This is surely symbolic, for the Otherworld is always to be found in the west!

And thereupon thirteen messengers of the emperor's set forth. And before them they saw a high mountain, which seemed to them to touch the sky. Now this was the guise in which the messengers journeyed; one sleeve was on the cap of each of them in front, as a sign that they were messengers, in order that through what hostile land soever they might pass no harm would be done to them. And when they came over this mountain, they beheld vast plains, and large rivers flowing there through. 'Behold,' said they, 'the land which our master saw.'

And they went along the mouths of the rivers, until they came to the mighty river which they saw flowing to the sea, and the vast city, and the many-coloured high towers in the castle. They saw the largest fleet in the world, in the harbour of the river, and one ship was larger than any of the others. 'Behold again,' said they, 'the dream that our master saw.' And in the great ship they crossed the sea, and came to the island of Britain. And they traversed the island until they came to Snowdon. 'Behold,' said they, 'the rugged land that our master saw.' And they went forward until they saw Anglesey before them, and until they saw Arvon likewise. 'Behold,'

said they, 'the land our master saw in his sleep.' And they saw
Aber Sain, and a castle at the mouth of the river.

The portal of the castle saw they open, and into the castle they
went, and they saw a hall in the castle. Then said they, 'Behold the
hall which he saw in his sleep.' They went into the hall, and they
beheld two youths playing at chess on the golden bench. And they
beheld the hoary-headed man beside the pillar, in the ivory chair,
carving chessmen. And they beheld the maiden sitting on a chair
of ruddy gold.

The messengers proclaim the young maiden as empress of Rome.
They tell her that the emperor of Rome has seen her in a dream
and would have her for his wife. Not fully believing the messengers,
she tells them, 'If the emperor loves me, let him come here and seek
me.' The rest of the story leaves the Otherworld concept behind, as
we are told how the emperor comes with his army to conquer the
island of Britain. He arrives at last in Arvon (Caernarvon) where
he finds the castle at Aber Sain and he marries the maiden; but the
emperor stays in Britain for the symbolic 7 years, and the Romans
decide to make a new emperor. He sends the famous taunting letter
to Maxen, saying only, 'If you come to Rome and if ever you
come.' To which Maxen replies saying, 'If I come to Rome and if I
come'. The remainder of the tale is recognizable as the career of
Magnus Maximus as he takes his army to conquer Rome and how
Kynan and his followers came to settle in Brittany.

Like all the tales of *The Mabinogion, The Dream of Maxen* is a
little confusing, the more so because the characters within it are
partly historical. The Otherworld imagery is strong within it; and
for the first time we find it linked with some definite geography and
with places that can be recognized.

In his dream, Maxen journeys westwards along the river that
runs through Rome, to its source in the highest mountain in the
world. Once beyond the mountain, he travels through a flat plain
and follows a broad river down to the sea. At the mouth of the
river lies a great city and a castle of many colours and high towers.
In the great ship, he sails over to a rugged island, from which he
looks back on his course. He sees an island and the mountain and
the river running down from it; and at the mouth of it is the castle,
which he enters (evidently without having to travel back across the
sea).

A curious reference then follows: between the rugged island and the castle lies a country of which 'the plain was as large as the sea'. Could this be a reference to the Irish Sea and the lost plain beneath it? The boundary of the Otherworld and the real world is ill defined in this story. Later, when the messengers arrive they at first see the Otherworld scene, but by the time they arrive at the island of Britain they have left the Otherworld and the geography is explained. The mountain that touches the sky is Snowdon and the island where the castle lies is the island of Anglesey – Ynys Mon. The story seems to be a genuine attempt to link the geography of the Otherworld with identifiable places. Could *The Dream of Maxen* be telling us where we should look if we wish to find the Otherworld?

There is also a resemblance here between the description of Mount Snowdon and some of the exaggerated accounts of Mount Atlas. Snowdon is described as the highest mountain in the world, reaching to the sky. Could it be that the classical legends of Mount Atlas originated from the same source as the story of Maxen's dream, namely the druids and bards of Britain?

The castle where Maxen finds the maiden in his dream is similarly a part of the Otherworld. The suggestion that it represents a description of the Roman fort at Caernarvon will not do at all, for no Roman fort on the edge of the empire was ever so luxuriously adorned. It is an otherworldly palace just like those described elsewhere in Welsh and Irish legend. It is a multicoloured castle with great high towers. The description of the interior has parallels too with Plato's description of the palace of Atlantis. Plato describes a similar temple there with a roof of gold, silver and red gold. The geography too is reminiscent of Plato. Here once again we have a vast castle within a great city. The city lies at the mouth of a broad river, flowing through a great level plain. The city is also a seaport with a fleet of many ships, just as Plato described his lost city.

The unknown bard who composed *The Dream of Maxen* set out to preserve the memory of the Otherworld. To preserve his secret, he wove it into a story. Maxen's dream appears to describe the view of the Otherworld as it would appear from the summit of Mount Snowdon. On a bright sunny day, the modern visitor who climbs its slopes may just make out the Isle of Man in the distance, away across the Irish Sea. There may be more than we had previously thought to an old Manx saying. It is said that on a clear day, from the highest point of Snae Fell on the Isle of Man, one may view six kingdoms. The first five are the kingdoms of Mann, England, Scotland, Ireland and Wales. The sixth is the Kingdom of Heaven.

15

In a Golden Age

It is often said that there is little evidence from either classical or Egyptian mythology to support Plato's story of a lost civilization in the west. It was Plato himself who made Atlas the central figure of his narratives and elsewhere in Greek mythology Atlas was one of the Titans, the son of Iapetus and the nymph Clymene. Among the many myths associated with him he is said to have fathered many groups of daughters: the Pleiades, the Hyades and the Hesperides, all with different mothers. He was also the father of the nymph Calypso who, according to Homer, detained Odysseus for 7 years on the island of Ogygia. Indeed, if we were to accept all the myths about Atlas then we would have to conclude that he is yet another composite figure. According to Apollodorus, he lived in the furthest west, beyond Oceanus, among the Hyperboreans.[1]

The Titans were the divine dynasty, from whom sprang all the Olympian gods. They were the children of Uranus and Gaea, the Earth goddess. Their names were Oceanus, Coeus, Hyperion, Crius, Iapetus and, the greatest of them all, Cronus, who killed his father and seized the throne. The Titanesses were Tethys, Themis, Rhea, Phoebe, Mnemosyne and Thia. Their children were also known as Titans, among them Zeus, mightiest of all the Greek gods.

The myths describe Zeus as the son of Cronus and Rhea. Cronus feared the prophecy of an oracle, warning that he would be overthrown by one of his own sons, just as he had overthrown his own father Uranus. To forestall the prophecy, Cronus swallowed up all his children as soon as they were born; but when Rhea was about to give birth to Zeus, she escaped and fled to a place called Cretea where she secretly gave birth to her son. The birthplace of Zeus was hotly disputed between the various Greek states. The Arcadians claimed he was born on Mount Lycaeus, but the Cretans insisted that he was born in a cave on Mount Ida, and that he was subsequently brought up by the Cretan nymphs.

When Cronus demanded of Rhea that she should give up her child, she instead gave him a stone wrapped up in a baby's swaddling clothes, which he duly swallowed. The infant Zeus lived on, looked after by the nymphs until he achieved manhood; he then set out to win his heritage. He consulted Metis, daughter of the Titan Oceanus, who offered him a potion to make Cronus heave up the children he had swallowed. Disguised as his cup-bearer, Zeus fed the potion to Cronus, who promptly became so nauseous that he expelled the stone and all the infants he had swallowed. These were the brothers and sisters of Zeus: Demeter, Hestia, Hera, Poseidon and Hades.

Allied with his brothers, Zeus then made war on Cronus and the Titans, who were led by Atlas. After 10 long years of fighting, still nothing was resolved. Zeus therefore sought to free the Cyclopes, whom Cronus had imprisoned in Tartarus. The myths describe these Cyclopes as 'one-eyed giants'; they were the sons of Uranus and possessed great powers. Armed with their thunderbolts, the Olympian gods finally defeated Cronus and the Titans. All except Atlas were then imprisoned in Tartarus, the lowest region of the underworld, where the hundred-handed Hecatoncheires were set to guard them. For his own punishment, Atlas was condemned for ever to hold the weight of the sky on his shoulders.

The victors then drew lots for control of the universe. Zeus drew the heavens, Hades the underworld, and Poseidon the sea; but no sooner was Zeus triumphant than he was forced to do battle with the giants and the serpent monster Typhon. Gaea was so angered by the treatment of her children, the Titans, that she had given birth to this monster as a punishment for Zeus. Zeus struck the serpent again and again with thunderbolts and eventually the wounded creature was defeated. Some versions say that the monster escaped to tend its wounds, others that it was flung into Tartarus. The calamity at the beginning of the age of Zeus is graphically described by Hesiod:[2]

> The boundless sea roared terribly around,
> The great earth rumbled, and broad heaven groaned,
> Shaken; and tall Olympus was disturbed
> Down to its roots, when the immortals charged.

Despite the warfare and calamity that ended his divine reign, a very different tradition remembered the reign of Cronus as a golden age. The story is found in Hesiod's *Myth of the Ages*. The gods of Olympus first created a golden race of men, who lived justly without any need for laws or their enforcement. They lived long and happy lives, without the burden of worry, in a world of eternal springtime. Their crops sprang from the earth without the need for planting. They enjoyed complete peace and happiness. Hesiod tells us that in the golden age iron had not yet been used to make swords and shields and hence there could be no wars. The golden race were hidden beneath the earth where they became the daemones; the beneficent spirits of the earth.

After the golden race came a silver race. These men were compelled to obey their mothers in all things; which angered Zeus, who hid this race too, away beneath the earth. There they became the much-honoured spirits of the underworld. After them came a race of bronze: warlike men who fashioned weapons of bronze in an age before iron was known. This race too was consigned to Hades to be replaced by the fourth race, the heroes who fought at Troy. The last race of all were the Greeks themselves.

The decline of mankind from this original state of paradise to its present miseries was vividly portrayed by the Roman poet Ovid, who in his years of exile had access to many mythological sources since lost to us. The Romans adopted most of the Greek myths virtually unchanged, substituting only their own names, Jupiter, or Jove, for Zeus, and Saturn for Cronus. Consider these few lines from the *Metamorphoses*:[3]

> Earth willingly, untouched, unwounded yet
> By hoe or plough, gave all her bounteous store;
> Men were content with nature's food unforced,
> And gathered strawberries on the mountainside
> And cherries and the clutching bramble's fruit,
> And Acorns fallen from Jove's spreading tree.
> Springtime it was, always, forever spring;
> The gentle zephyrs with their breathing balm
> Caressed the flowers that sprang without a seed;
> Anon the earth untilled brought forth her fruits,
> The unfallowed fields lay gold with heavy grain,
> And streams of milk and springs of nectar flowed
> And yellow honey dripped from boughs of green.

> When Saturn fell to the dark Underworld
> And Jove reigned upon earth, the silver race
> Replaced the gold, inferior, yet in worth
> Above the tawny bronze. Then Jupiter
> Curtailed the pristine spring and led the year
> Through winter, summer, autumn's varying days
> And brief precarious spring in seasons four.
> Then first the blazing sky with torrid heat
> Sweltered, and ice hung frozen in the gale;
> Then men sought shelter – shelter under caves
> And thickets and rough hurdles bound with bark;
> Then in long furrows first were set the seeds
> Of grain and oxen groaned beneath the yoke.

Ovid intended the *Metamorphoses* to represent a complete history of the world since the creation. The implications of his poetry are crystal clear. He recalls a golden age when the world enjoyed a climate of eternal springtime. Only with the fall of Saturn (Cronus) did the seasons commence and the transition was a time of great extremes in the weather!

The fundamental characteristics of the golden age may be recognized as a description of the world in an era when the climate was far more equable than now. It was a world without the extremes of summer and winter in which the year had little meaning. The poems of Ovid and Hesiod give us a remarkably sound description of the world's climate as it would be before and after an increase in the axial tilt. If we should seek a period in prehistory that these myths might describe there is but one suitable era: the Atlantic/Sub-Boreal transition around 3100 BC.

The Greeks believed in the existence of an underworld. They named it Hades (or the House of Hades) after the Titan who chose it for his kingdom. According to Hesiod, the deepest part of the underworld was Tartarus, where Cronus was confined. Tartarus must have existed even during the golden age, for it was there that Cronus imprisoned the Hecatoncheires, who would one day become his own guards in that gloomy place. Before him, Uranus imprisoned the Cyclopes there. It is an ancient place of punishment. Homer describes it as a region as far below Hades as the heaven is above the Earth. In Hesiod's *Theogony* it is a dark and misty place. A great wall of bronze surrounded it and Poseidon secured it with gates of bronze.

There are many myths about Hades. It was the place where the spirits of the dead and the daemones were believed to dwell. As the abode of the dead, it must not be equated with the Nordic concept of hell; that role more properly belongs to Tartarus alone. The land of Hades was said to be surrounded by five rivers, among them the Styx, over which Charon the ferryman would transport the souls of those who had been properly buried. Within Hades, the souls, or 'shades', seem to have carried on an existence much as they had in their earthly lives.

The House of Hades was also a place that could be visited by mortal men, for this is precisely what Homer has Odysseus do in the *Odyssey*. Returning from the Trojan Wars, Odysseus and his crew are swept away against their will to the island of Ogygia where, after various calamities, they encounter the sorceress Circe. She tells them that the only person who can direct them home is the shade Tiresias who dwells in Hades. Odysseus follows her directions and sets off across the stream of Oceanus until he arrives at Hades.

The *Odyssey* gives us a precise location for Hades. It lay beyond the stream of Oceanus at the very edge of the world. Odysseus is driven before a strong north wind to the place where the River of Lamentation and the River of Fire unite with the River Acheron, a branch of the Styx, around a rocky island. He leaves his boat near the city of the Cimmerians, whose land is eternally shrouded in mist. When the Sun rises in their land, no ray of sunlight can ever reach the ground. From there they walk on into Hades, where they encounter the multitudinous souls of the dead.

The 10-year voyage of Odysseus is conventionally rationalized as taking place entirely within the confines of the Mediterranean Sea; but it does not take 10 years to sail around the Mediterranean and there is no place within its confines that properly fits the description of the misty land of the Cimmerians. In any case, the Greeks would not have considered a location within the Pillars of Heracles to be at the edge of the world. It is, however, quite a fair description of the latitude of the British Isles on a cloudy day. Cloud and mist are the prevailing climate of Britain, in sharp contrast to the deep blue skies of the Mediterranean.

Homer's mythical Cimmerians should not be confused with the historical race of that name, first described by Herodotus. These Cimmerians were semi-nomadic horsemen who occupied the Black

Sea coast between the Danube and the Don – two rivers named after the goddess Danu. The strait that separates the Black Sea from the Sea of Azov was known as the Cimmerian Bosporus.[4] According to Herodotus they were driven from their lands by the Scythians and we subsequently hear no more of them.[5]

Diodorus Siculus equated these historical Cimmerians with the Galatians and the Cimbri who attacked Rome, and compared their reputed cannibalism with that of the Britons from the island called 'Iris'.[6] Homer's Cimmerii may in fact be a reference to the Cymry. The Welsh name for their nation derives from a Brythonic word *combrogos* meaning 'compatriot', and the regional names of Cumbria and Cambria are similarly derived. The Welsh triads do indeed describe the Black Sea region as the ancestral home of the Cymry, whence they migrated shortly after the Flood, and claim that all the Britons were descended from this ancestral stock. The tribe of Nemed in Irish myth are also said to have migrated by way of Scythia. Such stories may have been known to Posidonius, who similarly blamed the migrations of the Cimbri upon a sudden inundation by the sea.[7]

Perhaps it was also Celtic myth that led Plutarch to identify the British Isles as the abode of Cronus, for a story he tells has remarkable parallels in Arthurian legend. Shortly after the Roman conquest of Britain he wrote a short essay entitled *The Decline of the Oracles*.[8] He recounts the travels of Demetrius of Tarsus, an explorer sent out from Rome to survey the islands to the west of Britain. Demetrius describes a number of islands scattered in the sea, most of which were uninhabited and named after various *daemones* and heroes. On visiting 'one of the nearest' of these islands, occupied only by a few holy men, he was told of a nearby isle where Cronus lay eternally imprisoned, watched over as he slept by the hundred-handed Briareus. Around about him were many *daemones* who acted as his servants.

Precisely which island Demetrius visited is difficult to determine. Since it is described as a desolate place, with many other islands nearby, we may presume that it was one of the nearer Scottish islands. In another of his short 'Moral Essays', *The Face in the Moon*, Plutarch elaborates further on the subject of Cronus and proposes some interesting geography.[9] He reveals that Homer's island of Ogygia lay at a distance of some 5 sailing days westwards from Britain, in the direction of the summer sunset; which would suggest that Ogygia should be identified with Iceland. This identification is further reinforced by Plutarch's assertion that three other islands also lay in the general direction of Ogygia, 'equally distant from it and from each other' and which, in the summer, experienced only a single hour of darkness. It is apparently on one of these islands that Cronus was confined.

Clearly Plutarch did not believe that the voyages of Odysseus were confined to the Mediterranean. Possibly the islands he mentions may be identified with the Orkneys or the Shetlands, but Plutarch's geography is somewhat vague. He states that his source was native British tradition. The isle of Cronus, he says, was colonized in ancient times by Greeks, who intermingled with the people of Cronus. This statement cannot simply be dismissed, for it is wholly consistent with both Welsh and Irish mythology.

Hesiod preserves another somewhat different myth about Cronus. In *Works and Days* he describes him as ruler of the Island of the Blest, situated at the world's edge.[10] It is therefore quite likely that this was merely another name for Hades, or alternatively Hades was only a part of the Island of the Blest. In Pindar's *Odes* the Island of the Blest is a happy place where those who have lived honest lives may dwell contentedly alongside the honoured gods.[11] There also we find:

> Go by God's road to the Tower of Cronus
> Where the Airs, daughters of Ocean
> Blow round the Island of the Blest

Having said previously that no positive references to the British Isles are found in the Greek myths, that is not to say that none exists. It may be that they are just difficult to recognize. There are also references to an elusive northern race known as the Hyperboreans, whose name appears to mean, 'people from beyond the north wind'. There are sound reasons to suggest that these, too, represent a memory of the ancient inhabitants of Britain.

Later Greek and Roman geographers were at a loss where to place the land of the Hyperboreans. Initially Hyperborea was considered to lie somewhere immediately to the north of the known world. As the limits of the known world expanded, the location of the legendary land of Hyperborea was driven further and further north until eventually it reached the North Pole! Herodotus refused to believe in the existence of the Hyperboreans, on the grounds that the Scythians and other nations to the north knew nothing of them. We may therefore safely conclude that by the era when Herodotus wrote they had ceased to be recognizable as a nation.

In Pindar's *Odes* references to the land of the Hyperboreans are scarcely distinguishable from those of the Island of the Blest, or the Phaeacians of the *Odyssey*. In the *Odyssey*, the hero Odysseus takes part in the games of the Phaeacians, whereas Pindar similarly describes the games of the Hyperboreans.[12]

> He travels there
> To the furthest edge of sailing.
> But not in ships or on foot
> will you find the marvellous road
> To the games of the People beyond the North.

Herodotus cites a lost poem, the *Arimaspea* by Aristeas.[13] He states that Hyperborea lay along the shores of the sea, beyond the land of the Griffins, which in turn lay beyond the land of the Arimaspians, which itself lay beyond the land of the Issedones. All that can really be gathered from this is that it was a long way from Greece along the northern coasts of Europe.

The story goes that Aristeas was a magician of some kind who disappeared from his home in Proconnesus one day, and was presumed to be dead. He mysteriously reappeared again 7 years later and it was then that he composed his epic poem. Aristeas claimed to have visited the land of the Issedones, from whom he had learned certain mysteries of the Hyperboreans and had become converted to the worship of their god Apollo. He later disappeared again and set up an altar to Apollo in Sicily; but it is the absence of Aristeas for precisely 7 years that makes his story so interesting.

No one is quite sure when Aristeas lived, but he is usually considered to have composed his poetry before the time of Homer. If his disappearance for 7 years is more than a coincidence then we must place him earlier than 1000 BC while the 7-year Long Seasons were still influencing the climate. To recap, it has been proposed here that the combination of a 14-month nutation of the Earth's axis with the normal seasons would produce suppressed seasons alternating at 7-year intervals with severe enhanced seasons. Under such a climatic regime, there would have been a 'sailing season' every 7 years during which long sea voyages could have been attempted. Presumably Aristeas made his journey to the Issedones during one such opportunity and only returned in the next sailing season, 7 years later. This clue may be used to date the Hyperboreans to earlier than 1000 BC.

Diodorus Siculus quotes a fragment of a history of the Hyperboreans, written by Hecataeus of Abdera during the fourth century BC. It has been seen by many commentators as a clear reference to Britain.[14]

> Opposite to the coast of the Celts, there is an island in the ocean, not smaller than Sicily and lying to the north, which is inhabited by the Hyperboreans, who are so named because they dwell beyond the north wind. This island is of a happy temperature, rich in soil, and fruitful in everything, yielding its produce twice in the year.
>
> Tradition says that Leto was born there, and for that reason, the inhabitants venerate Apollo, more than any other god. They are in a manner, his priests, for they daily celebrate him with continual songs of praise, and pay him abundant honours.
>
> In this island, there is a magnificent grove of Apollo, and a remarkable temple of a round form, adorned with many consecrated gifts. There is also a city sacred to the same God, of which most of the inhabitants are harpists, who continually play upon their harps in the temple, and sing hymns to the God, extolling his actions.
>
> The Hyperboreans use a peculiar dialect, and have a remarkable attachment to the Greeks, especially to the Athenians, and the Delians, deducing their friendship from remote periods. It is related that some Greeks formerly visited the Hyperboreans, with whom they left consecrated gifts, of great value, and also that in Ancient times, Abaris, coming from the Hyperboreans, into Greece, renewed their friendship with the Delians.

This passage is remarkable for a number of reasons. It is difficult to see it as anything other than a reference to Britain, or just possibly to Ireland. Hecataeus wrote at a time when the Greeks applied the name 'Celt' to all the predominantly yellow or fair-haired tribes living north of the Alps. He seems to imply that the Celts were not in Britain at that era. However, Hecataeus probably drew his information from ancient poetry and legend just as Herodotus did. It cannot therefore be regarded as accurately recording the geography of the fourth century BC.

Whether Hyperborea may be equated with the land of the Phaeacians, or the Island of the Blest, is debatable. The reference to the mild climate and the production of crops twice each year is very reminiscent of Plato's island. However, it seems unlikely that the Hyperboreans can be equated with the Atlantians, although some authorities would hold that Atlas was a Hyperborean.

Hecataeus mentions Leto, the mother of Apollo. She was the daughter of the Titans Coeus and Phoebe; and according to some authorities, the first wife of Zeus. This would date the origin of the cult of Apollo to an era shortly after the end of the golden age; and therefore too late to have any connection with Atlantis. However, all this does help to reinforce the derived chronology. It seems reasonable to suggest that Hyperborea should be equated with memories of the British Isles during the second or third millennium BC.

The Hyperboreans were best known on the Aegean island of Delos, which was the centre of the cult of Apollo.[15] No Greek of the classical era ever claimed to have met a Hyperborean and contact seems to have been lost during or before the last Greek dark age. Delian legend claimed that Leto escaped from Zeus and was pursued all over the world by 'a great serpent'. When finally she reached Delos, she was allowed sanctuary and there she gave birth to her children Apollo and Artemis. There is a legend that two Hyperborean girls came with her to help with the birth of her children; later, the Hyperboreans sent two more girls accompanied by several men and various gifts. This custom continued until the Hyperboreans noticed that their messengers failed to return, after which they passed on their gifts via intermediaries.

When Leto arrived there, Delos was still a floating island! Apollo is said to have firmly anchored it as a reward for the Delians' hospitality to his mother. Interestingly, Herodotus records precisely the same phenomenon regarding the Egyptian shrine of Leto on an island in a lake near Buto.[16] The Egyptians told Herodotus that it too was a floating island, although he never saw it move! According to the Egyptian myths Apollo and Artemis were the sons of Demeter (Isis) and Dionysus (Osiris). Leto is said to have saved Apollo (Horus) from the serpent Typhon, which was evidently the same mythical creature as is remembered in the Delian version.

Other authors have suggested that this great serpent is an imagery of the very comet that collided with the Earth and was the cause of the Flood.[17] The memories of 'floating islands' would support this view, as they clearly remember the pole tides that would accompany a disturbance of the axis. How else are the many stories of floating islands to be rationalized? Clearly islands cannot truly float. The myths must remember an abnormal variation of the sea and this is only feasible if the figure and rotation axes of the Earth have become separated during a major geological upheaval. The era of Zeus and the Titans has already been placed at the Atlantic/Sub-Boreal transition, and this would therefore date the travels of Leto and the birth of Apollo to the 20-year period of instability following this impact. By the same device, the Titanic Wars and the advent of Zeus may be dated to a few years before the Flood.

Greek mythology recalls another paradise in the far west, known as Elysium, or the Elysian Fields. Later writers referred to it as a great plain, distinct from Hades, the abode of the virtuous dead. There is the famous line in the *Odyssey* where King Menelaüs is told that he will not die in his own land of Argos:[18]

> The Deathless Ones will waft you instead to the world's end, the Elysian fields where yellow-haired Rhadamanthus is. There indeed men live unlaborious days. Snow and tempest and thunderstorms never enter there, but for men's refreshment Ocean sends out continually the high-singing breezes of the west.

The gentle westerly breezes that blew across the Elysian Fields may well refer to the prevailing Atlantic westerlies, during a somewhat calmer age. As for Rhadamanthus, he is a comparatively minor deity whom Zeus appointed as one of the judges of the underworld. He is recalled in the *Iliad* as 'godlike Rhadamanthys' and Pindar describes him as the trusted counsellor of Cronus, who kept him continually at his side as he ruled in the Island of the Blest.[19, 20] Thus we may conclude that Hades, the Elysian Fields and the Island of the Blest are all names for the same place.

The description of yellow-haired Rhadamanthus is also a fairly typical description of the Titans. The gods were the golden race. Hesiod refers to fair-haired Rhea and grey-eyed Athene, golden-crowned Tethys and Phoebe, grey-eyed Tritogeneia and golden Aphrodite. This is precisely how the inhabitants of the Celtic Otherworld are described in Welsh and Irish sagas.

The Elysian Plain is similarly recalled in Phoenician myths, where it is called the Sad-El or Field of God. It is named for the home of the principal Phoenician god El, whom Philo identified with Cronus. This writer, during the first century AD, attempted to derive most of Greek mythology from Phoenician sources.

Philo's version of the Phoenician pantheon reads very similarly to that of the traditional Greek sources. It has Uranus, the sky, and Ge (or Gaea) as the parents of El, with Hermes Trismagistus as his trusted adviser. Atlas is there too, as the brother of El, who feared the ambitions of Atlas and, on the advice of Hermes, he buried him deep beneath the earth. The youngest son of El by his wife Rhea was recognized as a god at the moment of his birth and is therefore equated with Zeus.

There is no reason why the Greek version of the pantheon should be regarded as any more authentic than the Phoenician, or indeed any other. Diodorus Siculus gives another variant of it, which was described in chapter 2, and which is probably derived from Libyan sources.[21] He presented it as 'the teachings of the Atlantians about the gods'. These Atlantians, he said, 'lived in the remotest west'. The similarity between these myths is perhaps further confirmation that the Atlantians whom Diodorus describes are the same as those of Plato. By two entirely separate trains of argument, it has been possible to place both stories at approximately 3100 BC.

The Babylonians too, had their myths about the Land of the Dead. Their Flood story, in the *Epic of Gilgamesh*, tells how the gods feared the Flood and retreated into the highest heaven for safety. The Sumerian father of gods was called Anu or An and his children, the judges of the underworld, were known as Annuniki. Like the legendary Odysseus, Gilgamesh also visited the Land of the Dead. However, Gilgamesh is a historical figure who lived at about 2500 BC and the Gilgamesh Epic can be shown to be some 1,500 years older than Homer! Gilgamesh is said to have travelled the world and brought back stories of the days before the Flood.

In his search for everlasting life, Gilgamesh goes in search of his ancestor Utnapishtim to the land of Dilmun, in the Garden of the Sun. First he travels overland to the garden of the gods. He must then pass through the mountain of Mashu and through 12 leagues of total darkness. Then he meets with Siduri, the woman who sits by the edge of the sea and makes wine in a golden bowl that the gods gave her. He asks her how he may find Utnapishtim and the land of Dilmun. She tells him that to reach the Land of the Dead he must first cross the sea.[22]

Gilgamesh, there is no crossing the Ocean; whoever has come since the days of old, has not been able to pass that sea. The sun in his glory crosses the Ocean, but who beside Shamash has ever crossed it? The place and the passage are difficult, and the waters of death are deep which flow between. Gilgamesh, how will you cross the Ocean?

But Gilgamesh does succeed in crossing the ocean. He finds Urshanabi, the ferryman of Utnapishtim, who conveys him across the ocean to the Land of the Dead where he learns the story of the Flood from Utnapishtim.

This remarkable passage tells us a number of things. First, the Land of the Dead was a place that could be visited by the living, but only by a difficult voyage across the sea. Also, we learn that it was formerly possible to cross the sea, but in the time of Gilgamesh, for some reason, it was not. This echoes the statements made by Plato. He too says that the ocean was formerly navigable, but that it became impassable because the way was blocked by mud. The *Epic of Gilgamesh* confirms that this was a view prevalent in the Middle East during the third millennium BC.

The Gilgamesh Epic does not state specifically that the garden of the gods was in the west, but Mesopotamia is the likely place of inspiration for the biblical Garden of Eden story, which most definitely lay in the west. The Greeks, too, remembered a garden in the west, called the Garden of the Hesperides. The garden belonged to the daughters of the gods, the Hesperides; some sources even say that they were the daughters of Atlas. They guarded the tree on which grew the golden apples, which Heracles later stole as one of his labours.

The Egyptians, too, believed in a Land of the Dead situated in the far west, ruled over by the god Osiris. Egyptian mythology presents us with a baffling array of gods, many of whom are animal deities recognizable from pre-dynastic times. For most of the Egyptian gods, no theogony myths have survived. They were apparently so well known to the Egyptians themselves that they seldom bothered to write them down. We are fortunate even to have the myth of Osiris, for which we must again thank Plutarch who pieced it together from a number of sources.[23]

The story of the birth of Osiris was related in chapter 10, in connection with the origin of the Egyptian calendar. Osiris grew up to be a wise and powerful king of Egypt, respected by the people.

He is said to have instructed them in the rites of the gods for the first time, and to have abolished cannibalism and other primitive ways. He established a peaceful empire in Asia and travelled the world, spreading civilization. But his jealous brother Set coveted his throne and conspired to murder him.

At a feast-day celebration in Memphis, Set and his followers brought along a luxuriously adorned chest, announcing that it should belong to the person who could best fit within it. Osiris played along with the charade and agreed to try it out for size. At once, Set and his conspirators slammed the lid and nailed it down. The chest, containing Osiris, was cast into the Nile and carried out to sea where eventually it washed up on the coast of Phoenicia.

Set usurped the kingdom and ruled as a tyrant. But Isis, the wife (and sister) of Osiris retrieved the chest and brought the body back to Egypt. She hid it in the swamps of Buto, where Set discovered it and had the body of Osiris chopped into fourteen pieces in order to be rid of him for ever. Still the goddess Isis would not be beaten. She recovered all the pieces and put them back together; and then sought the help of her sister Nephthys and the gods Thoth and Anubis. Isis then performed for the very first time the process of embalmment and mummification, which restored Osiris to eternal life. From the union of Isis and Osiris the god Horus was conceived. Osiris then retired to rule in Amenti, the Land of the Dead in the west; the later Ptolemaic Greeks therefore equated him with their own gods Hades or Dionysus.

The Osirian myth goes on to describe the birth of Horus on the floating island of Chemmis. It is this Horus whom Herodotus equated with Apollo, while Set was equated with the serpent monster Typhon. He also states that Horus was the last of the gods to rule over Egypt. The name Horus was applied to many Egyptian gods; the early kings also bore the name as part of their title and each pharaoh was himself a god. During the early dynastic period we hear of persistent conflict between the 'followers of Horus' and the 'followers of Set'.

Egyptologists have suggested that the Osiris myth may represent a memory of a pre-dynastic king of Egypt. His rule seems to have been remembered as a golden age whereas that of Set is recalled as a harsh tyranny. Their relationship bears a strong resemblance to that between Cronus and Zeus in this respect. It may be that the myth of Osiris was just an attempt by the early dynastic kings to claim descent from the gods of the golden age.

As for fitting Osiris into the chronology, we can only rely on the accuracy of Plutarch. He involves the birth of Osiris intimately with the changes in the calendar. The extra days were added to the year by Thoth, in order that Osiris could be born! This would also seem to place his birth at around the time of the Flood. However, the birth of his own posthumous son Horus (Apollo) on a 'floating' island would argue that the death of Osiris occurred shortly after the Flood, as would the equating of Set with the serpent Typhon. According to Plutarch the deluge occurred during the age of Set when the Nile delta was first revealed.[24] Osiris may therefore have been the king of Egypt at the time of the Flood. The belief that he built a peaceful empire in Asia is a further clue to his era. It is at just this period that archaeologists find evidence of contact between Egypt and Mesopotamia.[25]

Whatever the reality of Osiris may be, to the later Egyptians he became a symbol of the rebirth of the immortal soul. When a pharaoh died he became united with Osiris and his son replaced him on the throne as the new Horus. Although originally the symbol of the ruler's divinity, by the time of the New Kingdom any wealthy Egyptian might claim the right to an eternal life in Amenti.

Throughout the 3,000-year history of Pharaonic Egypt, the religious beliefs and the ascendancies of the various gods changed many times, but the funerary customs remained surprisingly conservative. By the time of the New Kingdom, no prominent Egyptian would have been buried without a complex set of instructions detailing how to survive and behave in the Land of the Dead. In the earliest period, these instructions and spells were inscribed on the walls of the tomb, but they grew so voluminous that it became necessary to resort to papyrus scrolls. The Arab tomb robbers referred to these scrolls as 'the book of the dead' and the name has stuck. The Egyptians themselves referred to them as 'The Chapters of Coming Forth by Day'.

The various chapters and spells of the Book of the Dead are undoubtedly very old indeed. It was generally believed to be the work of Thoth, the scribe of the gods. There were three recensions, and at each revision the sequence was changed and a little more detail added. The earliest recension, the Heliopolitan, is known from as early as the Fifth Dynasty and is found in the Pyramid

Fig. 15.1 THE ELYSIAN FIELDS. From the papyrus of the scribe Nebseni. The scribe himself is depicted performing various agricultural labours in the fields. Rivers are shown dissecting the plain and discharging at the sea. At the mouth of the rivers is a bowl-shaped cartouche with the inscription 'The birthplace of the god of the city'. Below this is an island on which reside the company of gods. To the right is moored the boat of Tchetetfet. In the upper divisions a number of lakes or pools are depicted. These features appear in one form or another on all the Book of the Dead papyri.

Texts. The Theban Recension dates from the Eighteenth Dynasty and is found in Coffin Texts and papyri. The final recension took place during the Saite Dynasty, as part of the late religious revival. A comment attached to the Saite Recension indicates that the chapter to be recited on the birthday of Osiris was found in a cave-temple made by Horus for his father Osiris Wennefer.[26] This is usually taken to indicate the First Dynasty origins of the ritual. No such inscriptions have yet been found in pre-dynastic tombs.

The chapters of the Book of the Dead contain a variety of spells and prayers on behalf of the deceased. It opens with hymns in praise of Re and Osiris. The deceased is then judged on the sins of his lifetime to see if he may be granted land in the Field of Offerings and his heart is weighed by the judges of the dead against the Feather of Righteousness. There follows a spell which permits the deceased to enter the nether world on the day of internment. He hails Osiris, Lord of All, and all those who reside in 'the West', and implores them to let him enter.

Egyptian belief demanded that the body of the deceased must be preserved. Only then could his *Ka*, or soul, be released to enjoy the afterlife. Within Amenti, the deceased was required to perform various agricultural labours. A further spell forbade the deceased to do any work, instead his *shabti* figure was released to perform these duties on his behalf. This must have made the idea of the afterlife very appealing to the Egyptian agricultural labourer, who probably spent the greater part of his life engaged in such toil. The concept is similar to the 'shades' of the Greek underworld. Other spells provided for everyday needs during the afterlife and, curiously, another spell ensured that the deceased would not die a second time!

From the Book of the Dead we may glean a wealth of detail about the Land of the Dead itself. It is described as lying to the west or north-west of Egypt, although some later texts would place it in the sky, or beneath the earth.[27] The dead are often simply referred to as 'westerners'. In that region lies a mountain where the Sun sets, known as the Manu Mountain which is in the land of Manu. The name Amenti denotes the west generally, the hidden region through which the soul must pass in order to reach the next world, the *Tuat*, where Osiris reigns. Within the Tuat itself was the *Sekhet-Hetepet* or 'Fields of Peace' over which the company of gods presided. The Greeks equated it with their own Elysian Fields.

Within the Fields of Peace, another region may be identified. This was the *Sekhet-Aaru* or 'Field of Reeds', sometimes called the 'Field of Offerings'. Occasionally Aaru is referred to as a divine city. This was where the spirit of the deceased would dwell. The newcomer was expected to learn the geography of it and would be introduced to the other souls who dwelt there. Spells 109 and 110 describe respectively the souls of the 'westerners' and the 'easterners'.[28] In the Field of Reeds, the barley grows 5 cubits high and the Khus who reap it are each 9 cubits in height. If we take this as the biblical measure of the length of a man's forearm, then these are the spirits of giants some 4 metres tall.

The geography of the Elysian Fields is not at all easy to interpret. Fortunately, some Book of the Dead papyri hold maps of the Elysian Fields. A number of excellent examples of these are on display in the British Museum in London for all to see. They range from the papyrus of the scribe Userhat dating from about 1400 BC to the papyrus of the priest Hori of the second century BC. They show the Elysian Fields as a regular, flat, rectangular plain, divided into sectors by rivers and straight canals. The deceased is named personally within the papyri. His shabti figure is depicted within the fields carrying out various agricultural labours, such as ploughing, reaping and sowing seed.

Although each papyrus is an individual, they all obey certain rules of format. If we assume that they are intended to be aligned with north at the top, then the rectangular plain is usually drawn with the sides in the ratio 3:2 with the long sides running north to south, although sometimes the western boundary is depicted as the sea. In some later papyri of the Saite Recension, the rectangle is turned through a right angle, such that the long sides run east to west, but the ratio of the sides is still preserved.

One of the earliest representations shows rivers cutting through the regular channels and discharging into the sea. Opposite them lies a dish-shaped cartouche representing an island, which is described as 'the birthplace of the god of the city'. In the southernmost island, four gods and a flight of steps are depicted, described as 'the great company of gods who are in Sekhet-Hetep' or 'the Lords of the Tuat'. There are many lakes within the divisions, some of them named, including one that 'contains neither fish nor worms'. Leading off from one of the waterways is a canal which terminates abruptly. At the end of this canal is moored the Boat of Osiris Wennefer. Usually, the Boat of Re is also depicted.

However much the style may vary, even when the rectangle is rotated, the city of the gods is always placed near the south-western corner. The boats, and the blind channel, are always depicted in the southernmost division. In later versions, the rivers are lost.

Fig. 15.2 Sekhet-Hetepet (Papyrus of Anhai).
Reproduced by courtesy of the Trustees of the British Museum.

Usually, the straight waterways dividing the fields stand out quite clearly in blue, but the later papyri of the Ptolemaic period show them as just thin straight lines. They never entirely disappear.

The first comparison that may be made is between these representations of the Elysian Fields and the description of Atlantis that Solon brought back from Egypt. The similarity with the rectangular plain on the island of Atlantis is immediately apparent. Solon would have visited Sais in the midst of the Saite religious revival and what is more likely than that he was told a form of the Book of the Dead stories? He may even have seen a map of the Elysian Fields and received from the priests a rationalized historical version of their religious material.

It was probably also the Elysian Fields that Crantor saw inscribed on a temple column during his visit to Egypt, and which he equated with Plato's story. After the Saite Recension the depictions of the Elysian Fields became more stylized. Later examples (see figure 15.3) show the island birthplace of the gods lying off the southern edge of the plain; and this is very reminiscent of the way that the central island of Atlantis is depicted in most modern popular reconstructions. It is probably this late version of Elysium that Solon took away in his notes.

The second comparison that may be made is with Welsh and Irish descriptions of the Otherworld, and with the rectangular plain and submerged topography of the Irish Sea floor. The correspondence here is quite remarkable, the more so because it can be most clearly seen in the oldest papyri dating from the Theban Recension.

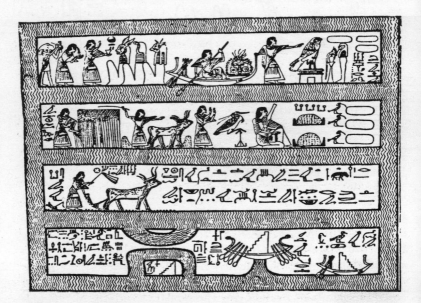

Fig. 15.3 Sekhet-Hetepet (Papyrus of Ani).
Reproduced by courtesy of the Trustees of the British Museum.

The sea lies to the west of the plain and the rivers are always drawn flowing from east to west, discharging themselves at the city. The Greenfield Papyrus in the British Museum is perhaps the best example of this, for it gives the sense of a river delta.

The Book of the Dead papyri give no indication that the Elysian plain was situated on an island. However, that piece of information is available from other sources. The Elysian Fields in Greek myth were situated on the Island of the Blest, already tentatively identified with the British Isles via a separate train of argument.

We must also take note of the reference to the 'Manu Mountain' and the 'Land of Manu' within the hymn to the Sun god Re. The Manu Mountain marked the place where the Sun set; and it is an observable fact that, when viewed from the eastern Irish Sea, the Sun does indeed set behind the Isle of Man. The name 'Manu' bears an obvious similarity to the names *Man* and *Manannan*, suggesting a common etymology. In various Roman documents we find the earliest names for the Isle of Man.[29] They refer to it variously as *Monapia*, *Manavia* and *Manavi*, which may be equated with the *Manau* of Nennius. For the island of Anglesey we similarly find *Mona* and *Manna* which may be compared with the modern Welsh name Ynys *Mon*.

There is also surprising correspondence here with another of the world's great mythologies: that of the Finno-Ugric races of northern Europe. In the Finnish epic known as the *Kalevala* we find the myths and legends of the Finns as preserved in songs and chants.

The underworld, or Land of the Dead, in Finnish mythology is known by two apparently equivalent names, *Manala* – 'the land of Mana' – and *Tuonela* – 'the home of Tuoni'. The journey to the Land of the Dead required a march of many weeks through dense forests, to the region of darkness. Within Tuonela was a river, both broad and deep, which had to be crossed to arrive at the isle of Manala and the shining hills, where Tuoni and his daughter Tuonetar were said to rule over the Land of the Dead. Here again, the correlation with Egyptian myth is quite striking. Such a degree of correspondence in the names for the Land of the Dead and the god of the underworld, from places so far removed as Finland and Egypt, points to a shared etymology. It suggests that perhaps both mythologies recall a real place intermediate between the two countries.

The similarity of the two names *Tuonela* and *Tuat* is also worth further examination. The god Tuoni may well be the same as the *Tiw* or *Tyr* of the Scandinavian and Germanic pantheon, who was later displaced by *Donar* or *Thor*. It is Tiw who is still recalled in English 'Tuesday'; and it is generally accepted that the same god is intended by the south Germanic *Ziu* and in other Indo-European gods such as Greek *Zeus* and the Latin word *deus*, meaning simply 'god'; from the Latin we derive the English word *deity*. Tuoni also appears in the mythology of the Norwegian Lapps, where he is called *Duodna*, meaning 'the dead one'.

A very ancient, possibly pre-Indo-European etymology is evident here. Wallis Budge, in his *Egyptian Hieroglyphic Dictionary*, lists *Tuaanu* as the name of a god; and *Tua-t neter* as a title of the high priestess of Amen.[30] No one can be certain how ancient Egyptian words were pronounced, but these names at least seem to be of a Finnic origin, suggesting that much of the associated mythology of the Tuat was ultimately borrowed from a north European source.

The various references to 'giants' are a further common thread within all the myths. The Egyptian Book of the Dead describes khus (spirits) of giants, who were 9 cubits (4 metres) tall, and it surely cannot be a coincidence that many Manx legends also refer to giants of similar height.[31] The occurrence of giants in both Greek and Celtic mythology has been discussed previously, and they are equally prominent within the Norse myths; the *Völuspa* tells us that a race of giants perished on the great plain of Vigred, along with the gods. Whatever you may think of all this talk of giants, they are present in all the relevant mythologies and this too requires an explanation.

In reality the 'giants' may not have been of such enormous stature as these exaggerated myths record. The Book of the Dead also describes giant barley which, in the Elysian Fields, grew to a height of 5 cubits. Now if we take the cubit to be about 0.4 metres then this would imply that the barley grew to a height of some 2 metres. Real barley simply does not grow this high and so, logically, a mistranslation of units must have occurred at an early stage in the evolution of the myths. If one accepts that Neolithic cereal crops grew to much the same height as they do today, then simple ratio would make the 'giants' only about 2 metres in height. This is not so formidable after all; and well in line with the upper limit for modern Europeans.

If the Elysian Fields may indeed be held to be the ultimate source of the Atlantis myth, then we may also have an explanation for the straight canals which Plato mentions, and the deep channels which he says surrounded the great plain. Neither Irish nor Welsh legends of the Otherworld make any reference to canals. The closest that we get to them are the 'dykes' described in the Welsh legends of Cantre'r Gwaelod. There is no indication that the various rivers of the underworld described in mythological sources are anything other than natural features. Perhaps, then, the irrigation channels were neither as prominent nor as regular as Plato makes them. They may simply result from the way the Elysian Fields were drawn, on rectangular papyri, or inscribed on the temple walls.

16

Druids and Standing Stones

It is never easy to suggest correspondence between archaeological evidence and mythology. It seldom seems to concern the archaeologists if their theories do not agree with the indigenous local mythology; but if archaeology is the bones of prehistory then mythology is surely the flesh on those bones. Ultimately the two must converge, for the past has only one true story to tell.

Archaeology confirms that a surprisingly sophisticated culture existed in western Europe during the Neolithic. From about 5500 BC onwards, evidence of settled farming communities begins to appear around the coasts of Spain and Portugal. A millennium later, portal tombs or 'dolmens' were being built along the Atlantic coast of southern Portugal. This term is often applied to a class of chambered tomb consisting of a circular arrangement of massive upright stones, sometimes capped with another large lintel stone. These collective burial sites mark the earliest known evidence of the megalithic culture, which was later to become widespread over much of western Europe.

From Iberia, the megalithic culture region expanded eastwards and northwards. To the east, on the island of Malta, Neolithic farmers arrived in about 5000 BC and by 4000 BC, they were carving extensive tombs from the rock. By 3500 BC the temple at Ggantija was built and that at Tarxien at about 3300 BC. These temples, with their spiral decoration and monumental sculpture, outshine anything so far found in pre-dynastic Egypt at this early date. To the north, megalithic tombs are abundant along the Atlantic coast of Europe, the oldest being that at Kercado near Carnac dating from about 4700 BC.[1] Elsewhere along the coast of France they occur increasingly from 4000 BC onwards.

Towards the northern limit of the megalithic culture on the flat peninsula of Denmark, portal tombs are again found, though only dating from after 3400 BC. There they are associated with the people of the Funnel Beaker Culture, so named from their distinctive style of pottery, which is found right across north Germany and Scandinavia.[2] They seem to have merged with a mainly pastoral culture which had spread across Europe from the Danube after about 5000 BC.[3]

In Ireland, the earliest evidence of farming communities comes from the north-east of the island. The Neolithic settlements are easily distinguishable from the older Mesolithic sites by the presence of pottery. There is no evidence that the Mesolithic people of Ireland made any pottery at all and were presumably hunter-gatherers. The introduction of agriculture is therefore usually taken to indicate an influx of settlers from the Continent. The oldest farming settlement so far found is the Neolithic house at Ballyna-gilly in County Tyrone dating from around 4500 BC.[4] Clearings in the forest can be dated to this time, together with traces of wheat pollen and the remains of domesticated animals.

The earliest tombs found in Northern Ireland are the so-called Court Cairns, a class of long burial mound of roughly trapezoidal shape. Their distinctive features include one or more galleried burial chambers with impressive crescent-shaped entrance passages and a predominantly east–west orientation. The greatest concentration is found around Carlingford Lough, but pottery and flint tools of a style similar to that found in the Court Cairns occur on the Isle of Arran, Islay, the Isle of Man and in southern Ireland.

On mainland Britain sites are concentrated in Kintyre, around the Clyde, in south-west Scotland, and in Wales, but elsewhere the British sites are comparatively few. The uniformity of this tomb style led to its identification as a distinct Neolithic culture province called the Clyde–Carlingford Culture.[5] The tendency more recently has been to differentiate the tombs further into Clyde cairns, Solway cairns, and so forth. Outlying tombs of a similar style occur all round the Irish Sea coasts.[6] A prominent group is found in Anglesey, of which the Trefignath tomb near Holyhead is perhaps the best preserved. Outlying examples of the Irish style are to be found in Pembrokeshire, the Calderstones at Liverpool, and possibly others as far afield as Cheshire and Derbyshire.

The Isle of Man lies roughly at the geographic centre of this culture province and a further group of Court Cairns is found along its eastern side. The Manx tombs are of the more elaborate design found also in Northern Ireland and Arran, those elsewhere being of a simpler form.[7] The two best examples on the island are King Orry's Grave, now cut in two by a modern road; and Cashtal yn Ard, a much despoiled tomb lying to the north-west of Port Cornaa. Cashtal yn Ard was provided with the crescent-shaped forecourt typical of all the Irish cairns. This crescentic feature displays similarities with tombs found in the Pyrenees, and with one of the temples at Hal Tarxien, Malta, which has led to suggestions of a common derivation for the style.[8]

Another class of tomb found on the Isle of Man are those referred to as Giants Graves – apparently for no reason other than their elongated shape. The mounds have been much devastated by tomb robbers and clumsy excavators. The Giants Grave, Liaght ny Foawr, near German survives only as a row of stones, like that found within other chambered tombs. The Cloven Stones at Baldrine is now entirely enclosed by houses. It was formerly an oval mound enclosing a double compartment gallery grave. A document in the Manx Museum records the opening of this tomb by a group of miners in the early nineteenth century.[9] Within, they discovered a skull and thighbones belonging to a person 'of gigantic stature'. The size of the 'giant' is sadly not recorded.

In the south west of Britain during the fourth millennium BC a slightly different, but clearly related tomb-building tradition can be discerned.[10] In a region extending from south Wales, the Severn valley, Wessex and the south coast, chambered graves of a similar trapezoidal form to the Court Cairns are found. The tombs lack the crescent-shaped entrance found in Ireland. Pottery styles are comparable and fit into the overall classification of Western Neolithic or Neolithic 'A'.[11] A style of pottery known as Lyles Hill or Grimston ware is found all around the Irish Sea coasts.[12] It first appeared at about 4600 BC, but is not found at all after 3000 BC.

At this early period the British built hilltop enclosures known as causewayed camps, or 'henges'. Tomb styles in southern England are typified by the earthen and chambered long barrows, of which that at West Kennet, Wiltshire, is the archetypal example. These predominate in the chalk downland of Wiltshire and Dorset and are thought to have been built in areas lacking suitable stone for the building of chambered cairns.[13] As the name suggests, they consist of an elongated mound of earth or chalk rubble, covering a collective burial. The West Kennet long barrow also originally

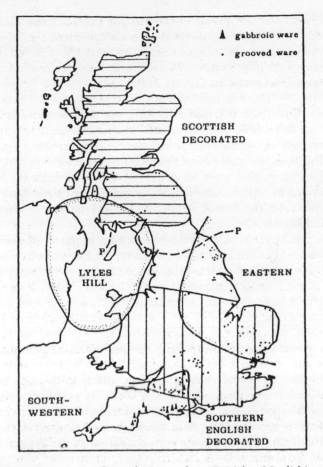

Fig. 16.1 Pottery styles during the British Neolithic (after Castleden 1987).
Reproduced by permission of International Thomson Publishing.

possessed a crescentic forecourt, before it was sealed by huge boulders about 1,000 years after it was built.

Excavations beneath the Wessex long barrows have revealed that they were built on top of farmland first cleared as early as 3500 BC. The criss-cross marks made by cross-ploughing were found beneath a long barrow at South Street, Avebury, Wiltshire.[14] Other so-called

'Celtic' field systems found in the west of England may also date from this early period – there is no way to date them.

In the west of Ireland, walled fields have been uncovered during the process of peat cutting. Whole field systems covering many acres have been found in County Mayo, which run on beneath the uncut peat.[15] There is little doubt that they should be associated with the Court Cairn builders. During the excavation of a Court Cairn at Behy, west of Ballycastle, field walls were discovered running right up to the edge of the cairn.[16] The blanket bogs have served to 'fossilize' these Neolithic fields in the state that they were abandoned and leave us in no doubt that they date from the fourth millennium BC. Similar pre-bog field walls and cairns have now been found on the Isle of Arran, Argyll and on the Orkney and Shetland Islands.[17]

The introduction of farming into Britain is put at about 4700 BC. Pioneering communities were clearing the forests in Cumbria at about this time and clearance accelerated after 4300 BC.[18] Many areas of the English chalk downland were also cleared for pasture, and at Hembury in Devon wheat and barley were grown from as early as 4200 BC.[19]

By 4000 BC, agriculture was well established throughout Britain. A hilltop enclosure at Carn Brea in the western tip of Cornwall has yielded radiocarbon dates in the range 3900–3150 BC, indicating the existence of cereal cultivation and animal husbandry at this early date.[20] At the northern extreme, on the remote Orkney island of Papa Westray, lies the Knap O'Howar site.[21] Here, querns for the grinding of corn have been found amidst the foundations of two stone houses. Dates given for occupation of the houses range between 3700 and 3100 BC.

Evidence for a growth of population towards the end of the fourth millennium BC is suggested by the clustering of radiocarbon dated finds, in the range 3600–3200 BC.[22] In the south of England, most of the causewayed camps and long barrows are from this period. A similar clustering is observed in the dates for the Neolithic fields and the Court Cairns, which also ceased to be built after about 3200 BC. The increase in the number of burials at this period would seem to imply a similar increase in the numbers of the living.

Shortly after 3200 BC, the building of gallery graves and long barrows came to an end, and the custom of collective burial ceased.

Ireland

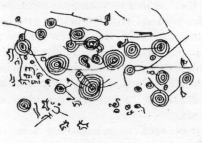

Sicily   North-West Spain

Northern Scotland   Malta

Fig. 16.2 Spiral carvings from Neolithic monuments around Europe (after Bradbery, A. and Bradbery J. 1979).
Reproduced by permission of G. Weidenfeld & Nicolson Ltd.

The focus of activity then switches away from the Irish Sea province to southern England. The extensive walled field systems of County Mayo were abandoned some time before 3000 BC and as the wetter Sub-Boreal conditions set in they began to be enveloped by layers of blanket bog.[23] Some archaeologists now think that they detect evidence of a 'Mid-Neolithic Crisis' at this period.[24] A cultural break occurs and the customs of burial, pottery styles and other indicators are totally changed. There is then a gap of some 200 or 300 years during which there is a dearth of recorded finds.[25] New types of monument, such as the stone circles and alignments, then make their first appearance.

The excavated remains may even indicate a complete change in human physical type.[26] Skeletal remains from the Neolithic are a comparative rarity, due to the general preference for cremation at that period. Those found in the Middle Neolithic cairns and long barrows tend to be tall, slender, dolichocephalic, or 'long-headed', individuals. These contrast strongly with the brachycephalic, or 'round-headed', population prevalent in the Late Neolithic round barrows.

It has been suggested that some kind of agricultural crisis developed during the Middle Neolithic as the population expanded rapidly, outstripping the capacity of the soil to support agriculture.[27] This idea is supported to some extent by the regrowth of woodland on formerly cleared land and a reversion to pastoralism in some areas.[28] A natural decline in the population over a number of centuries is then claimed to have set in, but it is difficult to see how this could explain all the changes noted at this period. The Mid-Neolithic Crisis is not just a British or Irish phenomenon; it has parallels elsewhere in Europe, notably in Scandinavia. It is synchronous with the recovery after the elm decline, the Atlantic/ Sub-Boreal transition, world-wide sea level variations and cultural changes noted as far afield as Egypt and China.

The radiocarbon revolution swept away most of the older theories of British and European prehistory. The then prevailing archaeological theories placed the Irish Sea cultures as late as 1900 BC on the basis of cross-dating.[29] Diffusionist theories had placed Britain and Ireland at the western end of a long chain of colonization and cultural exchange emanating from the eastern Mediterranean. While the advent of radiocarbon dating in the 1950s challenged this picture, this was as nothing compared to the upheaval that accompanied the first tree ring calibrated dates. The Neolithic culture of Atlantic Europe required total reassessment as an indigenous development.

Following the reappraisal of the chronology, it is now more usual to classify the Neolithic period into a preliminary phase

(4700–4300 BC), followed by the Early Neolithic (4300–3600 BC).[30] The succeeding period is termed the Middle Neolithic (3600–3200 BC) and the final phase is the Late Neolithic (3200–2000 BC). The case for the earlier divisions is not entirely proven, but it is only by the Middle Neolithic that evidence of a single homogeneous culture is discernible throughout the British Isles.

The Late Neolithic period is now considered as a time of recovery following the marked deterioration of the climate.[31] The most notable phenomenon for the archaeologist is the rapid spread of the distinctive Beaker pottery during the third millennium BC. This highly ornamented bell-shaped style of pot is found throughout Europe, from Ireland to the Black Sea and from Iberia to the Baltic. Beaker pottery is linked with a culture that buried its dead in single graves covered with mounds of earth, the so-called round barrows. This is in marked contrast to the communal internment customs of the earlier gallery grave and long barrow builders. The dead were inhumed in an upright crouching posture, together with various artefacts. Usually this included the characteristic Beaker urn, weapons of flint or copper and sometimes even ornaments of gold.

In Ireland, Beaker pottery has been found in the vicinity of Newgrange and other passage graves in the valley of the River Boyne.[32] Passage graves are generally to be found set within round cairns, in contrast to the long or trapezoid-shaped mounds of the earlier Neolithic. About 150 such passage graves are known throughout Ireland, but related groups are also found in Anglesey and in Brittany. In its restored form the passage grave at Newgrange is, without a doubt, the most impressive Neolithic monument surviving anywhere in Europe. The Tales of the Tuatha De Danann identify Newgrange with the legendary faery palace of Bruig na Boinde. It is by far the largest in the Boyne group, which includes Knowth to the west and another at Dowth to the east. The recently excavated frontage is of white quartz decorated here and there with darker material; and the entire mound is encircled by a ring of standing stones which may be somewhat later than the mound itself.

A narrow, almost straight passage leads to a corbelled cross-shaped chamber at the centre of the mound. Many of the stones comprising the passage walls are curiously decorated with engraved motifs. The style of carving is repetitive, exhibiting a variety of lozenge shapes, interlocking spirals, concentric rings, chevrons and zigzag lines. We can only speculate as to the meaning of this 'passage grave art'. The question of why only a few of the stones should be engraved is equally demanding of an answer. Recent investigation suggests that they may have astronomical significance and that perhaps Newgrange was more than just a tomb.

Carvings comparable with those in the Boyne valley tombs are found across the Irish Sea at the Bryn Celli Ddu passage grave on Anglesey. These similarities of style have led to suggestions that the Irish Sea coasts and the western peninsulas formed part of a single maritime culture province throughout the Neolithic.

Invasion theories are now out of favour as an explanation for cultural change. There is little real archaeological evidence to support any large-scale invasions of Britain or Ireland between that of the Beaker period and the intrusion of the Iron Age Belgae, just prior to Caesar's raids.[33] Some theorists would even claim that the changes that accompanied the arrival of the Beaker Culture can be explained without resort to large-scale population influx.[34] The evolution from the predominantly tall and slender, long-headed population of the Middle Neolithic into the robust, round-headed population of the Late Neolithic is explainable, they say, in other ways. The division is not altogether clear cut, as brachycephalic individuals are known from the earlier period and the population of the round barrows may be only representative of a small ruling elite. Skulls from Iron Age burials show evidence of a more varied population.[35]

However, the indigenous legends of the British Isles are unequivocal on the subject of prehistoric invasions. They tell of the arrival of many groups of settlers and invaders in Britain and Ireland. The Irish *Book of Invasions*, Geoffrey of Monmouth and the Welsh triads all recall an occupation of the British Isles following an era when they were virtually unoccupied. Only one period adequately fits this legendary 200 years when the British Isles were deserted and that is the Neolithic dark age.

The earliest Irish invaders of legend are said to have taken a northerly route from their Aegean home, via Scythia and the Baltic. Later waves of invaders made their way from the same region, but via Spain and the Mediterranean. It would be curious indeed if some of their number had not settled in Britain and the Atlantic coast of Europe along the way. The Welsh triads similarly recall an

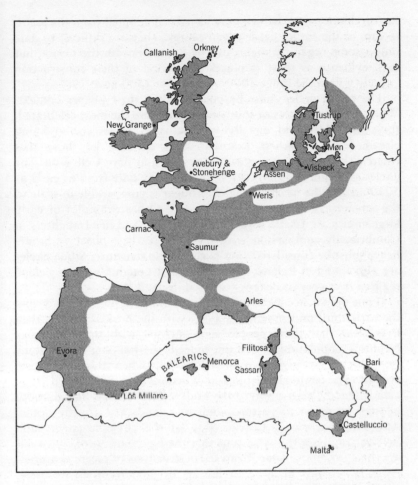

Fig. 16.3 The approximate boundaries of the megalithic culture region in western Europe (after Bradbery, A. and Bradbery, J. 1979). Reproduced by permission of G. Weidenfeld & Nicolson Ltd.

early migration from the regions around the Black Sea. They also hint at a whole series of later invaders, such as the Caledonians, and the Coranied, who settled about the Humber.

The third millennium BC is the age of stone circles and alignments. Stone circles and henge monuments seem to be a largely

British development, which may have been adapted from the architecture of the earlier causewayed camps. They are difficult to date unless some organic remains can be found beneath the stones, but such evidence as there is places the period of their construction entirely within the range 3000 BC to about 1500 BC.[36]

The stone circles must be considered in their proper context. While the giant circles of southern England are the most celebrated, there are older and equally impressive examples to be found elsewhere. The earliest examples may actually be those that encircle the passage graves at Newgrange and Bryn Celli Ddu. The circles at Stenness on Orkney Mainland may date from as early as 3040 BC and the nearby Ring of Brodgar is comparable in scale to the inner rings of the Avebury circle.[37] Other examples of early large circles are Castle Rigg, and Long Meg and her Daughters in Cumbria. By comparison with these, the earliest phase of Stonehenge must be considered as a fairly simple structure. Stone circles are also found in Ireland, where the main Lough Gur ring yielded the first discovery of Beaker pottery in Ireland.[38]

If one does concede the influx of an immigrant population during the early third millennium BC, along with the Beaker pottery, then it is clear that these people soon merged with the indigenous Neolithic population of Britain. Indeed, the building of the stone circles may already have been ongoing when the newcomers arrived. The circle at Avebury in Wiltshire was constructed in an area where the cultivation of the Middle Neolithic period had been allowed to revert to pasture land, in a landscape already dotted with long barrows.[39] Construction of the circle began around 2600 BC at about the same time that the Egyptians were constructing their pyramids. Apart from the destructions of recent centuries, Avebury remains in more or less its original form. By contrast, nearby Stonehenge began its life shortly after 3000 BC and was to undergo three successive phases of redevelopment.[40]

The first phase of construction at Stonehenge involved the building of the circular bank and ditch. There appears to have been originally no stone circle on the site, but the ring of fifty-six chalk-filled holes, known as Aubrey holes after the antiquarian John Aubrey, can also be dated to this period. The outlying Heel Stone and Slaughter Stone also belong to the first phase, together with a curious array of post-holes situated on the main avenue.

A second phase of building took place at about 2250 BC, when the first stone circle was constructed using the famous Bluestones from south Wales.[41] Originally they were laid out as two concentric rings, along with four outliers called the Station Stones set in a rectangle around the outer henge. The huge ring of sarsen stones and the central horseshoe of trilithons that we see today were only introduced at about 2100 BC and successive phases of reorganization continued up to about 1100 BC.

William Stukeley in the mid-eighteenth century first noted the alignment of the main axis of Stonehenge with the direction of midsummer sunrise. This alignment has existed from the earliest stage of the monument, as on Midsummer Day the Sun can be seen to rise approximately over the Heel Stone. Many subsequent writers took up this theme and in the popular imagination Stonehenge has come to be associated with Sun worship, or dubbed a druid temple. But the Sun does not rise exactly over the Heel Stone today due to the precession of the Earth's orbit since it was built. In the early twentieth century, the astronomer Sir Norman Lockyer attempted to date the building of Stonehenge by calculating when the Sun did rise precisely over the Heel Stone and arrived at the then highly controversial date of 1800 BC for its construction.[42]

Little notice was taken of the possibility of Neolithic astronomical alignments until the 1960s. In 1963 the American astronomer Gerald S. Hawkins published his book *Stonehenge Decoded* in which he claimed a whole series of astronomical alignments for Stonehenge, marking the solstice points and the extreme rising and setting positions of the Moon. He put forward a strong case for Stonehenge as an eclipse predictor. This was followed shortly afterwards by the investigations of Professor Alexander Thom into the alignment of other stone circles and megalithic monuments throughout Britain and France.[43] His comprehensive surveys show that many of the stone circles are complex ellipses and ovoids, laid out with a sound knowledge of geometry. The megalith builders were skilled mathematicians, aware of Pythagorean triangles long before the Greeks.

The subject of Neolithic calendrical alignments has been well explored by many able minds. The case is now virtually proven and the validity of many alignments claimed for stone circles is accepted here without further enquiry. The question that has never been satisfactorily answered is *why* the stone circles were built. Why was it necessary for Stonehenge to be totally redesigned twice over?

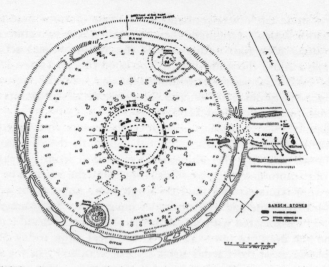

Fig. 16.4 Astronomical alignments at Stonehenge.

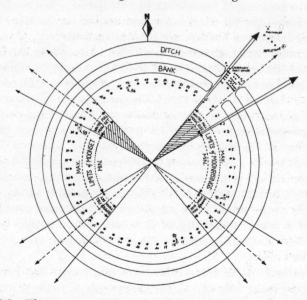

Fig. 16.5 The extreme rising and setting points of the Sun and Moon at Stonehenge. What was the function of the post-holes on the main avenue? (After C. A. Newham 1972.)

Reproduced by courtesy of Moon Publications.

Why should the Neolithic Britons have been so obsessively interested in astronomy?

The idea that Stonehenge and Avebury might be druid temples was originally proposed by John Aubrey in about 1690 and later by William Stukeley. In the twentieth century, these ideas have tended to be pushed aside as druidism has come to be associated almost exclusively with the Iron Age Celts. Even the official *Stonehenge Handbook* now disparages any connection between the druids and stone circles.[44]

In fact there is every reason to believe that the druids were a very ancient order traceable back to 3000 BC and perhaps even earlier. Evidence of druids is found throughout the area we associate with the Celts. The possibility that the stone circles and alignments might be the sacred groves of the early druids remains a reasonable theory. Unfortunately very little is known about the druids. Such positive information as we do have about them is largely derived from Roman sources and relates to Gaul rather than Britain. Nevertheless, an examination of this rather late evidence will bear useful fruit.

In Irish legend the druids of the Tuatha De Danann appear in a number of early sagas, and Manannan mac Lir, who navigated by astronomy, is said to have been a druid.[45] They also figure prominently within the *Book of Invasions* which, as has been suggested elsewhere, may describe events of the early third millennium BC. In the legendary battle between the children of Nemed and the Fomorians, we are told that 'A battle was begun first between their druids, and another between their druidesses.'[46] Taken at face value, this would seem to imply that the aboriginal Fomorians also possessed priests or shamans whose function was at least comparable to the druids, as the later story-tellers understood them.

Classical texts refer exclusively to the druids of Gaul and we cannot be entirely sure that they fulfilled precisely the same role within Irish society. The name derives from a common Indo-European root, *druid* being the Irish plural form.[47] Pliny derived the meaning of the word: *drus*, meaning 'oak-tree', with the second half of the word deriving from an Indo-European word implying knowledge, or wisdom. The Gaulish druids built sanctuaries or sacred groves within forest clearings and something of this may be intended by the Irish word *nemedh* which means 'a sanctuary'.[48]

This is common in many Celtic place-names, such as *Aquae Arne-metiae*, the English spa town of Buxton. There are numerous examples throughout the former Celtic areas, such as the Galatian sanctuary of Drunemeton in Asia Minor.[49] This points to an early arrival of druidism in Ireland associated with the legendary tribe of Nemed.

The customs of the Gaulish druids are preserved by several classical writers, notably Pliny, Diodorus Siculus, Strabo and Caesar, most of whom drew upon the lost histories of Posidonius.[50] Caesar described the Gaulish druids as one of the two privileged classes. Strabo calls them one of three privileged classes, along with the vates and the bards. They paid no taxes and took no part in warfare. As a result of these privileges, many young men were keen to join their order as novices. They acted as judges in all disputes and took a leading role in the ceremonial worship of the Celtic gods. Their judgement was accepted by kings and chieftains as settlement of intertribal disputes.

Although some of their practices were exceedingly brutal, the druids were undoubtedly philosophers of great wisdom and renown. Caesar records that they held long debates about the powers of the gods, the nature of the universe and the movements of the Sun, Moon and planets. They held that the universe was indestructible, but that at times 'fire and water may temporarily prevail'! This philosophy they jealously guarded as therein lay the ultimate source of all their power. Their novices were required to memorize all this information in the form of verse.

Astronomy is numbered among the achievements and most closely guarded secrets of the druids, and such detailed astronomical knowledge could only have been gained after a period of sound observation and recording of the bodies in the sky. The strongest case for astronomical alignments can be made for the very oldest stone circles.[51] Stonehenge, for example, may have degenerated into a temple only in its later phases, following a long period when the site served as a practical observatory.

Julius Caesar gives us the important piece of information that druidism originated in Britain and that those who wished to become truly proficient would go there to study. He states that the doctrine was 'discovered' in Britain and only later imported into Gaul. For all that, there is little information available as to the role of druidism in Britain, but this simple statement would seem to attribute it to the aboriginal inhabitants rather than to any later Celtic immigrants from the Continent.

It is known that the Romans found druidic rituals abhorrent and considered the order to be a constant threat to their authority in Gaul. The order was proscribed by Augustus and its eradication may have been one of the underlying motives behind the Claudian invasion of Britain. Nothing at all is heard of the druids in accounts of the early conquest. It is not until the conquest of Mona (Anglesey) by Suetonius Paulinus in AD 60, that we encounter them in Britain.[52] Tacitus records that the island was densely populated and that among the army that faced him as he crossed the Menai Straits were women clad in black robes and druids wailing curses. Suetonius conquered the island and demolished the sacred groves dedicated to 'Mona's barbarous superstitions'. Apparently the task was left incomplete as Suetonius hastened to deal with the Boudiccan revolt; and it was left to Agricola some years later finally to destroy the power of the druids in Anglesey.

This is really the only firm association that we have between the druids and Anglesey. The importance that the Romans attached to the island's conquest suggests that it was the very centre of their cult, and of Celtic resistance to Rome. However, there is much other circumstantial evidence to suggest that Anglesey was the sacred island of the druids. Caesar includes Mona in his description of Britain, but neglects the existence of the Isle of Wight or the Scilly Isles although they are closer to Gaul. Curiously he also refers to a number of islands west of Britain in which a month of perpetual darkness occurred at the winter solstice.

The geographer Strabo records that there was an island near to Britain on which sacrificial rites in honour of Demeter and Core were performed, after the manner of those performed on the Aegean island of Samothrace.[53] It is probable that this also refers to some rites of the Anglesey druids and may also explain a remark by Nennius: 'The sons of Liathan reigned in the country of the Demetians, where the city of Mynyw is.'[54] The tribe of the Demetians is usually placed in the modern county of Dyfed. The origin of the tribal name is not known, but it is interesting to postulate that it derives from the name of the goddess Demeter; perhaps a name applied to them by the Romans.

You may recall that Demeter was one of the daughters of Cronus and a much-revered Olympian goddess. She was worshipped as the golden-haired goddess of fertility. According to Greek mythology her daughter Core (perhaps better known as Persephone or Proserpine) was carried off by Hades and the rape of Persephone was said to symbolize the annual death and rebirth of the plants and animals.[55] This further supports Caesar's claim that the Celts knew the same gods as the Greeks and Romans. He also records the druids teaching that the Celts were all descended from Father Dis (Dis Pater). This is simply the Roman name of Hades and the case for linking Hades with the Irish Sea region need not be further elaborated here.

It was only shortly after the Roman conquest of Anglesey that the explorer Demetrius learned the tale of the eternal imprisonment of Cronus on an island to the west of Britain. We are only told that his source was a group of holy men. Plutarch says that they were 'held inviolate by the Britons' and were therefore presumably druids.[56] Although the Celts may have called their gods by quite different names, this need not preclude the possibility that they were essentially the same deities as those worshipped by the Greeks and Romans; and indeed that the same dynasty of ancient kings may underlie all the gods of western mythology.

Pliny gives us another interesting piece of information regarding Anglesey, in his discussion of the solstices.[57] He describes the phenomenon of the Arctic summer and winter, whereby six months of continuous daylight occur in the summer, and six months continuous night during the winter.

> Pytheas of Marseille writes that this occurs in the island of Thule, 6 days' voyage north from Britain, and some declare it also to occur in the Isle of Anglesey, which is about 200 miles from the British town of Colchester.

This apparently innocent geographical error by Pliny may in fact be highly revealing, for the ultimate source of the remark can only have been the astronomical knowledge of the Anglesey druids themselves. It seems to imply that at some period in the past the Arctic Circle strayed as far south as the latitude of Anglesey! Something like this may also be recalled at the beginning of the Welsh Annals which refer to 'days as dark as night'.[58]

There seems to be a genuine recollection here of a time when the Arctic Circle was much further south, and this in turn would imply a much greater axial tilt than the Earth has at present. The possibility that the Earth has experienced a nutation large enough to bring the Arctic Circle quite so far south seems unlikely. More credibly, it may have been lowered to the latitude of the Orkneys or the Hebrides, as is supported by Caesar's commentaries. Perhaps Pliny's remark may therefore be explained as a piece of misunderstood druidic astronomy.

The original purpose of the stone circles and alignments may therefore be ventured. It was no mere philosophical interest that drove their construction, but a very real need to understand the calendar and the complex cycle of the seasons. It is significant that the building of circles began in the north during the early third millennium BC and declined towards the end of the second millennium BC. This spans the Sub-Boreal period of climate change and the entire period during which it is postulated that the axial tilt and the calendar were evolving.

In order to understand the cycle of the year as it is experienced today, it is not necessary to build anything as complex as the stone circle alignments. All that would be needed is to set up a simple gnomon or sundial and measure the period between the extreme lengths of the shadow. Alternatively, an extreme rising or setting position of the Sun could be marked out by an alignment. During a period when the Earth's axial tilt was changing, and the number of days in the year were increasing, then the calendar would not be quite so simple. It would require constant checking and revision. Glitches in the rotation and episodes of nutation would spell disaster for agriculture at northerly latitudes unless their effects could be predicted. This was the original function of the stone circle observatories. The power of the druids grew out of their ability to predict the changing seasons by regular and careful observation of the stars.

According to Pliny's *Natural History* the druids operated a lunar calendar in which the months were measured from the sixth day following each new Moon.[59] He also refers to the use of longer units of 30 years called 'ages'. This interval is also mentioned by Plutarch, who states that at intervals of 30 years the Britons undertook regular sea voyages to the island of Ogygia.[60] The voyages commenced each time that the planet Saturn (the star of Cronus) entered the constellation of Taurus. This constellation holds the Pleiades star cluster, the rising of which traditionally marked the Celtic spring festival of Beltane; and clearly the arduous voyage to Ogygia (probably Iceland) could only have been attempted in the spring or summer.

The use of this long unit might imply that the synodic period of Saturn was used as an absolute check on the calendar, for much the same reason that Venus was observed by the Babylonians and the Mayans. The 30 year 'age' was therefore equivalent (or very nearly) to twenty-nine synodic periods of Saturn – the interval required for the planet to circuit the zodiac and return again to the Pleiades (see Appendix A). Some investigators have even suggested that Pleiades alignments may exist at Stonehenge and at Callanish in the Hebrides.[61]

There are just a few other indicators worthy of mention, which help to confirm the antiquity of druidic astronomy. The first of these is a recently excavated calendrical monument found at the Dacian capital of Sarmizegetusa, in the area of modern Romania. This druid-like temple, of wood and stone, was also demolished by the Romans and displays a superficially similar ground plan to the final phase of Stonehenge. At the centre of the circular monument lies a horseshoe of post-holes aligned on the midwinter sunrise, just as the axis of Stonehenge is aligned on the midsummer sunrise. This points to a continuity of astronomical knowledge between the Celts of Roman times and the Stonehenge era, 1,500 years earlier. Similar aligned wooden structures dating from the early third millennium BC have been found at Woodhenge near Amesbury, and also at Godmanchester in Cambridgeshire.

The writer John Michell has also pointed out the similarity between the Neolithic stone circle at Boscawen-un in Cornwall and the traditional *Gorsedd* circle used by the modern Welsh Bards.[62] These latter would claim to be the inheritors of ancient bardic tradition.

Yet a further clue to the antiquity of druidic astronomy is supplied by Hecataeus in his description of the fabled Hyperboreans. The Hyperboreans were also astronomers, who well understood the cycle of the Moon.

> It is also said, that, in this island, the moon appears very near to the earth, that certain eminences of a terrestrial form, are plainly seen in it, that the god (Apollo) visits the island once in a course of nineteen years, in which period the stars complete their revolutions, and that for this reason, the Greeks distinguish the cycle of nineteen years, by the name of the Great Year.

During the season of his appearance, the god plays upon the harp, and dances every night, from the vernal equinox, till the rising of the Pleiades, pleased with his own success.

The supreme authority in that city and sacred precinct, is vested in those who are called Boreadae, being the descendants of Boreas, and their governments have been uninterruptedly transmitted in this line.

This passage is a continuation of that quoted in the previous chapter. It refers to the 19-year Cycle of Meton, named after the Athenian astronomer who introduced it to Greece in the fifth century BC. Its significance lies in the reconciliation of the lunar and solar periods. After a cycle of 235 months, or 19 years, the Sun and Moon return to their starting positions, with an error of only a few hours. A calendar could therefore be constructed consisting of 12 years of 12 lunar months; and 7 years with 13 lunar months. This cycle lies at the heart of theories of astronomical alignments at Stonehenge as propounded by Hawkins, Hoyle and others.

Many authors have suggested that the 'spherical temple' of the fabled Hyperboreans is a reference to Stonehenge or to one of the other astronomically aligned circles. The reference to the Boreads may imply an early dynasty of all-powerful druids. If the Stonehenge connection is true then it would carry the origins of druidic astronomy back close to 3000 BC; but it may be possible to trace some elements of druidism back even earlier than this, to the Middle Neolithic cultures of the Irish Sea region.

The tumuli at Bryn Celli Ddu in Anglesey and at Newgrange in Ireland are of a generation even older than the stone circles. The construction of them apparently ceased just as the building of stone circles got under way. It had long been known that the passage at Newgrange was approximately aligned on the direction of the midwinter sunrise, but during the modern restorations a curious narrow slot feature was discovered above the main entrance, which has come to be called the 'roof-box'.

Around midwinter sunrise, the Sun briefly shines directly through this roof-box and illuminates the back wall of the chamber. In a recent survey, T.P. Ray, of the Dublin School of Cosmic Physics, concluded that the Newgrange alignment is deliberate and that Newgrange is therefore the oldest monument for which an astronomical function can be claimed.[63] However an earlier survey showed that the Sun would still illuminate the chamber if its declination lay anywhere within a range of 3° of arc. It was also possible to date the roof-box from charcoal samples found between the slabs and these gave a construction date of 3150 BC, within a probable accuracy of 100 years. The position of the rising Sun 5,150 years ago would have illuminated a three-leafed spiral figure on the back wall of the chamber. This date is crucial for the theories proposed here, as astronomical alignments are not to be expected from the period before the Earth's rotation was disturbed. The implication therefore is that the astronomical event that triggered the building of the mound occurred shortly before this date.

It should be appreciated that an increased Chandler wobble or a motion of the axis of the crust and mantle about that of the core would in no way invalidate the various alignments proposed for these ancient monuments. The gravitational factors influencing the Earth's axis (the astronomical precession) can be projected back with some validity in order to determine the ancient rising and setting positions of the Sun and Moon. However, between about 3100 BC and 1000 BC it is here proposed that the spiralling of the celestial pole would have carried the rising and setting points to the north and south of these average positions over a regular 7-year cycle. At Newgrange these changes in azimuth could have been tracked by the position of the beam along the walls of the chamber, while at Stonehenge similar alignments may have been achieved using an array of wooden posts across the main avenue. The transition from passage observatories to outdoor alignments may have had much to do with the decreasing amplitude of the phenomenon over the centuries.

The building of the so-called passage graves may therefore be linked with the arrival of the Nemedians in Ireland and the Cymry in Britain, just as the legends suggest. The wisdom of the later Iron Age Celts may therefore represent a fusion of the religion of these invading groups with that of the aboriginal population. In Irish tales, the indigenous Fomorians, the inhabitants of the Otherworld and the people of the Sidhe or faery mounds are often indistinguishable. The struggle between the Tuatha De Danann and the Fomorians is graphically described in a story called *The Fate of the Children of Tuirenn*.[64] Here we find Balor, the king of the Fomorians, holding a council of war along with Lobais the druid, and 'the nine deeply learned poets and prophetic philosophers of the Fomorians'.

Pliny describes a ceremony performed by the druids, which bears a striking resemblance to the bull sacrifice ceremony of Plato's narrative. On the sixth day after the new Moon, two white bulls would be ritually sacrificed with a golden sickle.[65] We cannot know how often this took place, but if it was indeed a monthly ceremony then the supply of white bulls must have been truly prodigious! This ritual of sacrificing oxen to the king of the underworld was clearly an important element of pagan belief. The early Christians dared not abolish the practice, instead redirecting the sacrifice towards the Christian god.[66] We should therefore be left in no doubt that some elements of Iron Age worship were very old indeed and belonged to the earliest religion of the Atlantic west.

The Mythological Triads date the founding of druidism to the time immediately after the Flood. Hu Gadarn is said to have been the first druid and it was he who first adapted poetry for the purpose of preserving records. The astronomy of the druids is celebrated in the triad of the Three Happy Astronomers of the Island of Britain.[67]

> Idris Gawr
> Gwyddion, the son of Don,
> And Gwyn, the son of Nudd.
>
> [So great was their knowledge of the stars, and of their nature and situation, that they could foretell whatever might be desired to be known, to the day of doom.]

Why should Anglesey, an obscure island on the western periphery of Europe, come to be the sacred island of the druids? The earliest colonists may have voyaged to the Irish Sea in search of the fabled Elysium, the Otherworld of eternal springtime of which their legends told them. Instead they discovered only a land of the dead, a landscape littered with the burial cairns, abandoned fields and the artefacts of a lost civilization; where dead and fallen trees lined the shores, alternately submerged and exposed by the fluctuating tides. The surviving monuments would have seemed far more impressive to these early colonists than the ruins of today.

This superstition that the Land of the Dead lay off the western coast of Britain remained prevalent in Britain and Gaul at least as late as the Roman period. The sixth-century writer Procopius records the myth.[68] For historians, Procopius is one of the few sources of information about early Anglo-Saxon England and his mythological references are usually considered an embarrassment! His geography is confused, for he attributes the myth to an island called Brittia, which he locates somewhere north of the Roman province of Britannia. Evidently he believed that Britannia and Brittia were two different islands. We may equate his Brittia with northern Britain in the sixth century AD, as he says it was inhabited by Angles, Britons and Frisians.

The myth relates that the men of Brittia once built an impassable wall to separate a part of the Land of the Dead from the habitable regions. To the east of this wall, the description given by Procopius is a familiar one, and perhaps this is another occasion when only a quotation will serve to illustrate.

> for to the east of the wall there is a salubrious air, changing with the seasons, being moderately warm in summer and cool in winter. And many people dwell there, living in the same fashion as other men, and the trees abound with fruits which ripen at the fitting season, and the corn-lands flourish as abundantly as any . . .

One may immediately recognize the Celtic Otherworld and elements of Geoffrey's Avalon yet again in the more sober description of Procopius. The story must have originated from one of the aboriginal tribes of the north; and once again the only era when the climate was sufficiently mild to fit this description is the warm Atlantic period. It is striking how often this climatic marker occurs in mythology. By this device the events may be assigned to the fourth millennium BC.

Procopius goes on to say that to the west of the wall there lay a region where the air was foul and unbreathable, inhabited only by snakes and wild beasts. Were a man to venture there he would surely fall down dead within less than half an hour. Here we have heaven and hell placed side by side, echoing many of the descriptions of Tartarus found within classical mythology. According to Hesiod, the gods surrounded Tartarus with a great wall of bronze.[69]

Procopius further records the myth, published he says by many writers of his day, that the souls of the dead are carried to the west of Britain for their final rest. The people of northern Gaul, he tells us, carried on a commerce with Brittia, upon which they paid no duty or tax, in recognition of a certain valuable service rendered since the most ancient times. The fishermen and traders along the coast were charged with the duty of ferrying the souls of the dead across to their final resting-place in Britain. Their boats, laden down by the weight of their invisible passengers, would require less than an hour's journey to arrive at their destination. The souls would then alight and the boatmen return home with all haste. As they departed, a voice might be heard, announcing the names of the new arrivals in the Land of the Dead.

17

A Neolithic Empire

It is likely that neither Plato nor his source Solon knew of the existence of the British Isles. They may have heard tales of the fabled Hyperboreans, or of the Island of the Albiones beyond the Celts, but they had no reason to associate any existing island with the Atlantis legend. Plato had inherited from Solon the belief that the island had been utterly consumed in the depths of the ocean some 9,000 years before his own time.

The earliest classical references to islands in the Atlantic that can be positively identified with Britain and Ireland occur at around the time of Solon. They are found in the *Massiliote Periplus* as preserved by Avienius. Although attributable to some unknown inhabitant of the Greek colony of Marseille, it is apparently based upon a sailing itinerary by the Carthaginian navigator Hamilco, dating from about 500 BC. It describes a journey to the Tin Islands (the Cassiterides or Oestrymnides) and is followed by a most curious reference to the British Isles.[1]

> But from here it is two days journey by ship to the sacred island, as the ancients called it. This spreads its broad fields amongst the waves and far and wide the race of the Hierni inhabit it. Near it again lies the island of the Albiones.

This reference to 'fields amongst the waves' is surely an odd way to describe an island. The sacred island mentioned is usually considered to be Ireland, since Aristotle, writing a little later, refers to the two 'Brettanic Islands' called Albion and Ierne.[2] The occurrence of Albion as the name for Britain steadily declined throughout the classical era until by the first century AD Pliny referred to it as an old name of the island.

The usually reliable Herodotus knew nothing of the British Isles, unless possibly it be in his references to the Hyperboreans. He appears not to know of any islands beyond the Celts, or even that there was a sea in that direction at all. He does record that tin and amber came from the Cassiteride Islands in the Atlantic, but confesses to know nothing about them.[3] In two places Herodotus refers to a people called the Cynetae 'furthest west of all', who lived somewhere along the Atlantic coast, beyond the Celts.[4] This may be a reference to the Cyn-men who are remembered in Welsh poetry; the bard Aneurin describes the Cynt as a division of the Celts of Britain, but there is no suggestion by Herodotus that his Cynetae lived on an island.[5]

The Greeks were long barred from trading beyond the Straits of Gibraltar by the Phoenicians and later by the Carthaginians, who monopolized the Atlantic tin trade. This monopoly was certainly in force throughout the sixth and early fifth centuries BC and explains why Herodotus was so vague about the geography of the west. The supply of tin in antiquity came almost exclusively from two sources, Cornwall, and the estuary of the River Loire. Various authors throughout the classical period refer to the source of tin as the Cassiteride Islands, which had an uncertain location. Ptolemy's map of AD 150 shows them lying off the north-west coast of Spain. Since no such islands exist, they are usually equated with Cornwall or the Isles of Scilly; but it is much more likely that the name refers to former islands in the Loire estuary, now joined to the mainland.[6]

The principal port of the tin trade was Gades: the modern Spanish port of Cadiz. The first city on the site was a colony built by the Phoenicians c.1100 BC on an island within the sheltered bay. Lying just outside the Pillars of Heracles, it represented the very limit of Greek knowledge of the Atlantic. It was from this base that the Phoenicians operated their western commercial empire and from which, later, the Carthaginians would colonize most of southern Spain. It was always a wealthy city and Strabo was later to record the wealth of the Gaditanian merchants at Rome.[7]

It was partly in an effort to break this tin monopoly, partly in the cause of exploration, that in about 325 BC a Greek sailor named Pytheas set out from Marseille to defy the Carthaginian blockade.[8] It is possible that Pytheas had heard vague Carthaginian reports about the islands in the Atlantic. He sailed through the Straits of Gibraltar, avoiding Gades, and on up the Atlantic coast in search of the Tin Islands.

The travels of Pytheas took him to Britain, which he called

the Prettanic Isles and on into the North Sea, where storms blew him away from the British coast. He claimed to have reached Thule (probably the coast of Norway in this case) and turned back south again, via the coasts of Germany and Holland. On returning to Marseille, he wrote an account of his voyage called *On the Ocean* of which, sadly, only fragments survive. Pytheas's book became the source for all Greek and Roman geography regarding the north-west of Europe for the next four centuries, until the Romans reached Britain. Later geographers refused to believe Pytheas. It may seem strange to us today that the inhabitants of southern France should know almost nothing about an island lying off the north of that same country. In antiquity the land was the true barrier. The sea was the open avenue of trade over great distances.

Plato's story of Atlantis falls entirely into this period of three centuries between the Massiliote Periplus and the voyage of Pytheas. Greek knowledge of the west ended at Gades. Any information about the Atlantic can only have come via the Carthaginians, whose sole objective was to confuse the geography and exaggerate the dangers of the ocean. A good deal of this confusion is evident from the geography of later Greek and Roman writers. These authors seldom undertook any exploration of their own and merely perpetuated the errors in their sources.

The classical geographers believed that the British Isles were much closer to Spain than they truly are. This geographical mistake is evident in Caesar's description.[9] Coming from a general who actually campaigned in Britain, it is useful both for its brevity and as an indication of the extent of geographical knowledge in the first century BC.

> The island is triangular, with one side facing Gaul. One corner of this side, on the coast of Kent, is the landing-place for nearly all the ships from Gaul, and points east; the lower corner points south. The length of this side is about 475 miles. Another side faces west, towards Spain. In this direction is Ireland, which is supposed to be half the size of Britain, and lies at the same distance from it as from Gaul.

Caesar's view of Britain as a triangular island is probably drawn from Eratosthenes, who drew upon Pytheas. The geographical error that the western side of Britain faced towards Spain, with Ireland in between, is a very persistent one. It is evident as late as Pliny, who describes it as facing Germany, Gaul and Spain across a broad channel.[10] The error is even more clearly seen in the geography of Strabo. He was not at all aware of the existence of the Brittany peninsula and thought that the western cape of Britain (Land's End) lay opposite the Pyrenees.[11] He too believed the Cassiteride Islands to lie somewhere off the north-west coast of Spain.

The Greek world, knowing so little of the geography beyond the Straits of Gibraltar, could only speculate idly on what lay there. The various legends of the Isles of the Blest, the Fortunate Isles, and of course, Mount Atlas, have their roots in this period when real knowledge of the west was restricted. The Greeks knew that the coast of Iberia turned north beyond Gades, but were apparently unaware that it turned east again beyond Cape Finisterre. Faced with reports of islands lying 'opposite' the coast of Iberia, they therefore quite naturally placed them out in the open ocean, facing the coast of Portugal. This error persisted as late as the description of Diodorus Siculus (*c*.30 BC), which is but one example:[12] 'Above the country of the Lusitani [Portugal] there are many mines of tin, and on the islets which lie near Iberia in the ocean, and because of this are termed Cattiterides.'

The Atlantis narratives reflect Greek, and perhaps Egyptian, understanding of the geography of the west in the sixth century BC. The known errors of the classical geographers must therefore be borne in mind when considering their geography. In the *Timaeus*, Atlantis is represented as lying 'opposite' or 'in front of' the Straits of Gibraltar. Elsewhere, as has already been discussed, Plato describes a peninsula or promontory of the island: 'the extremity of the island towards the pillars of Heracles, facing the country which is now called the region of Gades in that part of the world . . .' The geography is precisely the same as is found in later references to Britain and the Tin Islands, which similarly place them opposite the coast of Iberia. In view of what has been said previously, there is no reason at all why this peninsula should not be identified with Cornwall and the regions that now lie submerged off its coast. A little of the 'mystery' of Atlantis begins to dissolve away.

It may now be possible to make a little more sense of the fragment from the *Ethiopic History* of Marcellus which was quoted in chapter 2 and which it is worth while examining further.

That such and so great an island once existed, is evident from what is said by certain historians respecting what pertains to the external sea. For according to them, there were seven islands in that sea, in their times sacred to Proserpine and also three others of immense extent, one of which was sacred to Pluto, another to Ammon, and the middle [or second] one of which was sacred to Neptune, the magnitude of which was a thousand stadia. They also add, that the inhabitants of it preserved the remembrance from their ancestors, of the Atlantic island which existed there, and was truly prodigiously great; which for many periods had dominion over all the islands in the Atlantic sea, and was itself likewise sacred to Neptune.

We cannot know who these historians were, or precisely when their times might have been, but the uncertain geography is indicative of a very early source. The gods are Roman. Proserpine is the same as Greek Persephone, often referred to as Core ('Maiden'). Pluto is identical with Father Dis and Hades, while Ammon is identifiable with Ammon-Re, the Sun god, whom the Greeks called Zeus-Ammon.[13]

The seven sacred islands may be compared with accounts elsewhere of the Cassiteride Islands. Pomponius Mela (AD 40) says that there were 'several' Cassiteride Islands lying off the Brittany coast, on which lay an oracle, served by nine Gaulish priestesses sworn to perpetual virginity.[14] Strabo says that there were ten Cassiterides, inhabited by priests clad in black robes. The druidesses who confronted Suetonius in Anglesey are similarly described.[15] Possibly these islands sacred to Proserpine are merely another reference to the ceremonial worship of a virgin or 'earth-mother' type goddess, equivalent to the mysteries of Demeter and Core, which we know were performed 'on an island close to Britain'.

The three larger islands may be interpreted as a reference to the British Isles. There are two distinct possibilities here. The island sacred to Pluto must be equated with Britain as it is known that the British druids considered themselves to be descended from the god of the underworld. The other two islands are problematical. It may be that Iceland (Thule) and Ireland are intended, which would make Ireland the central island, in line with interpretations of Avienius. Alternatively, the island sacred to Ammon could be Ireland, which would imply that either Anglesey or Man was the 'central island' referred to as sacred to Neptune-Poseidon. It must not be forgotten that in Irish tradition the Isle of Man is the island of Manannan mac Lir. The reference by Marcellus is therefore perfectly logical if it refers to Ler – the Celtic god of the sea.

This central island (according to Marcellus) preserved a tradition that it had formerly been part of a single large island situated at the centre of a great empire, ruling over all the islands in the Atlantic Ocean. Possibly this tradition formed part of the teachings of the Celtic bards and survived at least long enough for some unknown classical historian to record it.

So it may be seen that the identification of Plato's lost island with the Middle Neolithic cultures of the British Isles is an entirely plausible one. The various strands of evidence offered here fit very well with existing chronologies and physical evidence. All that is required to accept them is a modification to our rigid ideas about the nature of the Earth's rotation. A recognition and understanding of the geophysical theory proposed here is crucial to an understanding of mythology. Plato's story is only the most lucid and compelling of many memories of a flood catastrophe found in ancient sources.

The preservation of the Atlantis myth among Egyptian religious texts becomes somewhat more explainable. The influence of the Neolithic Empire extended as far east as Libya and Scandinavia. As the hub of this great empire disappeared amidst the upheaval, the survivors in these two regions were able to preserve aspects of it in their mythologies. As the Sahara became progressively drier, the Libyan subjects sought refuge and security in the delta of the Nile, bringing with them the cult of their goddess Neit.

It is rather unfortunate that Solon translated all the proper names into Greek. It has therefore always seemed rather pointless to apply etymology to the Atlantis texts. However in view of the suggestion made previously, that Atlantis was based upon some form of the material preserved with the Egyptian Book of the Dead, then it is possible that a little progress may be made here. The name 'Atlantis' is nowhere found in Egyptian texts and it seems that it was a Greek name for some Libyan or Ethiopic tribe.

A better insight may be gained by examining the various names applied to the Land of the Dead and the home of the gods in mythology. The general correspondence of the Manau/Manu/Manala sequence of names has been previously noted. It is interesting that the name Manau was not only applied to the Isle of Man.

Welsh and Arthurian sources speak of another Manau – Manau Gododdin, identifiable with the central lowlands of Scotland around the modern city of Edinburgh. Beyond the Forth lies the town and county of Clackmannan – a name which means 'stone of Manu'. This suggests that the name may have possessed some meaning within the language of the Caledonian tribes.

Little is known for certain about the languages of northern Britain in pre-Roman times or of the ethnic origin of the north Britons, but there are a few clues available to us. Tacitus, in his *Germania*, lists a tribe called the Aestii who inhabited the shores of the Baltic Sea in the area of the modern Baltic states. Although he numbers them among the Germanic Suebi on account of their similar religion and customs, he also remarks that their language was not Germanic at all, but 'more like that of the Britons'.[16]

Now this is revealing, for the Aestii seem to have left their name to the modern nation of Estonia. Beyond the Aestii lived the Fenni, who are presumably related to the modern Finns and Lapps. Ethnically it is unlikely that these tribes were ancestral to the modern peoples, but these are names applied to them by foreigners. The Finns call themselves Suomi, from *suo*, 'a marsh', and it seems that Fenni is a Germanic translation of this. Indeed the Swedes still use the name Finns when referring to the Laplanders.

There is little doubt that Tacitus was not referring to any Celtic language. He was well aware that Brythonic was related to Gaulish, for he tells us so in his *Agricola*.[17] Elsewhere in the *Germania* he states that only two Celtic tribes had strayed into German territory: the Boii and the Helvettii.[18] He makes no mention of Celtic tribes on the Baltic shores and there is no evidence to support such an interpretation. The conclusion therefore must be that Tacitus was not referring to Brythonic at all, but to the language spoken by the Caledonians of the north. Tacitus was surely familiar with their language, for he translates the famous speech of Calgacus before the battle of Mons Graupus. In his *Agricola*, he makes no distinction between the British tribes on linguistic grounds, referring to them all alike as Britons.

The possibility that 'Pictish', or the language of the pre-Celtic Britain, may have been a language of the Finno-Ugric group and therefore related to Finnish and Estonian is no new suggestion. In fact, place-name evidence suggests that more than one language was spoken in the Pictish region right up to Roman times and beyond. There is evidence of another Celtic language, not Brythonic, but even closer to Gaulish. There are also river names which suggest another early Indo-European language that was neither Celtic nor Germanic. In addition, a number of place-names exist throughout the British Isles for which no Indo-European origin can be suggested, and for which analogues may be found within the modern Finnic languages.

There are a number of river and place-names containing the element *al* or *allen* which are generally accepted as pre-Celtic in origin. One may cite Alness on the Cromarty Firth, Alloa on the Forth, and further south in England Alcester (formerly Alencestre). A river Aln flows into the sea at Alnmouth in Northumbria, in Monmouthshire a river Alun, and there are many other examples throughout Britain. Scots Gaelic has a word *ailean* meaning 'a green plain', but this cannot explain the occurrence of the 'alan' names further south. In the modern Finno-Ugrian languages there are a whole series of words based on *al* which convey the sense 'low' as in Finnish *alas*, 'down', or *alanko*, 'lowlands'. One may also find *alue* meaning 'area' or 'territory'.

There are various other place-names which may contain pre-Celtic elements. Within the bounds of later Pictish Alban, there are a series of names commencing *pit* as in Pitlochry, Pitcaple, and many others; a possible analogue for this in Finnish is *pitäjä*, 'parish'. Many other associations may be suggested, such as *kylä*, 'a village or settlement', which may underlie at least some of the Kil or Kyle place-names of Scotland. There is also *maa* meaning the ground or the land which may be evident in Mar and Braemar. For most of the place-names of northern Britain, a Gaelic or Welsh root can be suggested, but many of these could still have ultimately originated from a pre-Celtic substratum. Certainly these are all elements that one would expect to find in place-names.

Of the possible evidence for archaic Finnic names within Egyptian texts one may cite a rather obvious association. One name that we know Solon did not translate is that of the goddess Neit, which would have become Athene. It is interesting to note that in Finnish *neiti* implies a young girl as in *neitsyt*, a virgin or maiden. Some sources do indeed describe Neit/Athene as a virgin goddess. Caesar equated one of the British gods with Minerva; and she may indeed be the same goddess as the Nerthus worshipped along the Baltic shores and whose sanctuary lay 'on an island in the ocean'.[19]

Other associations are suggested by such names as Sekhet-Aaru, the 'Field of Reeds' which was only a part of the Elysian Fields or Fields of Peace. There was another region called Sekhet-Aanru which had fourteen divisions within it, and was the part of the Land of the Dead where the khus were set to plough the fields. Now in these names one may perhaps detect the same roots which underlie Annan, Annwn and Arran as found in name of the Isle of Arran. There is no generally accepted derivation for any of these place-names, but the Welsh name Annwn has been translated as 'the abyss' or 'the very lowest part'.[20] Again in modern Finnish there is a word *aura* meaning 'plough' as in *auranala*, 'a plough land'.[21] Significantly the verb 'to plough' is *kyntää* as found in *kyntäjä*, 'a ploughman'; a related word is *kenttä*, 'field', and these roots may perhaps be discerned in the name of the peninsula of Kintyre. It is more usual to derive this from Gaelic *ceann-tire* meaning 'headland', but the proximity of the Kintyre peninsula to the Isle of Arran is another remarkable coincidence.

Still other associations of this kind may be ventured. The same name may perhaps be discerned in Kintore, a village in Aberdeenshire. Further south it may be present in the name of the county of Kent which Caesar called Cantium and the tribe of the Cantii who lived there. No definite Celtic root can be suggested for these names. More significantly there is the river name Kennet which old sources called Cynetan and Kinete. This is the river that flows just a few miles from Avebury, through some of the earliest farmland in southern England. The old form of the name is better preserved in the Berkshire village name Kintbury. Further north in Clackmannan there is another Kennet, this time a place-name; and various place-names with the element *kin* or *ken* occur throughout the length and breadth of Britain.

The same root may also underlie the Welsh Cynt, possibly identifiable with the people whom Herodotus called Cynetae, and for which one may therefore venture a meaning something like 'the people who plough', or more simply 'ploughmen'. It is possible that these Cynetae represent the aboriginal element in the British population whose language, as represented by 'Pictish', persisted in southern Britain until about 500 BC. Its northward retreat may be discernible in the progressive disuse of Albion within classical sources.

The myths identifying Britain as the Land of the Dead and as the home of the gods seem to have retreated northwards along with these aboriginal people. An examination of the writings of Procopius and Plutarch reveal this to be a native tradition of the island; and within the Finnic myths we encounter yet again the myth of the boat of the dead. It was believed that the dead were ferried across the river of Tuonela on their final journey to the Land of the Dead.

Other likely associations may be found in the various names by which the ancient paradise was known. The name Manala seems to derive from *maa* (the ground) + *alla* (under) and in modern Finnish *maan alla* also means 'underground'. Perhaps another may be found in the Avalon of Arthurian mythology. For although this sounds like the Welsh word for 'apple', hence 'Island of Apples', one may also venture a derivation something like *aava* or *avara*, a Finnish word implying 'vast' or 'extensive', together with the *alan* particle, and conveying the sense 'vast lowlands' or 'vast plain'.

It is not suggested that the Pictish language or the language of Neolithic Britain was identical with modern Finnish, rather that it was perhaps a branch of proto-Finnic or even of the parent Finno-Ugrian language. Make of these associations what you will, for they are freely given. Very little can be proven by etymology alone and it is only when placed alongside all the previous coincidences that these theories carry any weight.

As if to show that one must always be careful with etymology, we may recall the example of the Fomorians. Irish legends speak of the Fomarhaigh as the aboriginal inhabitants of the Scottish islands and the Irish Sea region, including both Arran and Man. One may derive the name of these people several ways. One is from Gaelic *fomhar* meaning 'autumn' or 'harvest-time', as in *fomharai*, 'a harvester'. This interpretation would again imply that the aboriginal people of Britain were farmers; and the name may therefore be a straight translation of Cynetae. But the name has also been derived from *fo* + *mara* meaning 'under-seas' and therefore implying 'the undersea people'. This sense is found in a modern Irish word *fomhuirean* meaning 'submarine'. Either of these derivations would equally serve the theories outlined here – but they surely cannot both be right!

If one may conclude this investigation with a final word of caution, it is simply this. There are too many references to flood and cataclysm within the mythologies of the world for them all to

be mere fiction. There are seen to be too many correspondences
between them. The question becomes not whether we should
believe them, but rather: how are they to be interpreted? You may
not agree with the interpretation given here, or with the methods
used to assign calendar dates to the events of myth and legend; but
there is no doubt that many of them can be adequately explained
as the consequence of changes in the Earth's rotation.

Wherever we encounter references to sea level fluctuations, submergence, abnormal seasons and climate changes within mythology
then we have an opportunity to attach those events to a chronology.
If we would only believe what our ancestors are telling us then we
may already possess far more history than we ever knew. For a
legend that can be attached to a chronology is a legend no longer –
it is history!

The Neolithic Calendar

For those who are sufficiently interested to pursue matters of the calendar, there is a further detail within the *Critias* which has not previously received the attention it deserves. Plato records that the kings of Atlantis gathered together for a religious ceremony: 'every fifth and every sixth year alternately'. In any thorough investigation, such an important clue to the past cannot be left uninvestigated, for it suggests the workings of a calendar.

Now if you are one of those who believes that Plato made up the whole Atlantis story, then ask yourself why he needed to include such a concise statement? Fiction does not require such precision. Alternate 5- and 6-year intervals have no place within the calendars of either Greece or Egypt. Every society requires a calendar of some kind, so it is worth while posing the question: can a working calendar be devised that employs these principles?

In the late nineteenth century a fragmentary Celtic calendar was discovered in a vineyard near Bourg, in the French district of Ain, which has come to be known as the Calendar of Coligny. In reconstruction, the fragments are seen to form about three-fifths of a bronze tablet. It is engraved in the Gaulish language, using the Roman alphabet and remains one of the earliest documents written in a Celtic language. In total the notation for 62 months can be discerned, including two 30-day intercalary months, which together make up 5 solar years.

This 5-year period cannot constitute the entire calendar, for 62 months contain 1,831 days – about 5 days more than is required for 5 solar years. Simply to repeat the extant calendar would give an accumulating error of 5 days every 5 years. The Coligny calendar in its entirety must therefore have contained a further cycle, alternated with this one, in order to pull back the divergence.

There can be little doubt that the Calendar of Coligny is the only surviving evidence we have of the calendar of the druids. Its fragmentary remains testify to the thoroughness of the Roman eradication of druidism in Gaul. If we believe Pliny, the druidic calendar was strictly lunar in operation. Unlike our modern calendar, which allows the lunar cycle to drift through a series of abstract 30- and 31-day months, a true lunar calendar must ensure that the Moon and the calendar month remain strictly in step. The difficulty in constructing such a calendar lies in reconciling the lunar month with the solar year to give a repeating cycle. This could be achieved by employing the 19-year cycle of Meton, or the less precise 84- or 76-year cycles; however it is known that the druids actually operated a cycle of 30 years within their lunar calendar.[1]

A period of 30 years is not easily reconciled with the lunar cycle, not least because 30 solar years contain 10,957½ days and half-days cannot be permitted in a calendar. If instead we double this and employ a 60-year cycle then this gives 21,915 days. This is very close to 742 lunar months with a discrepancy of only about 4 days. Sixty lunar years gives 720 months, leaving 22 intercalary months to be somehow fitted into the calendar.

Within the Coligny calendar there is only evidence of 2 such intercalary months. One of these occurs at the beginning of the 5-year period; the other is inserted in the middle of the third year, giving an interval of 2½ years. If this 5-year cycle were simply to be repeated it would give 12 intercalations in 30 years rather than the required 11. MacNeill in his study of the Coligny calendar suggested that a better result would be obtained if the intercalary months were spaced at alternate intervals of 2½ and 3 years.[2] Since we know that the 5-year period was also significant within the Coligny calendar, this suggests the following result for two consecutive 30-year periods:

$$2½ + 2½ + 3 + 3 + 2½ + 2½ + 3 + 3 + 2½ + 2½ + 3 = 30 \text{ years}$$
$$3 + 2½ + 2½ + 3 + 3 + 2½ + 2½ + 3 + 3 + 2½ + 2½ = 30 \text{ years}$$

It may therefore be seen that an alternating cycle of 5 years followed by 6 years does indeed give the required 22 intercalations in 60 years. The 30-year 'age' also falls neatly at the end of the middle 3-year period.

However there remains the problem of the 4-day divergence over the 60-year cycle. In the modern Gregorian calendar such discrepancies are corrected using leap years in which a day is added to the month of February according to strict rules. Also, since the true period of the month is 29.53 days, any lunar calendar must include both 29- and 30-day months. The Coligny calendar does indeed contain evidence of various devices to keep the Moon within its month. It has 5 months of 29 days and 6 of 30 days. The month of Eqvos (equivalent to February) was a special case. It had 30 days in years 1, 3 and 5 and only 28 days in years 2 and 4. The overall effect of this would be a net gain of 6 days over a 60-year cycle.

There is no evidence as to how the remainder of the calendar operated, but the workings of the extant portion would still leave the calendar deficient. This can be summarized as follows:

$$60 \text{ lunar years} = 60 \times 354 = 21{,}240 \text{ days}$$
$$\text{plus } 22 \text{ intercalary months} = 21{,}240 + (22 \times 30) = 21{,}900 \text{ days}$$

A further day gained in each of the six 5-year periods leaves a further 9 days to be gained elsewhere in the calendar, to equal 60 solar years (21,915 days).

Of course, the fact that the Calendar of Coligny could have operated on these principles does not prove that it actually did; still less can it prove that this was the calendar alluded to within Plato's narrative. However there is no doubt that the druids were responsible for the calendar and astronomy among the Gauls; and there is every reason to believe that their calendar was of ancient origin.

It has been suggested here that in Neolithic times there were only some 360 days in a solar year. If the calendar of the druids was indeed descended from an earlier calendar, devised as long ago as the fourth millennium BC then it would also have to operate under this regime. The first principle to appreciate is that a change in the length of the day alone does not affect any other astronomical phenomena. The true period of the year remains unchanged, as does the month and the synodic periods of all the planets. The only difference is the number of 'days' occurring within those periods. If we make the approximation that the year formerly contained precisely 360 revolutions then the former number of days in the month can be established by dividing the modern value in ratio:

1 synodic month	$= 29.53 \times 360/365.25$	$= 29.1$ old-days
1 lunar year	$= 12 \times 29.1$	$= 349.2$ old-days
60 solar years	$= 60 \times 360$	$= 21{,}600$ old-days

This is a much simpler world in which to operate. A lunar year of 349 old-days would have required only one 30-day month with all the rest being of 29 days. This gives the following result:

$$60 \text{ old-lunar years} = 60 \times 349 = 20{,}940 \text{ old-days}$$

To this must be added the 22 intercalary months:

$$20{,}940 + (22 \times 29) \quad = 21{,}578 \text{ old-days}$$

Now this is precisely 22 old-days short of 60 years and so it can be seen that if each of the intercalary months is increased to 30 days (as found in the Coligny fragment) then the calendar is complete:

$$20{,}940 + (22 \times 30) \quad = 21{,}600 \text{ old-days}$$

So it may be seen that this is a much simpler calendar to operate than the Coligny calendar, supporting a hypothesis that the Celtic calendar evolved gradually from a Neolithic progenitor – in much the same way indeed as the modern Gregorian calendar has evolved from its Roman origins.

There must have been an underlying reason why the 30-year age was considered so important; and why the druids chose to base their calendar around it. Far better calendrical devices than this are available and these must surely have been known to the druids. Indeed there is some evidence that the pagan Britons also operated another calendar based on an 84-year cycle; and Hecataeus also hints at a knowledge of the 19-year Meton cycle among the northern Hyperboreans.[3, 4] So why did they choose a 30-year cycle?

A possible answer may be that 30 solar years is very close to 29 synodic periods of the planet Saturn, the interval during which it completely circuits the zodiac. Plutarch informs us that the Britons ritually observed this phenomenon.[5] The correspondence is not exact; since the average synodic period of Saturn is 378.1 days, this means that Saturn would have returned to its twenty-ninth opposition some 7.5 days (or about a quarter-moon) later than it did in the previous age. It would therefore have been fairly easy to measure any deficiency against the absolute reckoning of the star of Cronus; and to correct it by inserting extra days into the calendar. The ancient astronomers were wise indeed to choose a time standard so totally independent of the Earth's motion.

APPENDIX B

A Postscript

You may wonder why the foregoing chapters have made no mention of such recent discoveries as the Chicxulub impact crater in the Yucatan, or the collision of comet Shoemaker-Levy 9 with Jupiter, the Ice-Man of the Alps, or a variety of other discoveries during the 1990s that have revolutionized the case for catastrophism in human prehistory. This is because the bulk of the research was performed between 1987 and 1992 and the first edition went to press only in late 1994.

Certainly, were I to begin the book *today* I should not feel the need to make quite such a strong case for the likelihood, or indeed the effect, of recent comet impacts on the Earth. The Jupiter impact has opened minds that were previously closed and catastrophist research is now being cited in many academic contexts, where formerly it would never have passed a referee. In the space of just a decade, catastrophist geology has begun its return to respectability as a subject for mainstream science.

In preparing this new edition, I have therefore resisted the temptation to revise the original text with sources that were not influential to the first edition. Any misconceptions it may contain must be judged in the light of subsequent discoveries. However, I have taken the opportunity to restore, in the endnotes, some geophysical detail that was edited out; and to include some comments about the significance of Indian calendars and cosmogony.

The Indian Calendar

A serious omission from the first edition was a proper examination of Hindu mythology and cosmogony; in fact it merits at least as much attention as the Chinese or Central American calendars.

Hindu Vedic traditions recall an eternal cosmic cycle of fire, flood and regeneration; and with each successive 'age' the world has become increasingly corrupt. The present age, called the Kaliyuga, began with events that are deeply shrouded in religious imagery. Following the most recent destruction by fire, the world sank into the ocean; the god Vishnu is then said to have incarnated in the form of a boar and lifted the world out of the abyss on his tusks.

From the extant Indian calendars, scholars have been able to retro-calculate the epoch of the Kaliyuga. It began at midnight on 18 February 3102 BC – when supposedly all the planets were in alignment with the Sun. It does in fact correspond to a close conjunction of the Sun, Moon and planets in the constellation Pisces. Early Vedic calendars employed a 360-day year interlocked with a further cycle of 432 days (about 14½ months) which had an obscure purpose in the cosmology, concerned with theoretical divisions of the ecliptic. This number is remarkably close to the period of the Earth's free wobble; recent observations give a period of 435 days for the Chandler wobble and 434–4 days for the 'core motion' of the axis in space.

We therefore have another indicator that the amplitude of this nutation may have been much more apparent before *c.*1500 BC; significant enough to be detected by the naked eye and important enough to warrant inclusion in the calendar.[1] As a method of authenticating the Flood, the Indian cosmology therefore falls into place alongside all the other 'coincidences'.

Catastrophism in Human Prehistory – Some Recent Studies

I would also like to take this opportunity to thank the various people who have written to me with evidence and suggestions for further research, especially Antony Rowe and Paul Devereux. Also David Furlong, who drew my attention to the Internet web-site of Dr Richard Meehan entitled *Whatever Happened in 3200 BC?* Beneath his whimsical treatment of the subject there lies some solid sea level and climate research. His investigation closely paralleled my own in both time and content, with much additional evidence that I missed.[2]

The year 1995 saw the publication of the first in a string of books by well-known authors on the subject of 'alternative Egyptology', catastrophism and Atlantis. Many of these theories have been so absurd that it is hard to believe even their authors ever took them seriously.

Among the best of recent Atlantis studies is *The Sunken Kingdom* by Peter James, archaeologist and author of *Centuries of Darkness*.[3] He gives probably the most thorough critique to date of recent 'Aegean Atlantis' and various other catastrophist theories. Peter James had proposed Megalithic Britain as Atlantis as long ago as the 1970s, but he now favours a site in Anatolia.

Another quite remarkable work is *When the Earth Nearly Died* by D.S. Allen and J.B. Delair,[4] a colossal study of the evidence for a close encounter with a comet, Phaeton, at the close of the Ice Age around 9500 BC. Although their conclusions are rather too 'Velikovskian' for my own taste, the depth of their research can only be truly appreciated by someone who has undertaken such work. Clube and Napier had preferred to place comet Phaeton at 1369 BC;[5] my own preferred date remains *c.*3100 BC. However, the extant flood stories are surely compound myths preserving aspects of more than a single impact event.

Recent studies of the Ice Age terminal event have confirmed that the switch from cold to warm conditions was completed within as little as 20 years;[6] an effect that, as I have argued, can be entirely explained by a pole shift and the associated Chandler wobble.[7] No doubt there was an asteroid or comet impact at the close of the Ice Age, but there have surely been others both before and since.

Impacts in the Ocean

Interest in the Jupiter impact and the K-T Event has also stimulated academic study of the dangers presented by comet and asteroid impacts. Among these papers is that of Hills et al., on the likely scale of tsunami damage consequent upon an impact in the ocean.[8] They conclude that an asteroid of only 400 metres in diameter, striking the North Atlantic, would generate a tsunami some 60 metres high that would travel up to 20 kilometres inland, with the capacity to: 'totally devastate small, flat coastal countries in Europe such as Holland or Denmark'. They further warn us that: 'the entire research field of geologic assessments of tsunami produced by impactors is virtually nonexistent and needs to be initiated.' Yet among papers in the same volume I note scarcely a word of understanding that these impacts would take place on a *rotating* planet. How much more important, then, that we should understand the effect of the pole tides resultant upon the Earth's wobble.

At the Earth's Core

Seismological studies have revealed that the Earth's inner core is anisotropic; and this may be explainable if the inner core rotates at a slightly different rate. Song and Richards conclude that the axis of the inner core rotates some 1° per year faster than the outer shell and may also be slightly tilted from the north–south axis.[9] The exchange of energy between inner core and mantle may explain the decade fluctuations in the length of day.[10] It is too soon to say whether this misalignment is archaic, or whether it is a relict of a recent transient phenomenon.

Radiocarbon Uncertainties?

Whereas from the 1970s archaeologists had come to believe that calibrated radiocarbon dates could provide calendar dates BC, within an accuracy of some 20–30 years, now they are no longer so confident. It has become clear that an average of many dates is needed to confirm the age of an artefact and that all calibrated dates must be treated as only a good approximation.[11] I hope that I never fell into this trap. An author who believes that the Earth's rotation has changed during prehistory could never entirely trust a dating method that is based upon assumptions about the Earth's magnetic field – which itself is a child of that rotation.

The Irish Sea

Between 1992 and 1995 the British Geological Survey published a series on the offshore geology of the UK continental shelf and the Irish Sea region. The debate about Holocene sea levels continues, but here at least it is acknowledged that the present sea level around the British Isles stabilized 'since about 5000 years BP'.[12]

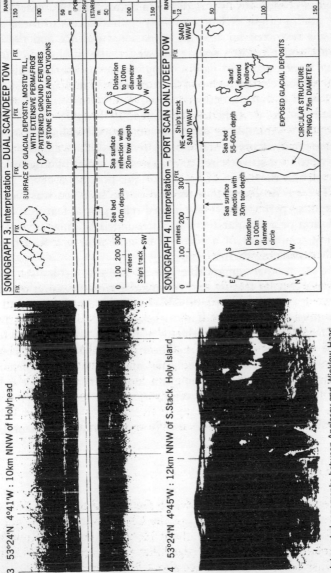

Interpreted sonographs between Anglesey and Wicklow Head.
R.T.R Wingfield, giant sand waves and relic periglacial features of the Irish Sea bed west of Anglesey, *Proceedings of the Geologists' Association*, 98, 4, 400–404.

Sonar surveys of the eastern Irish Sea have revealed the presence of numerous 'polygonal textures' on the sea floor; and 15 kilometres north-west of Anglesey lies a 'circular structure', which the geologists conservatively suggest is 'a drowned pingo scar of sub-aerial tundra origin'.[13] Unfortunately, public access to these sonographs is restricted for reasons of national defence and these are the only sonar records so far allowed to be published.[14] In his original paper, geologist Robin Wingfield described this feature as: 'a near perfect circle which has the form of a 75 m diameter shallow saucer with a sharply defined, raised rim'. Nearby are less well-resolved features described as 'sand filled hollows'.[15]

Perhaps we should not expect a submerged Neolithic settlement to differ greatly from contemporary remains that we find on land. If we were to discover circular features on aerial photographs we might suspect they were of human origin: possibly a henge or hill-fort? There is no doubt that the bed of the Irish Sea was formerly glaciated, so perhaps these are indeed relict glacial features. Plato's description of a circular fortress, surrounded by rings of water, is certainly reminiscent of a fortified *natural* structure; and he also describes quarries nearby.

It is yet another remarkable coincidence that geologists should discover a circular feature and rectangular structures on the seabed in an area where Welsh legends describe submerged cities, and just a few miles from where I had suggested that the city of Atlantis might lie. Whether or not the Irish Sea region does turn out to be the site of Elysium, the accumulation of coincidences will remain no less real. So was there a Neolithic catastrophe around the coasts of Britain and Ireland? And might a lost city lie beneath the Irish Sea? There is a case to be answered.

                                                        Paul Dunbavin

Notes and References

1. Lost Atlantis

1. The translation quoted here is that of Jowett, 1892.
2. Ibid.
3. Plutarch, *Parallel Lives, The Life of Solon*, 26; Plutarch also indicates that Plato himself visited Egypt: see *Isis and Osiris*, 354.
4. Strabo, *Geography*, 2. 3. 5–6; Posidonius considered the Earth to undergo rising and settling processes quite distinct from earthquakes and cited Atlantis as an example. See also chapter 15, note 7.

2. In Search of a Legend

1. Herodotus, II, 141–6. It is likely that all the Egyptian temples were plundered by the Persians in 525 BC. See Herodotus, III, 16; *Diodorus Siculus* 1,46.
2. Waterson, Barbara, *The Gods of Ancient Egypt*, p. 177. See also Hoffman, M.A., 1980, p. 296. Atlantis could not be older than the cult of Neit-Athene.
3. Taylor, Thomas, *The Commentaries of Proclus*, vol. 1, p. 64. See chapter 15 below.
4. Waddel, W.G., *Manetho*, appendix 1, p. 209.
5. Whiston, W., *Josephus, The Complete Works, Antiquities of the Jews*, book 1, chapter 2.
6. Waddel, W.G., *Manetho*, appendix 1, p. 211 and introduction.
7. Waterson, Barbara, *The Gods of Ancient Egypt*, pp. 176–8.
8. Taylor, Thomas, *The Commentaries of Proclus*, book 1, p. 148. A slightly different translation is available in Taylor, *Plato the Timaeus and the Critias*.
9. *Diodorus Siculus*, II, 55–9.
10. *Diodorus Siculus*, III, 53–60. The Amazon women were more conventionally located in Scythia, but perhaps this term was more widely applied to women warriors, wherever they arose.
11. Ibid., 54. Oldfather translation.

12. Ibid., 55. Oldfather translation.
13. Herodotus, IV, 181–8. See also chapter 15, note 21 below.
14. Pliny, *Natural History*, VI, 184–7.
15. Taylor, Thomas, *The Commentaries of Proclus*, book 1, p. 151. From the surviving fragments of Heraclitus (*c.*500 BC) he is thought to have believed in a periodic world conflagration.
16. *Diodorus Siculus*, III, 56.
17. Ibid., 60. See also chapter 15, note 21 below.
18. Pliny, *Natural History*, VII, lvi 201–4.
19. Hesiod, *Theogony*, 507.
20. Plato, *Critias*, 110. Jowett translation.
21. Taylor, Thomas, *The Commentaries of Proclus*, book 1, p. 65. He describes the west as 'a place of noxious demons'.
22. Strabo, *Geography*, 2. 3. 5–6. See chapter 1, note 4 above.
23. Pliny, *Natural History*, VII, 203.
24. I have preferred here not to engage in a critique of modern authors and their theories. However, Lewis Spence's books, particularly his final work, *The History of Atlantis*, merit special mention. They remain some of the best books ever written on the subject.
25. See Marinatos, Sp., 1971. I have not further pursued here the various Minoan theories of Luce, Mavor and others. Suffice to say that all these Aegean variants disdain or make no reference to *Diodorus Siculus* and the Phoenician links; and are all wholly untenable once this evidence is accorded the respect it is due.
26. Herodotus, IV, 43–5.
27. Herodotus, II, 141–6. See also *Diodorus Siculus*, I, 26–7 and chapter 9, note 9 below.

3. The Figure of the Earth

1. See Gold, T., *Nature*, 175, 526–9 (1955). The 'raising' of a hypothetical mountain is analogous to the 'sinking' of an island. Most Atlantis investigators have hitherto not appreciated that the 'traditional' Atlantis sinking must leave a world-wide signature of evidence and could not be neatly localized in the mid-Atlantic.
2. A summary of the 'uniformitarian' rejection of polar wandering theories is given by H. Jeffreys in *The Earth*, pp. 478–81, citing the work of Sir George Darwin and Thomas Gold. Darwin had considered that a maximum polar wander of 8° might be possible, but more likely just 1–2° by the elevation (or sinking) of a continent-sized mass. However, later researchers overturned his mathematics, leaving a consensus that polar wandering has been negligible over geological time.

3. For a discussion of possible gravitational or magnetic influences on the Earth's rotation, see Peter Warlow's *The Reversing Earth*, in which he argues that the Earth could turn over on its axis, rather like a 'tippie-top', upon the close fly-by of a rogue planetoid. Warlow admits to being strongly influenced by Velikovsky.

4. Taylor, Thomas, *The Commentaries of Proclus*, book 1, p. 92.

4. Target Earth

1. Pasachoff, J.M., 1987, pp. 261–72.

2. *The Times*, 21 April 1989. Since this chapter was written in the early 1990s we have witnessed the impact of comet Shoemaker-Levy-9 on the planet Jupiter, which spurred the astronomers to discover many more asteroids and comets in potentially Earth-crossing orbits.

3. Gault, D.E., and Wedekind, J.A., 1978, p. 3843, leading to earlier references.

4. Ibid., pp. 3483–4.

5. See Schultz, P.H., and Lianza, R. E., 1992, for the Argentine craters; oriented lakes occur near Point Barrow in Alaska and in the Carolina Bays of the eastern USA.

6. Baxter, J., and Atkins, T., 1976, p. 156.

7. Florensky, K.P., *Sky and Telescope*, 26, 268–9, (Nov. 1963).

8. Ovid, *Metamorphoses*, books 1 and 2.

9. *Diodorus Siculus*, III, 70.

10. See Schultz, P.H., and Gault, D.E., 1990 p. 257; in their opinion the oblique collision of a 10-km object at 15 km/s could have occurred, 'without a trace of an impact cavity in the geologic record'.

11. These extremes are from escape velocity to a head-on collision with a parabolic comet falling from rest at the edge of the solar system. The present author remains to be convinced that we do not, from time to time, encounter *hyperbolic* comets emanating from deep space, which must possess an even higher velocity. A pole shift in recent prehistory demands a low-mass, high-velocity impact.

12. See Lambeck, K., *Geophysical Geodesy*, pp. 49–54, for a discussion of pressure or inertial coupling.

13. See Morner, N.A., 1976 and 1980, for a uniformitarian discussion of geoid-eustasy. It is typical of the era that he did not include impact phenomena among the possible causes of geoid-eustasy.

14. Chamberlain, T.C., *The Origin of the Earth*, p. 82.

15. Wells, J.W., 'Coral growth and geochronometry', *Nature*, 197, 948–50 (1963). For a discussion of tidal deceleration over geological time, see also Jeffreys, H., *The Earth*, 6th edition, pp. 339–40.

5. The Chandler Wobble

1. See Jeffreys, H., *The Earth*, 6th edition, pp. 297–9 for a discussion of the harmonic analysis of the Chandler wobble over 7-year intervals.
2. Press, F., and Briggs, P., *Nature*, 256, 270–3 (1975).
3. Vincente, R.O., in *Physics and Chemistry of the Earth*, vol. 4.
4. This is the Kelvin-Hough model – see Jeffreys, H., *The Earth*, pp. 299–305.
5. See Lambeck, K., *Geophysical Geodesy*, pp. 49–54 and 569–71. I have assumed throughout that the free wobble is superimposed upon forcibly displaced axes. However the equations demand that the 'wobble' *relative to geography* must always be accompanied by a 'nutation' *in space* that is some 460 times greater in amplitude (see Lambeck, pp. 48–9 and 570, and Toomre, 1974). Thus a nearly diurnal wobble of just 23.5 arc seconds should be accompanied by a variation in the obliquity, of as much as 3° of tilt. Geophysicists, however, decline to speculate on the characteristics of this 'as yet largely unobserved motion'.
6. See Capitaine, N., and Xiao, N., 1982. Their data reveal a tiny retrograde motion (0.01 arc sec) in space of period 434–44 days, indicating a modification of the theoretical 460-day period analogous to that of the Chandler wobble. Compare this with 0.7 arc sec and recent observations of 435 days for the period of the Chandler wobble. Whereas in discussing the Chandler wobble the *spatial* motion is so small that the rotation axis can be treated as virtually coincident with the angular momentum, for the nearly diurnal wobble, it is instead the *body* motion that is negligible (see note 5 above) and the motion in space becomes significant.
7. See Jeffreys, H., *The Earth*, 6th edition, p. 312. More recent models also treat the shell as having elastic properties.
8. Fong Chao, B., and Gross, R.S., *Geophys. J. R. Astr. Soc.*, 91, 569–96 (1987).
9. Lambeck, K., *Geophysical Geodesy*, pp. 150–2 and 559–61.
10. The Milankovitch theory explains Ice Ages by gradual climate change, due to variations of the obliquity (41,000 years) combined with the precession of the equinoxes (25,920 years) together with variations in the Earth's orbital eccentricity.
11. I know of no suitable existing name for such a motion – unless it be the 'core nutation' (See Toomre, A., 1974, p. 339 and also note 5 above). This circular motion was first proposed by Hopkins in 1839 and further developed by Hough in 1895. Toomre describes the motion of the angular momenta of core and mantle

as 'precessing slowly retrograde', but in the past many geophysicists have used imprecise terminology. Therefore, in assigning a convenient 'plain English' name to the spatial motion, for the benefit of the general reader, I could perhaps have called it 'core–mantle nutation'. Geophysicists discuss the tiny modern wobble as arising due to movements in the core, whereas here I am discussing a similar misalignment arising from an external force on the surface – so 'core nutation' no longer seems appropriate. Geophysicist P. Melchior (in Federov, E.P. et al. (eds), 1980, pp. 17–21) bemoaned the lack of standard terminology to describe the Earth's various nutations. Using Poinsot's conic representation he defines this long-period motion in space as: the herpolhody of 'the retrograde principal free core nutation'. The accompanying motion relative to the rotating Earth is given by the polhody and it is *this part* that has a nearly diurnal period. It must be stressed that these are just views of the same motion. The name 'nearly diurnal wobble' arose because successive investigators had neglected the existence of the accompanying (and much larger) motion in space. A historical account is given by Rochester et al., 1974.

6. The Evidence of Sea Level Variations

1. Fairbridge, R.W., in *Physics and Chemistry of the Earth*, vol. 4. A general discussion of eustatic, isostatic and geodetic controls of sea level. The irregular Fairbridge sea level curves are now returning to favour after a period when researchers sought a more uniform 'eustatic' curve. But see Hardisty, 1990: 'It is now clear that the search for a "global" sea-level curve is probably fruitless and attention has focused on determining local peculiarities . . .'
2. Charlesworth, J.K., *The Quaternary Era*, pp. 1306–9 – leading to various older references.
3. Steers, J.A., *The Coastline of England and Wales*, p. 497.
4. West, G., 1968, pp. 169–73.
5. Fairbridge, ref. as note 1, p. 165.
6. Jensen, J., 1982, p. 84.
7. Glob, P.V., 1971, p. 49.
8. Schou, A., 'The Coastline of Djursland' in Steers, J.A. (ed.), *Applied Coastal Geomorphology*.
9. Jelgersma, S., 1961.
10. Devoy, R.J.N., 1977. Sea level curve for the Thames estuary.
11. De Beer, Sir Gavin, 1960, 'close to 2000 BC'. For other British dates see references in other chapters.

12. Prigent, D. et al., 1983, pp. 303–25.
13. Burl, H.A.W., *Megalithic Brittany*, p. 65.
14. Charlesworth, J.K., 1957, p. 1311. See also Evans, E., *Prehistoric and Early Christian Ireland*, p. 83.
15. Fairbridge, R.W., 1962 (5000 BP). See also chapter 8, refs 8–12.
16. Bell, B., 1970.
17. Herodotus, II, 8.
18. Herodotus, II, 13. See also Strabo's *Geography*, 1.3.4 and the remarks of Eratosthenes on the Nile delta.
19. Plutarch, Isis and Osiris, 367. Note also his remarks regarding the lighthouse at Pharos.
20. Kraft, J.C., Stanley, E., Aschenbrenner, S.E., and Rapp, G., Jr, 1977, p. 942.
21. Ibid., pp. 943–4.
22. Plato, *Timaeus*, 25.
23. Lloyd, S., *The Archaeology of Mesopotamia*, pp. 35–7.
24. Ibid.
25. Pliny, *Natural History*, VI, XXXI, 140.
26. Fairbridge, R.W., 1961, p. 164 (4370 ± 110 BP).
27. Ibid. (4150 ± -200 BP and 4190 ± 70 BP).
28. Fairbridge, R.W., *Encyclopaedia of Geomorphology*, p. 151 (4600 BP).
29. Fairbridge, R.W., 1961, p. 164 (4150 ± 80 BP).
30. Shepard, F.P., 1964.
31. Moore, G.W., in *Geological Research Survey*, 1960, p. B335 ('about 3000 BC'). Also Hopkins, D.M., in *The Bering Land Bridge*, p. 85. 'sea level has remained within a few metres of its present position since about 3000 BC'.
32. Laughlin, W.S., in *The Bering Land Bridge*.
33. Fuenzalida, H. et al., 1965, p. 477.
34. Richards, H.G., and Broeker, W.S., 1963, p. 1045 (5350 ± 200 BP).
35. Ireland, S., 1987, p. 60.
36. Shepard, F.P., and Curray, J.R., 1967, p. 289 (4800 BP).
37. Fuenzalida, H. et al., 1965, p. 488 ('about 6000 years ago').
38. Ibid., p. 480.
39. Clapperton and Sugden et al., in Van Zinderen Bakker, ed., 1978, p. 100.
40. John, B.S., and Sugden, D.E., 1971, pp. 105–7.
41. Ibid., p. 106 (4600 ± 200 BP).
42. Ibid., (6040 ± 250 BP).
43. Blake, W., Jr, 1975, p. 13.
44. Ibid.
45. Coatzee, J.A., in Van Zinderen Bakker, ed., 1978, p. 174.
46. Fairbridge, R.W., 1961, p. 163 (5570 ± 70 BP).

47. Bloom, A.L. (ed.) *The Atlas of Sea Level Curves*, D22. Sea level curves should be used with caution as they give a false impression that there is evidence for the dates between the plotted points.
48. Ibid., D23.
49. Einsele, G., Herm, D., and Schwarz, H.U., 1974.
50. Giresse, P., 1987, p. 268.
51. Chappel, J., 1987, pp. 297–331.
52. Fairbridge, R.W., 1961, p. 165 (equated with his 'Bahama Emergence').
53. Bird, E.C.F., 1984, pp. 184–5.
54. Shepard, F.P., and Curray, J.R., 1967, p. 286.
55. Montaggioni, L., 1976, D26 in Bloom, A.L. (ed.), *The Atlas of Sea Level Curves*.
56. Flood, Josephine, 1983.
57. Ibid.
58. Fairbridge, R.W., 1961, p. 164 (4400 BP).
59. Ota, Y., and Machida, H., 1987, pp. 182–224.
60. Fontaine, H., and Delibrias, G., 1974, D1 in Bloom, A.L. (ed.), *The Atlas of Sea Level Curves*.
61. Ronan, C.A., 1984, p. 21.
62. Yang H., and Xie, Z., 1984, p. 303.
63. Morner, N.-A., 1980, p. 544 citing earlier references.
64. Raikes, R.L., 1965.
65. Fairbridge, R.W., 1961, p. 166 (3710 ± 250 BP).
66. Ibid.
67. Ibid.
68. Ase, L.E., 1987, pp. 290–2.
69. Ireland, S., 1987, pp. 59–60.
70. Richards, H.G., and Broeker, W.S., 1963, p. 1044 (3000 + 200 BP).
71. Flemming, N., *Cities in the Sea*, 1971, p. 37.
72. Ibid., p. 57.

7. The Changing Climate

1. Figures based on Lamb, H.H., 1966. The Blytt–Sernander classification of pollen zones, based on European peat stratigraphy, has tended to disuse more recently as comparisons with the rest of the world have proceeded. The Atlantic-Sub-Boreal transition therefore principally represents a change from *warm/wet* to *warm/dry* conditions within north European lowlands.
2. Burenhalt, G., 1984, p. 170 – in reference to the 'landnam'.
3. Ibid., p. 172.
4. Lappalainen, V., 1965, p. 91 (2100–2800 BC).

5. Frenzel, B., in Sawyer, J.S. (ed.), *The International Symposium on World Climate 8000–0 BC*, 1966, p. 100.
6. Polunin, O., and Walters, M., 1985, p. 17.
7. Ibid.
8. Wilkinson, G., 1981, p. 32.
9. Frenzel, B., in Sawyer, J.S. (ed.), *The International Symposium on World Climate*, 1966, p. 111.
10. Ibid, p. 100.
11. Kind, N.V., in *The Bering Land Bridge*, pp. 184–6.
12. Lamb, H.H., 1977, pp. 391–2.
13. Ibid., plate IV.
14. Ibid., pp. 394–6.
15. Charlesworth, J.K., 1957, p. 1455.
16. Ibid., p. 1489.
17. Lamb, H.H., 1977, p. 391.
18. Charlesworth, J.K., 1957, p. 1490. See also Moar, N.T. in Sawyer, J.S. (ed.), *The International Symposium on World Climate*, 1966.
19. Herodotus, IV, 181–8.
20. Desmond Clark, J. (ed.) *The Cambridge History of Africa*, vol. 1, p. 562.
21. Ibid., p. 566.
22. Lamb, H.H., 1974, pp. 214–15.
23. Goodfriend, G.A., 1988.
24. Wright, H.E. Jr, in Sawyer, J.S. (ed.) *The International Symposium on World Climate*, 1966.
25. Lamb, H.H., 1974, p. 203.
26. Ibid.
27. Coatzee, J.A., in Van Zinderen Bakker, ed., 1978.
28. Wiseman, J.D.H., in Sawyer, J.S. (ed.), *The International Symposium on World Climate*, 1966.
29. Chu Ko-Chen, in *Scientia Sinica*, May 1973, pp. 226–8.
30. Ibid., p. 229.
31. Ota, Y., and Machida, H., in Tooley and Shennan: *Sea-level Changes*, pp. 211–13.
32. Lanning, E.P., 1967, p. 12.
33. Frenzel, B., in Sawyer J.S. (ed.) *The International Symposium on World Climate*, 1966, p. 104. The author refers to a short, sharp cold spell at the end of the Atlantic period, called the 'Piora Oscillation'.
34. Ibid.
35. Page, N.R., 1968, p. 694 (4550 ± 170 BP).
36. Ibid., p. 696.
37. Ibid., p. 695 (4700 ± 200 BP).
38. Porter, C.S., and Denton, G. H., 1967, p. 186 (4700 ± 300 BP).

39. Ibid., p. 183 (4770 ± 120 BP).
40. Ibid., p. 187 (4700 ± 450 BP).
41. Goldthwaite, R.P., in Sawyer, J.S. (ed.), *The International Symposium on World Climate*, 1966, p. 49.
42. Porter, S.G., and Denton, G.H., 1967, pp. 195–6.
43. Mercer, J.H., 1970, p. 22 (4060 ± 110 BP). See also Mercer, J.H., 1967, pp. 530–9.
44. Ibid. See also Page, N.R., 1968, p. 696.
45. Mercer, J.H., in Sawyer, J.S. (ed.), *The International Symposium on World Climate*, 1966, p. 350.
46. Mercer, J.H., 1970, p. 21.
47. Hammer, C.U., Clausen, H.B., and Dansgaard, W., 1980.
48. Baillie, M.G.L., and Munro, A.R., 1988.
49. Ibid.
50. Hammer, C.U., Clausen, H.B., and Dansgaard, W., 1980.
51. Manning, S.W., 1988.
52. Hammer, C.U., Clausen, H.B., Freidrich, W.L., and Tauber, H., 1987.
53. Ibid. See also Simpkin, T. et al., 1981, p. 111.

8. Memories of the Flood

1. Plato, *Timaeus*, 23.
2. Genesis, 6–10.
3. Sollberger, E., 1971.
4. Lloyd, S., 1978.
5. Roux, G., 1964, p. 123.
6. Wooley, Sir Leonard, 1982, pp. 24–35.
7. Ibid.
8. *Manetho Fr 52* – see Waddel, W.G., 1940, p. 113.
9. Exodus 14.
10. Josephus, XVI, 2.
11. Josephus, XVI, 3.
12. Josephus, III, 3.
13. Plutarch, *Isis and Osiris*, 367.
14. Wallis Budge, E.A., 1899, Introduction, p. ccii, chapter CLXXV.
15. Turville Petre, E.O.G., 1964.
16. *New Larousse Encyclopedia of Mythology*, p. 426.
17. Restelle, W., *Bibliotheca Sacra*, 64, 148–67 (1907).
18. Burland, Cottie, 1965, pp. 96–9.
19. Ibid., p. 99.
20. Ibid., p. 127.
21. Poignant, Roslyn, 1985, p. 118.

22. Ibid.
23. Flood, Josephine, 1983, p. 113.
24. Ibid., pp. 114–15.
25. Ibid., pp. 179–180.
26. *New Larousse Encyclopedia of Mythology*, p. 445.
27. Ibid., pp. 448.
28. Ibid., pp. 444–5.
29. Ibid., pp. 441–2.
30. *The Singing Match II*, see Matti, Kuusi et al., 1977.
31. Translation by Kirby, W.F., runo VIII.
32. Ibid., runo XLVII.
33. Poignant, Roslyn, 1985, p. 58.
34. Ibid., p. 60.
35. Ibid.
36. Ibid., p. 56.
37. Ibid.
38. Ibid.
39. Ibid.
40. Howells, W.W., 1973, pp. 223–363.
41. Poignant, Roslyn, 1985, pp. 74–5.
42. *New Larousse Encyclopedia of Mythology*, p. 405.
43. Piggot, Juliet, 1982, p. 11.
44. *New Larousse Encyclopedia of Mythology*, p. 409.
45. Piggot, Juliet. 1982, p. 12.
46. Bird, E.C.F., 1984, p. 52.
47. Werner, E.T.C., 1932, pp. 334–5.
48. Ronan, C.A., *The Shorter Science and Civilisation in China*, vol. 1, p. 84.
49. Werner, E.T.C., 1932, p. 334.
50. Ibid., pp. 623 and 334.
51. Ibid.
52. Watson, W., 1961, p. 17.
53. Waltham, Clae, 1971, p. 4.
54. Ibid., p. 5.
55. Ibid., p. 6.
56. Ibid., p. 21.
57. Ibid., p. 63 – quoting James Legge.
58. *Geoffrey of Monmouth*, from the translation by Lewis Thorpe, 1966, p. 237.
59. Baillie, M.G.L., *Current Archaeology*, 117, (1990).

9. Parallel Trends in Ancient Cultures

1. Harris, J.R., 1971, p. 17. Its mention in an Old Kingdom pyramid text would suggest that the epact is older than 2500 BC.
2. Long, R.D., 1974, *Orientalia*, 43: 261, p. 263.
3. Harris, J.R., 1971, p. 20.
4. Renfrew, C., 1973, pp. 27–8.
5. Ibid., pp. 28–9.
6. Long, R.D., 1974, p. 265.
7. Long, R.D., 1974.
8. Wilson, D., 1975, pp. 41–2.
9. Herodotus, II, 142.
10. Suess, H.E., 1970.
11. Wilson, D., 1975, p. 113.
12. Desmond Clark, J. (ed.), *The Cambridge History of Africa*, vol. 1, p. 484.
13. Ibid., p. 498.
14. Edwards, I.E.S. (ed.), *The Cambridge Ancient History*, vol. 1, p. 488.
15. Hoffman, M.A., 1980, p. 110.
16. Gardiner, Sir A., 1961, pp. 391–6.
17. Aldred, C., 1965, pp. 17–18.
18. Ibid., p. 493.
19. Ibid., p. 495.
20. Ibid., vol. 2, p. 1.
21. Hassan, F.A., and Robinson, S.W., 1986.
22. Edwards, I.E.S. (ed.), *The Cambridge Ancient History*, vol. 1, p. 6.
23. Jacobsen, T., 1939.
24. Manetho (Syncellus) Fr 7 – see Waddel, W.G., 1940.
25. Manetho (Syncellus) Fr 8 – see Waddel, W.G., 1940.
26. Manetho (Syncellus) Fr 11 – see Waddel, W.G., 1940.
27. Bell, B., *Geogr. J.*, 136, pp. 569–73 (1970).
28. Roux, G., 1964, p. 39 and appendix 1.
29. Plato, *Timaeus*, 22–3.
30. Hoffman, M.A., 1980, pp. 284–94.
31. Thallon-Hill, I.D., 1953, p. 3.
32. Hammond, N.G.L., 1967, pp. 37–9. See also Christopoulos, G., and Bastias, J.C., 1970, pp. 372–4.
33. Christopoulos, G., and Bastias, J.C., 1970, pp. 372–4.
34. Ibid., pp. 368–72.
35. Renfrew, C., 1973, p. 30.
36. Edwards, I.E.S. (ed.), *The Cambridge Ancient History*, vol. 1, part 1, pp. 413–14.

37. Ibid., pp. 407 and 415–16.
38. Jensen, J., 1982.
39. Ibid., p. 72.
40. Burl, H.A.W., 1979, pp. 113–15.
41. Bradley, R., 1978, pp. 6–10.
42. Ibid., p. 107. Here he says, 'this cannot be attributed to changes of sea level', but this probably reflects the conservatism in the prevailing sea level research cited.
43. Edwards, I.E.S. (ed.), The Cambridge Ancient History, 1, part 1, p. 408.
44. Jacobsen, T., 1939, pp. 203–5.
45. Renfrew, C., 1987, pp. 35–41, summarizing earlier references.
46. Dumond, D.E., 1987, p. 93.
47. Diamond, J.M., Nature, 336, pp. 307–8 (1988).
48. Rawson, Jessica, 1980, p. 16.
49. Ronan, C.A., 1984, p. 21 (2500 BC).
50. Lanning, E.P., 1967, pp. 59–65 (2500 BC).

10. The Calendar Confusion

1. Hawkes, Jaquetta, and Wooley, Sir Leonard, History of Mankind – Cultural and Scientific Development, vol. 1, 1964, pp. 677–80.
2. Ibid.
3. Ibid.
4. Ibid.
5. Roux, G., 1980, p. 337.
6. Ibid. – however, the precise era of the Venus tablets remains a subject of debate.
7. Ronan, C. A., 1984, vol. 1, pp. 184–7.
8. See ref 1, pp. 684–7.
9. Ibid.
10. Ibid.
11. The Document of T'ang. See Waltham, C., 1971, pp. 4–5. There have been numerous attempts to retro-calculate the date of the Hsi and Ho eclipse, ranging from 2166 BC to 1949 BC (see Needham, 1959, vol. 2, p. 409).
12. Thompson, J.E.S., 1974.
13. Ibid.
14. Gallenkamp, C., 1987, p. 78.
15. Ibid., p. 77.
16. Thompson, J.E.S., 1974, p. 84.
17. Thompson, J.E.S., 1974. Others prefer a Julian date of 8 September 3114 BC – see Gallenkamp, C., 1987, p. 77. The Vedic calendar of

India has a similar epoch of 18 February 3102 BC, which is associated with a close conjunction of all the planets.

18. Gallenkamp, C., 1987, pp. 74–6.
19. Thompson, J.E.S., 1974, p. 84.
20. Harris, J.R., 1971, p. 17. See also chapter 9, note 1 above.
21. Parker, R.A., 1950, p. 53. He suggests 2937–2821 BC.
22. Ibid., p. 34.
23. Ibid., p. 37.
24. Harris, J.R., 1971, p. 15.
25. Parker, R.A., 1950, p. 34.
26. Ibid., pp. 51–6.
27. Manetho, Egyptica Epitome Fr 49 – see Waddel, W.G., 1940, pp. 98–9.
28. Plutarch, Isis and Osiris, 355–8. Here he says a seventieth part of the Moon's light was taken away, but see also The Face in the Moon, 932: 'the Egyptians ... say that the moon is one seventy-second part [of the earth]'. If this also refers to the periods of light then: $360 \div 72 = 5$ days.
29. See also Plutarch's remarks regarding the eternal flame at the shrine of Ammon. Moralia, Obsolescence of Oracles, 410–11.
30. See chapter 5, notes 5, 6 and 11. The motion of the axis in space is accompanied by the nearly diurnal free wobble which must also generate a pole tide. This, however, should be of much lesser amplitude than that discussed for the Chandler wobble and may not have been noticed in ancient times.
31. Ishtar and Gilgamesh.
32. The Wooing of Etain. (See Chapter 13).
33. Genesis, 41:28–31.
34. See Vicente, R.O., 1961, in Physics and Chemistry of the Earth, p. 271. I have tried to simplify the arguments here for the general reader. In fact, the simultaneous presence of the nearly diurnal wobble should also act to modify the period of the Chandler wobble by perhaps one part in ten.
35. Hoffman, M.A., 1980, pp. 27–9.
36. Davidson, R., 1979, p. 246, note 27; See also Harris, J.R., 1971, p. 271. The inscription on Sehel Island is believed by Egyptologists to be a forgery of Ptolemaic age. It appears to associate Joseph with the Third Dynasty pharoah Djoser, however it seems probable that the story as extant is a composite myth, which may explain why it is not associated with a flood.
37. Emery, W.B., 1961, pp. 249–51.
38. See the discussion in Christopoulos, G., and Bastias, J.C., 1970, pp. 160–2.
39. Jacobsen, T., 1939, p. 71.

40. Genesis, 9:29.
41. Genesis, 5:27.
42. Waloff, Z., and Green, S. M., *Nature*, 256, pp. 484–5 (1975).

11. The World of the Fourth Millenium BC

1. See also chapter 10, note 17 above.
2. Plato, *Timaeus*, 40. From the translation by Desmond Lee.
3. See Lambeck, 1988, pp. 602–7 and pp. 636–7, regarding a small alteration to the secular rate of change in the rotation between AD 700 and AD 1000, as derived from ancient eclipse observations. Unfortunately eclipse records do not extend back beyond the first millennium BC.
4. See Gault, D.E., and Schulz, P.H., 1990, for a discussion of comet and asteroid ricochet.
5. Pliny, *Natural History*, V.iv. See also V.vii.

12.　Beneath the Irish Sea

1. Steers, J.A., 1973, pp. 45–9.
2. Herries Davies, G.L., and Stevens, N., 1978, p. 21.
3. Stevens, N., 1970, p. 127.
4. Herries Davies, G.L., and Stevens, N., 1978, p. 204.
5. Ibid., p. 185.
6. Burenhalt, G., 1984, p. 168.
7. Godwin, H., 1943 and 1948.
8. Churchill, D.M., 1965.
9. Kidson, C., and Heyworth, A., 1973, p. 574.
10. Ibid., p. 576 (6184 BP).
11. Campbell, J.A., and Baxter, M.S., *Nature*, 278, 409 (1979).
12. Heyworth, A., 1978, p. 287.
13. Taylor, J.A., *Prog. Geogr.*, 5, 286 (1974).
14. Kay Gresswell, R., 1953.
15. Kay Gresswell, R., 1957.
16. Kay Gresswell, R., 1967.
17. Godwin, H., 1959.
18. Tooley, M.J., 1978, p. 140.
19. Shennan, I., 1983, pp. 269–70.
20. Jardine, W.G., and Morrison, A., in Davidson, D.A., and Shackley, M.L., *Geoarchaeology*, 1976, p. 190.
21. Ibid.
22. Ibid., p. 192.

23. Steers, J.A., 1964, p. 258.
24. Taylor, J.A., *Prog. Geogr.*, 5, 272–3 (1974).
25. Mitchell, G.F., 1963, p. 342.
26. Mitchell, G.F., 1972, p. 197.
27. Naylor, D., and Mountenay, S.N., 1975, chapter 8.
28. Ibid.
29. Ibid.
30. Wright, J.E., Hull, J.H., McQuillin, R., and Arnold, S.E., 'Irish Sea Investigations 1969–70', 1971, p. 32.
31. See *Diodorus Siculus*, II, 50.
32. Thomas, T.M., 1961, p. 214.
33. Hibbert, F.A. et al., 1971.
34. Girling, Maureen. A., and Greig, J., 1985.
35. Moore, P.D., *Nature*, 256, 267–9 (1975).
36. Good, R., 1974, pp. 315–18.

13. The Land of Youth

1. Herodotus, IV, 50.
2. Arrian, I, IV.
3. This comparison was originally made by Douglas Hyde in 1899.
4. *Geoffrey of Monmouth*. From the Penguin translation by Lewis Thorpe, 1966, p. 184.
5. Peate Cross, T., and Harris Slover, C., 1936, p. 4.
6. Ibid., p. 8.
7. *The Second Battle of Mag Tured* (Moytura).
8. Hyde, D., 1899, p. 282.
9. Ibid., p. 96.
10. Rolleston, T.W., 1911 (reprinted 1985), p. 271.
11. Jackson, K.H., 1951, p. 150.
12. Ibid., p. 165.
13. Rolleston, T.W., 1911 (reprinted 1985), p. 160.
14. Peate Cross, T., and Harris Slover, C., 1936, pp. 504–5.
15. Hyde, D., 1899 (reprinted 1967), p. 98.
16. Peate Cross, T., and Harris Slover, C., 1936, p. 592.
17. Bromwich, Rachel, 1978, p. 441.
18. Skene, W.F., 1868, pp. 77–9.
19. Christopoulos, G.A., and Bastias, J.C., p. 371.
20. Ibid., p. 372.
21. Peate Cross, T., and Harris Slover, C., 1936, pp. 598–9.
22. Swire, O.F., 1966, pp. 66, 148.
23. *Folklore, Myths and Legends of Britain*, p. 434.
24. Hyde, D., 1899, (reprinted 1967), p. 283.

14. Sunken Cities – Lost Lands

1. *Geoffrey of Monmouth*. From the translation by Lewis Thorpe.
2. North, F.J., 1957, chapter XI.
3. Bromwich, Rachel, 1950.
4. Tacitus, *Annals* XIV, 27–9.
5. Crawford, O.G.S., 1927.
6. Guest, Lady Charlotte, 1877, pp. 453–5.
7. Bromwich, Rachel, 1978, Introduction.
8. See chapter 12.
9. Davies, E., 1804, p. 157. The Welsh texts are in the *Myvyrian Archaiology* (1870 version), pp. 400–11.
10. Skene, W.F., 1868, pp. 28–31. See also Thomas Parry, 1955, pp. 302 and 381, regarding the authenticity of the third series of Triads.
11. Davies, E., 1804, p. 157.
12. Ibid., p. 158.
13. Caesar, *The Conquest of Gaul*, V. 12.
14. Tacitus, *Agricola*.
15. See Davies, E., 1804, pp. 154–5.
16. Skene, W.F., 1868, pp. 99–100.
17. Dio Cassius, *Epitome*, LXII, 1–2.
18. Tacitus, *The Agricola*, XI.
19. Tacitus, *Annals*, XIV, 30–6.
20. Ibid., XII, 39–40.
21. Rhys, J., 1891, Llanerch edition, p. 107.
22. Caesar, *The Conquest of Gaul*, V. 14.
23. Bede, *History of the English Church and People*, I.I.
24. In *The Destruction of Da Derga's Hostel*.
25. From the Penguin translation by Jeffrey Gantz, 1976.
26. Gwyn Jones and Thomas Jones, 1974.
27. Gantz, Jeffrey, 1976.
28. Guest, Lady Charlotte, 1877. See also the comments by North, 1957.
29. Ibid.
30. Gantz, Jeffrey, 1976.
31. Rivett, A.L.F., and Smith, C., 1979, p. 238.
32. Bede, *History of the English Church and People*, II.2., The Conference at Augustine's Oak.
33. From the translation by Lady Charlotte Guest, 1877.

15. In a Golden Age

1. Apollodorus, *The Library*, II.v.ii.
2. Hesiod, *Theogony*, 666–97. From the Penguin translation by Wender, Dorothea, 1973.
3. Ovid, *Metamorphoses*, book 1. From the translation by Melville, A.D., 1986. A similar story occurs in Hesiod's *Works and Days*.
4. Avery, C.B., and Johnson, J. (eds), *The New Century Classical Handbook*.
5. Herodotus, IV, 9–13.
6. *Diodorus Siculus*, V, 32, 2–6. See also Strabo, *Geography*, 3.2.12.
7. Strabo, *Geography*, 2.3.5–7, citing Posidonius.
8. Plutarch, *Moralia, The Decline of the Oracles*, 419, 184.
9. Plutarch, *Moralia, The Face in the Moon*, 941–2.
10. Hesiod, *Works and Days*, 165–95.
11. Pindar, *Olympian Odes*, II, 70–5. From the translation by C.M. Bowra.
12. Pindar, *Pythean Odes*, X, II. From the translation by C.M. Bowra.
13. Herodotus, IV, 12–20.
14. *Diodorus Siculus* II, 46, 47. Translation by E. Davies, 1804.
15. Avery, C.B., and Johnson, J. (eds), *The New Century Classical Handbook*.
16. Herodotus, II, 154–5.
17. Clube, V., and Napier, W., 1982. These authors suggest that Enke's comet is a fragment of a much larger comet that struck the Earth in recent pre-historical times.
18. Homer, *Odyssey*, IV, 519–643. From the translation by Walter Shewring.
19. Homer, *Iliad*, 14, 316.
20. Pindar, *Olympian Odes*, II, 75–80.
21. See chapter 2. Herodotus says that Poseidon was originally known only to the Libyans (Herodotus, II, 50); also Tritogeneia as a title of Athene means something like 'born of Trito' – the Libyan lake. Statues of Athena were dressed in the Libyan style (Herodotus, IV, 88). The ultimate equivalence of many Mediterranean myths is a subject to which classical scholars have long closed their minds.
22. From *The Search for Everlasting Life*; translation by N.K. Sandars, 1960.
23. Plutarch, *Isis and Osiris*, 355, 12–13.
24. Ibid., 367, 40–1.
25. See chapter 9.
26. Wallis Budge, E.A., 1899 (1989 edition), Introduction, clxxvii.
27. Ibid. (1977 edition), Introduction, lxxiv.

28. Faulkner, R.O., 1972 (revised 1985), Spell No. 109, pp. 101–2.
29. Rivett, A.L.F., and Smith, C., 1979, pp. 41 and 210–11.
30. Wallis Budge, E.A., 1920, pp. 870–1. The names occur in pyramid texts of the Vth and VIIth dynasties.
31. See the story of the giants of Castle Rushen in Grose, F., 1772, also quoted (with errors) in the Swarbreck Manuscript (Manx Museum).

16. Druids and Standing Stones

1. Bradbery, A., and Bradbery, J., 1979, p. 45.
2. Jensen, J., 1982, chapter 8.
3. Ibid., see also 1 above.
4. Ap Simon, A. M., 1969 (c.3795–c.3550 BC).
5. Piggott, S., 1954, leading to earlier refs.
6. De Valera, R., 1960, pp. 78–9.
7. Piggott, S., 1954, p. 157.
8. Ibid., p. 186, leading to earlier refs.
9. *The Swarbreck MS* (1815) pp. 121–2. The document contains a drawing of the Cloven Stones in their former state.
10. De Valera, R., 1965, p. 19.
11. Childe, V.G., 1931.
12. O'Kelly, M., 1989. See also Castleden, R., 1987, p. 83.
13. Adkins, Lesley and Adkins, R.A., 1982.
14. Fowler, P.J., and Evans, J.G., 1967.
15. Caulfield, S., in Bowen, H.C., and Fowler, P.J., (eds), 1978, pp. 137–43.
16. Ibid.
17. Mercer, R., in Bowen, H.C., and Fowler, P.J., (eds), 1978, pp. 133–6.
18. Castleden, R., 1987, leading to earlier references.
19. Thomas, C., 1985, leading to earlier references.
20. Mercer, R.J., 1981.
21. Bradbery, A., and Bradbery, J., 1979, p. 191, leading to earlier references.
22. Burl, H.A.W., 1979, chapter 5. See also Bradley, R., 1978, pp. 105–7.
23. Caulfield, S., 1978, p. 142.
24. Castleden, R., 1987, pp. 24–31, leading to earlier references.
25. Burl, H.A.W., 1979, chapter 5.
26. Brothwell, D., 1974. For a discussion of older references see also Rice-Holmes, T., 1936.
27. Burgess, C., 1980, p. 36 and chapter 4.

28. Bradley, R., 1978, p. 106.
29. Piggott, S., 1954, chronological appendix.
30. Castleden, R., 1987, p. 7.
31. Ibid., p. 27.
32. O'Kelly, J., 1982.
33. Burgess, C., 1980, pp. 15–17.
34. Ibid., chapter 4.
35. Brothwell, D., 1974.
36. Laing, L., and Laing, J., 1982 (r. 1987), p. 201. See also Burl, H.A.W., 1976, p. 11.
37. Castleden, R., 1987, p. 141.
38. O'Kelly, M.J., 1989, chapter 4.
39. Burl, H.A.W., 1979, p. 114.
40. Castleden, R., 1987, p. 101.
41. Ibid., pp. 102–3.
42. Lockyer, J.N., 1906.
43. Thom, A., 1967.
44. Newall, R.S., 1959 (1981 edition), p. 29.
45. See Skene, W.F., 1868, quoting the *Yellow Book of Lecan*.
46. *The Book of Invasions*.
47. Piggott, S., 1968, pp. 100–1.
48. Rivett, A.L.F., and Smith, C., 1979, pp. 254–5.
49. Piggott, S., 1968, pp. 100–1.
50. See Tierney, J.J., 1960, for a collection of the ethnographies of Posidonius from various authors.
51. MacKie, E.W., 1977.
52. Tacitus, *Annals*, XIV, 29.
53. Strabo, *Geography*, 4.4.6.
54. Nennius. See Morris, J., *Arthurian Period Sources*, vol. 8. Regarding the Demetae, see also Rivett, A.L.F., and Smith, C., 1979, p. 333.
55. Avery, C.B., and Johnson, J. (eds), *The New Century Classical Handbook*.
56. Plutarch, *The Decline of the Oracles*, 419, 18.
57. Pliny, *Natural History*, II, LXXV, lxxvii, from the Loeb translation by Rackham H.
58. Nennius, see Morris, J., *Arthurian Period Sources*, vol. 8.
59. Pliny, *Natural History*, XXX, xiii.
60. Plutarch, *The Face on the Moon*, 941.
61. See, for example, Peter Lancaster-Brown, 1976, pp. 77–81. It is debatable whether the so-called 'great year' of the druids was the 30-year cycle of Pliny, or the 19-year cycle as assumed by Hecataeus. This is further explored in appendix A.
62. Michell, J., 1977 (r. 1989), p. 47. See also the article by Griffiths, J., in *Nature*, May 1907, pp. 9–10.

63. Ray, T.P., Letter to *Nature*, 377 (January 1989).
64. See the translation by Peate Cross, Tom, and Harris Slover, Clark, 1936.
65. Pliny, *Natural History*, XXX, xiii.
66. Pope Gregory's letter to Mellitus – see Bede, *History of the English Church*, i. 30.
67. Davies, E., 1804, p. 161.
68. Procopius, *History of the Wars*, VIII, xx.
69. Hesiod, *Theogony*, 726–37.

17. A Neolithic Empire

1. Avienius, *Ora Maritima*, 94–134.
2. Aristotle, *De Mundo*, iii.
3. Herodotus, III, 112–13.
4. Ibid., IV, 46–50 and II, 32–3.
5. Davies, E., 1804, p. 129.
6. De Beer, Sir Gavin, 1960.
7. Strabo, *Geography*, 3.5.3.
8. See Rice Holmes, T., 1936, chapter 4, for a discussion of the various fragments of Pytheas.
9. Caesar, *The Gallic War*, V, 13. From the translation by Handford, S.A.
10. Pliny, *Natural History*, IV, 101–2.
11. Strabo, *Geography*, 4.5.1–5.
12. *Diodorus Siculus*, V, 38, 4–5.
13. Avery, C.B., and Johnson, J., (eds), *The New Century Classical Handbook*.
14. Pomponius Mela, *De Chorographica*, II, 6.
15. See chapter 16.
16. Tacitus, *Germania*, 45.
17. Tacitus, *Agricola*, 11.
18. Tacitus, *Germania*, 28.
19. Ibid., 40.
20. Williams Ab Ithel, J., 1862, p. 172.
21. The Finnic word for 'plough' is often classed as an early Indo-European loan word. See Hajdu, P., 1975, p. 74, and Buck, C.D., 1949, p. 492.

Appendix A

1. Pliny, *Natural History*, 30.13.
2. MacNeill, E., 1928.

3. Bede, *History of the English Church and People*, II.2.
4. *Diodorus Siculus*, II.46.47.
5. Plutarch, *The Face in the Moon*, 941.

Appendix B

1. See chapter 5, note 6 and the general discussion in chapter 10 here above.
2. *http://www.stanford.edu/meehan/donnelly/index.html*.
3. James, P., *The Sunken Kingdom*, London (1995).
4. Allen, D.S., and Delair, J.B., *When the Earth Nearly Died*, Bath (1995).
5. Clube, V., and Napier, B., *The Cosmic Serpent*, London (1982).
6. Charles, C., 'The ends of an era', *Nature*, 394, 422–3 (1998); Severinghaus, J.P. et al., 'Timing of abrupt climate change at the end of the Younger Dryas interval from thermally fractionated gases in polar ice', *Nature*, 391, 141–6 (1998).
7. See the various arguments in chapter 10 here above.
8. Hills, J.G. et al., 'Tsunami generated by small asteroid impacts', in Hills, J.G. et al. (eds), *Hazards Due to Comets and Asteroids*, Arizona University Press (1994).
9. Song, X., and Richards, P., 'Seismological evidence for the rotation of the Earth's inner core', *Nature*, 382, 221–4 (1996).
10. Buffet, B.A. 'A mechanism for decade fluctuations in the length-of-day', *Geophys. Res. Lett.*, 23, 3803–6 (1996).
11. Aitken, M.J., *Science-based Dating in Archaeology*, Longman, London (1990).
12. *The Geology of Cardigan Bay and the Bristol Channel*, HMSO, London (1994), p. 90.
13. *The Geology of the Irish Sea*, HMSO, London (1995), p. 102.
14. James, J.W.C., British Geological Survey, personal communication.
15. Wingfield, R.T.R., 'Giant sand waves and relict periglacial features on the Irish Sea bed west of Anglesey', *Proceedings of the Geologists' Association*, 98, 4, 400–4 (1987).

Bibliography

The following is a list of all sources quoted, cited, or consulted in the making of this book.

Adkins, L., and Adkins, R.A., *A Thesaurus of British Archaeology*, David and Charles, Newton Abbot, Devon (1982)

Aldenderfer, M.S., 'Late Preceramic ceremonial architecture at Asana, southern Peru', *Antiquity*, 64, 479–93 (1990)

Aldred, C., *Egypt to the End of the Old Kingdom*, Thames and Hudson, London (1965)

Allegre, C., *The Behaviour of the Earth*, Harvard University Press, Cambridge, Mass. and London (1988)

Anwyl, E., *Celtic Religion in Pre-Christian Times*, Banton Press, Largs (facsimile of the 1906 edition) (1991)

Ap Simon, A.M., 'An early Neolithic house in County Tyrone', *J.R.S.A.I.*, 99, 165–8 (1969)

Arribas, A., *The Iberians*, Thames and Hudson, London (undated)

Ase, L.E., 'Sea-level changes on the east coast of Africa during the Holocene and Late Pleistocene', in Tooley, M.J., and Shennan, I. (eds), *Sea-level Changes*, Basil Blackwell, Oxford (1987)

Ashbee, P., *Ancient Scilly*, David and Charles, Newton Abbot, Devon (1974)

Avery, C.B., and Johnson, J. (eds), *The New Century Classical Handbook*, George G. Harrap, London (1962)

Babbitt, F.C., *Plutarch's Moralia*, vol. V, William Heinemann, London (1936)

Baillie, M.G.L., 'Irish oaks record prehistoric dust veils drama', *Archaeology Ireland*, 2(2), 71–4 (1988)

Baillie, M.G.L., 'Do Irish bog oaks date the Shang Dynasty?', *Current Archaeology*, 117, 310–13 (1990)

Baillie, M.G.L., and Munro, M.A.R., 'Irish tree rings, Santorini and volcanic dust veils', *Nature*, 332, 344–6 (1988)

Barber, C., *Mysterious Wales*, David and Charles, Newton Abbot Devon (1982)

Barger, V., and Olsen, M., *Classical Mechanics – A Modern Perspective*, McGraw-Hill, Maidenhead (1973)

Barrow, R.H., *Plutarch and his Times*, Indiana University Press, Bloomington and London (1967)

Baxter, J., and Atkins, T., *The Fire Came By*, Macdonald and Jones Publishers, London (1976)

Bell, B., 'The oldest records of the Nile floods', *Geogr. J.*, 136, 569–73 (1970)

Bell, B., 'The Dark Ages in ancient history – the first dark age in Egypt', *Am. J. Archaeol.*, 75, 1–26 (1971)

Bennet, L.V., 'Development of a desert locust plague', *Nature*, 256, 486–7 (1975)

Berlitz, C., *Atlantis – The Lost Continent Revealed*, Macmillan, London (1984)

Berresford Ellis, P., *A Dictionary of Irish Mythology*, Constable, London (1987)

Bird, E.C.F., *Coasts – An Introduction to Coastal Geomorphology*, (3rd edition), Basil Blackwell, Oxford (1984)

Black, R.F., and Barksdale, W.F., 'The oriented lakes of northern Alaska', *Journal of Geology*, 57, 105–18 (1949)

Blake, W., 'Radiocarbon dating of raised beaches in Nordouslandet, Spitsbergen', in Raasch, G.O. (ed.), *Geology of the Arctic*, University of Toronto Press, pp. 133–45 (1961)

Blake, W., Jr, 'Radiocarbon age determinations and post-glacial emergence at Cape Storm, Southern Ellesmere Island, Arctic Canada,' in *Geografiska Annaler*, 57A, 1–71 (1975)

Bloom, A.L. (ed.) *The Atlas of Sea Level Curves*, Cornell University, New York (1977)

Bomford, G., *Geodesy* (4th edition), Oxford Science Publications, Clarendon Press (1980)

Bond, A., 'Multiple sources of pumice in the Aegean', *Nature*, 259, 194–5 (1976)

Booth, B., and Fitch, F., *Earthshock*, J.M. Dent, London (1979)

Bott, M.H.P., 'The geological structure of the Irish Sea basin', in Donovan, D.T. (ed.), *Geology of Shelf Seas*, Oliver Boyd, Edinburgh, pp. 93–113 (1968)

Bottema, S., *Late Quaternary Vegetation History of North Western Greece*, VRB Offset Drukerij, Groningen (1974)

Bottema, S., 'Pollenanalytical investigations in Thessaly', *Paleohistoria*, 21, 19–40 (1979)

Bowen, E.G., *Britain and the Western Seaways*, Thames and Hudson, London (1972)

Bowra, C.M., *Pindar – The Odes*, Penguin Books, Harmondsworth (1969)

Bradbery, A., and Bradbery, J., *Megaliths and their Mysteries – The Standing Stones of Europe*, George Weidenfield and Nicolson, London (1979)

Bradley, R., *The Settlement of Britain*, Routledge and Kegan Paul, London (1978)

Brennan, M., *The Stars and the Stones*, Thames and Hudson, London (1983)

Briggs, C.S., 'Early observations on early fields', in Bowen, H.C., and Fowler, P.J. (eds), *Early Land Allotment in the British Isles*, BAR British Series 48 (1978)

Brodrick, M., and Morton, A.A., *A Concise Dictionary of Egyptian Archaeology*, Methuen, London (1902)

Bromwich, R., 'Cantre'r Gwaelod and Ker-Is', in Fox, Sir Cyril, and Dickens, Bruce (eds), *The Early Cultures of North-West Europe*, pp. 217–41 (1950)

Bromwich, R., *Troiedd Ynys Prydein – The Welsh Triads*, University of Wales Press, Cardiff (1978)

Bromwich, R. (ed.), *Studies by Sir Ifor Williams*, University of Wales Press, Cardiff (1980)

Brothwell, D., and Kzanowski, W., 'Evidence of biological differences between early British populations from Neolithic to Medieval times as revealed by eleven commonly available cranial vault measurements', *J. Archaeol. Sci.*, 1, 249–60 (1974)

Brunt, P.A., *Arrian – Anabasis of Alexander and Indica*, William Heinemann, London (1976)

Brush, S.G., 'Discovery of the Earth's core', *American Journal of Physics*, 48, 705–24 (1980)

Buck, C.D., *A Dictionary of Selected Synonyms in the Principal Indo-European Languages*, University of Chicago Press, Chicago and London (1949)

Burenhalt, G., *The Archaeology of Carrowmore, Co. Sligo. Theses and Papers in North European Archaeology*, 14, Institute of Archaeology, University of Stockholm (1984)

Burgess, C., *The Age of Stonehenge*, J.M. Dent, London (1980)

Burgess, C., 'Volcanoes, catastrophe and the global crisis of the late second millennium BC', *Current Archaeology*, 117, 325–9 (1990)

Burl, H.A.W., 'Henges: internal features and regional groups', *Arch. J.*, 126, 1–28 (1969)

Burl, H.A.W., *The Stone Circles of the British Isles*, Yale University Press, London (1976)

Burl, H.A.W., *Prehistoric Avebury*, Yale University Press, London (1979)

Burl, H.A.W., ' "By the light of the Cinerary Moon": Chambered tombs and the astronomy of death', in Ruggles, C.L.N., and Whittle, A.W.R., *Astronomy and Society in Britain during the Period 4000–1500 BC*, BAR British Series 88, pp. 243–75 (1981)

Burl, H.A.W., *Megalithic Brittany*, Thames and Hudson, London (1985)

Burl, H.A.W., *The Stonehenge People*, J.M. Dent, London (1987)

Burland, C., *North American Indian Mythology*, Paul Hamlyn, London (1965)

Burn, A.R., and Burn, M., *The Living Past of Greece*, Herbert Press, London (1980)

Bury, R.G., *Plato* vol. IX, William Heinemann, London (1929)

Campbell, J.A., and Baxter, M.S., 'Radiocarbon measurements on submerged forest floating chronologies', *Nature*, 278, 409–13 (1979)

Capitaine, N., and Xiao, N., 'Some terms of nutation derived from the BIH data', *Geophys. J. R. Astr. Soc.*, 68, 805–14 (1982)

Cary, E., *Dio Cassius – Roman History*, vol. VIII, William Heinemann Ltd, London (1925)

Castleden, R., *The Stonehenge People*, Routledge and Kegan Paul, London (1987)

Caulfield, S., 'Neolithic fields: the Irish evidence', in Bowen, H.C., and Fowler, P.J. (eds), *Early Land Allotment in the British Isles*, BAR British Series 48 (1978)

Chamberlain, T. C., *The Origin of the Earth*, University of Chicago Press, Chicago (1916)

Champion, T., Gamble, C., Shennan, S., and Whittle, A., *Prehistoric Europe*, Academic Press, London (1984)

Chappell, J., 'Late Quaternary sea-level changes in the Australian region', in Tooley, M.J., and Shennan, I. (eds), *Sea-level Changes*, Basil Blackwell, Oxford (1987)

Charlesworth, J.K., *The Quaternary Era*, Edward Arnold, London (1957)

Cherniss, H., and Helmbold, W., *Plutarch's Moralia*, vol XII, William Heinemann, London (1957)

Childe, V.G., 'The continental affinities of British Neolithic pottery', *Arch. J.*, 88, 37–66 (1931)

Childe, V.G., *The Dawn of European Civilisation*, (6th edition), Routledge and Kegan Paul, London (1957)

Christopoulos, G.A., and Bastias, J.C., *History of the Hellenic World, Prehistory and Protohistory*, Heinemann Educational Books, London (1970)

Chu Ko-Chen, 'A preliminary study on the climatic fluctuations during the last 5,000 years in China', *Scientia Sinica*, XVI, no. 2, May 1973 (1973)

Churchill, D.M., 'The displacement of deposits formed at sea-level 6500 years ago', in *Quaternia*, vol. VII, 239–49 (1965)

Clancy, J.P., *The Earliest Welsh Poetry*, Macmillan, London (1970)

Clausen, H.B., Friedrich, W.I., and Tauber, H., 'Dating of the Santorini eruption', *Nature*, 332, 401 (1988)

Cleator, P.E., *Lost Languages*, Robert Hale, London (1959)

Close, A.E., 'Living on the edge: Neolithic herders in the eastern Sahara, *Antiquity*, 64, 79–96 (1990)

Clube, V., and Napier, B., *The Cosmic Serpent*, Faber and Faber, London (1982)

Coles, B., and Coles, J., *The Sweet Track to Glastonbury*, Thames and Hudson, London (1986)

Collins, R., *The Basques*, Basil Blackwell, London (1986)

Cotterell, A., and Joseph, M., *The Minoan World*, Joseph, London (1979)

Crawford, O.G.S., 'Lyonesse', *Antiquity*, 1, 1927, 5 (1927)

Crossley-Holland, K., *The Norse Myths*, Penguin Books, Harmondsworth (1982)

Cubbon, A.M. (ed.), *The Prehistoric Sites in the Isle of Man, Manx Museum and National Trust*, Norris Modern Press, Douglas, I.O.M (1986)

Cymmrodomon, The Honourable Society of, *Dictionary of Welsh Biography down to 1940*, Blackwell, London (1959)

Daniel, G., *A Short History of Archaeology*, Thames and Hudson, London (1981)

Darvil, T., *Prehistoric Britain*, B.T. Batsford, London (1987)

Davidson, D.A., and Shackley, M.L (eds), *Geoarchaeology*, Gerald Duckworth, London (1976)

Davidson, R., *The Cambridge Bible Commentary, Genesis 12–50*, University Press, Cambridge (1979)

Davies, E., *Celtic Researches*, J. Booth, London (1804)

Davies, E., *The Mythology and Rites of the British Druids*, J. Booth, London (1809)

De Beer, Sir G., 'Iktin', *Geographical Jour.*, 126, 160–7 (1960)

Delibrias, G., and Guillier, M.T., 'The sea-level on the Atlantic Coast and the Channel for the last 10,000 years by the 14C method', *Quaternaria*, 14, 131–5 (1971)

Derricourt, R.M., 'Radiocarbon chronology for Egypt and North Africa', *Journal of Near Eastern Studies*, 30, 4, 271–92 (1971)

De Selincourt, A., *Herodotus – The Histories*, Penguin Books, Harmondsworth (1954)

Desmond Clark, J. (ed.), *The Cambridge History of Africa*, Cambridge University Press, Cambridge (1982)

De Valera, R., 'The Court Cairns of Ireland', *Proc. R. Irish. Acad.*, 60C, 9–140 (1960)

De Valera, R., 'Tranceptal Court Cairns', *Jour. R. Soc. Ant. Ireland*, 95, 5–37 (1965)

Deveraux, P., 'Three dimensional aspects of apparent relationships between selected natural and artificial features within the topography of the Avebury complex', *Antiquity*, 65, 249, 894–8 (1991)

Devoy, R.J.N., 'Flandrian sea level changes in the Thames estuary and the implications for land subsidence in England and Wales', *Nature*, 267, 712–15 (1977)

Devoy, R.J.N., 'Quaternary shorelines in Ireland: An assessment of their implications for isostatic and relative sea level changes', in Smith, D.E., and Dawson, A.G., *Shorelines and Isostasy*, Academic Press, London (1983)

Dewing, H.B., *Procopius*, vol. V, William Heinemann, London (1928)

Diamond, J.M., 'Express train to Polynesia', *Nature*, 336, 307–8 (1988)

Diamond, J.M., 'The earliest horsemen', *Nature*, 350, 275–6 (1991)

The Dictionary of Imaginary Places, Granada Publishing (1981)

Dillon, M., *Early Irish Literature*, University of Chicago Press, Chicago (1948)

Donnelly, I., *Atlantis: The Antediluvian World*, Harper, New York (1882)

Donnelly, I., *Ragnarok: The Age of Fire and Gravel*, University Books, New York (1970) (originally published 1883)

Doumas, C.G., *Thera – Pompeii of the Ancient Aegean*, Thames and Hudson, London (1983)

Dumond, D.E., *The Eskimos and Aleuts* (revised edition), Thames and Hudson, London (1987)

Edwards, I.E.S. (ed.), *The Cambridge Ancient History*, vol. 1, Prologomena, Cambridge University Press (1977)

Ellis Davidson, H.R., *Gods and Myths of Northern Europe*, Penguin Books, Harmondsworth (1964)

Ellis Davidson, H.R., *Scandinavian Mythology*, Hamlyn, London (1982)

Emery, W.B., *Archaic Egypt*, Penguin Books, London (1961)

Encyclopaedia of Religion, ed. Mercea Eliade, Macmillan Publishing, London (1987)

Encyclopaedia of Religion and Ethics, ed. James Hastings, T. and T. Clark, Edinburgh (1909)

Evans, Estyn, A. *Prehistoric and Early Christian Ireland*, B.T. Batsford, London (1968)

Fairbridge, R.W., 'Eustatic changes in sea level', in *Physics and Chemistry of the Earth*, vol. 4, Pergamon Press (1961)

Fairbridge, R.W., 'New radiocarbon dates of Nile sediments', *Nature*, 196, 108–10 (1962)

Fairbridge, R.W. (ed.) *The Encyclopaedia of Oceanography*, Reinhold, New York (1966)

Fairbridge, R.W. (ed.) *The Encyclopaedia of Geomorphology*, Academic Press, Dowden Hutchinson and Ross, Stroudsberg, Pennsylvania (1968)

Fairbridge, R.W. (ed.) *The Encyclopaedia of World Regional Geology, Part 1 (Western Hemisphere)*, Academic Press, Dowden Hutchinson and Ross, Stroudsberg, Pennsylvania (1975)

Faulkner, R.O., *The Ancient Egyptian Book of the Dead*, British Museum Publications, London (1972)

Faulkner, R.O., *The Ancient Egyptian Pyramid Texts*, Aris and Williams, Warminster (1993)

Flemming, N.C., *Cities in the Sea*, New English Library, London (1971)

Flood, J., *The Archaeology of the Dreamtime*, Collins, London (1983)

Florensky, K.P., 'Did a comet collide with the Earth in 1908?', *Sky and Telescope*, 26; 268–9 (Nov. 1963)

Folklore, Myths and Legends of Britain, Readers Digest Association, London (1973)

Fong Chao, B., and Gross, R.S., 'Changes in the Earth's rotation and low-degree gravitational field induced by earthquakes', in *Geophys. J. R. Astr. Soc.*, 91, 569–96 (1987)

Foucault, A., and Stanley, D.J., 'Late Quaternary paleoclimatic oscillations in East Africa recorded by heavy minerals in the Nile delta', *Nature*, 339, 44–6 (1989)

Fowler, P.J., *The Farming of Prehistoric Britain*, Cambridge University Press, Cambridge (1983)

Fowler, P.J., and Bowen H.C., (eds), *Early Land Allotment in the British Isles*, BAR British Series 48, Oxford (1978)

Fowler, P.J., and Evans, J.G., 'Ploughmarks, lynchets and early fields', in *Ant.*, XLI, 289–301 (1967)

Francey, R.J., and Hubrick, K.T., 'Tree-ring carbon-isotope ratios re-examined', *Nature*, 333, 712 (1988)

Frazer, Sir J.G., *Apollodorus – The Library*, William Heinemann, London (1921)

French, E.M., *The Periglacial Environment*, Longman, London (1976)

Fries, M., 'Vegetational and climatic history, Sweden', *Spec. Pap. Geol. Soc. Am.*, no. 84 (1965)

Fuenzalida, H., et al., 'High stands of Quaternary sea level along the Chilean coast', *Spec. Pap. Geol. Soc. Am.*, no. 84 (1965)

Funnel, B.M., 'History of the North Sea', *Bull. Geol. Soc. Norfolk*, 21, 2–10 (1972)

Gallenkamp, C., *Maya* (3rd revised edition), Penguin Books, Harmondsworth (1959)

Gantz, J., *The Mabinogion*, Penguin Books, Harmondsworth (1976)

Gantz, J., *Early Irish Myths and Sagas*, Penguin Books, Harmondsworth (1981)

Gardiner, Sir A., *Egypt of the Pharoahs*, Clarendon Press, Oxford (1961)

Garland, G.D., *The Earth's Shape and Gravity*, Pergamon Press, London (1965)

Gault, D.E., and Wedekind, J.A., 'Experimental studies of oblique impact', *Proc. Lunar Planet. Sci. Conf.* 9th, pp. 3843–75 (1978)

Gelkie, A., 'Emergence and submergence of land', *Nature*, 70, 111–15 (1904)

Gibb, J.G., 'A New Zealand regional Holocene eustatic sea-level curve and its implications', *R. Soc. N.Z. Bull.*, 24, 377–95 (1986)

Giles, J.A., *Six Old English Chronicles*, London (1848)

Giresse, P., 'Quaternary sea-level changes on the Atlantic coast of Africa', in Tooley, M.J. and Shennan, I. (eds), *Sea-level Changes*, Basil Blackwell, Oxford (1987)

Girling, M.A., and Greig, J. 'A first fossil record for *Scolytus scolytus* (F.) (Elm Bark Beetle): its occurrence in elm decline deposits from London and the implications for Neolithic elm disease', *Journal of Archaeological Science*, 12, 347–51 (1985)

Glob, P.V., *Danish Prehistoric Monuments*, Faber and Faber, London (1971)

Godwin, H., 'Coastal peat beds of the British Isles and North Sea', *Journal of Ecology*, 31, 199–247 (1943)

Godwin, H., 'Studies of the post-glacial history of British vegetation. X. Correlation between climate, forest composition, prehistoric agriculture and peat stratigraphy in Sub-Boreal and Sub-Atlantic peats in the Somerset levels'. *Phil. Trans. R. Soc.*, B 233, 275–86 (1948)

Godwin, H., 'Studies of the post-glacial history of British vegetation. XIV. Late-glacial deposits at Moss Lake, Liverpool'. *Phil. Trans. R. Soc.*, B. 242 (689), 127–49 (1959)

Godwin, H., 'Prehistoric wooden trackways of the Somerset Levels: their construction, age and relation to climatic change', *Proceedings of the Prehistoric Society*, 26, 1–36 (1960)

Godwin, H., *The History of the British Flora*, Cambridge University Press, Cambridge (1975)

Godwin, H., and Newton, L., 'The submerged forest at Borth and Ynyslas', *New Phytologist*, 37, 333–44, (1938)

Gold, T., 'Instability of the Earth's rotation', *Nature*, 175, 526–9 (1955)

Gold, T., 'Irregularities in the Earth's rotation', *Sky and Telescope*, 17, 284–6 (1958)

Goldstein, H., *Classical Mechanics*, Addison Wesley, USA (1980)

Good, R., *The Geography of Flowering Plants* (4th edition), Longman, London (1974)

Goodfriend, G.A., 'Mid-Holocene rainfall in the Negev Desert from 13C of land snail shell organic matter', *Nature*, 333, 757–60 (1988)

Gorenstein, S. et al., *Prehispanic America*, Thames and Hudson (1974)

Grant, M., *Tacitus – The Annals of Imperial Rome*, Penguin Books, Harmondsworth (1956)

Green, R.M., *Spherical Astronomy*, Cambridge University Press, Cambridge (1985)

Greenly, E., 'Some recent work on the submerged forest in Anglesey', *Proc. Liverpool Geol. Soc.* (1928)

Greenwood, J.J.D., 'Three-year cycles of lemmings and Arctic geese explained', *Nature*, 328, 577 (1987)

Gregor, D.B., *Celtic – A Comparative Study*, Oleander Press, Cambridge (1980)

Greig, J.R.A., and Turner, J., 'Some pollen diagrams from Greece and their archaeological significance', *Journal of Archaeological Science*, 1; 177 94 (1971)

Gresswell, R.K., *Sandy Shores in South Lancashire: The Geomorphology of South-West Lancashire*, University of Liverpool Press (1953)

Gresswell, R.K., 'Hillhouse coastal deposits in South Lancashire, *Lpool. Manchr. Geol. J.*, 2, 60–78 (1957)

Gresswell, R.K., 'The Post-glacial raised beach in Furness and Lyth, North Morecambe', *Trans. Inst. Br. Geol.*, 25, 79–103 (1958)

Gresswell, R.K., 'The Geomorphology of the Fylde', in Steel, R.W., and Lawton, R. (eds), *Liverpool Essays in Geography: a Jubilee Collection*, pp. 25–42, Longman, London (1967)

Griffith, J., 'The astronomical and archaeological value of the Welsh Gorsedd', *Nature*, 76, 9–10 (1907)

Grinsell, L.V., *Folklore of Prehistoric Sites in Britain*, David and Charles, Newton Abbot (1976)

Grinsell, L.V., *Barrows in England and Wales*, Shire Publications, Princes Risborough, Buckinghamshire (1979)

Grose, F., *The Antiquities of England and Wales: being a collection of views of the most remarkable ruins and ancient buildings accurately drawn on the spot* (1772)

Guest, Lady Charlotte, *The Mabinogion*, J.M. Dent, London.

Gurney, R., *Bardic Heritage*, Chatto and Windus, London (1969)

Hadingham, E., *Circles and Standing Stones*, William Heinemann, London (1975)

Hafsten, U., 'Biostratigraphical evidence for late Weichselian and Holocene sea level changes in southern Norway', in Smith, D.E., and Dawson, A.G., *Shorelines and Isostasy*, pp. 161–81, Academic Press, London (1983)

Hawkes, Jaquetta, and Wooley, Sir Leonard, *History of Mankind – Cultural and Scientific Development*, vol. 1, George Allen and Unwin, London (1964)

Hajdu, P., *Finno-Ugrian Languages and Peoples*, translated and adapted by G. Cushing, André Deutsch, London (1974)

Hakulinen, L., *The Structure and Development of the Finnish Language*, translated by J. Atkinson, Indiana University Press, Bloomington, Indiana (1961)

Hallam, A., *Great Geological Controversies*, Oxford University Press, Oxford (1983)

Hamilton Paterson, J., and Andrews, C., *Mummies: Death and Life in Ancient Egypt*, W. Collins, Glasgow (1978)

Hammer, C.U., Clausen, H.B., and Dansgaard, W., 'Greenland ice sheet evidence of post-glacial volcanism and its climatic impact', *Nature*, 288, 230–5 (1980)

Hammer, C.U., Clausen, H.B., Friedrich, W.L., and Tauber, H., 'The Minoan eruption of Santorini in Greece dated to 1645 BC?', *Nature*, 328, 517–19 (1987)

Hammond, M., *Homer – The Iliad, A New Prose Translation*, Penguin Books, Harmondsworth (1987)

Hammond, N.G.L., *A History of Greece to 322 BC* (2nd edition), Clarendon Press, Oxford (1967)

Hammond, N.G.L., and Scullard, H.H., *The Oxford Classical Dictionary* (2nd edition), Clarendon Press, Oxford (1970)

Handford, S.A., *Caesar – The Conquest of Gaul*, Penguin Books, Harmondsworth (1951)

Hanle, P.A., and Chamberlain, V.D., *Space Science Comes of Age*, Smithsonian Institution Press (1981)

Harbison, P., *Prehistoric and Early Christian Ireland*, Thames and Hudson, London (1982)

Hardisty, J., *The British Seas*, Routledge, London (1990)

Harris, J.R., *The Legacy of Egypt*, Clarendon Press, Oxford (1971)

Harrison, R.J., 'Origins of the Bell Beaker cultures', *Antiquity*, 48, 99–109 (1974)

Harrison, R.J., *The Beaker Folk*, Thames and Hudson, London (1980)

Hassan, F.A., and Robinson, S.W., 'High precision radiocarbon chronometry of ancient Egypt and comparisons with Nubia, Palestine and Mesopotamia', *Antiquity*, 231, 119–31 (1987)

Hawkes, J., *History of Mankind, Prehistory and the Beginnings of Civilisation*, published for the International Commission for a History of the Scientific and Cultural Development of Mankind, Allen and Unwin, London (1963)

Hawkins, A.B., 'Sea level changes around South-West England', *Colston Papers*, XXIII, Bristol (1971)

Hawkins, G.S., *Stonehenge Decoded*, Souvenir Press, London (1966)

Heath, Sir Thomas L., *Greek Astronomy*, J.M. Dent, London (1932)

Henderson, I., *The Picts*, Thames and Hudson, London (1967)

Henshall, A.S., *The Chambered Tombs of Scotland*, vols 1 and 2, Edinburgh University Press, Edinburgh (1972)

Herity, M. and Eogan, G., *Ireland in Prehistory*, Routledge and Kegan Paul, London (1977)

Herries Davies, G.L., and Stevens, N., *The Geomorphology of the British Isles, Ireland*, Methuen, London (1978)

Hess, H.H., 'Drowned ancient islands of the Pacific basin', *American Journal of Science*, 244, 772–91 (1946)

Heyworth, A., 'Submerged forests around the British Isles: their dating and relevance as indicators of post-glacial land and sea-level changes', in Fletcher, J.M. (ed.), *Dendrochronology in Europe*, pp. 279–88, Oxford, British Archaeological Reports International series 51 (1978)

Hibbert, F.A. et al., 'Radiocarbon dating of Flandrian pollen zones at Red Moss, Lancashire', *Proc. R. Soc. B.*, 177, 161–76 (1971)

Hide, R., and Roberts, P.H., 'The origin of the main geomagnetic field, in *Physics and Chemistry of the Earth*, Pergamon Press, London (1961)

Hilliar, J. et al., 'English Neolithic Dendrochronology', *Antiquity*, 243, 210–20 (1990)

Hoffman, M.A., *Egypt before the Pharaohs*, Routledge and Kegan Paul, London (1980)

Holland, C.H., *A Geology of Ireland*, Scottish Academic Press, Edinburgh (1981)

Holmberg, Uno, 'Finno-Ugric Mythology', in *Mythology of all Races*, vol. 4, Boston (1964)

Hopkins., A.A., 'Legendary islands of the North Atlantic', *Scientific American Monthly*, 4, 362–3 and 4, 14–18 (1921)

Hopkins, D.M. (ed.), *The Bering Land Bridge*, Stanford University Press, Stanford, California (1967)

Hopkins, W., 'Researches in physical geography', *Phil. Trans. R. Soc. London*, 129, 381–423 (1839)

Hopley, D., 'Deformation of the North Queensland continental shelf' in Smith, D.E., and Dawson, A.G., *Shorelines and Isostasy*, pp. 356–61, Academic Press, London (1983)

Hoppe, G., and Fries, M., 'Submarine peat in the Shetland Islands', *Geografiska Annaler*, 47, A, 195–203 (1965)

Hough, S.S., 'The oscillations of a rotating ellipsoidal shell containing fluid', *Phil. Trans. R. Soc. London*, 186, 469–506 (1895)

Howarth, H.H., 'Recent changes in circumpolar lands', *Nature*, 5, 162–3 (1871)

Howarth, H.H., 'Circumpolar land, *Nature*, 5, 420–2 (1872)

Howarth, H.H., 'Recent climate changes', *Nature*, 6, 24–5 (1872)

Howells, W.W., *The Pacific Islanders*, Weidenfeld and Nicolson, London (1973)

Hoyle, F., *On Stonehenge*, Heinemann Educational Books, London (1977)

Hsu, K.J., 'When the Mediterranean dried up', *Scientific American*, 227, 26–36 (1972)

Hughes, M.K., 'Ice layer dating of eruption at Santorini', *Nature*, 335, 211–12 (1988)

Hull, M.A., *A Textbook of Irish Literature*, M.H. Gill, Dublin (1906)

Hutton, M.A., *The Tain*, Maunsel, Dublin (1907)

Hyde, D.A., *Literary History of Ireland* (1967 edition), Ernest Benn, London (1899)

Ireland, S., *Roman Britain – A Source Book*, Croom Helm, Beckenham, Kent (1980)

Ireland, S., 'The Holocene sedimentary history of the coastal lagoons of Rio de Janeiro State, Brazil', in Tooley, M.J., and Shennan, I. (eds), *Sea-level Changes*, Basil Blackwell, Oxford (1987)

Jackson, J.E., *Sphere, Spheroid and Projections for the Surveyor*, Granada Publications (1980)

Jackson, K.H., *A Celtic Miscellany*, Penguin Books, Harmondsworth (1951)

Jackson, K.H., *The Gododdin – The Oldest Scottish Poem*, Edinburgh University Press, Edinburgh (1969)

Jacobsen, T., *The Sumerian King List – Assyriological Studies No. 11*, University of Chicago Press, Chicago (1939)

James, E.O., *Seasonal Feasts and Festivals*, Thames and Hudson, London (1961)

Jamieson, J., *An Etymological Dictionary of the Scottish Language*, Alexander Gardner, Paisley, Scotland (1874)

Jardine, W.G., 'Form and age of late quaternary shore-lines and coastal deposits of South-West Scotland: critical data', *Quarternaria*, V14, 103–14 (1971)

Jardine, W.G., 'Chronology of Holocene marine transgression and regression in South-western Scotland', *Boreas*, 4, 173–96 (1975)

Jardine, W.G., 'Holocene raised coastal sediments and former shore-lines in Dumfriesshire and eastern Galloway', *Trans. J. Proceedings of Dumfries and Galloway Nat. Hist. Antiq. Soc.*, 55, 1–59 (1980)

Jeffreys, Sir H., *The Earth, its Origin, History and Physical Constitution* (5th edition), Cambridge University Press (1970)

Jelgersma, S., 'Holocene sea level changes in the Netherlands', *Med. Geol. Stitching*, Serie C-VI, No. 7 (1961)

Jensen, J., *The Prehistory of Denmark*, Methuen, London (1982)

Jephcoat, A., and Olson, P., 'Is the inner core of the Earth pure iron?', *Nature*, 325, 332–5 (1987)

John, B.S., and Sugden, D.E., 'Raised marine features and phases of glaciation in the South Shetland Islands', *British Antarctic Survey*, Bulletin No. 24 (1971)

Johnstone, D.E., *The Channel Islands – An Archaeological Guide*, Philimore, London (1981)

Johnstone, J.B., *The Place Names of Scotland*, S.R. Publishers (1892)

Jones, E., *Folk Tales of Wales* (1978 edition), Gomer Press, Llandysul, Wales (1947)

Jones, Glynis, and Legge, A., 'The grape in the Neolithic of Britain', *Antiquity*, 233, 452–5 (1987)

Jones, H.L., *Strabo: Geography*, vol. I, William Heinemann, London (1917)

Jones, J., and Jones, T., *The Mabinogion*, J.M. Dent, London (1974)

Jones, Owen et al., *The Myvyrian Archaiology of Wales* (2nd edition), Thomas Gee, Denbigh (1870)

Jowett, B., *The Dialogues of Plato*, vol. III, Oxford University Press, London (1871)

Katz, F., *The Advanced Civilisations of Mesoamerica*, (English translation 1982), Weidenfeld and Nicolson, London (1969)

Kelly-Simpson, W. (ed.), *The Literature of Ancient Egypt*, with translations by Faulkner, R.O., Wente, E.F., Jr, and Simpson, W.K., Yale University Press (1972)

Khan, Mohammed Zafrulla, *The Koran*, Curzon Press (1971)

Kidson, C., and Heyworth, A., 'The Flandrian sea level rise in the Bristol Channel', *Proc. Ussher Soc.*, 2, 565–84 (1973)

King, E.A., *Space Geology*, John Wiley, New York (1976)

King, C.A.M., *Beaches and Coasts*, Edward Arnold, London (1972)

King, C.A.M., *The Geomorphology of the British Isles – Northern England*, Methuen, London (1976)

Kinsella, T., *The Tain*, Oxford University Press (1970)

Kinslow, R. (ed.), *High Velocity Impact Phenomena*, Academic Press, New York (1970)

Kirby, W.F., *Kalevala; The Land of Heroes*, J.M. Dent, London (1907 – republished by the Athlone Press, 1985)

Kirk, G.S., *The Nature of Greek Myths*, Penguin Books, Harmondsworth (1974)

Kraft, J.C., Aschenbrenner, R.S.E and Rapp, G., Jr, 'Paleographic reconstructions of coastal Aegean archaeological sites', *Science*, 195, 941–7 (1977)

Krupp, E.C., *In Search of Ancient Astronomies*, Chatto and Windus, London (1979)

Krupp, E.C., *Echoes of the Ancient Skies*, Harper and Row, New York (1983)

Kukal, Z., *Atlantis in the Light of Modern Research*, Elsevier, London (1984)

Kuusi, M., Bosley, K., and Branch, M. (eds), *Finnish Folk Poetry – Epic: An Anthology in Finnish and English*, Helsinki (1977)

Laing, L., and Laing, J., *The Origins of Britain*, Routledge and Kegan Paul, London (1980)

Lamb, H.H., Lewis, R.P.W., and Woodroffe, A., 'Atmospheric circulation and the main climatic variables between 8000 and 0 BC: meteorological evidence', *Quart. J. R. Met. Soc. Special issue, Conference on World Climates 8000–0 BC*, London (1966)

Lamb, H.H., 'Climate, vegetation and forest limits in early civilised times', *Phil. Trans. R. Soc. Lond.*, A. 276, 195–230 (1974) [195] (1974)

Lamb, H.H., *Climate, Past, Present and Future*, vol. 2, *Climatic History and the Future*, Methuen, London (1977)

Lambeck, K., *Geophysical Geodesy – The Slow Deformations of the Earth*, Clarendon Press, Oxford (1988)

Lampert, R.J., and Hughes, P.J., 'Sea level change and Aboriginal coastal adaptations in southern N.S.W.', in *Archaeology and Physical Anthropology of Oceania*, vol. 9 (3) (1974)

Lancaster Brown, P., *Megaliths, Myths and Men*, Blandford Press, London (1976)

Lanning, E.P., *Peru before the Incas*, Prentice-Hall, New Jersey, USA (1967)

Lappalainen, V., 'Postglacial pollen, Finland', *Spec. Pap. Geol. Soc. Am.*, no. 84 (1965)

Last, H., 'Rome and the Druids – a note', *Journ. Rom. Stud.*, XXXIX, 1–5 (1949)

Lee, H.D.P., *Plato – Timaeus and Critias*, Penguin Books, Harmondsworth (1965)

Lehner, M., *The Egyptian Heritage – Based on the Edgar Cayce Readings*, The Edgar Cayce Foundation, Virginia Beach, USA (1974)

Le Roux, C.T., 'New excavations at Gavrinis', *Antiquity*, 227, 183–7 (1985)

Levin, M.G., and Potapov, L.P., *The Peoples of Siberia*, University of Chicago Press, Chicago and London (1964)

Lloyd, S., *The Archaeology of Mesopotamia*, Thames and Hudson, London (1978)

Lockyer, J.N., *Stonehenge and other British Stone Monuments Astronomically Considered* (2nd edition), Macmillan, London (1909)

Long, R.D., 'A Re-examination of the Sothic Chronology of Egypt', *Orientalia*, 43, 261–73 (1974)

Loomis, R.S., *The Development of Arthurian Romance*, Hutchinson University Library, London (1963)

Luce, J.V., *The End of Atlantis*, Thames and Hudson, London (1969)

Lynch, F., *Prehistoric Anglesey*, Llangefni (1970)

Lynch, J., *Horizon – Time of Darkness*, script of the programme transmitted 26 June 1989, BBC Broadcasting Support Services (1989)

Mac Cana, P., *Celtic Mythology*, Hamlyn, London (1970)

MacKenzie, A., *Archaeology in Romania – The Mystery of the Roman Occupation*, Unified Printers and Publishers, London (1986)

Mackie, E.W., 'Astronomer priests in Iron Age Britain, in Archaeological Texts on Supposed Astronomical Sites in Scotland', *Phil. Trans. R. Soc. Lond.*, A. 276, 169–94 (1974)

Mackie, E.W., *Science and Society in Ancient Britain*, Elek Books, London (1977)

Mackie, J.B., *The Elements of Astronomy for Surveyors*, Charles Griffin, High Wycombe (1985)

MacNeill, E., 'On the notation and calligraphy of the Calendar of Coligny,' *Eriu*, X (1926–8), 1–67 (1928)

MacNeish, R.S., 'Ancient Mesoamerican civilisation', *Science*, 143, no. 3606, 531–8 (1964)

Maddox, J., 'Halley's Comet is quite young', *Nature*, 339 (1989)

Mallory, J.P., *In Search of the Indo-Europeans*, Thames and Hudson, London (1986)

Mansinha, L., and Smylie, D.E., 'Effect of earthquakes on the Chandler Wobble and the Secular Polar Shift', *Journal of Geophysical Research*, 72, 4731–43 (1967)

Marinatos, Sp., *Some Words about the Legend of Atlantis* (2nd edition), Athens (1971)

Massey, G., *The Egyptian Book of the Dead and the Mysteries of Amenta* (facsimile edition), Banton Press, Largs (1991)

Mattingley, H., *Tacitus – The Agricola and the Germania*, Penguin Books, Harmondsworth (1948)

Mattingley, H., *Tacitus on Britain and Germany*, Penguin Books, Harmondsworth (1960)

Mavor, J.W., *Voyage to Atlantis*, Souvenir Press, London (1969)

McGraw-Hill Encyclopaedia of Science and Technology – An International Reference Work in Fifteen Volumes, McGraw Hill, New York (1960)

Melchior, P.M., 'Latitude variation', chapter 7, in *Physics and Chemistry of the Earth*, vol. 2, Pergamon Press, Oxford (1957)

Melchior, P.M., *Rotation of the Earth*, D. Reidel Publishing, Holland (1972)

Melville, A.D., *Ovid – Metamorphoses*, Oxford University Press, Oxford (1986)

Mercer, J.H., 'Glacier resurgence at the Atlantic/Sub-Boreal transition', *Royal Meteorol. Soc. Quart. Jour.*, 93, 528–34 (1967)

Mercer, J.H., 'Variations of some Patagonian glaciers since the late-glacial: II', *Am. J. Sci.*, 269, 1–25 (1970)

Mercer, R., 'Field survey in the Blackwaterfoot and Machrie areas of the Isle of Arran, Bute', in Bowen, H.C., and Fowler, P.J., *Early Land Allotment in the British Isles*, BAR British Series 48 (1978)

Mercer, R.J., 'Excavations at Carn Brea, Illogan, Cornwall', *Cornish Archaeology*, 20 (1983)

Merril, G.P., 'The Siberian Meteorite', *Science*, 67, 489–90 (1928)

Michell, J.A., *Little History of Astro-Archaeology*, Thames and Hudson, London (1977)

Miller, H., *Scenes and Legends of the North of Scotland*, W.P. Nimmo, Hay and Mitchell, Edinburgh (1834)

Mitchell, G.F., 'The Pleistocene history of the Irish Sea', *Advancement of Science*, 17, 313–25 (1960)

Mitchell, G.F., 'Morainic ridges on the floor of the Irish Sea', *Irish Geogr.*, 4, 335–44 (1963)

Mitchell, G.F., 'An Irish vegetational record', *Spec. Pap. Geol. Soc. Am.*, no. 84 (1965)

Mitchell, G.F., 'Some chronological implications of the Irish Mesolithic', *Ulster Journal of Archaeology*, vol. 33 (1970)

Mitchell, G.F., 'The Pleistocene history of the Irish Sea: Second Approximation', *Sci. Proc. R. Dubl. Soc.*, A.4. 13, 181–99 (1971)

Montague, J. (ed.), *The Faber Book of Irish Verse*, Faber and Faber, London (1974)

Moore, D. (ed.), *The Irish Sea Province in Archaeology and History*, Cambrian Archaeological Association, Cardiff (1970)

Moore, G.W., 'Recent eustatic sea level fluctuations recorded by arctic beach ridges', *US Geol. Surv.*, prof. papers, 400B (1960)

Moore, P.D., 'Origin of Blanket Mires', *Nature*, 256, 267–79 (1975)

Moore, P.D., 'Tree-ring chronology', *Nature*, 272, 578–9 (1978)

Moore, P.D., 'Blow, blow thou winter wind', *Nature*, 336, 313 (1988)

Moore, P.D., 'Ancient climate from fossils', *Nature*, 340, 18–19 (1989)

Morner, N.-A., 'The Holocene eustatic sea level problem'. *Geol. en Mijnbouw*, 50, 699–702 (1971)

Morner, N.-A., 'Eustasy and geoid changes', *Jour. Geol.*, 84, 123–52 (1976)

Morner, N.-A., 'The Fennoscandian uplift and late Cenozoic geodynamics: geological evidence,' *GeoJournal*, 3.3, 287–318 (1979)

Morner, N.-A. 'Eustasy and geoid changes as a function of core/mantle changes', in Morner, N.-A. (ed.), *Earth Rheology, Isostasy and Eustasy; Scientific Reports of the Geodynamics Project No. 49*, John Wiley, Chichester (1980)

Morrice, Rev. J.C., *A Manual of Welsh Literature*, Bangor (1909)

Morris, J. (ed.), Nennius, *Arthurian Period Sources*, vol. 8, *British History and the Welsh Annals*, Philimore Press, London and Chichester (1980)

Morrison, J., 'Ancient Greek measures of length in nautical contexts', *Antiquity*, 65, 247, 298–305 (1991)

Muck, O., *The Secret of Atlantis* (English edition), William Collins, London (1976)

Muir-Wood, 'Shear waves show the Earth is a bit cracked', *New Scientist*, 21 April 1988, 44–8 (1988)

Munk, W.H., and Macdonald, G.J.F., *The Rotation of the Earth*, Cambridge University Press (1960)

Munksgaard, E., *Denmark – An Archaeological Guide*, Faber and Faber (1970)

Naylor, D., and Mountenay, S.N., *The Geology of the North-west European Continental Shelf*, vol. 1, Graham Trotman Dudley Publishers, London (1975)

Newell, N.D., 'Recent terraces of tropical limestone shores', *Zeitschrift fur Geomorphology* Supplementband 3, 87–106 (1961)

Newell, R.S., *Stonehenge*, Department of the Environment Official Handbook, HMSO, London (1959)

Newham, C.A., *The Astronomical Significance of Stonehenge*, Moon Publications, Shirenewton, Gwent, Wales (1972)

New Larousse Encyclopedia of Mythology, Hamlyn, London (1959)

Newman, W.S. et al., 'Eustasy and deformation of the geoid: 1000–6000 radiocarbon years BP', in Morner, N.-A. (ed.) *Earth Rheology, Isostasy and Eustasy*, John Wiley, Chichester (1980)

Newman, W.S. et al., 'Holocene delevelling of the United States' east coast', in Morner, N.-A. (ed.), *Earth Rheology, Isostasy and Eustasy*, John Wiley, Chichester (1980)

Nicolaisen, W.H.F., *Scottish Place Names*, B.T. Batsford, London (1976)

North, F.J., *Sunken Cities*, University of Wales Press, Cardiff (1957)

O'Kelly, M., *Newgrange*, Thames and Hudson, London (1983)

O'Kelly, M.J., *Early Ireland*, Cambridge University Press, Cambridge (1989)

Oldfather, C.H., *Diodorus Siculus Library of History*, vol. I, William Heinemann, London (1933)

Oldfather, C.H., *Diodorus Siculus Library of History*, vol. II, William Heinemann, London (1935)

O'Neil, W.M., *Time and the Calendars*, Sydney University Press (1975)

Ota, Y., and Machida, H., 'Quaternary sea-level changes in Japan', in Tooley, M.J., and Shennan, I. (eds), *Sea-level Changes*, Basil Blackwell, Oxford (1987)

Owen, A.L., *The Famous Druids*, Oxford University Press, Oxford (1962)

Page, N.R., 'Atlantic/Early Sub-Boreal glaciation in Norway', *Nature*, 219, 694–7 (1968)

Parker, R.A., *The Calendars of Ancient Egypt*, University of Chicago Press, Chicago (1950)

Parrinder, G., *African Mythology*, Hamlyn, London (1982)

Parry, T.A., *History of Welsh Literature*, Clarendon Press, Oxford (1955)

Pasachoff, J.M., *Astronomy: From the Earth to the Universe* (3rd edition), Saunders College Publishing, Holt, Rinehart and Winston, USA (1987)

Patrick, J. 'Midwinter sunrise at Newgrange', *Nature*, 249, pp. 517–19 (1974)

Pears, N.V., 'Interpretation problems in the study of tree-line fluctuations', in Taylor, J.A. (ed.), *Research Papers in Forest Metrology, An Aberystwyth Symposium*, pp. 31–45 (1972)

Pearson, G.W., 'How to cope with calibration', *Antiquity*, 61, 98–103 (1987)

Pearson, R., 'Radiocarbon dates from China', *Antiquity*, XLVII, 141–3 (1973)

Peate Cross, T., and Harris Slover, C. (eds), *Ancient Irish Tales*, George G. Harrap, London (1935)

Pellegrino, C., 'The fallen sky', *Astronomy*, April 1981, 66–71 (1981)

Pichler, H., and Schiering, W., 'The Thera eruption and the late Minoan I-b destructions on Crete', *Nature*, 267, 819–22 (1977)

Piggot, J., *Japanese Mythology*, Hamlyn, London (1982)

Piggott, S., *Neolithic Cultures of the British Isles*, Cambridge University Press, Cambridge (1954)

Piggott, S., *The Druids*, Thames and Hudson, London (1968)

Pilot, G., *The Secret Code of the Odyssey* (translated from French by F.E. Albert), Abelard Schuman, London (1972)

Pirazzoli, P.A., 'Sea level relative variations in the world during the past 2000 years', *Z. Geomorph. N.F.*, 21, 3, 284–96 (1977)

Poignant, R., *Oceanic and Australasian Mythology*, Newnes Books, London (1985)

Polunin, O., and Walters, M.A., *Guide to the Vegetation of Britain and Europe*, Oxford University Press (1985)

Porter, S.C. and Denton, G.H., 'Chronology of neoglaciation in the North American Cordillera', in *Am. Jour. Sci.*, 256, 177–210 (1967)

Press, F. and Briggs, P., 'Chandler Wobble, earthquakes, rotation, and geomagnetic changes', *Nature*, 256, 270–3 (1975)

Prigent, D., Visset, L., Morzadec-Kerfourn, M.T., and Lautrido, J.P., 'Human occupation of the submerged coast of the Massif Armoricain and postglacial sea level changes', in *Quaternary Coastlines and Marine Archaeology*, Academic Press, New York (1983)

Prouty, W.F., 'Carolina Bays and their origin', *Geological Society of America, Bulletin*, 63, 167–224 (1952)

Rackham, H., *Pliny Natural History*, vol. I, William Heinemann, London (1938)

Rackham, H., *Pliny Natural History*, vol. II, William Heinemann, London (1942)

Rackham, H., *Pliny Natural History*, vol. VII, William Heinemann, London (1963)

Raikes, R.L., 'The Mohenjo-daro Floods', *Antiquity*, 39, 196–203 (1965)

Rammage, E.S., *Atlantis Fact or Fiction?*, Indiana University Press, Bloomington and London (1978)

Rawson, J., *Ancient China – Art and Archaeology*, British Museum Publications, London (1980)

Ray, T.P., 'The winter solstice phenomenon at Newgrange, Ireland: accident or design?', *Nature*, 337, 343–5 (1989)

Renfrew, C., *Before Civilisation – The Radiocarbon Revolution*, Penguin, London (1973)

Renfrew, C. (ed.), *British Prehistory: A New Outline*, Duckworth, London (1974)

Renfrew, C., *Archaeology and Language – the Puzzle of Indo-European Origins*, Cape/Cambridge University Press (1987)

Renfrew, C., and Daniel, G., *The Idea of Prehistory* (2nd edition), Edinburgh University Press (1988)

Restelle, W., 'Traditions of the Deluge', *Bibliotheca Sacra*, 64, 148–67 (1907)

Rhys, J., *The Early Ethnology of the British Isles*, reprinted 1990 by Llanerch Enterprises, Llanerch, Dyfed (1890)

Rice Holmes, T., *Ancient Britain and the Invasions of Julius Caesar*, Oxford University Press, Oxford (1936)

Richards, H.G., and Broeker, W.S., 'Emerged Holocene South American Shorelines', *Science*, 141, 1044–5 (1963)

Rieu, E.V., *Homer – The Odyssey*, Penguin Books, Harmondsworth (1946)

Rieu, E.V., *Appolonius of Rhodes*, Penguin Books, Harmondsworth (1959)

Ritchie, J.C., and Haynes, C.V., 'Holocene vegetational zonation in the eastern Sahara', *Nature*, 330, 645–7 (1987)

Rivet, A.L.F., and Smith, C., *The Place-Names of Roman Britain*, B.T. Batsford, London (1979)

Roberts, A., *Giants in Myth and History*, Rider, London (1978)

Robinson, H.S., and Wilson, K., *The Encyclopedia of Myths and Legends of all Nations*, Kaye and Ward, London (1962)

Rochester, M.G., Jensen, O.G., and Smylie, D.E., 'A search for the Earth's "nearly diurnal free wobble"', *Geophys. J. R. Astr. Soc.*, 38, 349–63 (1974)

Rolleston, T.W., *Myths and Legends of the Celtic Race*, George G. Harrap, London (1911)

Romer, J., *Romer's Egypt*, Michael Joseph, London (1982)

Ronan, C.A., *The Shorter Science and Civilisation in China*, vols I, II and III, Cambridge University Press (1984)

Rose, J., *The Sons of Re – Cartouches of the Kings of Egypt*, J.R.T. Croft, Warrington, Cheshire (1985)

Roux, G., *Ancient Iraq*, George Allen and Unwin, London (1964)

Rundle Clark, R.T., *Myth and Symbol in Ancient Egypt*, Thames and Hudson, London (1959)

Rycroft, M.J., 'Magnetosphere forcing of upper atmosphere dynamics', *Nature*, 326, pp. 747–8 (1987)

Sandars, N.K., *The Epic of Gilgamesh*, Penguin Books, Harmondsworth (1960)

Sandars, N.K., *Poems of Heaven and Hell from Ancient Mesopotamia*, Penguin Books, Harmondworth (1971)

Saunders, A., 'Putting continents asunder', *Nature*, 332, 679–80 (1988)

Saville, S., *Pears Encyclopedia of Myths and Legends*, Pelham Books, London (1976)

Sawyer, J.S. (ed.), *Proceedings of the International Symposium on World Climate 8000–0 BC*, Royal Meteorological Society, London (1966)

Scaife, R., 'Flag Fen: the vegetation environment', *Antiquity* 66, 251, 462–6 (1992)

Scholl, D., 'Recent sedimentary record in mangrove swamps and rise in sea level over the south west coast of Florida', in *Mar. Geol.*, 1, 344 (1964)

Schou, A., 'The coastline of Djursland', in Steers, J.A. (ed.), *Applied Coastal Geomorphology*, Macmillan Press, London (1971)

Schultz J., *The Movement and Rhythms of the Stars*, Floris Books, Edinburgh (1986)

Schultz, P. H., and Gault, D. E., 'Prolonged global catastrophes from oblique impacts', in *Geological Society of America Special Papers*, 247, 239–61 (1990)

Schultz, P.H., and Lianza, R.E., 'Recent grazing impacts on the Earth recorded in the Rio Cuarto crater field, Argentina', *Nature*, 355, 234–7 (1992)

Scott-Kilvert, I., *Plutarch – The Rise and Fall of Athens: Nine Greek Lives*, Penguin Books, Harmondsworth (1960)

Scuderi, L. A., 'Late-Holocene upper timberline variation in the southern Sierra Nevada', *Nature*, 325, 242–4 (1987)

Shennan, I., 'Sea-level changes and crustal movements in England and Wales', in Smith, D.E., and Dawson, A.G., *Shorelines and Isostasy*, Academic Press, London (1983)

Shennan, I., 'Holocene sea-level changes in the North Sea', in Tooley, M.J., and Shennan, I. (eds), *Sea-level Changes*, Basil Blackwell, Oxford (1987)

Shepard, F.P., 'Sea level changes in the past 8,000 years, possible archaeological significance', *Science*, 143, 574–6 (1964)

Shepard, F.P., and Curray, J.R., 'Carbon-14 determination of sea level changes in stable areas', *Progress in Oceanography*, 4, 283–91 (1967)

Sherley-Price, L., *Bede – A History of the English Church and People*, Penguin Books, Harmondsworth (1955)

Shewring, W., *Homer's Odyssey*, Oxford University Press, Oxford (1980)

Shoemaker, E.M., 'Interpretation of lunar craters', in Kopal, Z. (ed.), *Physics and Astronomy of the Moon*, Academic Press, New York, pp. 283–341 (1962)

Silverberg, R., *The Challenge of Climate*, Windmill Press (1971)

Simpkin, T. (ed.), *Volcanoes of the World*, Smithsonian Institution, Hutchinson Ross Publishing, Pennsylvania (1981)

Singh, G., 'The Indus Valley Culture – seen in the context of post-glacial climatic and ecological studies in North-West India', Archaeol. Phys. Anthropol. in *Oceanea*, 6, 177–89 (1971)

Skene, W.F., *Four Ancient Books of Wales*, Edmonston and Douglas, Edinburgh (1868)

Skene, W.F. (ed. D. Bryce), *Arthur and the Britons in Wales and Scotland*, Llanerch Enterprises, Lampeter, Dyfed (1988)

Smith, A.G., and Pilcher, J.R., 'Radiocarbon dates and vegetational history of the British Isles', *New Phytol.*, 72, 903–14 (1973)

Sollberger, E., *The Babylonian Legend of the Flood*, British Museum Publications, London (1971)

Spanuth, J., *Atlantis of the North* (translated from the German), Sidgwick and Jackson, London (1979)

Spence, L., *Myths of Ancient Egypt*, George Harrap, London (1915)

Spence, L., *The Problem of Atlantis*, New York (1924)

Spence, L., *The History of Atlantis*, Citadel Press, New Jersey (1973)

Spence, L., *The Encyclopedia of the Occult*, Bracken Books, London (1988)

Steers, J.A., *The Coastline of England and Wales*, Cambridge University Press (1964)

Steers, J.A., *The Sea Coast*, Collins, London (1972)

Steers, J.A., *The Coastline of Scotland*, Cambridge University Press (1973)

Stenton, Sir F., *Anglo-Saxon England* (2nd edition), Clarendon Press, Oxford (1947)

Stephens, N., 'The coastline of Ireland', in *Irish Geographical Studies*, Queens University Press, Belfast (1970)

Stephens, N., and Collins, A.E.P., 'The Quaternary Deposits at Ringneill Quay and Ardmillan, Co. Down', *Proceedings of the Royal Irish Academy* (Series C), 61, 41–77 (1960)

Suess, H.E., 'Bristlecone-pine calibration of the radiocarbon time-scale 5200 BC to the present', in Olsson, I.U. (ed.), *Radiocarbon Variations and Absolute Chronology, Proceedings of the Twelfth Nobel Symposium*, Uppsala, Sweden, 303–11 (1970)

Swire, O.F., *The Outer Hebrides and their Legends*, Oliver and Boyd, Edinburgh and London (1966)

Sykes, E., *Everyman's Dictionary of Non-Classical Mythology*, J.M. Dent, London (1961)

Synge, J.L., and Byron, A.G., *Principles of Mechanics* (3rd edition 1981), McGraw Hill Kogakusha, Maidenhead (1960)

Tallis, J.H., 'Tree remains in southern Pennine peats', *Nature*, 256, 482–4 (1975)

Taylor, J.A., *Prog. Geogr.*, 5, 247–334 (1974)

Taylor, T., *Proclus – Commentary on the Timaeus of Plato*, London (1820)

Taylor, T., *Plato the Timaeus and the Critias – Bollingen Series 3*, Pantheon Books, Washington (1944)

Thallon-Hill, I.D., *The Ancient City of Athens*, Camelot Press, London and Southampton (1953)

Thom, A., *Megalithic Sites in Britain*, Oxford University Press, Oxford (1967)

Thom, A., 'Prehistoric monuments in Western Europe', *Phil. Trans. R. Soc. Lond.*, A. 276, 149–56 (1974)

Thom, A., and Thom, A.S., *Megalithic Remains in Britain and Brittany*, Clarendon Press, Oxford (1978)

Thomas, C., *Exploration of a Drowned Landscape – Archaeology and History of the Isles of Scilly*, B.T. Batsford, London (1985)

Thomas, T.M., *The Mineral Wealth of Wales and its Exploitation*, Oliver and Boyd, Edinburgh and London (1961)

Thompson, J.E.S., 'Maya astronomy', *Phil. Trans. R. Soc. Lond.*, A. 276, 83–98 (1974)

Thorpe, L., *Geoffrey of Monmouth – The History of the Kings of Britain*, Penguin Books, Harmondsworth (1966)

Thorpe, L., *Gerald of Wales – The Journey through Wales: The Description of Wales*, Penguin Books, Harmondsworth (1978)

Tierney, J.J., 'The Celtic ethnography of Posidonius', *Proc. Royal Irish Acad.*, LX (C) 189–275 (1960)

Tooley, M.J., 'Sea-level changes during the last 9,000 years in North-West England', *Geogr. J.*, 140, 18–42 (1974)

Tooley, M.J., *Sea Level Changes: North-West England during the Flandrian Stage*, Clarendon Press, Oxford (1978)

Tooley, M.J., 'Floodwaters mark sudden rise', *Nature*, 342, 20–1 (1989)

Toomre, A., 'On the "Nearly Diurnal Wobble" of the Earth', *Geophys. J. R. Astr. Soc.*, 38, 335–48 (1974)

Tripp, E., *Dictionary of Classical Mythology* (1988 edition), Collins, London and Glasgow (1970)

Turville Petre, E.O.G., *Myth and Religion of the North*, Weidenfeld and Nicolson, London (1964)

Valmore, C.L., Jr, 'Tree-ring evidence of past climatic variability', *Nature*, 276, 334–8 (1978)

Van Andel, T.H., 'Prehistoric and historic shorelines of the southern Argolid peninsula', *International Journal of Nautical Archaeology and Underwater Exploration*, 12, 303–4 (1983)

Van Andel, T.H., 'High resolution seismic reflection profiles for the reconstruction of postglacial shorelines – an example from Greece', *Quaternary Research* 22, 31–45 (1984)

Van Andel, T.H., 'The emergence of civilisation in the Aegean', *Antiquity*, 62, 234–45 (1988)

Van Andel, T.H., 'Late Quaternary sea level changes and archaeology', *Antiquity*, 63, 733–45 (1989)

Van Zinderen Bakker, E.M. (ed.), *Antarctic Glacial History and World Paleoenvironments*, A.A. Balkema, Rotterdam, Netherlands (1978)

Vicente, R.O., 'The theory of nutation of the Earth', in *Physics and Chemistry of the Earth*, vol. 4, Pergamon Press, London (1961)

Waddel, W.G., *Manetho*, William Heinemann, London (1940)

Wait, G.A., *Ritual and Religion in Iron Age Britain*, parts 1 and 2, BAR British series 149(i), Oxford (1985)

Walker, C.B.F., 'Eclipse seen at ancient Ugarit', *Nature*, 338, 204–5 (1989)

Wallis Budge, E.A., *Egyptian Religion*, Kegan Paul, Trench, Trubner, London (1899)

Wallis Budge, E.A., *The Book of the Dead*, Kegan Paul, Trench, Trubner, London (1899)

Wallis Budge, E.A., *Egyptian Magic*, Kegan Paul, Trench, Trubner, London (1899)

Wallis Budge, Sir E.A., *An Egyptian Hieroglyphic Dictionary*, John Murray, London (1920)

Waloff, Z., and Green, S.M., 'Regularities in duration of regional desert locust plagues', *Nature*, 256, 484–5 (1975)

Waltham, C., *Shu Ching – Book of History*, George Allen and Unwin, London (1971)

Warlow, P., *The Reversing Earth*, J.M. Dent, London (1982)

Warner, R., *Plutarch – Moral Essays*, Penguin Books, Harmondsworth (1971)

Waterson, B., *The Gods of Ancient Egypt*, B.T. Batsford, London (1984)

Watkins, T. (ed.), *Radiocarbon: Calibration and Prehistory*, Edinburgh University Press (1975)

Watson, W., *China*, Thames and Hudson, London (1961)

Weast, R.G., and Astle, M.J. (eds), *Handbook of Chemistry and Physics – A Ready Reference Book of Chemical and Physical Data*, CRC Press (1981)

Webster, G., *The British Celts and their Gods under Rome*, B.T. Batsford, London (1986)

Wells, J.W., 'Coral growth and geochronometry', *Nature*, 197, 948–50 (1963)

Wender, D., *Hesiod and Theognis*, Penguin Books, Harmondsworth (1973)

Werner, E.T.C., *A Dictionary of Chinese Mythology*, Kelly and Walsh, Shanghai (1932)

West, M.L. (ed.), *Hesiod's Works and Days – edited with prologomena and commentary*, Clarendon Press, Oxford (1978)

West, R.G., *Pleistocene Geology and Biology* (2nd edition), Longman Group, Harlow (1977)

Weyer, E.M., 'Pole movement and sea levels', *Nature*, 273, 18–21 (1978)

Whiston, E.M., *Josephus – The Complete Works*, Pickering and Inglis, London (1960)

Whitehouse, D., and Whitehouse, R., *Archaeological Atlas of the World*, Thames and Hudson, London (1975)

Wilkinson, G., *A History of Britain's Trees*, Hutchinson, London (1981)

Williams, E., 'Dating the introduction of food production into Britain and Ireland', *Antiquity*, 63, 511–21 (1989)

Williams, T., *Iolo Manuscripts. A Selection of Ancient Welsh Manuscripts*, Welsh Manuscripts Society, London (1848)

Williams Ab Ithel, J., *Barddas*, vol. 1, Welsh Manuscripts Society, Longman, London (1862)

Williamson, J.B., 'Megalithic units of length', *Journal of Archaeological Science*, 1, 381–2 (1974)

Wilson, A.T., 'Past surges in the West Antarctic ice sheet and their climateological significance', in Van Zinderen Bakker, E.M. (ed.), *Antarctic Glacial History and World Paleoenvironments*, A.A. Balkema, Rotterdam, Netherlands (1978)

Wilson, D., *Atoms of Time Past*, Allen Lane, London (1975)

Wilson, I., *The Exodus Enigma*, Weidenfeld, London (1985)

Winterbottom, M. (ed.), *Gildas – The Ruin of Britain*, Phillimore Press, Chichester (1978)

Wood, A., 'Erosional history of the cliffs around Aberystwyth', in Steers, J.A. (ed.), *Applied Coastal Geomorphology*, Macmillan Press, London (1971)

Wood, J.E., *Sun, Moon and Standing Stones*, Oxford University Press (1978)

Woodman, P.C., 'Filling in the spaces in Irish prehistory', *Antiquity*, 66, 251, 295–314 (1992)

Wooley, Sir L., revised and updated by Mooney, P.R.S., *Final Account of the Excavations at Ur*, Herbert Press, London (1982)

Wright, J.E., Hull, J.H., McQuillin, R., and Arnold, S.E., 'Irish Sea Investigations, 1969–70', *Rep. Inst. Geol. Sci.*, 71/19 (1971)

Yang, Huai-Jen, and Xie, Zhiren, 'The evolution of the East Asian environment. Sea level changes over the past 20,000 years', in White, R.O., *Centre of Asian Studies Occasional Paper No. 59* (1984)

Yenne, B., *The Atlas of the Solar System*, Bison Books, London (1987)

Zvelebil, M., and Zvelebil, K.V., 'Agricultural transition and Indo-European dispersals', *Antiquity*, 236, 574–83 (1988)

Index

104 — _____ & . 3000 b.c.

205 — first _____ c. 3000 b.c.
P 217 — _____ line

266/65 — _____
267

268/ — _____
271

290 — _____
297 — _____

letc̄